PRAISE F⟨✓⟩ P9-DXO-755

JESUS ON TRIAL

"I have long admired David Limbaugh for tackling difficult issues in the media and public square. While his public persona as a lawyer sometimes invites critical scrutiny, I have seen his tender heart and winsome witness to the love and truth of Jesus Christ. As he relates, after years as a skeptic, he discovered the Bible to be 'intellectually, emotionally, and spiritually attractive, and probative of the truth of Christianity.' His book is quite an exhaustive summary and interaction with numerous apologists and challenges to Christianity. His keen mind and practical wisdom combine to present a clear articulation of the truth and will stir every reader's thinking. It is a great resource for both skeptics and believers alike."

—**RAVI ZACHARIAS**, author and speaker

"*Jesus on Trial* is a *tour de force*. Even more: this compelling book is an elegant, personal, and enriching *tour de faith*. In his passionate defense of Christianity, my friend David Limbaugh combines intellectual rigor and deep research with a refreshing candor and resounding grace. David forges an intimate relationship with the reader by detailing his own remarkable journey from skeptic to believer. His enthusiasm for scripture and theology is infectious. This invaluable addition to the literature of Christian apologetics is guaranteed to change minds and open hearts!"

—**MICHELLE MALKIN**, bestselling author and
founder of Hot Air and Twitchy

"I've never read a book quite like this. In *Jesus on Trial*, David Limbaugh interweaves the story of his own spiritual journey with powerful, factual arguments for Christianity's truth claims. Taken together, these narratives form a passionate paean to the Bible and to our Lord Jesus Christ. In an age when Christianity has become a popular whipping boy for our social ills, David Limbaugh has penned a wonderful and convincing defense of our Savior that is infused with beauty, excitement, and awe."

—**ERICK ERICKSON**, radio host and editor of RedState.com

"Clear and convincing, powerful and persuasive, *Jesus on Trial* is a spiritual adventure story—the fascinating account of a lawyer's intellectual journey toward Christianity. I wish this book had been available when I was an atheist investigating faith!"

—**LEE STROBEL,** *New York Times* bestselling author of *The Case for Christ* and professor at Houston Baptist University

"Many people know my friend David Limbaugh as a bestselling author and political commentator. But he is also a lawyer trained to analyze evidence—and in *Jesus on Trial* he provides his personal journey to the truth of the Bible. A fantastic book!"

—**SEAN HANNITY,** host of *The Sean Hannity Show* and Fox News Channel's *Hannity*

"*Jesus on Trial* provides far more than a great intellectual case for Christianity. David Limbaugh takes you on an enlightening journey through highlights of the world's most influential book while he tackles the big questions he had about the faith. You're left marveling at the tapestry of scripture and the Savior who wove it."

—**FRANK TUREK,** founder and president of CrossExamined.org and co-author of *I Don't Have Enough Faith to Be an Atheist*

JESUS
ON TRIAL

JESUS ON TRIAL

A LAWYER AFFIRMS THE TRUTH
OF THE GOSPEL

DAVID
LIMBAUGH

REGNERY
PUBLISHING
A Division of Salem Media Group

Copyright © 2014 by David Limbaugh

All rights reserved. No part of this publication may be reproduced or transmitted in any form or by any means electronic or mechanical, including photocopy, recording, or any information storage and retrieval system now known or to be invented, without permission in writing from the publisher, except by a reviewer who wishes to quote brief passages in connection with a review written for inclusion in a magazine, newspaper, website, or broadcast.

Regnery® is a registered trademark of Salem Communications Holding Corporation

Scripture quotations are from the following sources: The ESV® Bible (The Holy Bible, English Standard Version®) copyright © 2001 by Crossway, a publishing ministry of Good News Publishers. ESV® Text Edition: 2011. The ESV® text has been reproduced in cooperation with and by permission of Good News Publishers. Unauthorized reproduction of this publication is prohibited. All rights reserved; THE HOLY BIBLE, NEW INTERNATIONAL VERSION®, NIV® Copyright © 1973, 1978, 1984, 2011 by Biblica, Inc.® Used by permission. All rights reserved worldwide; The NEW AMERICAN STANDARD BIBLE®, Copyright © 1960, 1962, 1963, 1968, 1971, 1972, 1973, 1975, 1977, 1995 by The Lockman Foundation. Used by permission; The New King James Version®. Copyright © 1982 by Thomas Nelson, Inc. Used by permission. All rights reserved; and the King James Version.

First paperback edition published 2015; ISBN 978-1-62157-411-8
First hardcover edition published 2014; cataloging information below

Library of Congress Cataloging-in-Publication Data

Limbaugh, David.
  Jesus on trial : a lawyer affirms the truth of the gospel / David Limbaugh.
     pages cm
  ISBN 978-1-62157-255-8
  1. Christianity--Essence, genius, nature. 2. Apologetics. I. Title.
  BT60.L475 2014
  239--dc23
                          2014026242

Published in the United States by
Regnery Publishing
A Division of Salem Media Group
300 New Jersey Ave NW
Washington, DC 20001
www.Regnery.com

Manufactured in the United States of America

10 9 8 7 6 5 4 3 2 1

Books are available in quantity for promotional or premium use. For information on discounts and terms, please visit our website: www.Regnery.com.

Distributed to the trade by
Perseus Distribution
250 West 57th Street
New York, NY 10107

To Ravi Zacharias and his important world ministry,
Ravi Zacharias International Ministries;

To Dr. Norman Geisler and the apologetics-centered seminary he founded,
Southern Evangelical Seminary;

And to Dr. Frank Turek and his organization CrossExamined.org for
spreading the gospel and the truth throughout our society and
especially among university students, who are bombarded with
messages of skepticism and unbelief.

CONTENTS

CHAPTER 1

~~~~~~~~~~~~~~~~~~~~~~~~~~~~~~

FROM SKEPTIC TO BELIEVER

I have been fascinated with Christian apologetics—that is, the defense of the Christian faith—and theology since before I became a believer several decades ago. I have studied these subjects, off and on, with a fair amount of intensity, and I hope my studies have prepared me for this task.

As corny as this might sound, I believe the circumstances leading to my writing this book may have been providential. A few months ago I was having dinner with two longtime friends and one of them began talking about Christianity, as he had done on numerous occasions before. Both guys are nonbelievers, and the one who invariably brings up religion seems to want to discuss it, perhaps to test the sincerity of his own beliefs by challenging mine. I don't remember our discussion word for word, but I clearly recall that at one point he announced that he couldn't understand how any person who uses his reasoning powers could possibly believe in Christianity. He claims, lightheartedly I think, to be a deist—

a person who believes in a god who brought creation into existence and then abandoned it to its own devices. I'll get back to that in a moment.

EARLY DOUBTS

I remember at an early age my incredulity upon learning that Soviet Premier Nikita Khrushchev, like all good Communists, was an atheist. When we were leaving church one Sunday, I asked my dad how anyone could believe that all of this—the wondrous glory of God's creation— came from nothing. I instinctively knew that could not be true.

I am not suggesting I had sophisticated thoughts at age eight or nine. To the contrary, my point is that if I had gained such a clear awareness of God's existence simply through what I observed about His creation, there must be a self-evident quality about this truth.

I knew God was real—because God created us to know Him and has shown Himself in creation. The Bible confirms it: "For what can be known about God is plain to them, because God has shown it to them. For his invisible attributes, namely, his eternal power and divine nature, have been clearly perceived, ever since the creation of the world, in the things that have been made. So they are without excuse" (Romans 1:19–20).

Sure, I wondered how God could have always existed, and it gave me a headache contemplating it, but I accepted it because it was the only thing that made any sense at all. I would later learn that contrary to arguments from humanists, atheists, and anti-theists, there is a world of difference between the idea that the universe has always existed or sprang from nothing, and the idea that God, an uncaused cause Who has always existed, created it. Even at age sixty-one I don't have the capacity to comprehend infinity fully, or that God exists wholly apart from time, but I do believe there is no other plausible explanation for the existence of the universe or for man's presence in it. It is much more difficult to believe that matter spontaneously erupted from non-matter and life from non-life without a non-material, uncaused creator.

My brother and I had an ordinary, but wonderful, Midwestern child-hood with loving parents who took us to Sunday school and church every

Sunday. Our entire extended family was very involved with the church, and I will always have the fondest memories of those days. Going out to eat after church was a family ritual I will always especially cherish. I trusted my parents, and I had no reason to distrust Christianity or the Bible, but the truth is that, like many kids, I probably wasn't engaged enough at a young age to give them the attention they deserved. I was more interested in figuring out ways to sneak out of church with my mischievous friends.

We learned about the Bible in Sunday school, and I went through the confirmation process. Whether or not I actually believed in the ideas, I certainly didn't embrace them actively, and as the years passed I slowly began to have doubts. This was no fault of my upbringing, or of the fine church we attended, but probably stemmed from my lack of seriousness at the time and my other interests. I either didn't sufficiently absorb the lessons I'd learned from the Bible or they gradually diminished in my memory from disuse. I'm sure this sounds familiar to many people, especially of that era.

By the time I was in college, I don't think I was a believer, but I often wondered about philosophical questions, including Who God was and what He was like. Like many, I thought I could bootstrap my way to an understanding of spiritual truths through my reasoning powers alone, largely unaware of the actual content of God's special revelation in the Bible.

I was unconvinced that Jesus Christ is the Son of God. Though I always believed in a creator god, I had great difficulty believing in the God of the Bible—as little as I knew about Him, as it turns out. I couldn't accept that an all-powerful God, if He were also all-loving, would permit such evil, pain, and suffering as we see in the world when it is in His power to prevent it. The concept of an eternal hell was also difficult for me to square with the notion of an omnibenevolent creator.

Additionally, I couldn't comprehend why God would establish a system of salvation whereby one could attain eternal life simply by believing in Him, or more specifically, in Jesus Christ. I wondered how He could judge us on the basis of what we believe, which we can't control, rather than on our behavior, which we can. Then again, at the time I didn't grasp that the biblical concept of faith involved more than mere intellectual belief, but I'll get to that later. So without even investigating the Bible as a young adult, I had serious doubts about Christianity.

Like my old friend, I flirted with deism for a time when I was initially exposed to it in an American literature course in college. Deism was popular during the Enlightenment, and a few high-profile American Founders such as Ben Franklin and Thomas Jefferson were thought to be deists. In the course we read a fascinating letter from Ben Franklin to his friend Ezra Stiles, the president of Yale College, in which Franklin expressed some doubts about the divinity of Jesus Christ.[1] But in retrospect, I doubt that Franklin was a deist, because in the letter he clearly acknowledged his belief in a superintending god. Furthermore, four years earlier he had called the delegates to the Constitutional Convention to prayer during a deadlock[2]—and why would he have prayed if he thought God did not intervene in human affairs? Nonetheless, it was mildly reassuring to me as a skeptic that someone as brilliant as Franklin had doubts about Christianity.

Deism sounded right to me because it seemed to solve the dilemma of evil. It allows one to believe in an all-powerful creator God Who is not responsible for the evil and pain in the world, since He is not active in it. What a relief. Finally, I could believe what I'd always known in my gut to be true: that God exists, but that He is a good God, not the God of the Bible Who permits, or possibly even causes, suffering.

On closer inspection, however, we might discover that deism doesn't resolve the problem of evil at all. If some regard the God of the Bible as morally unacceptable because He actively intervenes in His creation yet permits or causes human suffering, how much more repugnant is the god of the deists, who for no apparent purpose at all, cynically created this suffering-infested world and then completely abandoned it? Does this mythical god even have a plan of redemption for us? If so, why doesn't he tell us about it through revelation like the "mean" God of the Bible? How does he exact justice, or is there any such concept in this belief system? How does he account for evil? How does he draw his creatures closer to him—assuming he cares in the slightest bit? Where is he, anyway?

My purpose isn't to ridicule skeptics—as I said, I used to be one. But at some point I realized it was foolish and arrogant of me to pretend to form final conclusions about the Bible and Jesus Christ when I hadn't begun to seriously study Scripture or Christian doctrine. It was reckless of me to make a potentially life-determining decision on nothing more than my naked ruminations. So I resolved to examine the evidence.

As it turned out, the more I studied it the more I came to believe that Christianity is true. It is important for doubters to understand that many of us believers came to the point of faith by first studying the evidence and using—not abandoning—our reasoning powers to analyze it. I discovered that to believe in Jesus Christ does not require us to discard our intellect. Reason is perfectly compatible with Christian doctrine—though admittedly, saving faith in Christ requires more than sterile analysis and intellectual assent to the basic propositions of the Christian faith.

Yes, we must believe that Christ is the Son of God, that He took on human form, lived a sinless life, and died a sacrificial death for our sins (2 Cor. 5:21). We must acknowledge our own sinful state and repent (Luke 13:3), turn to Christ, and trust Him for the forgiveness of our sins and for our eternal salvation, based solely on His grace and nothing we have merited. But the Christian faith *requires* more than the intellect because it *involves* more than the intellect. It involves the will: a conscious decision to place our trust (faith) in Christ for eternal salvation as if our life depended on Him—because it does. But it's a little difficult to take that final step of faith when you have serious doubts about Christianity and the Bible.

I want to tell you a little bit about my own spiritual journey from this point forward, not because it's anything to be proud of, or even that remarkable, but because it might be encouraging or helpful to some who are open to believing but are plagued with doubts similar to those I experienced.

INVISIBLE SEEDS

I was constantly seeking the truth, but usually through my own feeble efforts and presumptuous ponderings, and without studying the Bible itself or examining Christian doctrine more carefully. One Christmas not many years after I'd graduated from law school, my close friend Peter Kinder (who is now lieutenant governor of Missouri) invited me to his parents' home to visit with a few of his law school classmates who were in town.

Somehow the subject of Christianity came up, and Peter's friend Steve Springer began to talk to me about it. I shared with Steve certain doubts I had about the God of the Bible and told him I just didn't buy into Christianity. I will never forget a couple of things about this exchange. Steve did not fit my perception at the time of the stereotypical young Christian—a judgmental holy roller who accepted Christianity uncritically. He exhibited an extraordinary measure of grace. He not only didn't take offense at my skepticism, but he patiently retrieved his Bible from his bedroom and began to walk me through a few fascinating verses. This might have been the first time outside of Sunday school or church that someone went directly to the source and shared it with me.

Undaunted and unoffended by my challenge, he gave a model Christian response. Despite my skepticism, I was not close-minded and was genuinely interested in learning. I knew, after all, that I hadn't really given the Bible itself a hearing, much less a fair one. To my surprise—and this is embarrassing to admit—Steve showed me how verses of Scripture, both Old and New Testaments, were tied to others in content and theme with remarkable frequency. Amazingly, I had never looked at a reference Bible before, and I was blown away. My ignorance was on display, but Steve wasn't remotely judgmental—to help me learn more, he even gave me that Bible.

I was genuinely intrigued to discover that the Bible was not simply a mishmash of stories, allegories, alleged historical events, and moral lessons. There was obviously a pattern here, and for the first time in my life the Bible appeared to me to be thematically integrated. The scales on my eyes started peeling away.

Though Steve didn't realize it at the time, he had planted a very important spiritual seed. But sometimes it takes the planting of many such seeds before the Christian root springs up in one's life. As often as not, the planter won't even be aware he planted the seed, much less that it would later grow and bloom. So believers should not be discouraged by an apparent lack of response to their witnessing, as it won't always be clear to them or to the person to whom they are witnessing that they made an impact. We must do what we can and leave the rest to the Holy Spirit.

While I was intrigued by Steve's demonstration that Scripture was connected, I was still far from becoming a believer. Yet the planting of that seed was pivotal in my ultimate acceptance of Christ, which I would only realize many years later. The happy ending to this story is that a few years ago Steve was again in town visiting his old friend Peter and they both came by my house to say hello. I had never told Steve about the impact he had on me spiritually, and when we were all seated at the kitchen table I asked them to wait a minute while I went to my library to retrieve the very Bible he'd given me years ago. I brought it back and handed it to him as I told him the story and gave him my brief testimony. I believe he was deeply moved and quite surprised to discover that his gesture years earlier—his winsome witness to me—yielded fruit. I am very grateful for his role.

I don't remember everything that happened in my spiritual journey. But from that point forward my interest in learning about the Bible and theology intensified, and I became more of what you might call a seeker. I wanted to become a Christian—somewhere inside I felt Christianity was true—but certain things still bothered me. I had become interested in learning about the Bible instead of pronouncing judgment on it from a position of abject ignorance.

I took another spiritual step forward in the early eighties, while I was in England on a mini-vacation with my grandfather. We toured the sites there, from the courts to the famous cathedrals to Stonehenge. At one of the cathedrals—perhaps Canterbury—I visited the bookstore and bought a helpful-looking paperback by evangelist and apologist Paul Little: *Know What and Why You Believe*. It was a combination of two of Little's books, *Know What You Believe* and *Know Why You Believe*. The first of those is a primer on Christian doctrine, and the second is a book on apologetics—a defense of the faith. God must have led me to this book because, true to its title, it is a concise yet thorough overview of what and why Christians believe.

When I got back home I read the book and learned a great deal about Christian doctrine that I'd simply never been exposed to before in this accessible format. Little talks in depth about heaven and hell, angels, the divinity of Jesus Christ, the attributes of God, God's redemptive plan for mankind, and more. He addresses skeptics' challenges to the faith and deals with them persuasively. I was not fully on board yet, mind you, but this was the planting of another important seed.

Around this time I also came across the writings of Josh McDowell, who had become a believer by vigorously studying the evidence for the resurrection and other Christian beliefs in an effort to disprove them. I bought his *Evidence That Demands a Verdict*, in which he lays out many abundant proofs for the core claims of Christianity. This book had a significant impact on me and was particularly appealing, I think, because McDowell makes the case for Christianity systematically, thoroughly, and comprehensively—as if he were presenting his case to the court of appeals. I was well on the way to believing in Christianity's truth claims intellectually.

One thing I learned on my sporadic spiritual journey was that mainstream culture's disdain and disrespect for the intellectual integrity of Christianity is unwarranted, and its conceited assumption that Christian beliefs are a product of blind faith, bereft of reason and intellect, is completely false. The formidable arguments Paul Little, Josh McDowell, and others had marshaled were intellectually rigorous and anchored in historical evidence.

It also didn't hurt seeing Ravi Zacharias on television laying out the philosophical foundations of the Christian faith. When I first watched Ravi I was taken by the profound force of his intellect and his ability to articulate and defend the faith. I remember thinking, *Wow, I'd like to see any Christian skeptic listen to Ravi and dare claim that intellectuals can't be Christians or that Christians can't be intellectual.* By then, I had begun to shift sides. I had become sympathetic to Christianity and was rooting for that team, even if I still hadn't joined it. My exposure to Ravi Zacharias, who would later become my friend, was one of the most important seeds yet, not just because of what he said, but how he said it. It was one of the turning points. Ravi and his organization, Ravi Zacharias International Ministries (RZIM), win hearts and minds to Christianity every day all over the world through intellectually vigorous and winsome apologetics and evangelism.

Interestingly, in my exchange with Steve Springer many years ago, though he had no formal training in apologetics, he instinctively employed one of the techniques Ravi Zacharias encourages his students to use. Ravi stresses that when someone approaches a believer with a question about the Christian faith, it is just as important to focus on the questioner as on his question. We must try to understand what is actually bothering him, which may or may not involve intellectual doubts, and try to respond to him in a way that will reach him. Steve instinctively understood that I had intellectual doubts, or at least that I thought I did. He somehow sensed that I wasn't that familiar with the Bible, and that he might reach me by introducing me to certain aspects of it. He narrowed his sights on the questioner: me. Before talking, he listened closely, and then tailored his response to fit my specific needs. This has been a very important lesson for me.

FIRST STEPS

I continued to pursue God, or maybe, more accurately, He pursued me. I was open to learning more and occasionally reading things on the subject that caught my eye. But it wasn't until I attended a Christian Business Men's Committee (CBMC) prayer breakfast in my hometown that the final seeds were planted. At the end of the program, one of the organizers of the event told us that if we were interested in learning more about Jesus Christ, we should complete the information card that had been left on our tables. Something led me to fill out that form.

Within a few days of the breakfast I received a call from a friend who said he'd been given my card. He asked if I'd be interested in joining a short Bible study with him, another gentleman from CBMC, and two of my other close friends in the community who had also completed their cards at the breakfast. I said, "Sure, why not?"

So the five of us began to meet. The leaders gave us each a *Life Application Bible* and began to lead us through a short introductory booklet titled *First Steps*. The booklet contained four short chapters introducing us to important issues: "Is the Bible Credible?" "Who Is Jesus Christ?" "The Work of Jesus Christ," and "Eternal Life in Christ."

At the direction of the CBMC leaders we worked through and discussed a chapter each week.

In the first pages of the booklet we learned that the Bible consists of sixty-six books written by some forty different authors over a period of about 1,500 years. The authors came from every imaginable background—"kings, peasants, philosophers, fishermen, poets, statesmen and scholars. It was written on at least three different continents in three different languages—Hebrew, Aramaic, and Greek—yet, there is a thread of continuity from Genesis to Revelation." Indeed, Scripture is remarkably integrated on a wide variety of subjects and themes, a topic I explore in Chapter 7.

The pamphlet continued, "The Bible contains blatantly honest accounts of the lives of its main characters, exposing their strengths and their weaknesses."[3] The more I've read and learned about the Bible, the more I've confirmed this to be true. As R. A. Morey writes,

> One of the proofs of the inspiration of the Bible is its realism. It describes the great men and women of God who lived in biblical times as they really were. These great heroes of the faith were men and women with the same weaknesses that plague us.... The Bible paints the portraits of the saints of old with all their warts, moles, and wrinkles intact.... Abraham lied...Jacob was a skunk at times...Moses lost his temper...David had a problem with lust and committed murder.... The Bible could not have been man's idea. If we had written it, we would have never recorded all the evil things the patriarchs, prophets, and apostles did. We would have presented them as "perfect" examples for us to follow.[4]

Indeed, Professor Leland Ryken observes that the Bible is realistic precisely because of its "portrayal of unidealized human behavior.... It paints its characters as Cromwell wished to be painted—warts and all."[5] One Bible scholar notes that the patriarchs of Genesis are so deeply flawed that "they have almost more shadow than light."[6] As a great example, notice how the apostles show themselves in a bad light, such as when they argue over which of them will be greatest in the Kingdom of God (Luke 9:46–48). Another instance is when John tries to prevent someone from driving out demons in Jesus' name, presumably because he jealously thinks the disciples' standing might be diminished if others got in on the act.[7]

In the first chapter of the booklet we examined whether the Bible is the inspired Word of God and were introduced to Old Testament prophecies about Jesus Christ. I don't know if I slept through *all* the Sunday school lessons and sermons at my childhood church, but somehow I was woefully unaware of any of these things. I hadn't given much real thought to whether the Bible is actually the Word of God as opposed to a book written by spiritual men laying out traditional moral lessons. I was surprised to discover that the Bible clearly asserts its own divine authority. There is no ambiguity in this passage from the apostle Paul, in 2 Timothy 3:16–17: "All Scripture is God-breathed and is useful for teaching, rebuking, correcting and training in righteousness, so that the man of God may be thoroughly equipped for every good work."

All Scripture comes directly from God. That's a pretty bold claim. Note that Paul does not say that certain biblical passages come from God and others are just man's opinion. "All Scripture is God-breathed." All! I've since learned that this is a strikingly consistent theme of Scripture, and there are no contrary claims within the Bible. Consider a few examples in the Old Testament: "Every word of God is tested" (Prov. 30:5); "The words of the Lord are pure words, as silver tried in a furnace on the earth, refined seven times" (Psalms 12:6); "And, Forever, O Lord, thy word is settled in heaven" (Psalms 119:89).

In the New Testament, Jesus affirms, "For truly I say to you, until heaven and earth pass away, not the smallest letter or stroke shall pass from the Law until all is accomplished" (Matt. 5:18). In his gospel, John says, "The Scripture cannot be broken" (10:35). In his first letter, Peter writes, "But the word of the Lord endures forever" (1 Peter 1:25). And in his second letter he writes, "Knowing this first of all, that no prophecy of Scripture comes from someone's own interpretation. For no prophecy was ever produced by the will of man, but men spoke from God as they were carried along by the Holy Spirit" (2 Peter 1:20–21).

This idea is carried forward all the way through to Revelation, which unequivocally reaffirms that the Bible takes itself seriously. "Blessed is the one who reads aloud the words of this prophecy, and blessed are those who hear, and who keep what is written in it, for the time is near" (1:3). The book ends with a stern admonition regarding the gravity of Scripture and our duty not to distort its sacred words: "I warn everyone who hears the words of the prophecy of this book: if anyone adds to them, God will add to him the plagues described in this book, and if anyone takes away from the words of the book of this prophecy, God will take away his share in the tree of life and in the holy city, which are described in this book" (22:18–19).

What particularly caught my attention in the *First Steps* pamphlet was its discussion of some of the most important Old Testament prophecies about Jesus Christ (messianic prophecies) that were fulfilled in the New Testament. This is where things really got interesting for me.

- The prophet Micah, around 700 BC, wrote, "But you Bethlehem Ephrathah, though you are small among the clans of Judah, out of you will come for me one who will be ruler over Israel, whose origins are from of old, from ancient times" (Micah 5:2). The Gospel of Matthew records, "Jesus was born in Bethlehem in Judea" (2:1).

- The prophet Isaiah (ca. 700 BC) prophesied, "The virgin will be with child and will give birth to a son, and will call him Immanuel" (Isaiah 7:14).[8] Matthew says, "His mother Mary was pledged to be married to Joseph, but before they came together she was found to be with child through the Holy Spirit" (Matt. 1:18).

- Zechariah wrote in 500 BC, "Rejoice greatly, O Daughter of Zion! Shout, daughter of Jerusalem! See, your King comes to you, righteous and having salvation, gentle and riding on a donkey, on a colt, the foal of a donkey" (Zech. 9:9). In his gospel, John says, "They took palm branches and went out to meet him, shouting, 'Hosanna! Blessed is he who comes in the name of the Lord! Blessed is the King of Israel!' Jesus found a young donkey and sat upon it" (12:13–14).

- In the tenth century BC David wrote, "Even my close friend, whom I trusted, he who shared my bread, has lifted up his heel against me" (Psalms 41:9). In his gospel, Mark writes, "Then Judas Iscariot, one of the Twelve, went to the chief priests to betray Jesus to them" (14:10).

- Isaiah further adds, "He was despised and rejected by men...Like one from whom men hide their faces he was despised, and we esteemed him not" (Isaiah 53:3). John notes, "He came to that which was his own, but his own did not receive him" (John 1:11).

- Isaiah recounts, "He...was numbered with the transgressors" (Isaiah 43:12). Matthew tells us, "Two robbers were crucified with him, one on his right and one on his left" (Matt. 27:38).

- In Psalms we read, "They have pierced my hands and my feet" (22:16). John writes, "Put your finger here; see my hands. Reach out your hand and put it into my side" (John 20:27).

- Again from Psalms: "You will not abandon me to the grave, nor will you let your Holy One see decay" (16:10). In Acts, the book describing the history of the early Church, it says, "You killed the author of life, but God raised him from the dead" (3:15).

- Psalms says, "You ascended on high" (68:18). In Acts we see the fulfillment of this prophecy: "He was taken up before their very eyes, and a cloud hid him from their sight" (1:9).

These are but a small sampling of the messianic prophecies of the Old Testament that were fulfilled, in minute detail, in the New. I trust if you haven't been exposed to these they will impress you as they did me. I discuss these further in Chapter 8.

Learning of these prophecies represented a tipping point for me. We can always make excuses for why we won't believe; we can challenge the authenticity of the Old Testament writings that recorded these prophecies or the New Testament writings that documented their fulfillment. Or we can say the Old Testament writings were referring to something else or the New Testament writers conformed their writings to falsely claim fulfillment. But at that point I knew. I didn't doubt that these prophecies had been written in antiquity, long before Jesus was born, and I knew that His life and death represented a specific fulfillment.

A light went on. I knew I was reading a holy book that claimed to be a holy book—*the* holy book. I knew, for the first time in my life, that the Bible was the inspired Word of God. When it finally dawned on me that I was holding in my hands a written communication from the God of the universe, my life changed. I was beyond the point of pretending that intellectual obstacles precluded me from accepting Christianity as true. Sometime later I accepted Jesus Christ as my savior.

I had spent considerable time reading the classics and had given a great deal of thought to philosophical questions. At one point I believed I had developed, pretty much on my own, an idea of what God was like. I was attempting to mold Him to conform to my worldview at the time. When it hit me that the Bible was the revealed Word of God, I realized how foolish I had been in trying to reinvent the wheel to remake God in my image. I believe philosophy can be a worthy field of study, but I don't think we can improve on the Bible's revealed truths in conveying God's nature and His plan of redemption and salvation for mankind.

The brilliant G. K. Chesterton highlights the distinction between man-generated philosophy and divine revelation. In describing his purpose in writing *Orthodoxy*, he humbly admits that he had attempted "in a vague and personal way…to state the philosophy in which I have come to believe." But he adds this caveat: "I will not call it my philosophy; for I did not make it. God and humanity made it; and it made me."[9] Dr. Douglas Groothuis, professor of philosophy of religion, captures the significance of Chesterton's admission. "This stress on God's authority and ownership of truth," writes Groothuis, "should give followers of Christ a deep sense of anchorage in a divine reality beyond themselves. Their faith is not a 'religious preference' but has an indissoluble reference to revealed truths."[10]

GOD'S INSPIRED WORD

Having come to believe the Bible really is God's Word, I decided to begin reading it purposefully and in an entirely different light—with reverence and awe, realizing that as I was reading it, God was literally speaking to me. As Rev. Hugh McIntosh wrote in 1902, "From the viewpoint of practical religion, a Bible believed to be originally true, because inspired of God, is received with deepest reverence as the Word of God."[11] So, on the advice of believers I trusted, I began with the Gospel of John, the last of the four gospels in the New Testament canon and the one that is the most theological in nature.[12]

It's hard to deny that in John's gospel Jesus strongly asserts His own divinity. Yet that is precisely what many do. Granted, on the surface, there are some troubling passages wherein Jesus appears to be deferring to the Father and acknowledging that He is subordinate to Him. But the meaning of those passages becomes clear when we understand that Jesus is not denying His essential equality with the Father, but referring to certain functions within the Triune Godhead. Throughout, Jesus unambiguously maintains that He is God, that He is equal to the Father, and that He and the Father are one.

So as I read and reread this book, I was unable to deny that Jesus clearly claimed to be God, which was powerful stuff, considering that I had now come to believe that the Bible is inspired. Simply stated: God says that Jesus claimed to be God. Wow.

At this point I was on fire and began reading the Bible and everything about the Bible and theology I could get my hands on. I was impatient to accelerate my learning curve so that I could grasp the Bible's full picture. I remember searching in vain for a quick fix that would get me where I wanted to be without having to spend so much time in the dark. I dabbled in various books and software packages, but I soon realized there was simply no good shortcut. I would need to really put my nose to the grindstone and spend some time in Scripture if I hoped to get a better understanding of it.

I resolved to read through the Bible and achieved that goal after a few false starts. For those who would like to read the Bible from cover to cover, I found a relatively painless way to do it. Not that reading the Bible is painful, but it's daunting to read the entire book. However, I came across *The Daily Bible* by F. LaGard Smith, which presents the books of the Bible in their chronological—as opposed to canonical—order, and breaks it down into 365 daily readings, with a helpful introductory comment for each day's reading. There is no substitute, in my view, for reading the Bible itself in its original form, but this is a great way to get through it the first time. There are endless ways and methods to read the Bible, but I've read from experts, and can confirm from personal experience, that it is important at some point to read the Bible from beginning to end so you can begin to see the big picture—God's story of redemptive history—and understand how it all fits together.

Over the years, I attended numerous Bible studies, participated in many small groups, eventually taught some Sunday school classes, and took a correspondence course on the Old Testament. More recently, I took an Old Testament survey course online from Southern Evangelical Seminary, taught by Dr. Thomas Howe, which was enormously informative. I have been blessed with extremely helpful biblical and spiritual mentors along the way, including, among many others, my pastor Ron Watts, my former neighbor Pastor Steve Johnson, whose brain I picked every chance I had, and my friend—apologist extraordinaire—Frank Turek.

I must admit that even after intellectually embracing the truth of Christianity, I still faltered from time to time. Every once in a while I had to pinch myself and go back through the evidence in my mind. Do I really believe? Do I *really*? I spent so long as a skeptic I suppose it was only natural I'd have some residual baggage for some time.

But I also don't think there's anything wrong with a healthy element of doubt among believers. This doubt spurred me to study, think more, and consider the evidence even more thoroughly. In fact, I must admit that I did not come to believe in Christianity by exhausting all doubts or by understanding God's entire plan. I still had nagging issues about evil and pain and suffering in the world. The notion of eternal damnation also continued to bother me. But at a certain point I could no longer deny the overwhelming weight of the evidence in favor of Christianity. I am now convinced that when you study the evidence in earnest with an open mind and a willing heart, you can come away with no other conclusion. There are still things I can't fully explain—especially not to the stubborn doubter's satisfaction—but by far, the most reasonable conclusion from the evidence is that the Triune God of the Bible is real, the Bible is the inspired Word of God, the Bible is God's direct, special revelation to us and informs us about God's plan of salvation for mankind, and we ignore it at our peril.

What I want to tell my skeptical high school friends and any other nonbelievers is that I am sure I can't answer every one of your questions to your satisfaction, but if you approach the evidence objectively, you just might come to see the truth of the faith. Even the famous skeptic David Hume, in one of his arguments against the existence of miracles, acknowledged ironically, "A wise man, therefore, proportions his belief to the evidence."[13]

If you read the Bible itself with an open spirit, God will reveal Himself to you. "So faith comes from hearing, and hearing through the word of Christ" (Romans 10:17). "From infancy, you have known the holy Scriptures, which are able to make you wise for salvation through faith in Christ Jesus" (2 Tim. 3:15). The great British preacher Charles Haddon Spurgeon says, "It is God's Word, not our comment on God's Word, that saves souls. Souls are slain by the sword, not by the scabbard, nor by the tassels which adorn the hilt of it. If God's Word be brought forward in its native simplicity, no one can stand against it. The adversaries of God must fail before the Word as chaff perishes in the fire. Oh, for wisdom to keep closer and closer to that which the mouth of the Lord hath spoken!"[14]

Rev. Hugh McIntosh makes this bold claim about the divine authority of Scripture: "The clearness and decisiveness of the Bible claim to thorough truthfulness, entire trustworthiness, and Divine authority of all Scripture is the first impression made on every candid mind, on looking at this evidence and the vast amount of it—the immense mass, the impressive array of it; reminding one in its wide scope and massive strength of great mountain ranges, or vast, solid, imposing lines of impregnable fortifications. Even the most cursory view of it must impress this on every open mind."[15] But notice particularly his admonition about the fundamental importance of Scripture to those who are genuinely seeking after truth: "It certainly cannot be ignored or passed by lightly by anyone that wishes to know the truth."[16]

The *New American Commentary* on Romans also puts the power of the Bible in perspective: "Faith is awakened by the message."[17] British evangelist and Bible scholar G. Campbell Morgan (1863–1945) affirms the point, saying that Jesus' words, as revealed in the Bible, "constitute the very medium of life, for if a man hear His word, it is the word which reveals the Father; and the man receiving it will believe the Father; and so the word will become the medium through which he will receive life."[18]

SEEKING GOD

I would also suggest to skeptics that if you're interested in discovering whether God might be real, you ought to give Him a chance. Try approaching Him instead of always putting it off. What do you have to lose?

The Scriptures promise, "Draw near to God and he will draw near to you" (James 4:8). Seek God with an open heart and He will reveal Himself to you.[19] The greatest assurance of this comes from Jesus Himself, who teaches, "Ask, and it will be given to you; seek, and you will find; knock, and it will be opened to you. For everyone who asks receives, and the one who seeks finds, and to the one who knocks it will be opened" (Matt. 7:7–8).

I firmly believe that despite our fallen nature, we are, after all, made in God's image, and we are built to receive His message. As surely as we are fallen and apart from God, we crave being reunited with Him and won't find fulfillment until we are,[20] even if some of us are oblivious to that reality. We are empty without God, and only God can fill our God-shaped void. French Christian philosopher Blaise Pascal (1623–1662), in his *Pensées*, writes of the misery of man without God. All men, he argues—"princes and subjects, noblemen and commoners old and young, strong and weak, learned and ignorant, healthy and sick, of all countries, all times, all ages, and all conditions"—seek happiness, but their search will be for naught unless they find faith. "A trial so long, so continuous, and so uniform, should certainly convince us of our inability to reach the good by our own efforts.... What is it then that this desire and this inability proclaim to us, but that there was once in man a true happiness of which there now remains to him only the mark and empty trace, which he in vain tries to fill from all his surroundings, seeking from things absent the help he does not obtain in things present? But these are all inadequate, because the infinite abyss can only be filled by an infinite and immutable object, that is to say, only by God Himself."[21]

Elsewhere, Pascal is more specific about Christianity's singular ability to fill our void because it is not only true, but it correctly addresses our fallenness. He writes that "the true religion," in order to make man happy, must prove to him

> that there is a God; that we ought to love Him; that our true happiness is to be in Him, and our sole evil is to be separated from Him; it must recognize that we are full of darkness which hinders us from knowing and loving Him; and that thus, as our duties compel us to love God, and our lusts turn us away from Him, we are full of unrighteousness. It must give us an explanation of our opposition to God and to our own good. It must teach us the remedies for these infirmities, and the means of obtaining these remedies. Let us therefore examine all the religions of the world, and see if there be any other than the Christian which is sufficient for this purpose.[22]

None of the brilliant philosophers can provide the answer, he claims. Some of them, intoxicated by human pride and the desire to place man "on an equality with God," foolishly think the chief good can be found in man. Other religions have not provided the answer either. It can only be found in the one true religion—Christianity.[23]

Paul, in addressing the "men of Athens" about the gospel, tells them that God made "every nation of mankind...that they should seek God, and perhaps feel their way toward him and find him. Yet he is actually not far from each one of us" (Acts 17:26–27). So we see that one of God's aims "in revealing Himself both in creation and in history is that people would seek Him."[24]

The Old Testament contains the same promise. Job 8:5 says, "If you will seek God and plead with the Almighty, if you are pure and upright, surely then he will rouse himself for you." In Psalms God assures us, "And those who know your name put their trust in you, for you, Oh Lord, have not forsaken those who seek you" (9:10). Proverbs reaffirms the guarantee: "I love those who love me, and those who seek me diligently find me" (8:17). Deuteronomy 4:29 says, "But from there you will seek the Lord your God and you will find him, if you search after him with all your heart and with all your soul." And Jeremiah tells the Jews who are in exile in Babylon, "For thus says the Lord...You will seek me and find me, when you seek me with all your heart" (29:10, 13).

The message is clear and consistent. Come to God with a contrite, open, and humble heart. Seek Him in earnest and you will find Him. As Raymond Ortlund of Trinity Evangelical Divinity School declares, "If you seek God through his Word, with an open, receptive heart, you *cannot* miss him. He will not *let* you miss him. He will meet you and touch you. He will rekindle your spiritual fire through the power of the gospel."[25]

ROADBLOCKS

Finding and accepting God may not be as simple as it sounds. People will put all kinds of roadblocks in their own spiritual paths. Some rationalize that they don't want anything to do with Christianity because of the hypocrisy of so many churchgoers—and, admittedly, that's a problem. But the critic would do well to study his own heart and make sure he's not just making excuses for himself. Ravi Zacharias tells the story of the British journalist Malcolm Muggeridge, then a skeptic and later an ardent believer, who wrote to Mother Teresa and told her he had no interest in Christianity because of all its duplicity. Mother Teresa responded, "Your problem is a finite one. God is infinite. Let the infinite take care of your finite struggle." With that, says Ravi, "Muggeridge bent his knee to Christ and called it the most fulfilling step he had ever taken in his life."[26]

A friend once told me he had a far more serious barrier, confessing that he feared he was born with an intrinsic inability to believe. Talk about a paradox: a nonbeliever who is more convinced of predestination than a five-point Calvinist!

May I humbly suggest to my friend that his seeming inability to believe may well be something that is not intellectually based? Some people reject the gospel because they don't want to make a change in their lifestyle. For others, pain or pride may have alienated them from God. Toward the beginning of this chapter I cited Romans 1:19–20 to affirm my childhood experience of instinctively knowing that God exists: "For what can be known about God is plain to them, because God has shown it to them. For his invisible attributes, namely, his eternal power and divine nature, have been clearly perceived, ever since the creation of the world, in the things that have been made. So they are without excuse." So, Paul tells us, we are without excuse to deny God's existence.

But there is an important verse—verse 18—that precedes these two and provides insight into why certain recalcitrant people resist the truth. It says, "For the wrath of God is revealed from heaven against all ungodliness and unrighteousness of men, who by their unrighteousness suppress the truth." Some people blind themselves to the truth because of sin in their lives or because they don't want to have to account to a moral God. I am not moralizing here, because we are all sinners and this is a common obstacle to faith, even among some people whom we consider to be morally upright and good people. This especially applies to my friend who maintains he is incapable of believing. He is one of the finest people I know.

Concerning pride, some people have difficulty becoming humble enough to admit they need something beyond themselves—a personal savior. That's one reason I have come to believe that pride ranks high in the hierarchy of sins: pride leads us to believe we are spiritually self-sufficient and keeps us from drawing close to God—the very thing for which we were created. As J. N. Oswalt writes, "For those who depend for their very existence on the continued grace of a loving Creator to act as if they are somehow ultimate is the worst trespass upon reality imaginable."[27]

Pride is *the* sin that led to the fall of the human race. According to Paul, a person is not to think of himself "more highly than he ought to think" (Romans 12:3). Similarly, in Philippians 2, he says, "Have this mind among yourselves, a mind of Christ, who humbled himself."[28] It's quite ironic, but actually not unexpected, that a major obstacle for some to the Christian faith is an unwillingness to humble themselves before Christ, "Who, being in very nature God, did not consider equality with God something to be grasped, but made himself nothing, taking the very nature of a servant, being made in human likeness. And being found in appearance as a man, he humbled himself and became obedient to death—even death on a cross" (Philip. 2:6–8).

We must acknowledge our sinful state and our complete and utter inability to save ourselves apart from God. Only if we repent and place our faith in Christ will we receive God's gift of salvation. And this is true, by the way, no matter how much we may believe, intellectually, Christianity's truth claims—as even demons "believe" in Him, as James assures us: "You believe that God is one; you do well. Even the demons believe—and shudder" (James 2:19).

RELATING TO SKEPTICS

I noted at the beginning that I felt I might have been receiving providential promptings to write this book. Not only did my two old friends present me with an opportunity to defend the faith—an opportunity on which I failed to capitalize adequately—but within days my publishers suggested that for my next book I switch gears from politics to theology. They suggested I use my legal background to investigate the truth and reliability of the Gospel.

My initial response was ambivalent. As much as I've studied the Bible, theology, and apologetics, so much has been written about these topics by people who know more on the subject than I do, that I wondered, frankly, what I could add to the mix. But after prayerfully considering it for days, I warmed to the idea for a number of reasons.

On reflection, it occurred to me that I might be able to relate to nonbelievers in a way that some experts cannot because of my long-held skepticism and my protracted faith journey. We each communicate differently, we all have an opportunity to reach different people, and every single person is profoundly important. Thankfully, those of us who examine the evidence today are doing so on the shoulders of the megagiants of Christian apologetics, who have laid out the evidentiary case for Christianity compellingly.

So in this book I present evidence for the truth of Christianity's claims and also address some of the nagging questions that persist in the minds of many Christians even after they accept the faith, such as questions concerning science, the problems of pain and suffering, and alleged inconsistencies in the Bible. These questions have answers, and in some cases, while they may not wholly satisfy, they will give us a better understanding and a peace of mind that there are plausible explanations, the full depth of which we just might not be able to comprehend this side of heaven.

I also thought that in addition to presenting a defense of the faith in my own way, I could share some discoveries I've made and insights I've acquired on my spiritual path that have inspired and excited me about the Bible and about Jesus Christ, since such ideas might pique the interest of skeptics and also appeal to believers.

In terms of this book's structure, I don't strictly follow the systematic approach used by some classical apologists, such as that of Dr. Geisler in his classic *Christian Apologetics*. Nor do I exactly follow the twelve-point logical progression laid out by Dr. Geisler and Frank Turek in their book *I Don't Have Enough Faith to Be an Atheist*, for which I was honored to write the foreword.

I do cover all these points in the book, some in much greater detail than others. They are all important to a comprehensive apologetic, but I spend more time on the ones that had the most impact on me, thinking that I will have a better chance to reach doubters if I address those issues that contributed to my own skepticism. For example, while I discuss the abstract proofs for God's existence and address the question of whether miracles are possible, I don't dwell extensively on these points because I have never doubted the existence of a creator God, nor the existence of miracles, which are hard to deny if you believe in a creator God. I devote much more space to those things that turned my head directly toward the God of the Bible, such as biblical prophecy, the Bible's unity and historical reliability, other internal and external evidence that the Bible is true, and the attractiveness of biblical teaching, which has had enormous apologetic value for me.

Notice that many of these topics are focused directly on the Bible itself. There is a reason for that. When I told one of my nonbelieving friends I was writing this book, he suggested I refrain from quoting a lot of biblical passages. "You have to understand," he said, "that many of us don't share your high opinion of the Bible, so that's not going to make much of an impression on us." I told him that I respected his opinion, but I couldn't oblige his request. You see, I ultimately arrived at the point of faith not because of what others said about the Bible, as much as their ideas impressed me. It was the Bible itself that won me over—its prophecies, its unity, Jesus' authoritative and attractive teachings, and its overall divine glow. I would rather abandon writing this book altogether than omit quotations from and discussions of the Bible—a vital part of my mission here is to convey its incomparable majesty. But I am only a human being writing about Scripture. To fully grasp its wonder, you must read it for yourself and give it a fair hearing, as I ultimately did.

Another reason I quote abundantly from Scripture is that simply defending the faith might be inadequate if people don't understand something substantive about the faith itself. What's the point of apologetics if the people to whom you are addressing your arguments don't know much about Christianity? I admit that all Christians don't agree on every doctrinal point. But just calling oneself a Christian does not make one a Christian. There are essential beliefs that most Christians do agree on, and it does no one any good to pretend that Christianity can be all things to all people or that it can be molded to fit what we prefer our religion to be. As Alister McGrath laments, "At least some of what passes for Christianity in the world is a pathetic distortion of the real thing."[29]

As such, I discuss a number of theological concepts, with the hope that you will follow up and further explore them. I don't present these in the form of a discussion on theology or Bible doctrine. Instead, I introduce them more in the context of interesting passages that particularly affected me, thinking they might have some faith-enhancing quality for you.

Some of the insights I share in this book may strike the more mature believer as mundane, but I trust that some will find them as fascinating and riveting as I did. These are insights about the real, living God, Who made us in His image, and Who loved us so much, despite our sinfulness, "that He gave His only Son, that whoever believes in Him should not perish but have eternal life" (John 3:16).

But to avail ourselves of this opportunity—of this unmerited gift—we, as sinners, must act. We have a choice, but our choice doesn't include doing nothing. We must either accept Him or reject Him. "Neutrality is impossible." We must "become reconciled with God."[30]

I realize that some Christians are put off by the very idea of apologetics. "Why can't we just believe and quit trying to over-analyze everything?" they wonder. "Don't you understand that conversion is a matter of the heart, not of the intellect?"[31] Let me suggest to them that the Bible itself encourages apologetics. "But in your hearts honor Christ the Lord as holy, always being prepared to make a defense to anyone who asks you for a reason for the hope that is in you" (1 Peter 3:15). Even if you have never had doubts of the sort I address in this book, many of us have, and many of us have benefitted immensely from apologetics. As I can attest from personal experience, apologetics is not only for the nonbeliever, but also for Christians who experience doubt and need their faith reinforced from time to time.

I am also convinced that Christianity is under fierce attack in our culture and throughout the world, and those interested in truth have a duty to defend the faith and the Christian worldview. Our ready defense could have important consequences. Indeed, our children are bombarded with secularist indoctrination from the culture, our educational institutions, the media, and the entertainment industry, all of which tend to glamorize secularism and disparage—and often demonize—Christianity. Christian philosopher and apologist William Lane Craig agrees. He writes,

Christian laymen, too, need to become intellectually engaged. Our churches are filled with Christians who are idling in intellectual neutral.... People who simply ride the roller coaster of emotional experience are cheating themselves out of a deeper and richer Christian faith by neglecting the intellectual side of that faith.... But the results of being in intellectual neutral extend far beyond oneself. If Christian laymen don't become intellectually engaged, then we are in serious danger of losing our children. In high school and college Christian teenagers are intellectually assaulted on every hand by a barrage of anti-Christian philosophies and attitudes.... As I speak in churches around the country, I continually meet parents whose children have left the faith because there was no one in the church to answer their questions. For the sake of our youth, we desperately need informed parents who are equipped to wrestle with the issues at an intellectual level.[32]

Douglas Groothuis makes a related point: "One reason Christianity has failed to exert much influence on the major intellectual institutions of America is that too many Christians hold their beliefs in an uninformed and precarious fashion. Instead of pursuing answers to the toughest questions an unbelieving world can marshal, they attempt to preserve certainty through ignorance and isolation, relying on platitudes rather than arguments."[33]

While we don't have to over-intellectualize our faith, we mustn't shy away from its intellectual riches either. The Bible itself rejects anti-intellectualism. It exhorts us to engage our minds. "Love the Lord your God with all your mind" (Matt. 22:37). As God is the ultimate rational being, He wants us to be rational beings as well. He created us that way. "The mind is an essential ingredient of the Christian life," exclaims Jeffrey Spencer. "The mind is the main battleground of spiritual warfare."[34] Christians use their minds to develop Christ-likeness. Paul directs us to be "transformed by the renewing of your mind" (Romans 12:1–2). Only with our mind can we discern truth from error, so let's not disengage it. At the very least, as Christians, we must try to strike a balance between the intellectual and experiential aspects of the faith.

As you turn the page to the next chapter, I ask only that you try to approach what follows with an open mind and see where the evidence, the stories, the Bible, Jesus Christ, and the Holy Spirit take you. After having studied the evidence in depth, I am convinced that it proves that the fundamental doctrinal truth claims of Christianity are true beyond a reasonable doubt. I wouldn't have written this book if I didn't have some hope that by reading it, some doubters, with the illuminating work of the Holy Spirit, might begin to see this as well. Immediately following the scriptural charge that we must defend our faith is the further admonition, "yet do it with gentleness and respect" (1 Peter 3:15). I sincerely pray that in the pages that follow I approach this subject with the gentleness and respect that it requires.

CHAPTER 2

<figure>✕✕✕✕✕✕✕✕✕✕✕✕✕✕✕✕</figure>

"AHA" MOMENTS, PART 1

I n Chapter 1 I told you a bit about my spiritual journey and the pivotal moments leading me from unbelief to belief. In this chapter and the next I want to share with you certain stories I've run across and discoveries I've made as I've studied the Bible and theology, whether on my own, in preparation for teaching Sunday school, in connection with the seminary courses I've taken and audited, or from simply listening and talking to other people.

I will not pretend these insights are original or that everyone will find them profound. But they have all been meaningful to me, moving me spiritually, giving me a deeper understanding of Scripture, or strengthening my faith. My hope is that they will resonate with you as well.

I didn't keep a spiritual diary or a daily journal. But I do vividly remember my enthusiasm upon encountering each of these ideas. They may seem unrelated, but the common thread uniting them is the significant spiritual impact they each had on me. Conventional apologetics helped me arrive at the point of faith, and I went on to place my trust in Christ. But the story didn't end there. No Christian's spiritual journey ends at his conversion. In fact, it begins again, or it should, with a renewed intensity. So let me share a number of these discoveries and insights that have meant so much to me.

"THE ONLY LIFE EVER LIVED BACKWARD"

At some point in my early Christian walk, I bought a book that would change my thinking about Jesus Christ: *Life of Christ* by Archbishop Fulton Sheen. Though I am not a Catholic, this book is on my list of all-time favorites because it uniquely captures Christ's glory and the reasons for His incarnation. I highly recommend this book to everyone—Catholics, Protestants, and nonbelievers alike.

"If we leave the Cross out of the Life of Christ," writes Sheen, "we have nothing left, and certainly not Christianity. For the Cross is related to our sins. Christ was our 'stand-in' on the stage of life. He took our guilt as if He were guilty and thus paid the debt that sin deserved, namely, death. This made possible our resurrection to a 'new life' in Him. Christ, therefore, is not just a teacher or a peasant revolutionist, but our Savior. Our modern world does not like the word 'sin.'"[1]

Sheen says that three facts distinguish Jesus Christ from any other man who ever lived, and I ask you to ponder these. First, history is replete with those who claimed they came from God or were God, and that will always happen. But Jesus Christ is the only one of them Who satisfies the tests of "reason and history." He is the only person in history who was pre-announced, whose very birth, life, and death were prophesied, and who validated those prophecies. "What separates Christ from all men is that first He was expected," Sheen observes. "Even the Gentiles had a longing for a deliverer, or redeemer. This fact alone distinguishes Him from all other religious leaders."[2]

The second thing distinguishing Him from all others "is that once He appeared, He struck history with such impact that He split it in two,

dividing it into two periods: one before His coming, the other after it."
No one else did this. "Even those who deny Christ is Who He said He
was," writes Sheen, "are forced to date their attacks upon Him, A.D. so
and so, or so many years after His coming."[3] I've thought about that a
great deal. Christ is the only one Who divided history. He had to have
made a supernatural impact on the world for that to be true.

As fascinating as the first two examples are, the third one particularly grabbed me because I'd never heard, read, or thought about it quite
in this way. According to Sheen,

> Every other person who ever came into this world came into
> it to live. He came into it to die. Death was a stumbling block
> to Socrates—it interrupted his teaching. But to Christ, death
> was the goal and fulfillment of His life, the gold that He was
> seeking. Few of His words or actions are intelligible without
> reference to His Cross. He presented Himself as a Savior
> rather than merely as a Teacher. It meant nothing to teach
> men to be good unless He also gave them the power to be
> good, after rescuing them from the frustration of guilt. The
> story of every human life begins with birth and ends with
> death. In the Person of Christ, however, it was His death that
> was first and His life that was last.[4]

And this to me was the culminating eye-opener: "It was not so much
that His birth cast a shadow on His life and thus led to His death; it was
rather that the Cross was first, and cast its shadow back to His birth.
His has been the only life in the world that was ever lived backward."[5]

Imbibing these truths caused me to look at Christ and Christianity
in an entirely different way; it provided a new prism through which to
understand the faith, one that infused salvation history with fuller meaning and helped me to understand Scripture with greater depth.

This perspective illuminates why Jesus, Who had no fear, was so
intent on escaping the crowds that wanted to kill Him. It explains why
He rebuked Peter for defending Him with a sword when the soldiers

came to arrest Him. It helps us to understand why the disciples were often mystified by some of His teachings and didn't fully grasp the gravity of His message until *after* He died and was resurrected.

He didn't come to deliver His people by defeating the Roman Empire and establishing an earthly kingdom—not in His first coming, anyway. He came to die. He had to die so that He could conquer sin and death. And people like Peter who interfered with that were, in His words, doing Satan's work. Satan brought death into the world, and Christ came to vanquish it. Once He'd lived His sinless life and given us His teachings, it was time for Him to go. True, He didn't want to suffer and experience the anguish that separation from the Father would entail. He didn't want to feel, with every molecule of His existence, all God's wrath as He stood literally in our place as if He had committed every one of our past, present, and future sins Himself. He so dreaded this anguish in His human form that He asked if the Father could relieve Him of His misery.

But He knew better. He had come to die so that we could live, which is why, I think, He didn't lift a finger in His own defense when He was on trial. If Judas Iscariot hadn't betrayed Christ, He would have been delivered into the hands of the authorities in some other way, and no person or authority in the world would have been able to interfere with God's sovereign will that His mission—to die on our behalf—be fulfilled. There is no other person in human history about whom such truths apply. This realization leads us straight into the next insight I want to share with you.

DOES GOD HIDE HIMSELF FROM US?

I've often heard the question, "Why does God hide Himself?" It makes me think of the scene in *The Wizard of Oz* where the wicked witch writes with her smoke-emitting broom across the sky, "Surrender Dorothy." I have sometimes wondered why God didn't reveal Himself in some dramatic way like that so that we could all know that He's God. Some atheists even argue that God's failure to reveal Himself so conspicuously proves He doesn't exist. For me, the main flaw in this argument is that it assumes everyone is open to belief, which Scripture makes clear is not the case, as we've already seen.

Those arguments aside, I must tell you that at some point it dawned on me that God actually did (and continues to) reveal Himself. He reveals Himself in nature (Romans 1:19–20), and in the human conscience.[6] More important, He revealed Himself in a much more dramatic, content-rich, and sustaining way than any skywriting could have achieved: God the Father sent His Son to live among us. He performed many miracles, and some still did not believe. Not only did God send the Son, but He left us His Holy Word, written over a period of a thousand years. This Scripture includes not just the Law and the words of the prophets—which Jesus validated, often fulfilling their specific prophecies—but also contains Christ's own timeless words to us. We didn't have to be alive when Jesus was on this earth in order to profit from His message. Though He was here but a brief time, His words, in Scripture, endure forever.

Those who say God hides Himself and wonder what He's like need look no further than the person of Jesus Christ as revealed in Scripture. Christ said so Himself: "If you had known me, you would have known my Father also. From now on you do know him and have seen him.... Whoever has seen me has seen the Father. How can you say, 'Show us the Father'? Do you not believe that I am in the Father and the Father is in me?" (John 14:7, 9–10). William Barclay declares, "It may well be that to the ancient world this was the most staggering thing Jesus ever said. To the Greeks God was characteristically *The Invisible*, the Jews would count it as an article of faith that no man had seen God at any time."[7]

Indeed, how can we claim God hides Himself from us or is invisible to us when He showed Himself to us in Jesus? Jesus is the Son. The Son is a mirror image of the Father. Jesus' life and teachings are recorded in the gospels and we know precisely what He is like because He showed us Who and What He is. Consider John 1:14: "And the Word became flesh and dwelt among us, and we have seen his glory, glory as of the only Son from the Father, full of grace and truth." As D. A. Carson observes, "The glory John and others saw was *the glory of the One and Only*.... Thus it is nothing less than God's glory that John and his friends witnessed in the Word-made-flesh."[8]

Yes, God has revealed Himself generally in the wonder of His creation and specifically in His incarnation, and He continues to reveal Himself through His Holy Word—it's ongoing in the sense that we will always have it, and it will continue to speak to us afresh. So it seems that with the incarnation and the Bible, God has given us far more than skywriting, which is by definition temporal, fleeting, ephemeral, and non-sustaining.

The Bible is not merely a simple message from God saying, "I am here." It is a book of salvation history, a book of pure and absolute Truth, a book of Life, a book that explains for us our entire reason for existence. It is a book that lets us touch God and savor His words on a daily basis, a book that tells us Who He is and gives us instruction for acquiring wisdom, right living, and forming a relationship with Him. In his six-volume work *God, Revelation and Authority*, Dr. Carl F. H. Henry describes the Bible as "The Awesome Disclosure of God." He writes,

> Divine revelation palpitates with human surprise. Like a fiery bolt of lightning that unexpectedly zooms toward us and scores a direct hit, like an earthquake that suddenly shakes and engulfs us, it somersaults our private thoughts to abrupt awareness of ultimate destiny. By the unannounced intrusion of its omnipotent actuality, divine revelation lifts the present into the eternal and unmasks our pretensions of human omni-competence. As if an invisible Concorde had burst the sound barrier overhead, it drives us to ponder whether the Other World has finally pinned us to the ground for a life-and-death response.... Even once-for-all revelation that has occurred in another time and place fills us with awe and wonder through its ongoing significance and bears the character almost of a fresh miracle.[9]

Henry most assuredly rejects the idea that God hides Himself from us. "Revelation is God's unmasking of himself," he notes, "his voluntary act of disclosure. It comes from eternity, from beyond an absolute boundary that separates man from God."[10]

The Bible tells us that it is indeed the living Word of God (Heb. 4:12). I think this means that the divine revelation it contains is timeless and relevant to all generations, even though written in different historical contexts, and that when reading it we are actually communicating with the Living God of the universe. The Bible is so alive and supernatural that through its words God speaks to each of us personally and distinctly. By that I mean that when we read it, God is actually present with us and communicates His words to us through the Holy Spirit. So, for example, when I read the Bible, God illuminates the Scripture for me and shows how it applies to my life—if I'll listen. He does the same for every other Bible reader.

The message of the Bible is timeless and supernatural. If you're a believer, how many times have you listened to a sermon in church only to wonder how the pastor knew exactly what you were experiencing, as if he were talking to you and no one else in the congregation? Yet talk to your fellow congregants and you'll often find they had the exact same feeling. What he was saying to them, however, may be slightly or greatly different than what you heard as applying to yourself. This is part of what I think the Bible means when it says the Word of God is *living*. God inheres in the Word and speaks directly to us from the Word as we are reading and interacting with it. That may sound a little "out there" to some of you, and I fully understand that because I don't incline toward a charismatic approach, but I nevertheless believe it to be true.

On the other hand, maybe what I'm suggesting is not that strange. Doug Groothuis writes, "The word of God is a revelation from a transcendent, holy and communicative being, and so has an inner dynamism that rises above the psychology, sociology and politics of its readers, even though it is mediated through the particular cultural forms of its original context."[11] Professor Ben Witherington speaks to the living power of the Word. He observes, "It is interesting that in the plotting of the narratives in Luke and Acts there is a paradigmatic speech in each volume that sets in motion the mission of the good news: the speech of Jesus in Nazareth in Luke 4, and the speech of Peter in Acts 2 in Jerusalem. Over and over again, the living Word of God changes things either by transforming or scandalizing the audience."[12]

Theologian W. A. Criswell comes even closer to the concept I'm describing. He writes,

> The Word of God is always alive, fresh, and pertinent; it addresses itself to our present hour. If every drop of the Pacific Ocean were to dry up and turn into a dead lake, this Book would still be the fountain of the water of life. If that vast, granite, flint-rock mountain range called the Sierra Nevada should finally turn into heaps of dust, this Book would still be the rock of ages. If the very stars were to grow old and dim and go out, this Book would still be the light of the world. If the time were to come when the very atomic elements of this creation were to melt with fervent heat, this Book would still be witness to the coming of a new heaven and a new earth. This is the immutable, unchanging Word of God. "Heaven and earth may pass away, but my word will never pass away." It is quick. It is alive.[13]

Criswell also rejects the rather impersonal perspective that the Bible "contains" the Word of God. He insists that the Bible *is* the Word of God.[14]

The Bible claims to be "sharper than any two-edged sword, piercing to the division of the soul and of spirit, of joints and of marrow, and discerning the thoughts and intentions of the heart" (Heb. 4:12). It is dynamic—active, not passive—and is "full of living energy to carry out the will of God by either blessing or cursing as the case may be," as R. C. H. Lenski declares. He adds, "What folly to treat the Word of God as though it is subject to our minds, our 'views,' our opinions! It is electric and smites him who tampers with it; it is electric to light him who bows beneath it."[15] Lenski explains that the practical effect of this is that the Bible is convicting—in its light we recognize our vanity and sinfulness, even when the world is lauding the very activities in which we are engaging. "The Word," he exclaims, "pierces right through and shows what the soul is doing to the spirit."[16] But at the same time, "The Word approves and thus upholds, strengthens [and] comforts all who believe and obey."[17]

THE BIBLE WRITERS' CLAIMS OF SINCERITY AND INSPIRATION

While this next topic may not be considered part of a formal apologetic, it is probative to me of the Bible's divinity, and so I am compelled to discuss it. I don't think my bias is skewing my judgment, but I concede that my firm belief that the Bible is the Word of God heightens my sensitivities to the many profundities it contains.

What I have in mind are the multiple places in Scripture where the writers earnestly and conscientiously assure us they are telling the truth. Granted, one's own attestation that he's telling the truth may not seem unique; we all want people to believe we're telling the truth almost every time we open our mouths or commit words to writing. But we don't usually go to such lengths to make that assurance unless we feel our credibility might be in question, or to place a particular emphasis on what we are saying in order to impress upon our audience the utter importance of our message.

Whether or not these writers were always cognizant that they were writing under the inspiration of the Holy Spirit, they all surely had a sense of the immense weight of what they were writing and were personally invested in convincing their readers of their sincerity, reliability, and accuracy. As already noted, had their purpose been to deceive or to conspire to concoct a favorable tale, they would not have included so many things that placed them and their colleagues in an unfavorable light.

I want to share with you a number of passages that illustrate this point, and I ask you to consider the likelihood that the writers genuinely believed they were being truthful. This is no scientific test, and it's not hard, objective evidence, but it's an important part of the mix for me—just another reason I am so in awe of God's Word.

One of my favorite passages is the one that opens up the Gospel of Luke. Luke was a physician, a serious man who was obviously intent on our believing the authenticity of his record. I stop and reread this several times every time I come across it: "Many have undertaken to draw up an account of the things that have been fulfilled among us, just as they were handed down to us by those who from the first were eyewitnesses and servants of the word. Therefore, since I myself have carefully investigated everything from the beginning, it seemed good also to me to write an orderly account for you, most excellent Theophilus, so that you may know the certainty of the things you have been taught" (1:1–4).

It is crucial to Luke that Theophilus (and all other readers) "know the certainty" of the information he is passing along—because it is so important. Luke emphasizes that his evidence is reliable because it came from actual eyewitnesses and "servants of the word." It's another way of saying, *These aren't mere hearsay accounts.* Luke makes a point of assuring Theophilus that he has "carefully investigated" the entire record—"everything from the beginning"—and arranged it in an orderly manner. These are the assurances of a studious, meticulous scholar with a deep dedication to truth—and to *the Truth*, Jesus Christ, to Whom he had devoted his life.

We see a similar assurance from Peter, who writes,

> For we did not follow cleverly devised myths when we made known to you the power and coming of our Lord Jesus Christ, but we were eyewitnesses of his majesty. For when he received honor and glory from God the Father, and the voice was borne to him by the Majestic Glory, "This is my beloved Son, with whom I am well pleased," we ourselves heard this very voice borne from heaven, for we were with him on the holy mountain. And we have the prophetic word more fully confirmed, to which you will do well to pay attention as to a lamp shining in a dark place, until the day dawns and the morning star rises in your hearts, knowing this first of all, that no

prophecy of Scripture comes from someone's own interpretation. For no prophecy was ever produced by the will of man,
but men spoke from God as they were carried along by the
Holy Spirit (2 Peter 1:16–21).

Peter wants us to know he isn't purveying "myths," but providing
factual, eyewitness accounts. He obviously realizes he is reporting stories
that might seem fantastical—it's not every day that a person witnesses
the voice of God. But he is unafraid to make the claim clearly and
matter-of-factly. He tells us that the words of the Old Testament prophets were confirmed in the transfiguration, by which he is vouching for
the accuracy and inspiration of the Old Testament. He bolsters his point
with his claim that scriptural prophecy wasn't generated by the naked
interpretations of human beings, but by the Holy Spirit moving in men.
It's almost as though Peter is saying, *Hey, I realize I am telling some
bizarre stories here. So it's all that much more important that you understand I am telling you the whole truth. It's not like I would make up
such unlikely events, with nothing to gain but persecution.*

Paul, on a number of occasions, also labors to convince us of his sincerity and the accuracy of his accounts and of his message. He greets the
Galatians as "Paul, an apostle—sent not from men nor by man, but by
Jesus Christ and God the Father, who raised him from the dead" (Gal.
1:1). He adds, "I want you to know, brothers, that the gospel I preached
is not something that man made up. I did not receive it from any man, nor
was I taught it; rather, I received it by revelation from Jesus Christ" (Gal.
1:11–12). Notice he says, "I want you to know" that he didn't make these
things up. He couldn't have invented the story of the gospel. It was revealed
to him by no less an authority than the Son of God; this, from the most
notorious persecutor of Christians in his day, prior to his conversion.

Similarly, Paul tells the Corinthians, "For I received from the Lord
what I also delivered to you, that the Lord Jesus on the night when he
was betrayed took bread" (Cor. 11:23). And he informs the Thessalonians, "Because our gospel came to you not only in word, but also in
power and in the Holy Spirit and with full conviction. You know what
kind of men we proved to be among you for your sake" (1 Thess. 1:5).

Here's another gem from Paul to the Thessalonians:

> For our appeal does not spring from error or impurity or any
> attempt to deceive, but just as we have been approved by God
> to be entrusted with the gospel, so we speak, not to please
> man, but to please God who tests our hearts. For we never
> came with words of flattery, as you know, nor with a pretext
> for greed—God is witness. Nor did we seek glory from people,
> whether from you or from others, though we could have made
> demands as apostles of Christ. But we were gentle among you,
> like a nursing mother taking care of her own children. So,
> being affectionately desirous of you, we were ready to share
> with you not only the gospel of God but also our own selves,
> because you had become very dear to us (1 Thess. 2:3–8).

Here Paul is giving it a little twist. His motive, he says, isn't to please
man, but to please God, Who is well aware of the "hearts" of the men
conveying this message. They considered themselves honor-bound to
God to convey the truth—a higher motive, I dare say, even than to be
truthful to men.

There are a number of similar verses where the writers either assure
the readers of their veracity or that they were witnesses of the history
they record. I'm including the passages themselves, because I don't know
how many of you will go to the trouble to look all these up, and reading
them all makes the point in a way that paraphrasing them can't.

John writes, "Now Jesus did many other signs in the presence of the
disciples, which are not written in this book; but these are written so
that you may believe that Jesus is the Christ, the Son of God, and that
by believing you may have life in his name" (John 20:30–31). Here again
we have scriptural validation that the Bible itself can lead to our eternal
salvation. The gospel accounts were written so that we could read and
believe the essential facts about Jesus Christ, and that by so believing,
we could attain eternal life. Nothing could better underscore the importance of the writers getting their facts straight than their affirmed conviction that men's eternal destiny could depend on their accuracy.

John also declares, "That which was from the beginning, which we have heard, which we have seen with our eyes, which we looked upon and have touched with our hands, concerning the word of life" (1 John 1:1). Not only were they intellectually sure these things occurred, they experienced them with the full array of their physical senses.

Jesus Himself also makes the point that His followers would truthfully report accounts of His life because they had personally witnessed them. He says, "And you also will bear witness, because you have been with me from the beginning" (John 15:27).

John closes his gospel with, "Now there are also many other things that Jesus did. Were every one of them to be written, I suppose that the world itself could not contain the books that would be written" (21:25). This passage doesn't fall neatly into the category of verses I'm including here, but it makes a similar point. John is repeating that Jesus did many wonderful things beyond those recorded in the gospels. It is an example of the gospel writers' self-attestation—only in a different way. John is claiming credibility on reports he did not include, as well as those he did. Fascinating.

Luke writes in the Book of Acts, "For we cannot but speak of what we have seen and heard" (4:20). Similarly, "And we are witnesses of all that he did both in the country of the Jews and in Jerusalem" (10:39).

Also from Acts: "But Paul said, 'I am not out of my mind, most excellent Festus, but I am speaking true and rational words'" (26:25). I find it particularly interesting that right after this statement, Paul says that the king is well aware of all the facts about Jesus—"for this has not been done in a corner" (26:26). These things were publicly known, and Christianity was not some small, secret cult. As scholar F. F. Bruce argues, "The events which fulfilled the ancient promises were well known and public: this was no hole-and-corner esoteric mystery, whose initiates were pledged to secrecy. The ministry and death of Jesus were matters of common knowledge; his resurrection was amply attested; the gospel had been openly proclaimed in his name." And Bruce adds this: "Anyone who believed the prophets and compared their predictions with the historical facts concerning Jesus of Nazareth must acknowledge the truth of Christianity."[18]

In Acts, Luke says of Jesus, "He presented himself alive to them after his suffering by many proofs, appearing to them during forty days and speaking about the kingdom of God" (1:3). Also in Acts, Peter declares, "But what God foretold by the mouth of all the prophets, that his Christ would suffer, he thus fulfilled" (3:18). Here, Peter is affirming the authenticity of the Old Testament record and that Jesus historically fulfilled its prophecies about Him.

The writer of the letter to the Hebrews states, "How shall we escape if we neglect such a great salvation? It was declared at first by the Lord, and it was attested to us by those who heard, while God also bore witness by signs and wonders and various miracles and by gifts of the Holy Spirit distributed according to his will" (2:3–4).

"I CURSED THE ONE BY WHOSE WOUNDS I AM HEALED"

In his *Adventuring through the Bible*, Ray Stedman tells a moving story involving an encounter between his mentor Dr. H. A. Ironside and an unbelieving young man during the early years of Ironside's ministry when he was an officer in the Salvation Army. Every night Ironside held evangelism meetings in a large hall in a major city. He often noticed an attentive young man sitting in the rear of the meeting room and wanted to talk to him but could never catch him before he left at the end of the meetings.

Arriving late one night, the young man was forced to take a front row seat, allowing Ironside the opportunity to invite him to sit down and talk. In their conversation the man admitted he wasn't a Christian but said he wouldn't really call himself an atheist either, though he used to be one. When Ironside asked the young man what caused him to move away from atheism, he pointed to another man sitting nearby and said, "It's the change in that man right over there." Ironside recognized the man as a former bar owner and former alcoholic whose life was transformed when he had a religious awakening.

The young man said he'd known the former bar owner for years, and after witnessing his many failed attempts to quit drinking, concluded

that there may be something real to Christianity if it had finally turned
the guy's life around. As a result, the young man had begun reading the
Bible, but lamented that he wasn't getting much out of the New Testament. Recently, however, he'd been reading Isaiah in the Old Testament
and was impressed with the beauty of the language. "If I could become
a Christian by believing Isaiah," he said, "I think I would."

Seizing the opportunity, Ironside asked the man if he would listen
to a short chapter in Isaiah and then guess whom it was describing. The
young man was initially reluctant, saying he didn't know the Bible well
enough to answer that question. But he eventually agreed, and Ironside
proceeded to read Isaiah 53. (In his account of the story, Ray Stedman
didn't reprint the entire chapter, but I am choosing to, with your indulgence, to capture its full impact):

> Who has believed our message
>> and to whom has the arm of the LORD been revealed?
> He grew up before him like a tender shoot,
>> and like a root out of dry ground.
> He had no beauty or majesty to attract us to him,
>> nothing in his appearance that we should desire him.
> He was despised and rejected by mankind,
>> a man of suffering, and familiar with pain.
> Like one from whom people hide their faces
>> he was despised, and we held him in low esteem.
>
> Surely he took up our pain
>> and bore our suffering,
> yet we considered him punished by God,
>> stricken by him, and afflicted.
> But he was pierced for our transgressions,
>> he was crushed for our iniquities;
> the punishment that brought us peace was on him,
>> and by his wounds we are healed.
> We all, like sheep, have gone astray,
>> each of us has turned to our own way;

and the LORD has laid on him
> the iniquity of us all.

He was oppressed and afflicted,
> yet he did not open his mouth;
he was led like a lamb to the slaughter,
>> and as a sheep before its shearers is silent,
>> so he did not open his mouth.
By oppression and judgment he was taken away.
> Yet who of his generation protested?
For he was cut off from the land of the living;
> for the transgression of my people he was punished.
He was assigned a grave with the wicked,
> and with the rich in his death,
though he had done no violence,
> nor was any deceit in his mouth.

Yet it was the LORD's will to crush him and cause him to suffer,
> and though the LORD makes his life an offering for sin,
he will see his offspring and prolong his days,
> and the will of the LORD will prosper in his hand.
After he has suffered,
> he will see the light of life and be satisfied;
by his knowledge my righteous servant will justify many,
> and he will bear their iniquities.
Therefore I will give him a portion among the great,
> and he will divide the spoils with the strong,
because he poured out his life unto death,
> and was numbered with the transgressors.
For he bore the sin of many,
> and made intercession for the transgressors.

After he was done reading, Ironside asked the young man whom the passage was describing. The man asked Ironside to let him read it himself, and Ironside agreed. He read the entire chapter and then abruptly dropped the Bible in Ironside's hands and, without saying another word, raced out of the building. Dr. Ironside prayed for him.

The young man didn't return to the hall until three nights later. Ironside noticed he had a different look on his face as he approached and, voluntarily this time, took a seat in the front row. When it came time for people to share their personal testimonies, the young man stood up and began to speak.

Having been raised in an atheistic family, he said he'd been exposed to all the critics and was convinced that Christianity wasn't true. But he said that when he was in British-controlled Palestine working for the British government, he was exposed to influences that suggested to him the Bible might be true after all. Apparently he was far from convinced, however, because while he was still in Jerusalem with a tourist group, he was taken to Golgotha, the location where Christianity had begun, according to their guide. Feelings of anger welled up inside the man as he surmised that this is where "the Christian *deception* began." He began to curse, and the people he was with ran down the hill, afraid that God would strike him dead for blaspheming on that sacred spot.

Then the young man broke down in tears as he related the next chapter in his journey. "You know, friends, these last few nights I have learned that the one I cursed on Calvary was the one who was wounded for my transgressions and by whose wounds I am healed."

Stedman observes that it took an Old Testament prophecy to prepare this young man's heart for the good news of the New Testament. "His experience is a beautiful demonstration of the purpose and power of the Old Testament," he notes.[19]

I have read that story more than a dozen times, and almost every time it moves me—emotionally and spiritually—because it illustrates the power of the Bible itself to move human hearts. Isaiah 53 is indeed a striking chapter that shows the magnitude of suffering that Jesus endured on our behalf and vividly describes the agony of Christ in minute detail, hundreds of years before He was born.[20] This passage hits me like a smack in the face. It's as if each time I'm reading it, God is crying out to me, *Know that I am God and understand that I love you.* I treasure this opportunity to share this rich and powerful story with you.

In the next chapter, I will share some equally moving stories and additional insights into Scripture that have been especially meaningful to me.

CHAPTER 3

⟨⟨⟨⟨⟨⟨⟨⟨⟨⟨⟨⟨⟨

"AHA" MOMENTS, PART 2

A MAN SET APART

⟨⟨⟨⟨⟨⟨⟨⟨⟨⟨⟨⟨⟨⟨⟨⟨⟨⟨⟨⟨⟨⟨⟨⟨⟨⟨⟨⟨⟨

In his book *Deliver Us From Evil*, Ravi Zacharias tells a compelling story of God's pursuit of a man who, try as he might, could not escape God's clutches. The man was Hien Pham, a "devoted young Christian" interpreter who traveled with Ravi in 1971 during his ministry in South Vietnam. Ravi and Hien became close friends but lost contact when Ravi left the country that year. He didn't hear from Hien until 1988, when Hien called him out of the blue.

When Ravi asked Hien how he escaped from Vietnam, Hien said that not long after the South fell to the Communists, he was arrested and imprisoned for allegedly aiding the Americans. During one of his jail terms, his jailors persistently tried to indoctrinate him against democratic ideals and Christianity. He was not allowed to read anything in English and was fed only Communist propaganda in French or Vietnamese.

Gradually, he began to soften to this barrage and started to doubt his beliefs, wondering whether he had been deceived all his life. So he resolved to discontinue praying or even thinking about Christianity beginning the following day.

The very next day he was assigned to latrine cleaning duty. As he was cleaning out a can full of toilet paper he noticed a piece of paper with English writing on it. He quickly cleaned it off and put it into his pocket. Later, after his roommates had fallen asleep, he used a flashlight to read the paper. At the top corner of it he saw, "Romans, Chapter 8." Hien was moved as he started to read:

> And we know that in all things God works for the good of those who love him, who have been called according to his purpose.
>
> ...What, then, shall we say in response to this? If God is for us, who can be against us? He who did not spare his own Son, but gave him up for us all—how will he not also, along with him, graciously give us all things?
>
> ...Who shall separate us from the love of Christ? Shall trouble or hardship or persecution or famine or nakedness or danger or sword?...No, in all these things we are more than conquerors through him who loved us. For I am convinced that neither death nor life, neither angels nor demons, neither the present nor the future, nor any powers, neither height nor depth, nor anything else in all creation, will be able to separate us from the love of God that is in Christ Jesus our Lord.[1]

Hien wept. A camp official was using a Bible as toilet paper—and God chose this means to supply Scripture to Hien at the point of his greatest need, refusing to allow Hien to reject Him. Moreover, He could not have furnished "a more relevant passage of conviction and strength for one on the verge of surrendering to the threat of evil."[2] As Ravi poignantly describes it, "He cried out to God, asking for forgiveness, for this was to have been the first day in years that he had determined not to pray. Evidently, the Lord had other plans."[3]

The story contains an amazing postscript, also showcasing God's sovereignty and faithfulness. After "an equally providential set of circumstances" led to his release from prison, Hien began to make plans to flee the country. He was going to escape with fifty-three other people, but a few days before their departure, four Communists interrogated him about the plot. After convincingly denying it, he grew disgusted with himself for resisting what he believed was God's intervention. He vowed to God he would never do that again. Shortly before they were set to escape, the four men came back and renewed their questioning. Hien replied honestly this time, thinking it would be the end of him. To his surprise, the men told him they wanted to escape too.

Even this turn of events was not the end of God's role in this story. All fifty-eight people—Hien, his fifty-three colleagues, and the four Communists—were on the high seas when an overwhelming storm deluged their boat. Hien began to doubt God again, wondering if He had done all this just to bring them to the seas to die. But as providence would have it, the extraordinary sailing ability of the Communist escapees enabled them to weather the storm, and the ship made it safely to Thailand.

Some may scoff at the suggestion that God played a role in any of this, much less that His superintending hand guided Hien back to Him before he'd really had a chance to leave, then eventually on to safety. But others know that sometimes what we think of as a coincidence is, in the words of my pastor Ron Watts, a "God-incidence." The Book of Genesis has one remarkable string of such God-incidences involving Joseph, a story to which I now turn.

PRODUCING GOOD FROM THAT WHICH WAS INTENDED FOR EVIL

Beginning in Chapter 37 of Genesis, the familiar story of Jacob's son Joseph demonstrates God's sovereignty over human affairs. The story involves God's thwarting of the sinister plans of Joseph's jealous brothers to kill Joseph and, through a series of twists and turns, Joseph's unexpected promotion to the second-highest office in pharaoh's Egypt. The account shows how God can cause the most unlikely chain of events to work in furtherance of His ultimate plans. His sovereign plan to nurture and preserve the emerging Hebrew nation is consummated in spite of, and sometimes because of, the sinful actions of certain people, including Joseph's brothers.

Notice the unfolding of God's sovereignty at every turn: had Jacob not doted on Joseph in the presence of his brothers, they would not have become jealous and hateful toward him. Had the brothers not harbored such hatred, they would not have plotted against him. Had the Ishmaelites not been on the road to Egypt, Joseph's brothers probably would have killed him instead of selling him into slavery in Egypt. Had the cupbearer not been imprisoned with Joseph, he would not have been impressed by Joseph's dream-interpreting gift. Had the cupbearer chosen to "remember" Joseph when the cupbearer was released (as Joseph implored him to do), Joseph may have been released from prison and would not have been available to interpret pharaoh's dreams later.

But since the cupbearer opportunistically remembered Joseph's ability a few years later, when pharaoh was in need of such services, Joseph was able to prove himself in pharaoh's sight. Had Joseph not interpreted the dream as forecasting a famine, he would not have been placed in charge of the land of Egypt. Had Joseph not been elevated to that position of authority, he would not have been able to implement his God-given counsel to store 20 percent of the grain produced during the seven years of abundance. Had it not been for the God-induced abundance and then famine in fulfillment of pharaoh's God-induced dream, Egypt would not have prospered, and other nations, specifically Canaan, would not have needed her grain. Had Canaan not been experiencing famine, Jacob would not have sent his other sons to Egypt to buy grain. Had Jacob not done so, he and his family would never have settled in Egypt during the years of famine, and the entire nation of Israel would likely have died in its incipiency.

This valuable story shows us so many things about God. He is in control. This is *His* planet. He is a completely faithful God Who keeps His word. He promised Abraham that He would bless him, that He would make a great nation out of him, that He would make his name great, that he would be a blessing, that He would bless those who blessed him, that whoever cursed him He would curse, that all peoples on earth would be blessed through him, that his descendants would be as numerous as the sand on the seashores, and that they would inherit Canaan as their everlasting possession—all these are elements of the Abrahamic Covenant.[4] None of these commitments could have been fulfilled but for the bizarre and extremely improbable series of events involving Joseph.

As a result of these events, the burgeoning nation of Israel was allowed to settle and incubate in Goshen, the choicest land of Egypt. Israel was preserved, and it preserved God's law; the tribe of Judah was preserved, and through it would come Jesus Christ, the Messiah, who would fulfill the Abrahamic Covenant by blessing all people through Abraham and offering forgiveness of sins and salvation to all who would believe in Him. Throughout, God used sinners and their sinful acts in furtherance of His Divine Plan. "And we know that in all things God works for the good of those who love him, who have been called according to his purpose" (Romans 8:28).

Beyond the powerful demonstration of God's sovereignty and faithfulness, we also see in this story the exemplary faith and obedience of Joseph. He never complains, but always accepts God's will. He trusts and waits on God to do things in His own time and in His own way. The story illustrates that although we are often unaware of God's presence or of the intricacies of His plan, He nevertheless is present and has a plan, and our ignorance of it doesn't make it any less real. "He has made everything beautiful in its time. He has also set eternity in the hearts of men; yet they cannot fathom what God has done from beginning to end" (Eccl. 3:11).

As Christian writer Allen Ross says, "In the final analysis the human and the divine perception of evil come together in the wisdom of Joseph, who explained that what his brothers did for him was intended for *evil* but that evil was actually part of God's plan for *good*. Here we see how God's persistent plan to bless can actually triumph over evil and turn it back into good, as it had at the beginning of creation."[5]

MANNA FROM HEAVEN

I've always found this story appealing because of the faith lessons it teaches. In the wilderness wanderings, the Israelites begin to grumble because they are unable to find water in the desert (Exodus 15:24). So God shows Moses a tree and "when he threw it into the water, the water became fit to drink" (Exodus 15:25). Next, the people complain because they are hungry. In response, God provides them manna from heaven, but He tells them to gather just as much as they need and no more. He tells Moses that He will only provide enough for them to get by each day in order to test them to see if they will "walk in my law or not" (Exodus 16:4). God isn't teasing them or playing some kind of game—by allowing the Israelites only enough for one day at a time, He is teaching them to depend on Him.

If I had contemplated this story before becoming a Christian, I likely would have projected human qualities onto God and concluded that a perfect God wouldn't have treated the Israelites that way. He wouldn't have been so egotistical. What I wouldn't have understood is that God didn't withhold extra provisions so they would come groveling to Him as part of some divine ego trip. It was not about Him; it was about them—and the indispensability of their learning to depend on Him, not for His sake, but solely for theirs.

God was teaching them that He was their ultimate provider. He knew better than they what they needed, and He would give them what they needed, not what they wanted.[6] They were required to believe that He would give them just enough to supply their daily needs and not to fret over it and second-guess Him. But by only giving them enough for a day at a time, they would have to rely on Him and stay focused on Him. Otherwise, out of sight, out of mind. Obviously, this lesson transcended their physical needs. It had to do with matters far more important than their appetites; it was about their spiritual needs.

Nor was this some abstract exercise. God was teaching them a lesson about discipline and obedience when some of the manna, which had been reserved for the following morning in violation of His directive, "bred worms and stank." The Israelites learned that disobedience entailed consequences.

Then some of them sinned again by disobeying His command that they bake and boil leftovers for the Sabbath, as they were not to gather food on that day. They disobeyed both parts of the command by failing to properly preserve the food for the Sabbath and by going out to gather more on the sanctified day of rest. Those who obeyed were rewarded because the baked and boiled portions "did not stink and there were no worms in it." But those who went out on the seventh day to gather bread found none.

I think this is a lesson that we can't pick and choose what to obey in God's Word.[7] God was precise in His instructions, and the Israelites needed to be precise in their hearing and obeying. There would be enough food each day *except the Sabbath*. So the day before they'd need to make provision to ensure that they'd have enough left over to eat. As Charles Spurgeon warns, "Do not leave one single part of God's Word to lie void."[8]

God didn't merely teach them dependence by providing only enough for one day at a time. He taught them that He was present among them. He was on the scene and accessible. He was their provision.

These were transcendent messages, just as applicable to us today as to the Israelites in the wilderness. Just as they were to be dependent upon God each day for their physical sustenance, Christians today are to lean on Him daily for their spiritual nourishment. It is God's wish that we commune with Him in prayer and read the Bible daily in furtherance of our personal relationship with Him. Our spiritual manna must be sought daily. We must not try to live on last year's, last month's, or yesterday's supply.

"Stale experiences are poor food," says Spurgeon.[9] When we fail to stay in the Word or fail to pray or exercise other spiritual disciplines, we inevitably backslide because we are living in a fallen world and are subject to enormous temptations. God actively desires that we have an intimate relationship with Him. He does not want us to rely on our own power, but to humble ourselves before Him and seek the strength of His spirit to empower us for daily living.

Jesus uses this historical lesson when calling Himself the "bread of life" (John 6:32–33, 35, 41, 48). He is telling us that He is the heavenly manna, the spiritual sustenance the Father gives to those who seek and knock (John 6:45; Matt. 7:7–8).[10] Spurgeon says, "If you have spiritual life, you must feed it, and God will give you manna from heaven, that is, Christ himself, with which to feed your soul. He is that Bread of life which came down from heaven, and you must feed on him."[11]

God is teaching us an important lesson through the life experiences of the Israelites and their relationship with Him. We must depend on Him not for His sake, but for ours, and by doing so, in humility, obedience, and in trust, we grow in our love relationship with Him.

THE BOOK OF LAMENTATIONS

I now turn to the Book of Lamentations to illustrate another altogether different aspect of the beauty of Scripture: its literary quality. In his Old Testament survey course at Southern Evangelical Seminary, Dr. Tom Howe introduced us to the wondrous structure of Lamentations. Not only is the book brilliantly designed, but its structure unmistakably corresponds to the message of the book. I want to share this with the acknowledgment that I would never have noticed it but for Dr. Howe's course.

The book is organized as an alphabetic acrostic poem or a series of such poems in which each successive line or stanza begins with sequential letters of the Hebrew alphabet.[12] This structure is difficult to craft. For example, the first line or stanza begins with "aleph," the first letter of the Hebrew alphabet, the second with "bet," the second letter, the third with "gimel," and so on. This doesn't come through in the translations, but here's a crude example in English I found on the internet to illustrate the concept:

> Acrostic poetry is fun to write,
> Because nearly anyone
> Can do it.

Lamentations consists of five chapters, each containing a distinct poem of twenty-two stanzas. In Chapter 1, each stanza is composed of three lines, and the first line of each stanza begins with the next letter of the Hebrew alphabet. Chapter 2 has the same structure as Chapter 1. Chapter 3, which biblical scholars agree is the most highly constructed,[13] also has twenty-two stanzas of three lines each, but here each line in the stanza, not just the first line, begins with the *same* letter of the Hebrew alphabet, and all three lines for each successive stanza begin with the next letter of the Hebrew alphabet. Here's an example:

> Acrostic poetry is fun to write,
> And it is fun to read
> As you can see.
> Before trying it yourself,
> Be prepared for a challenge
> But don't get discouraged.

Imagine pulling that off for twenty-two stanzas without sounding sophomoric. Chapter 4 is composed of twenty-two stanzas of two lines each, with the first line of each stanza beginning with the next letter of the Hebrew alphabet. Chapter 5 has twenty-two stanzas, but each is only one line, and there is no acrostic structure involved, though Old Testament scholars La Sor, Hubbard, and Bush note that it "even seems to reflect the influence of the acrostic pattern."[14]

So we see a deliberate intensification of the poetic structure from Chapters 1–3, moving from a simple acrostic pattern to a more complex pattern, which eases off in Chapter 4, and then there is no strictly acrostic pattern at all in Chapter 5. Chapter 3 represents the culmination, structurally.

At the same time, there is a similar intensification of content and tone through the midpoint of Chapter 3, where there is lamenting over the destruction of Jerusalem, which intensifies into absolute despair about the people being carried away into captivity. The poet reaches the ultimate expression of his grief in verse 18, when he wails, "My strength has perished, and so has my hope from the Lord."

But then, just as his grief is about to overtake him, in verses 19–21 the poet recalls his suffering, affliction, and bitterness, but he also remembers something that gives him hope. It is that God was gracious to His people in keeping them from being totally consumed as a result of their sins. Because of His lovingkindness, God's compassion did not cease (3:22), even though there was great destruction and affliction. God was faithful to His promises and to His covenant (3:23), and so the poet can hope in God, Who is his salvation (3:24). The despair of Israel was not a state of utter hopelessness because the God of Israel still reigned. This is the climactic section and turning point of the entire book, whose perfect synchronicity of story and structure affects me much like a beautiful symphonic melody.

Dr. Howe observed that what we see in Lamentations, as in so many other books, both Old Testament and New Testament, is that Scripture is always pointing back to things and connecting those things, which illustrates the unity of Scripture I've been describing. By looking back and remembering God's faithfulness, our own faith is restored and strengthened, because we know God has always been reliable in His past dealings with us. The structure of the literature, as well as the content, is designed to make us remember what God has done for us, and how we should not repeat our (or Israel's) sinful behavior. This is a recurring theme throughout the Bible.

IS THE GOD OF THE OLD TESTAMENT DIFFERENT FROM THE GOD OF THE NEW TESTAMENT?

It is not just unbelievers who are sometimes mystified by the seeming harshness of God in certain Old Testament stories; it is also troubling for many Christians. Along the same lines, just as people often fail to recognize God's love in the Old Testament, they mischaracterize Jesus Christ as one Who is always gentle—a nonjudgmental milquetoast Who is infinitely tolerant, including of sin. If there is anything harsh coming out of the New Testament, they say, it comes from that "sexist" Paul. Nothing could be further from the truth. This is a case where, I think, myths of the popular culture have corrupted our true understanding. Yes, Jesus is absolutely loving, but He also embodies Truth, and like the Father, He abhors sin.

Seminary professor Cyril Barber tells the story of a colleague who said he couldn't preach from the Old Testament because he found "the

God of the Old Testament to be harsh and uncaring. He sends down fire and brimstone on Sodom and Gomorrah, destroys the firstborn in Egypt, commands the people to exterminate the Canaanites and Amorites, and punishes sin with unsparing severity. It is only when we come to the New Testament that we encounter a God of grace." Barber comments, "As the years have gone by I have found that this attitude is widespread."[15]

It's as if people impute human characteristics to God, assuming somehow that God is changeable, that the "mean" God of the Old Testament morphed into this wonderful, nonjudgmental God of the New Testament. But God is, in His very essence, unchangeable (Psalms 102:27; Heb. 1:12; Mal. 3:6; Heb. 13:8; James 1:17). The God of the Old Testament *is* the God of the New Testament. Though God has revealed Himself progressively, He is not two separate entities.

As Scottish theologian Thomas Torrance explains, "What God is toward us in the Gospel as Father, Son and Holy Spirit he is antecedently, inherently and eternally in himself." He did not become a Trinity in the incarnation. He has always been a Triune God. "God was not always incarnate. He was always God the Son as well as God the Father and God the Holy Spirit, but not always God become man in Jesus Christ in whom divine and human nature are forever united in the one incarnate Person of God the Son."[16] But just because the Son became man doesn't mean that God changed in nature. He still has the exact same essence He always had and always will have.

Professor Barber says his colleague could not have been more wrong. He points out that in Numbers 14:18–19 Moses tells the Israelites that "Yahweh is slow to anger and abundant in lovingkindness, forgiving iniquity and transgression." At Moses' request, God, in His grace, pardons the iniquity of his people. "God is a God of grace, but His grace does not give people a license to sin."[17] In Ezekiel, God is quoted as saying, "Have I any pleasure in the death of the wicked…and not rather that he should turn from his way and live?" (18:23).

As for the New Testament, we must not casually remake Jesus in the image in which we prefer to see Him or which conforms to the popular culture's misperceptions about Him. Our politically correct culture may, presumptuously, choose to recast Jesus as indifferent to sin and saccharine sweet, no matter the circumstances, but this Jesus is God, and God cannot look upon sin. What do these revisionists make of the Jesus Who made a whip of cords and drove the moneychangers out of the Temple (John 2:15)? Does that square with the image the modern-day pacifists have of Jesus? He clearly showed His righteous anger in that episode, but that's no detraction from His perfection. As Ron Rhodes notes, "One could forcefully argue that to stand idly by and turn one's face from blatant sin would be a sign of imperfection."[18]

What do the revisionists say about the Jesus Whom Paul describes as "revealed from heaven with his mighty angels in flaming fire, inflicting vengeance on those who do not know God and on those who do not obey the gospel of our Lord Jesus" (2 Thess. 1:7–8)? What of the difficult moral standard Jesus laid down in the Sermon on the Mount? Did He show indifference to sin there?

In fact, Jesus wasn't shy about dealing with difficult issues. He "talked more about hell than anybody else," says Pastor Timothy Keller. "You want to blame hell on Paul or somebody nasty like that, I'm sorry. Go take a look."[19]

Fulton Sheen argues that our culture, which refuses to deal with the idea of sin, has divorced Christ from His cross. Our culture, writes Sheen, sees "Christ as weak, effeminate, with no authority to drive buyers and sellers out of temples, and never speaks of self-discipline, restraint and mortification."[20]

This idea that Jesus is meek, mild, indifferent, and non-judgmental is the stuff of pure myth. Pastor Mark Driscoll says he used to believe Jesus was dull, boring, passionless—in short, unappealing—until he read the Bible. He didn't recognize in its pages the Jesus about Whom he'd always been told. Driscoll challenges us to read the Gospel of Mark, which will "spin your head around." Jesus, says Driscoll, tells people to "repent." He tells people to quit their jobs and follow him. He tells a demon to shut up. After He heals a leper He swears him to silence, too. Then He picks a fight with Sunday school teachers, He tells His mom He's busy, He rebukes the wind, He kills two thousand pigs, and "he offends people, but doesn't go to sensitivity training." He calls people hypocrites and calls Peter "Satan," He curses and kills a tree, He tells people they're going to hell, and He rebukes the disciples for falling asleep on Him in the garden.[21] Driscoll's point is not that Jesus was mean or bad in any way; merely that the lukewarm, pacifist image this culture has created of Him is as ridiculous as it is inaccurate.

In *The Jesus I Never Knew*, Philip Yancey says that the more he studied Jesus, the more he realized He bore little resemblance to his prior image of Him. He was not like a *Star Trek* Vulcan who "remained calm, cool and collected as he strode like a robot among excitable human beings on spaceship earth." As he studied the gospels more, Yancey discovered that "other people affected Jesus deeply: obstinacy frustrated him, self-righteousness infuriated him, simple faith thrilled him. Indeed, he seemed more emotional and spontaneous than the average person, not less. More passionate, not less."[22]

People just need to think through this a little bit. The God of the Old Testament is the God of the New Testament. Jesus Christ is the Second Person of the Triune Godhead, who became man in the incarnation but did not change His essence. His essence is an exact reflection of the Father's essence. If you have seen Jesus, you have seen the Father because Jesus and the Father are one. The Holy Spirit likewise is identical to the Father and Son in essence. Those who believe that God changed His character between the Old Testament and New Testament should understand that Jesus Himself validated the Old Testament in its entirety (Matt. 5:17–20) and demonstrated His exalted view of it by summarizing its teachings with the two commandments to love God and love your neighbor (Matt. 22:37). Jesus also affirmed that God in the Old Testament preferred love and mercy over sacrifice (Matt. 9:13; 12:7).

In addition, there are not two separate strains of Christianity in the New Testament, one taught by Jesus and the other by Paul, known by certain liberal critics as Pauline Christianity.[23] The New Testament is a unified whole, and Paul's epistles reflect a message wholly consistent with that delivered by Jesus—Who personally converted Paul and imparted the gospel message directly to him.

Let's not fool ourselves; Jesus hated sin. The great Christian writer A. W. Tozer says that modern Christians have been brainwashed into believing that to be good Christians we must be able "to purr softly and accept everything that comes along with Christian tolerance and understanding." To the contrary, we need to "show a zealous concern for the cause of Christ" and stand for the Truth, which includes opposing "iniquity with a deep, compelling revulsion."[24]

Among the real dangers of seeing Jesus as the contemporary culture portrays Him is that we entirely miss His uniqueness. He is like no one who has ever lived, and to rob Him of His distinctiveness is to wholly misunderstand Him. We can't rewrite the Bible to make it fit our modern notions of what is fair and just. And we dare not presume to remake our God.

Just to ensure I do not leave you thinking Jesus was obnoxious or terrifying, let me remind you that as Jesus is God, Jesus is love. He teaches us to love God and our neighbor above everything else (Matt. 22:37, 39). While He talks a great deal about hell, He also offers a guaranteed way out of any brush with it. His warnings about hell do not proceed from mean-spiritedness—how could He possibly be indifferent to hell? How could He fail to warn us about it when He sacrificed so much just so we could avoid it? His warnings are grounded in unbounded, unconditional love for us, which led Him to sacrifice His holy blood in payment for our sins to make possible our eternal life with Him.

THE BOOK OF THE COVENANT AND LAW SCHOOL

The next insight I want to share is something I discovered when I was reading through the Bible for the first time after becoming a Christian. As a young lawyer, I was intrigued when I came across the laws immediately following the Ten Commandments in Exodus (20:22–23:19), which collectively are described as the Book of the Covenant (24:7). I was taken by how many of our laws are obviously derived from the Bible. There are laws in the Book of the Covenant pertaining to torts, contracts, and property—three of the five subjects I took in my first semester of law school.

I remember studying in torts class the rules regarding an owner's liability for harboring a dangerous animal, most often applied to dogs. Our professor told us that many mistakenly believed that dog owners were exempted from liability for their dog's first bite. The rule is actually a bit more nuanced. Rather, a dog owner (or owner of any other animal) is responsible if he has knowledge of his animal's vicious propensities prior to the animal's injuring a person, even if the animal has never bitten or injured anyone before. From the way the discussion evolved I had always assumed this rule was a later development, replacing the simplistic "first-bite" rule.

When I read Exodus 21:28–29, I was genuinely surprised to discover that the nuanced rule was not new at all, but had derived from this passage: "If a bull gores a man or a woman to death, the bull must be stoned to death, and its meat must not be eaten. But the owner of the bull will not be held responsible. If, however, the bull has had the habit of goring and the owner has been warned but has not kept it penned up and it kills a man or woman, the bull must be stoned and the owner also must be put to death." As you can see, the animal owner's knowledge of his animal's vicious propensities is what triggers his liability. I realize that the penalty prescribed virtually puts this in the category of criminal law, but this does not detract from my point that the legal principle concerning the animal owner's knowledge of his animal's vicious propensities emanates from this biblical law. A reading of the other specific laws in the Book of the Covenant unsurprisingly reveals other striking similarities to laws still in force today.

POWER IN POSITIVE THINKING?

Frequent Bible readers typically discover they have certain favorite passages that are particularly encouraging or illuminating. One of my favorites is Philippians 4:4–9, in which Paul declares,

> Rejoice in the Lord always; again I will say, rejoice. Let your reasonableness be known to everyone. The Lord is at hand; do not be anxious about anything, but in everything by prayer and supplication with thanksgiving let your requests be made known to God. And the peace of God, which surpasses all

understanding, will guard your hearts and your minds in
Christ Jesus. Finally, brothers, whatever is true, whatever is
honorable, whatever is just, whatever is pure, whatever is
lovely, whatever is commendable, if there is any excellence, if
there is anything worthy of praise, think about these things.
What you have learned and received and heard and seen in
me—practice these things, and the God of peace will be with
you.

I ask you to notice that Paul is not telling us Christians merely to
wish ourselves into a happier existence through our own power; he's not
advocating some kind of psychological mood candy. He is telling us to
wrap our arms around Christ and avail ourselves of the comfort He
provides. He encourages us not to worry, to be reasonable, and to enjoy
the peace of God in Jesus Christ. We are to think of the true, the lovely,
the pure, anything worthy of praise, all of which are other-directed and
Christ-centered, not self-centered. We are not lifting ourselves up through
our own effort or works, or through psychological suggestion, but by
dwelling on the wonderful and true things God created and on Him.
This passage has been uplifting to me and many others with whom I've
shared it, and so I wanted to include it here for you.

Paul's exhortation is in stark contrast to the "power of positive thinking" movement popularized by Dr. Norman Vincent Peale, which, in
my view, was not altogether biblical because it seemed to suggest that
people could change the future just by willing positive outcomes. Like
the "prosperity gospel," which tells us we can all be rich if we just have
enough faith, it tends to detract from our proper emphasis on Christ-
centeredness. There is nothing wrong with pursuing success and material
blessings, but as Christians we must try to remember that our true con-
tentment is embodied in Jesus Christ, and we should organize our lives
around this truth. But this passage of Scripture does remind us that God
wants us to experience the peace and joy of the Lord. We must set our
hopes "on God, who richly provides us with everything to enjoy" (1 Tim.
6:17). As Christians we don't have to be stern, legalistic scolds, and we
won't be if we are Christ-focused.

SLAIN BY THE EVIDENCE
◇◇

Some particularly intelligent people use their God-given intellect to argue against the existence of their Maker. Two men in eighteenth-century England set out to do just that. Lord Lyttelton and Gilbert West were lawyers and committed nonbelievers. One day one of them said to the other, "Christianity stands upon a very unstable foundation. There are only two things that actually support it: the alleged resurrection of Jesus Christ and the alleged conversion of Saul of Tarsus. If we can disprove those stories, which should be rather easy to do, Christianity will collapse like a house of cards." Gilbert West agreed to write a book on the "alleged resurrection of Jesus Christ and disprove it." Lord Lyttelton vowed, in turn, to write a book to refute Saul's conversion.[25]

Sometime later they met again and one of them told the other, "I'm afraid I have a confession to make. I have been looking into the evidence for this story, and I have begun to think that maybe there is something to it after all." The other said, "The same thing has happened to me. But let's keep on investigating these stories and see where we come out." By the time they had completed their books they had become believers, and their tomes, West's *The Resurrection of Jesus Christ* and Lyttelton's *The Conversion of St. Paul*, reflected their newfound, evidence-based beliefs.[26]

Sometimes when we are certain we are on our own, completely independent, utterly self-sufficient, and without need of a savior, God actively intervenes with a gracious and timely lesson in humility. We sometimes fail to appreciate that our God is an infinitely loving God, Who pursues us not for His benefit, but for ours. Whether off the coast of Thailand with Vietcong sailors, on the road to Egypt with treacherous brothers, or wandering in the wilderness just outside the Promised Land, God can find us.

In the next two chapters I will discuss a number of paradoxes in biblical teachings that are fascinating because they are not what we would expect, and are faith-enhancing because they are mostly tied together by the common theological thread of grace abounding.

CHAPTER 4

✧✧✧✧✧✧✧✧✧✧✧✧✧✧

PARADOXES OF CHRISTIANITY, PART 1

I mentioned that biblical teachings draw me to the faith and help assure me of its truthfulness. I particularly enjoy the counterintuitive messages we often find in the Bible—the paradoxes we see throughout Christ's teaching and in the rest of Scripture as well.

There are many lessons in Christianity that may strike us as contradictory or unfair. But if we explore those teachings we will see they are neither. In fact, difficult teachings can lead us to a deeper faith, as was the case for me as I grew to better understand Christ's dual nature, as I explain in Chapter 6. Please permit me to cite, paradoxically, a renowned existentialist on the virtues of the paradoxical, Søren Kierkegaard, who advises, "One should not think slightingly of the paradoxical; for the paradox is the source of the thinker's passion, and the thinker without a paradox is like a lover without feeling: a paltry mediocrity."[1]

I've often thought that some Christian ideas are so weird that no human mind could have devised them. At first blush they seem so wrong but end up being so right—they must be from God. As G. K. Chesterton remarks, "Whenever we feel there is something odd in Christian theology, we shall generally find that there is something odd in the truth."[2]

There may be a plausible explanation for this. When something doesn't make sense at first, we are forced to think it through and try to resolve the difficulty. As a result, we end up grasping the concept better than if it had been simple and straightforward. Interestingly, Dr. Howe, an expert in biblical languages, described in his Old Testament survey course how Proverbs teaches that the acquisition of wisdom involves just such a process.

Dr. Howe introduced us to the various Hebrew words for "wisdom," such as *hokmah* and *binah*. Proverbs, of course, emphasizes the importance of acquiring wisdom and teaches that it begins with the fear of the Lord. Getting your mind focused on God and having reverence for Him are the keys to having a correct understanding of the world. To have wisdom is to possess a proper grasp of the basic issues of life and of the relationship of man to God, and having the understanding to skillfully apply knowledge to life's situations. This wisdom is not something one is born with; it must be taught and learned. But it can't all be acquired through book learning.

It is analogous to a craft that one learns and refines through experience. The word *hokmah* is used in Exodus 28:1–3 to describe the skill of the tailor in sewing the curtains for the Tabernacle and in Exodus 31:2–3 to portray the ability of the metal craftsman. A tailor or metal craftsman learns his craft through experience, gradually perfecting his skills over time. The more challenges he experiences in his craft, the more knowledgeable he becomes. He develops a sense of when to use certain tools and how best to manipulate each of them. Through hard work and trial and error, he refines his skills and eventually becomes a wise craftsman.

Proverbs teaches that we should apply these principles to our lives in our pursuit of wisdom. Like the craftsman, the wise person learns basic principles of life through application and experience, gaining knowledge from his mistakes. Wisdom, however, isn't merely a matter of accumulating and retaining knowledge. It's understanding how much you don't know (knowing one's limitations), being willing to learn what you don't know (being teachable), and exercising prudence and good judgment in life.

We can also acquire wisdom through Scripture by applying the craftsman's principles. We don't just read Scripture superficially; we read it, study it, mull it over, meditate on it, digest it, and then apply the principles we've learned in our everyday living. In turn, we learn from our successes and failures in applying these principles in our lives, after which we revisit Scripture again and continue this process. Through this back and forth—this interaction between our life experiences and our Scripture meditation—we grow in wisdom.

One consistent theme of the Bible is that we profit from struggling through problems; we grow when we confront our difficulties squarely and work through them. We are often better for having gone through the struggle than we'd have been if we never had encountered the difficulties. Proverbs 1:6 tells us that among the reasons we should study the proverbs is "to understand a proverb and a saying, the words of the wise and their riddles." The Hebrew word used for "riddle" means "an indirect, oblique, or enigmatic statement (like a figure of speech) which needs interpretation."[3]

If there were no enigmas—no riddles in Scripture—and all biblical truth were completely straightforward and comprehensible without the necessity to think deeply about it, we wouldn't learn the principles as thoroughly or grow as much. It is in the process of working through these riddles, untying their knots, and figuring out their meanings that we acquire understanding, wisdom, and even righteousness. The challenge then is on two levels: we struggle with the material when we read it, and we struggle as we endeavor to apply it to our lives.

If we properly grasp what is meant by wisdom, then we will better appreciate why the Bible, and particularly Jesus, often teaches in this manner. It is not to play mind games or to hide the truth from us. As always, He does what He does for our benefit. As we struggle through these concepts, we learn them more completely, and as a result we grow in wisdom, righteousness, and godliness.

One could doubtlessly write an entire book on Christian paradoxes—things that just don't sound right to us, until closer examination vindicates them, as it almost always does. As Millard Erickson says, "A paradox is a sign of intellectual indigestion; had it been more completely chewed, it would have disappeared."[4] In this chapter and the next I examine many paradoxes of Christianity that I believe will, if we wrestle with them, strengthen our understanding of Scripture and our faith.

MANY PARADOXES

Consider: Christians believe that God is one, yet He is also three. We believe Jesus is God and also man. We're assured that God is in control—He's completely sovereign—yet we are responsible for our own actions. We believe the Bible is the inspired Word of God, yet it was written by man. We are told that we have to give up our life to gain our life, that we must die through Christ so that we can live for Him, that we must serve in order to triumph, and to give away to gain. We learn that "he who is least among you all is the one who will be great," and that Jesus sometimes seems to condemn the rich and give comfort to the poor, but He also says that those who have plenty will be given an abundance. We are told that the servant is inferior to the master but that we should be servants. We are taught that we are inherently sinful yet we are commanded to be perfect, "just as your Father is perfect."

We are told that we gain strength in our weakness and experience joy in our suffering. We are admonished to fear God at the same time we are instructed to love Him. We are advised to have the faith of an innocent child but also commanded to love the Lord with all our heart, soul, strength, and mind. We are taught that we are saved by grace through faith alone, yet that we must take the initiative to exercise spiritual disciplines to grow in holiness.

What about the confusion between law and grace? Are Christians still under the Law? If not, why do we still consider it relevant to our faith, and why do we still talk about the Ten Commandments? We are told that through faith our sins are forgiven and that we are no longer under the Law, but that this doesn't give us the license to sin. We discover that in Christ we gain our freedom yet we are supposed to live as sinlessly as possible. We find out that everything in the world that God made is "good," yet we are warned against being "of this world."

In the parable of the prodigal son, the ungrateful and rebellious son is rewarded while the obedient older son seemingly receives no benefits.

As Christians, why do we pray? What difference will it make? Isn't God in control? He never changes His mind, does He? Why are we Christians told we have to forgive our enemies—people we believe with every fiber of our being don't deserve forgiveness and often aren't even repentant? Let's look more closely at some of these apparent contradictions.

GOD'S PLAN OF SALVATION

Consider, for example, God's plan for our salvation. It runs counter to everything in our bones to believe that we don't have to earn our way into heaven. Indeed, Christianity is the only major religion that is grace-based—Christ sacrifices Himself and offers His payment for our sins freely to all, by grace. How can the Bible teach that we are so thoroughly corrupt and yet offer us a way to overcome our depravity by accepting an unmerited gift? Are you serious? Apart from the biblical instructions we impart to them, that is certainly not how we teach our children to conduct themselves. We tell them they must work for what they get in life; otherwise they won't appreciate it. We tell them not to rely on handouts, but to make their own way.

Don't misunderstand—there is nothing inconsistent in our instruction of our children and the Christian doctrine of grace. But the point is, there *appears* to be a conflict.

Many skeptics ridicule the notion that Christ was sacrificed for *our* sins. To them it's not even a morally sound idea that we should be able to profit—much less attain forgiveness, expiation, and eternal life—based on what someone else, even God Almighty Himself, did for us. How does it make sense in the scheme of cosmic justice for us to be cleansed by the substitutionary death of the incarnate God? Isn't it unjust for someone to take credit for what someone else has done—and to which he has contributed absolutely nothing? Perhaps so in the case of mortals dealing solely with mortals, but we're talking about the Author of Life bestowing this gift.

Since becoming a Christian, it's occurred to me that God's salvation plan for us is so far-fetched and so foreign to our way of thinking that there must be something to it. It is just too bizarre an idea for human beings to have concocted it on their own and expected others to believe it. If the organizers of a new religion were conspiring to construct a believable scenario, this might be the last idea they'd contrive. Just as Christianity's paradoxical teachings paradoxically bolster the credibility of Christianity's truth claims, the apparent unlikeliness of Christianity's grand plan of salvation increases its believability.

The more I've thought through this divine salvation plan, the more I've concluded that it is the only plan that makes sense, as weird as it may seem at first. Given the human condition and God's perfection, His perfect justice and His desire to make us free agents capable of personal love, there is no other salvation plan that could work nearly as well, if at all. St. Thomas Aquinas agrees that there was no more "suitable way of delivering the human race than by Christ's passion." He adds, "Many other things besides deliverance from sin concurred for man's salvation." Among those things, says Aquinas, are that "man knows how much God loves him, and is thereby stirred to love Him in return," and "man is all the more bound to refrain from sin, when he bears in mind that he has been redeemed by Christ's blood, according to 1 Cor. 6:20: *You are bought with a great price: glorify and bear God in your body.*"[5]

Many people quite naturally think to themselves, *If I live a good life and my good deeds outweigh my bad ones, I should be saved.* Yes, in the abstract that sounds good, but it ignores so many things that a perfect God cannot allow to be ignored.

Would the Son have agreed with the Father to such a salvation plan if there were a less excruciating but equally effective method? If the Father could have satisfied His sense of perfect justice without having His Son take on human form and suffer immeasurable pain and separation from the Father, wouldn't He have done so? Wouldn't He have answered His Son's prayer in Gethsemane and "taken His cup from Him" if He could have spared His Son that sorrow and still accomplished His plan of redemption for humankind in accordance with His perfect nature? Indeed, if human sinners could have been made righteous in any other way, then God suffered for no reason at all.[6] As Paul wrote to the

Galatians, "I do not nullify the grace of God, for if righteousness were through the law, then Christ died for no purpose" (Gal. 2:21).

God's salvation plan wasn't just one plan that He chose among many. It was the perfect solution. The Son had to acquire a human nature, in addition to His divine nature, in order to save us. He had no choice other than the one He exercised for our salvation because His moral perfection, His Holiness, and His perfect justice inhere in Him. Unless He was willing to deny His own nature and compromise and violate His perfect holiness and justice, He couldn't just wipe the slate clean without requiring a sufficient satisfaction of our debt. Far from violating His nature, He vindicated it with this brilliant salvation plan. "For all have sinned and fall short of the glory of God, and are justified by his grace as a gift, through the redemption that is Christ Jesus, whom God put forward as a propitiation by his blood, to be received by faith. This was to show God's righteousness, because in his divine forbearance he had passed over former sins. It was to show his righteousness at the present time, so that he might be just and the justifier of the one who has faith in Jesus" (Romans 3:23–26).

Even if God's perfect justice can't be satisfied without a real payment for our sins, how can His sense of justice allow the satisfaction of our sins through the sacrifice of another? How does that square with anything we have ever perceived about justice, let alone perfect justice?

First, let's recognize that no sinful human being can save himself. Not one of us is without sin, so we better hope Christ can do it in our place or we're out of alternatives. But how can it work? How can God do this for us and still give us the credit?

In one of his debates with a Christian about the existence of God, the late self-professed atheist Christopher Hitchens seemed to be making this point. "How moral is the following?" he asked. "I am told of a human sacrifice that took place two thousand years ago, without my wishing it and in circumstances so ghastly that, had I been present and in possession of any influence, I would have been duty-bound to try and stop it. In consequence of this murder, my own manifold sins are forgiven me, and I may hope to enjoy everlasting life." Hitchens rejects the idea that he is responsible for Christ's flogging and crucifixion, in which he had no say and no part. He denies that Christ's agony was necessary to compensate for the sin of Adam, of which he also had no part. Hitchens further seems to be saying that the idea of atonement through Christ's substitutionary death is inconsistent with our personal accountability for sin, and he objects to the idea that our salvation depends on whether we "believe" Christ died for us.

What Hitchens seems to have overlooked is that we are not condemned for Christ's death but for our own sinfulness. Christ's death and resurrection are not our condemnation. They are our avenue to deliverance. Furthermore, "faith in Christ" does not mean mere intellectual assent to the proposition that Christ died for you. Rather, it's a full-blown commitment to placing your very life in His hands and trusting in Him for the remission of your sins and for eternal life. Saving faith involves genuine repentance—admitting that you're a sinner and deliberately turning away from your sins in complete humility—and turning toward Christ and trusting Him for your salvation. I'm not saying "saving faith = faith + repentance." I'm saying repentance is part of placing one's faith (trust) in Christ.

There's plenty of accountability in sincere contrition. There is nothing immoral in someone voluntarily sacrificing his life for you, especially when that someone is the very Giver of life, the Judge of all things. Nothing could be more moral; nothing could be more loving. And Christ's substitutionary sacrifice was unquestionably voluntary. The Father didn't pressure or coerce Him to do it. They were in complete accord. Jesus removes all doubt about this when He says, "Greater love has no one than this, that he lay down his life for his friends" (John 15:13). And more specifically, "The reason my Father loves me is that I lay down my life—only to take it up again. No one takes it from me, but I lay it down of my own accord" (John 10:17–18). Nor was this an act of selfishness or cruelty on the part of the Father, who suffered as much as Christ did in the process, as they are in perfect harmony and One, in essence.

Theologian Millard Erickson responds to the argument that it is unfair and unjust for the Father to have substituted His Son to bear our penalty. He considers the analogy of a judge imposing a penal sentence on an innocent bystander instead of the just-convicted defendant. The analogy fails, says Erickson, because God didn't impose the sentence on some innocent third party; He imposed it on Himself. "God is both the judge and the person paying the penalty," notes Erickson. "In terms of our courtroom analogy, it is not as if the judge passes sentence on the defendant, and some innocent and hitherto uninvolved party then appears to pay the fine or serve the sentence. Rather, it is as if the judge passes sentence on the defendant, then removes his robes and goes off to serve the sentence in the defendant's place."[7]

But what Hitchens (and others) might really be objecting to is not the giving of the sacrifice by Jesus—that's His business—but the unfairness or injustice in our receiving it and taking credit for it. How can Christ's righteousness be imputed to us, even through His sacrifice? If one of my kids does the other's assigned chores, that's a credit to the child doing the work, but how is it fair and just for the one who neglected his chores to take credit for it? Doesn't Christian morality teach that we are responsible and accountable for our own behavior?

I struggled with this at one time and satisfied myself with the realization that those to whom Christ's righteousness is being imputed—those who have placed their trust in Him—are not wholly passive. Again, it's not just a matter of naked, intellectual belief, as some mistakenly assume. They make a choice to identify with Him. They decide to turn from their former life and toward Him. They do nothing to earn their salvation, but they do consciously choose to place their faith in Him. We make a decision to align ourselves with Him, to unite with Him. This is not our abstract claim or credit for what some stranger has done. Millard Erickson explains it more eloquently:

> This objection would be to a considerable extent valid if our relationship with Christ were this detached and he were quite aloof from us. Then it would be as if a total stranger paid the fine for a convicted criminal. But the individual believer is actually united with Christ.... The transfer of the righteousness of Christ, and of what was accomplished by the atonement, is not an arm's-length transaction. Rather, it is a matter of the two, Christ and the believer, becoming one in the sight of God. Thus, Paul is able to speak of the believers having died with Christ and having been made alive with Christ (Rom. 6:3–4). It is as if, with respect to one's spiritual status,

a new entity has come into being. It is as if Christ and I have been married, or have merged to form a new corporation. Thus, the imputation of his righteousness is not so much a matter of transferring something from one person to another as it is a matter of bringing the two together so that they hold all things in common. In Christ I died on the cross, and in him I was resurrected. Thus, his death is not only in my place, but with me.[8]

This, to me, is a beautiful explanation. We are not riding Christ's coattails. We are sewed onto them—and Him.

But there's another important point we're missing here, perhaps the most important of all, that hadn't occurred to me until I'd thought through this numerous times. The whole idea of grace, as opposed to works, is that we can't save ourselves, and our salvation is an unmerited gift from God. "For by grace you have been saved through faith. And this is not your own doing; it is the gift of God, not as a result of works, so that no one may boast" (Eph. 2:8–9). It is a gross insult to Christ's finished work on the cross to challenge God's salvation scheme simply because we believe we shouldn't be entitled to credit for the sacrifice Christ chose to make on our behalf. We are insisting on setting the terms.

Our discomfort with the idea of His substitutionary sacrifice may very well arise from our human-based resistance to letting go and surrendering our destiny to Him. What might seem noble on our part—our insistence on earning our way, which is all this boils down to as you think through it—is, in effect, a sign of our pride and rebellion. That's because this isn't about fairness, in our customary way of assessing situations. It's *not* fair in human terms. We *don't* deserve this grace. But in His boundless mercy, He's offering to give it to us anyway.

It took me a while to understand that this one last objection is actually little more than a works-based argument disguised as humility. This is what finally hit me and what has helped me better embrace the idea of grace. I truly believe that this whole concept of salvation being God's gift to us, as believers, is one of the most difficult things for people to comprehend. So, yes, in one sense, salvation can be simple for us to the extent we don't have to do any work to earn it, but it's not simple at all for some people to set aside their pride and humbly turn to Christ with the admission that they need Him and the plea that He save them.

That's what we mean when we say that apologetics, examining the evidence, or reason alone can't save us. It can only get us to the point of faith. In the end, no matter how much our intellect tells us that Christianity's truth claims are valid, for salvation we must surrender and place our trust in Christ, and that's a matter of the will, not the intellect. But to say that saving faith involves more than the intellect is not the same thing as saying it is unreasonable or that it involves abandoning our rational faculties and embracing our faith blindly. Our faith is based on abundant evidence, rationally weighed and considered, as this book intends to demonstrate. It isn't taking some blind leap; it's taking a fully informed plunge of the will into the arms of Christ.

Christians don't place their faith in just anything; it can't be content-free. We must have knowledge of the nature of God and Who Christ is in order to put our trust in Him. Sean McDowell states it well: "The more we know about [God's] character, his heart, and his motivations and desires, the deeper our convictions will grow and the stronger our faith will be in his person. Faith and evidence work hand in hand in that way."[9]

Keep in mind that God doesn't have as low an opinion of faith as some skeptics do. He clearly tells us it is impossible to please Him without it (Heb. 11:6). While faith and reason are complementary, compatible, and mutually beneficial, reason is not our final destination. Our ultimate goal isn't to reason with God, although that would be delightful too. Saving faith isn't experiencing a mind-meld with God. Our goal is to have a saving relationship with God through Christ. That means intellectually understanding Who He is and what He's done for us and then placing our firm trust in Him for the remission of our sins. If we don't take that final step of trusting Christ, we do not "believe" or have "faith" in Christ for purposes of our salvation.

In the end, no matter what we may think of God's salvation scheme, it is good enough for Him. As explained in 2 Corinthians, "God made him who had no sin to be sin for us, so that in him we might become the righteousness of God" (5:21). And as Peter puts it, "Christ died for sins once for all, the righteous for the unrighteous, to bring you to God" (1 Peter 3:18).

WE ARE SAVED BY FAITH ALONE, BUT ISN'T OUR EFFORT ALSO REQUIRED TO FIGHT SIN?

The cross pierces our self-centeredness and pride because it conveys that we are incapable of saving ourselves. The heart of the gospel message is that we can be saved through faith in Christ. But while we are saved through no effort of our own, we still need to exert some effort as we battle sin during our journey toward holiness. Is this a contradiction?

There are three important words pertaining to salvation: justification, sanctification, and glorification. We are saved by grace through faith alone. Christ died a substitutionary and atoning death on our behalf. Placing our trust in Him leads to our justification, where we are declared righteous in a judicial sense and His righteousness is imputed to us, as we have seen. "But now apart from the law the righteousness of God has been made known, to which the Law and the Prophets testify. This righteousness is given through faith in Jesus Christ to all who believe. There is no difference between Jew and Gentile, for all have sinned and fall short of the glory of God, and all are justified freely by his grace through the redemption that came by Christ Jesus. God presented Christ as a sacrifice of atonement, through the shedding of his blood—to be received by faith" (Romans 3:21–25).

As nineteenth-century evangelist Charles H. Spurgeon powerfully argues,

> If God shall look upon us as we are He must be displeased; but when He sees us in Christ Jesus He is well pleased for His righteousness sake. When the Lord looks this way we hide behind the veil, and the eyes of the Lord behold the exceeding glories of the veil, to wit the person of His own dear Son, and He is so pleased with the cover that He forbears to remember

the defilement and deformity of those whom it covers. God will never strike a soul through the veil of His Son's sacrifice. He accepts us because He cannot but accept His Son, who has become our covering.[10]

As a result of justification, which occurs at the moment we place our faith in Christ, we are freed from the *penalty* of sin—death. We are regenerated, or given a new birth in Christ, which is where the term "born-again Christians" originated. It is a mistake to think of "born-again Christians" as some special subset of Christians. By definition, every Christian is born again and is made a new creature in Christ. If he isn't, he isn't saved and he isn't a Christian—it's that simple. One doesn't have to call himself "born again" to be a Christian, but becoming a Christian does involve a new birth.

This is purely biblical and not the brainchild of some fanatic. Jesus Himself told Nicodemus, when he asked Him how to attain eternal life, "I tell you the truth, no one can see the kingdom of God unless he is born again." "How can a man be born when he is old?" Nicodemus then asked. "Surely he cannot enter a second time into his mother's womb to be born!" Jesus answered, "I tell you the truth, no one can enter the kingdom of God unless he is born of water and the Spirit. Flesh gives birth to flesh, but the Spirit gives birth to spirit. You should not be surprised at my saying, 'You must be born again.' ... No one has ever gone into heaven except the one who came from heaven—the Son of Man. Just as Moses lifted up the snake in the desert, so the Son of Man must be lifted up, that everyone who believes in him may have eternal life" (John 3:3–15).

Once a person is born again or justified, his Christian walk is just beginning. At the point of justification, or conversion, he is freed not just from the *penalty* of sin, but also from the *power* of sin. The Holy Spirit dwells in the new Christian and empowers him to begin his walk toward holiness, a process known as "sanctification." He is no longer a slave to sin (Romans 6:6), but is instead empowered by the Holy Spirit to resist it—though it will be a daily struggle, where "sin remains, but no longer reigns."[11] At the moment he accepts Christ, then, a conflict arises: "For the desires of the flesh are against the Spirit, and the desires of the Spirit are against the flesh, for these are opposed to each other, to keep you from doing the things you want to do" (Gal. 5:17).

Sanctification is a lifelong process. The Christian will never be able to wholly avoid sinning this side of heaven. But remember that the process of sanctification has nothing to do with salvation. We are already saved at the point we begin our sanctification process.[12] We become sanctified through relying on the Holy Spirit and exercising the spiritual disciplines—prayer, worship, Bible study, meditation, memorization, giving, fasting, service, etc. Not until we meet Christ face to face, however, will we totally overcome sin and complete our process of becoming holy, at which point we will be glorified—freed from the *presence* of sin.

As the Christian grows and matures in his Christian walk through obedience to God and reliance on the Holy Spirit, he begins to exude what Paul refers to as the "fruit of the Spirit," which he defines as "love, joy, peace, patience, kindness, goodness, faithfulness, gentleness and self-control" (Gal. 5:22–23).

Here a paradox arises because the act of justification occurs through absolutely no effort of our own, but by complete reliance on the finished work of Christ. The process of sanctification, however, is different, because in a sense it requires our effort. And there is a further paradox, because while a certain effort on our part is involved, we overcome sin not through our own power, but solely through the power of the Holy Spirit. By "effort" I mean we must take the initiative to exercise the disciplines that facilitate our sanctification, but our spiritual growth through exercising the disciplines is empowered by the Holy Spirit, not by our own efforts.

Think of it this way: our effort comes into play in placing ourselves before the Holy Spirit so that He can transform us. We can't ignore the spiritual disciplines and expect to grow much in holiness. We put forth the "effort" of presenting ourselves before God through prayer, scripture, reading, etc., and He does the work of making us more holy. As Paul says, "Therefore, my dear friends, as you have always obeyed—not only in my presence, but now much more in my absence—continue to work out your salvation with fear and trembling, for it is God who works in you to will and to act according to His good purpose" (Philip. 2:12–13).

William Hendrikson comments, "To be sure, no one can continue in the faith in his own strength (John 15:5). The enabling grace of God is needed from start to finish (Phil. 2:12, 13). This, however, does not cancel human responsibility and activity. Yes, activity, continuous, sustained, strenuous effort (Heb. 12:14). It should be noted, however, that this is distinctly the activity of faith (cf. 1 Tim. 2:15)."[13]

Peter makes the same point when he says, "For this very reason, make every effort to add to your faith goodness; and to goodness, knowledge; and to knowledge, self-control; and to self-control, perseverance; and to perseverance, godliness; and to godliness, mutual affection; and to mutual affection, love. For if you possess these qualities in increasing measure, they will keep you from being ineffective and unproductive in your knowledge of our Lord Jesus Christ" (2 Peter 1:5–8). Notice that he says "make every effort." Dr. Thomas R. Schreiner explains that Peter's "exhortation to holiness is grounded in God's work of salvation as it has been accomplished in Jesus Christ. As is typical in the New Testament, grace precedes demand. The priority of grace, however, does not cancel out strenuous moral effort. Believers are to 'make every effort' or apply 'all diligence' (NASB) in carrying out Peter's commands. A godly character does not emerge from passivity or lassitude."[14] Schreiner's formulation that we must exert "strenuous moral effort" and not be passive nicely punctuates the point.

Richard Foster, in his *Celebration of Discipline*, put it this way: a farmer is helpless to grow grain; all he can do is provide the right conditions for its growth. He cultivates the ground, plants the seed, waters the plants, and then the natural forces of the earth take over and the grain comes up. This, says Foster, is how it is with the spiritual disciplines. "They are a way of sowing to the Spirit. The disciplines are God's way of getting us into the ground; they put us where he can work within us and transform us."[15] The farmer works hard and the disciplines likewise require effort on our part, but the farmer can't produce fruit without God and we can't produce spiritual fruit without God. So sanctification is a process, one in which we, as believers, are actively involved, but it is not a partnership with the Spirit in the sense that we each do our respective tasks. It is His "work" that drives the process; we can only grow spiritually as He empowers us. He works in us and through us.[16]

Another way to understand the Christian's sanctification process is through the words of Jesus in John 15: "I am the true vine, and my Father is the vine-dresser. Every branch in me that does not bear fruit he takes away, and every branch that does bear fruit he prunes, that it may bear more fruit" (1–2). He adds, "Abide in me, and I in you. As the branch cannot bear fruit by itself, unless it abides in the vine, neither can you, unless you abide in me. I am the vine; you are the branches. Whoever abides in me and I in him, he it is that bears much fruit, for apart from me you can do nothing" (4–5).

I mentioned Paul's explanation that when we grow in holiness through the sanctification process we begin to bear fruit. The evidence of our spiritual growth is called "the fruit of the Spirit." Jesus is saying essentially the same thing here. The whole point of all the spiritual disciplines is to become more Christ-like. Sanctification—the process of becoming more holy—is the process of becoming more like Christ, the picture of perfect holiness. Through the power of the Holy Spirit we want to abide in Christ so that He will abide in us. It's all about Christ-likeness, and it's all about love—mutual love between us and Christ. In Jesus' words, "By this my Father is glorified, that you bear much fruit and so prove to be my disciples. As the Father has loved me, so have I loved you. Abide in my love" (John 15: 8–9).

Christians, it should be noted, are not required to study theology formally or to understand all the doctrinal terms, though I believe that increasing our knowledge can help us grow in the faith, as long as we don't make it a purely intellectual exercise and ignore the rest, and as long as we don't grow proud of our acquisition of biblical knowledge. Understanding the definition of "sanctification," for example, isn't nearly as important for the believer as is keeping his focus on Christ and putting into practice the spiritual disciplines to grow in the faith.

THE PERVASIVENESS OF EVIL

Having saving faith in Christ doesn't mean the believer never experiences doubts—minor doubt sometimes creeps back into my own psyche. We Christians are still challenged by the flesh and by the spiritual enemy. Apologetics—the body of evidence that led me to the point of faith in the first place—is a great place to go to replenish our faith. But there's something else that reinforces my belief system more quickly than anything else, and this too is counterintuitive: the sheer extensiveness and pervasiveness of evil in the world.

For many, the overwhelming presence of evil is a major stumbling block, just as it used to be for me. But this was before I knew much about the Bible or Christian doctrine. Now it serves as a check on my doubt. It is invariably a wake-up call to consider the world's fallenness, for no other worldview comes close to so accurately describing the true state of the world and the human condition as Christianity does. As Malcolm Muggeridge astutely observes, "The depravity of man is at once the most empirically verifiable reality but at the same time the most intellectually resisted fact."[17]

Contrast the Christian view of the fall with the humanist's view of the perfectibility of mankind. The humanist worldview, whether consciously or not, presupposes that man can be his own god—he has the ability to remake and perfect himself over time. But as the last century has shown, these godless ideas have led to totalitarian regimes that enslave and murder millions. Even if you deny that godlessness has led to this depravity, you will still have a difficult time making the case that mankind is on a linear path to enlightenment.

Holy Scripture captures the world as it really is, not as some utopian or humanist idealists imagine or wish it to be. Shakespeare's timeless question from *King Lear*—"Who is it who can tell me who I am?"—makes sense only in terms of the Christian worldview, which can explain the coexisting qualities of both greatness and misery in the human condition.[18] They are only intelligible together in light of our creation in God's image and our subsequent fall—greatness and misery rolled into one. We know that mankind is not in the process of perfecting itself and that the human condition is unchanged since Adam and Eve disobeyed God in the Garden. While arguing that only Christianity accurately portrays the human condition, French philosopher Blaise Pascal writes, "The greatness and the wretchedness of man are so evident that the true religion must necessarily teach us both that there is in man some great source of greatness, and a great source of wretchedness."[19]

How we deal with this question of evil, and how the Christian comes to understand the reason for it and the answer to it, is more complicated. I address this in Chapter 13, where I also discuss another way in which acknowledging the existence of evil serves as a proof for God's existence. But trust me when I tell you that one of the most efficient recipes for overcoming my own sporadic doubt impulses is to focus on the world's evil and contemplate its complete harmony with the Bible's message.

YOU ARE HOPELESSLY SINFUL BUT MUST BE PERFECT

Is it really fair for the Bible to teach that we are intrinsically evil and then for Jesus to instruct us, "Be perfect, therefore, as your heavenly father is perfect" (Matt. 5:48)? The question reminds me of a discussion in a Bible study at my house not long after I became a Christian. We were reading through books of the Bible and discussing each and every verse as we went along, no matter how long it took. My neighbor Steve Johnson, who has a Master of Theology from Dallas Theological Seminary and a Doctor of Philosophy in Reformation History and Theology from Westminster Seminary, spent hours with me during and away from the study patiently answering questions and trying to help me overcome certain lingering questions. I distinctly recall one particular Saturday morning when we discussed the issue of righteousness.

The passage was in the Gospel of Matthew: "For I tell you that unless your righteousness surpasses that of the Pharisees and the teachers of the law, you will certainly not enter the kingdom of heaven" (5:20). I was not at all pleased by this verse, especially after having recently accepted the Bible as the Word of God. *Okay*, I thought, *all hope is lost. I might as well just withdraw from this study right now. There's no way I can ever enter the kingdom of heaven because I'll never attain, much less surpass, the righteousness of the Pharisees.*

Do you realize what kind of standard that is? I did, even at that stage of my Christian infancy. Pharisees devoted their entire lives to living by the rules. After his conversion to Christianity, Paul related that he had been "as to the law, a Pharisee; as to zeal, a persecutor of the church; as to righteousness under the law, blameless" (Philip. 3:6). Pharisees prided themselves in keeping God's law. I knew this was a high bar indeed.

I indignantly disputed the point while Steve, with his usual indulgence and tact, explained to me that I wasn't quite getting it. To be Christ-like—to be righteous in Christ—is not about obeying a set of rules. It is wholly different from engaging in good works as a result of our own efforts and fueled by our own power. Our righteousness comes with giving ourselves up to Christ and being empowered by the Holy Spirit to resist sin. It is avoiding sin for the right reasons and with the right attitude toward God. It involves the shedding of our pride and the willingness to be empowered by God to live rightly, thereby acquiring a more intimate relationship with Him.

Even as immature Christians, if we are acting in the power of the Spirit, our righteousness should exceed that of the Pharisees, because it is not just a matter of obeying rules. It is about living a spirit-filled life in Christ. This does not only involve one's conduct, but also concerns the motives for one's conduct. There is nothing Christ-like, for example, in grudgingly following rules. Rules are external and righteousness is from within. Jesus confirms this when He says, "You are those who justify yourselves before men, but God knows your hearts. For what is exalted among men is an abomination in the sight of God" (Luke 16:15).

I don't believe Christ teaches us to be perfect because He expects any of us actually to be perfect, for He knows that will not happen—as my pastor, Ron Watts, recently mentioned in a sermon. What He's telling us is that He is the standard of perfection. He models that standard in His earthly life and teaches us about it in His Sermon on the Mount and other lessons. He is telling us, in effect, how rigid the standard of perfection is, that we cannot possibly attain that standard through our own power, and that we need to surrender to Him in order to grow spiritually and morally.

But just because we can't reach the standard doesn't mean we shouldn't aspire to it, a lesson every bit as relevant and valuable for us today—especially in this often decadent culture—as it was in Jesus' time. So when He commands us to be perfect, He's telling us to fix our hearts on becoming more like Him. We must repent of our sins and turn to Him in faith, surrender to Him, and acquire the power of the Holy Spirit to begin a new path of righteousness that will indeed exceed that of the Pharisees.

There is another important and related point. For purposes of salvation, when we believe in Jesus Christ, we are justified, as we have seen, and take on His righteousness. But "to declare righteous" does not mean "to make righteous."[20] We are adjudicated innocent of all our sins, forgiven, and declared righteous before God. We take on the righteousness of the sinless, perfect God in the flesh by appropriating, through faith, His finished work on the cross. Justification, then, is a declaration whereby Christ's perfect righteousness is imputed to those who believe in Him. Taking on Christ's righteousness, we are declared more righteous than the Pharisees. This reflects Christ's teaching that while no human being (apart from the saving grace of God) was greater than John the Baptist, all who are *least* in the kingdom of God are greater than John. Membership in the kingdom of God—those declared righteous by faith—is more wonderful than being the greatest of human beings.[21]

The point is, then, that we can't do this on our own, "None is righteous, no, not one" (Romans 3:10); we are declared righteous in God's sight, not based on our own works, but because we placed our faith in Him.[22] As the Book of Isaiah relates, "All our righteous acts are like filthy rags" (64:6). Paul discusses the point in Romans 4:5: "And to the one who does not work but believes in him who justifies the ungodly, his faith is counted as righteousness." He further explains, "For all have sinned and fall short of the glory of God, and are justified by his grace as a gift, through the redemption that is in Christ Jesus, whom God put forward as a propitiation by his blood, to be received in faith.... Then what becomes of our boasting? It is excluded. By what kind of law? By a law of works? No, but by the law of faith. For we hold that one is justified by faith apart from works of the law" (Romans 3:23–25, 27–28). The Old Testament path to salvation was not perfect adherence to the Law either, as Paul makes clear in Romans 9:32: "Why [has Israel] not [attained the law of righteousness they pursued so zealously]? Because they pursued it not by faith but *as if* it were by works."[23]

So in two ways the righteousness of the believer should be greater than that of the Pharisees: it should be greater *in fact* if he is acting Christ-like via the power of the Holy Spirit, and it should be greater as a "legal" matter, based on God's declaration of our righteousness through the blood of Jesus Christ. Both of these require faith in Christ.

In the Sermon on the Mount, then, Jesus is saying that we are going to be judged according to the highest possible standard and, since the only way we can reach that standard is to have saving faith in Him, we better make it our business to trust Him.

THE LAW AND FAITH

Many people mistakenly believe that because Moses was given the Ten Commandments (the Law) on Mount Sinai, eternal salvation in Old Testament times was through works (adherence to the Law). In fact, as noted above, the passages from Genesis and Romans make it clear that even then, justification was by faith alone and not by works of the Law. According to Paul, the Israelites "stumbled" over this principle (Romans 9:32). Dr. Warren Wiersbe puts it this way: "How was Abraham saved? Not by keeping the Law, for the Law had not yet been given, nor by circumcision, for that was not established until he was ninety-nine years old. He was saved by faith in God's Word."[24] *The Bible Knowledge Commentary* agrees: "The Bible clearly teaches that in all ages imputed righteousness (i.e., salvation) comes by faith."[25]

The matter is handled straightforwardly in Genesis: "Abram believed the Lord, and He credited it to him as righteousness" (Gen. 15:6). In arguing that we are saved by faith, Paul explains that this was also true in Old Testament times, citing Genesis 15:6: "What then shall we say that Abraham, our forefather discovered in this matter? If, in fact, Abraham was justified by works, he had something to boast about—but not before God. What does the Scripture say? 'Abraham believed God and it was credited to him as righteousness'" (Romans 4:1–3). He adds, "It was not through law that Abraham and his offspring received the promise that he would be heir of the world, but through the righteousness that comes by faith" (Romans 4:13).

Why, then, did God give the Law? Dr. Warren Wiersbe sets out various reasons:

1. To reveal His glory and holiness (Deut. 5:22–28).
2. To reveal man's sinfulness (Romans 7:7, 13; 1 Tim. 1:9–11; James 1:22–25).
3. To mark the Israelites as His chosen people and to separate them from the other nations (Psalms 147:19–20; Eph. 2:11–17; Acts 15).
4. To give the Israelites a standard for godly living so they might enjoy God's blessings (Deut. 4:1ff; 5:29ff; Judges 2:19–21).
5. To prepare the Israelites for the coming of Christ (Gal. 3:24).
6. To illustrate in type and ceremony the Person and work of Christ (Heb. 8–10).[26]

So the Law was never meant to provide a means to salvation; the road to salvation has always been by faith. "If a law had been given that could give life, then righteousness would indeed be by the law. But the Scripture imprisoned everything under sin, so that the promise by faith in Jesus Christ might be given to those who believe. Now before faith came, we were held captive under the law, imprisoned until the coming faith would be revealed. So then, the law was our guardian until Christ came, in order that we might be justified by faith" (Gal. 3:21–24).

Thus, one central purpose of the Law was to show our need for forgiveness. As evangelist John Stott says, "We cannot come to Christ to be justified until we have first been to Moses to be condemned. But once we have gone to Moses and acknowledged our sin, guilt and condemnation, we must not stay there."[27] Similarly, Dr. Martin Lloyd-Jones observes, "The trouble with people who are not seeking for a Savior, and for salvation, is that they do not understand the nature of sin. It is the peculiar function of the Law to bring such an understanding to a man's mind and conscience."[28] This dovetails with my point that repentance—

turning from our sins and toward Christ, trusting Him for remission of our sins and eternal life—is part of saving faith.

Does the Law, then, apply to the New Testament believer? Paul repeatedly insists it does not: "For sin shall not have dominion over you, for you are not under law but under grace" (Romans 6:14); "But if you are led by the Spirit, you are not under the Law" (Gal. 5:18); "For the law of the Spirit of life in Christ Jesus has made me free from the law of sin and death" (Romans 8:2).

This gives rise to two questions:

1. Is the Christian, being free from the shackles of the Law and forgiven for all sins because of the blood of Jesus Christ, permitted to sin at will?
2. Is the Law abolished or invalidated, meaning the Ten Commandments are no longer valid?

Paul answers the first question directly in his most theological letter, his Epistle to the Romans. He is responding to a heresy in the early Church to the effect that if Christians are not under the Law, they are free to sin. He flatly and emphatically rejects that notion: "What then? Shall we sin because we are not under the law but under grace? Certainly not!" (6:15). The Christian, though technically not under the Law, is nonetheless motivated to be pure and holy in imitation of Christ, out of love for and obedience to God. "For all the law is fulfilled in one word, even in this: 'You shall love your neighbor as yourself'" (Gal. 5:14).

In this sense, the Christian is under an even more exacting standard than the Old Testament Jew. As John Stott notes in his commentary on Romans, quoting Professor C. E. B. Cranfield, "Being united to Christ, we are dead to sin but alive to God, and being enslaved to God we are ipso facto committed to obedience, pledged to the total belongingness, the total obligation, the total commitment and the total accountability which characterize the life under grace."[29] Paul further explains, "For what the law could not do in that it was weak through the flesh, God did by sending His own Son in the likeness of sinful flesh, on account of sin; He condemned sin in the flesh, that the righteous requirement of the law might be fulfilled in us who do not walk according to the flesh but according to the Spirit" (Romans 8:3–4).

As to the second question—does the Christian's liberation from the Law render it a nullity?—Jesus Himself provides the answer: "Do not think that I came to destroy the law or the Prophets. I did not come to destroy but to fulfill. For assuredly, I say to you, till heaven and earth pass away, one jot or one tittle will by no means pass from the law till all is fulfilled. Therefore, whoever relaxes one of the least of these commandments and teaches others to do the same will be called least in the kingdom of heaven, but whoever does them and teaches them will be called great in the kingdom of heaven" (Matt. 5:17–19).

Though you will doubtlessly find different views on this passage, I believe Christ is saying a number of things here. First, He is the Messiah promised throughout the Old Testament ("the Law and the Prophets"). After all, He is part of the Triune Godhead who gave this Law. He did not nullify the Law, but validated it by His incarnation. Moreover, through His sinless life and sacrificial death, He once and for all fulfilled all the Old Testament requirements of sacrifice as a means to forgiveness. Perhaps we can think of it this way: the Law is still God's perfect standard, but faith in Christ completely fulfills it, for purposes of our salvation.

In a parallel passage in the Gospel of Luke, Jesus states it a different way, which also shows the paradox: "The Law and the Prophets were until John; since then the good news of the kingdom of God is preached, and everyone forces his way into it. But it is easier for heaven and earth to pass away than for one dot of the Law to become void" (16:16–17). Here, He seems to be saying that the Law (and the Prophets) ended with John, at which time the New Covenant of grace arrived, but the Law is still valid.

So we see that just because the Christian is under grace and the Law of the Spirit does not mean God's Old Testament laws are any less perfect. God's laws are perfectly holy as He is holy. They were mainly bestowed as rules of conduct for the chosen Israelites, but they are nevertheless sound, indeed perfect, moral pronouncements.[30] And though the Christian is not technically under the stricture of the Old Testament law, the New Testament restates all but one of the Ten Commandments as being applicable today. The only exception is the commandment regarding keeping the Sabbath holy, which some people believe the New Testament nullifies: "So let no one judge you in food or in drink, or regarding a festival or a new moon or sabbaths, which are a shadow of things to come, but the substance is of Christ" (Col 2:16).[31]

IN GOD'S IMAGE BUT FALLEN

Is there an inconsistency in Christianity's teaching that man is totally depraved yet entitled to dignity because he was created in God's image? No. Despite the fall, we still have a glimmer of that image. Theologian Wayne Grudem explains that God makes that clear; otherwise, after the flood He wouldn't have established the death penalty for murderers. The harshness of the penalty is based on the gravity of the offense of murdering a human being created in God's image. Grudem says God's image in us "is distorted, but not lost." Yes, men are sinful, but "there is still enough likeness to God remaining in them that to murder another person…is to attack the part of creation that most resembles God, and it betrays an attempt or desire to attack God himself. Man is still in God's image."[32] James confirms this, testifying that men "are made in the likeness of God" (James 3:9).

God made us in His image for a purpose and He made us redeemable through the blood of His Son. Regeneration—at the point of our justification—begins the process of restoring God's moral image in our lives. But not until we are glorified (which as previously noted, will not happen this side of heaven) shall we reflect God perfectly in thought and action as mankind was originally made to do, and as the incarnate Son of God in His humanity did and does.[33]

THE TRIUNE GOD

How about the idea that God is one, yet also three? Christians are monotheists. We believe there is only one God. But we also believe He is triune—He is one God in three Persons. This is not something that egg-headed theologians or wishful thinkers concocted. Though the word "trinity" is not in the Bible, the doctrine is based on clear scriptural teachings, and there has long been consensus in the Church on the matter, both with the early Church fathers and the Church councils.[34] There is one God (Deut. 6:4, Mark 12:29, 32; 1 Cor. 8:4; Gal. 3:20; Eph. 4:5–6; 1 Tim. 2:5; James 2:19). But He is three distinct Persons, each equal in essence with the Others. The Son is equal with the Father (John 5:18, 23, 8:16, 14:9, 17:10; Philip. 2:6; Col. 2:9; Romans 1:7), and the Holy Spirit is equal with the Father and the Son (2 Cor. 13:14; Matt. 28:19; 1 Peter 1:2; Rev. 1:4–5). Many other passages teach that the three Persons are each eternal, They work in harmony, They are united, They are all-knowing, They are holy, They are interrelated, and They are united in one Godhead. There is nothing contradictory about God's being one in essence and having three united Persons in that essence. It is a mystery, but not a contradiction.[35]

Another fascinating aspect of our Triune God is that He is a relational God and a God of infinite love within the Trinity. We were created as relational human beings because the Triune God is relational. His love within the Trinity (John 17:24) flows into the world (John 3:16). The love of the community of Christian believers should overflow to a lost and hurting world because the love for the saved precedes the love for the lost.[36] So apologetics and evangelism are in service to the model God establishes in His relational and loving being and in His work on our behalf for our salvation.

CHRIST'S DUAL NATURE

I find it intriguing that there is a rough analogy between the doctrine of the Trinity and the so-called "hypostatic union" in Christ—that He is both fully human and fully divine. This idea that Christ has a dual nature, which is based on numerous scriptural passages, has long been settled in the Church, though many heresies have been promoted by the doctrine's opponents. It's conceptually analogous to the Trinity but also different. Instead of three Persons in one essence, there are two natures—human and divine—in one Person. This is foreign to us—we are all completely human, and there has never been any other being like Christ in this respect.[37]

    This too is a mystery, but not a contradiction. The analogy between the Trinity and Christ's dual nature, of course, is that there is a plurality and a unity in each. I called it a "rough analogy" because the two natures of Christ are not separate Persons, as are the Father, the Son, and the Holy Spirit, the three Persons of the Trinity. Understand, however, that Christ's two natures are distinct and not commingled. As Rev. Charles Spurgeon says, "Take heed never to commingle his Godhead and his humanity. Remember, Christ was not a deified man, neither was he a humanized God. He was perfectly God, and at the same time perfectly man, made like unto his brethren in all things."[38]

    I also see another basic difference in that God is Triune by nature. The Son had no beginning (John 1:1); He has always existed. However, He did not always have a dual nature but acquired it by choice with the incarnation. The heavenly Second Person of the Trinity antedated the earthly Jesus of Nazareth. That is, there was no such being as the earthly Jesus of Nazareth before He was conceived in the Virgin Mary's womb.[39] "The Word became flesh and made his dwelling among us" (John 1:14). Christ's dual nature is also different from the Trinity because Christ's natures have seemingly contradictory attributes—one infinite, the other finite.[40]

    There is another important analogy between Christ's dual nature and God's Triune nature. As I mentioned, our Triune God is a relational God within the Trinity and toward us, with love defining both sets of relationships. Similarly, the Son's incarnation is not only about our salvation. Christ's humanity makes possible our close relationship with Him. If the incarnation were solely about our salvation, then we might expect Christ to lay aside His body of flesh and bone and return to His solely spiritual form. But we are assured He will retain His humanity forever[41] by John (Rev. 1:13), Paul (1 Tim. 2:5), and by Jesus Himself, who promises to drink wine with His disciples in His Father's kingdom (Matt. 26:29). "Jesus, though crowned with glory and honor, remains man forever" because it was His eternal plan to be "with men."[42] By retaining His humanity, He enables us to continue to have a human relationship with Him "so that we can see Him, touch Him, fellowship with Him and worship Him, as our incarnate, divine, but also human savior.… Yes, indeed, we shall know Him by the print of the nails in His hands."[43]

I discuss Christ's dual nature in greater depth in Chapter 6.

GIVING UP LIFE TO GAIN IT

Scripture admonishes that we must give up our lives for Christ's sake in order to gain our lives. This means we must check our pride at the door and surrender our old lives to Christ so that we can be regenerated to a new life in Him. We are getting a far superior life in exchange for the one we are shedding, and this is for our own sake, not for Christ's. As Paul declares, "For to me to live is Christ and to die is gain" (Philip. 1:21). He explains this idea in more detail:

> But whatever gain I had, I counted as loss for the sake of Christ. Indeed, I count everything as loss because of the surpassing worth of knowing Christ Jesus my Lord. For his sake I have suffered the loss of all things and count them as rubbish, in order that I may gain Christ and be found in him, not having a righteousness of my own that comes from the law, but that which comes through faith in Christ, the righteousness from God that depends on faith—that I may know him and the power of his resurrection, and may share his sufferings, becoming like him in his death, that by any means possible I may attain the resurrection from the dead (Philip. 3:7–11).

Jesus says, "For whoever wants to save his life will lose it, but whoever loses his life for me will find it. What good will it be for someone to gain the world, yet forfeit his soul?" (Matt. 16:25–26). The life Jesus is offering His followers will involve suffering and hardship, but in the process they will find a better, more fulfilling life.[44] While being wealthy, comfortable, or powerful is certainly no bar to eternal life, we must understand that anything that competes with our love for and faith in Christ is idolatrous, and that we should aim for Christ-centeredness. Sometimes material blessings can impair our spiritual growth because they tend to distract or separate us from God or make us feel that we don't need Him, whereas the person who endures hardship and suffering might be more likely to call out to God.

THE LEAST IS GREAT BUT THE SERVANT IS NOT GREATER THAN HIS MASTER

Jesus tells His disciples that "the least among you all is the one who is great" (Luke 9:48). He also instructs them, "Let the greatest among you become as the youngest, and the leader as one who serves" (Luke 22:26). But He says elsewhere that the servant is not greater than his master (John 13:16). Is there a conflict here?

When He says the least among them will be great, He isn't trying to upend ordinary rankings. In terms of their hierarchical relationship, we know servants are subordinate to their master, and we know that as Christ's servants we are vastly inferior to Him.

He is making a larger point about our vitally important attitude toward Him and about serving our fellow man. Consider the context: in responding to His disciples' bickering over which of them is the "greatest," Jesus "took a child and put him by His side and said, 'Whoever receives this child in my name receives me and whoever receives me receives him who sent me.'" It is only after that preface that He jars them with His "least is great" remark. Just as He tells us to have the innocent faith of a child, He is telling the disciples that what He values is not what is often considered "great" in human terms, but a person's willingness to humble himself in order to serve others[45]—just as He did, and continues to do. He wants us to be like Him.

Christ, the greatest man Who ever lived, was the ultimate servant. Through His sinless life and substitutionary death, He performed the greatest act of selfless service in human history and is now glorified at the right hand of the Father. The disciples shouldn't have been thinking about their service as an avenue to their own glory, but about their relationship with Christ and their service to Him. To serve is to become Christ-like, because servant-hood was the essence of Christ's earthly mission. There is no greater goal we can have than to become Christ-like and no better path to achieve it than to follow Christ's example through serving. The disciples more than vindicated themselves following Christ's return, of course, living exemplary lives of service and dedicating themselves to the cause of Christ by spreading the gospel message at great risk to themselves.

HE WHO HAS MUCH—BLESSING OR CURSE?

Jesus says, "Blessed are you who are poor, for yours is the kingdom of God" (Luke 6:20), and "But woe to you who are rich, for you have received your consolation" (Luke 6:24). But with the parable of the talents He teaches, "For to everyone who has will more be given, and he will have an abundance. But from the one who has not, even what he has will be taken away" (Matt. 25:29). Why does He sympathize with the poor and admonish the rich in one sermon and seem to reverse himself in the other? Is there really a contradiction here?

No, of course not. He doesn't simply say the poor are blessed, but that they are blessed because they have the Kingdom of God. They are following Jesus and placing their trust in Him instead of in the world's riches. Some commentators believe He is only addressing His poor followers, not all the world's poor. Regardless, any who place their faith in Him, rich or poor, are blessed because they have Him, eternal life, and the Kingdom of God. Other commentators believe that Jesus, in the passages quoted by Luke, was not talking about those who are poor in a financial sense, but in a spiritual sense. Interestingly, Matthew reports Jesus as saying "poor in spirit" (5:3), meaning humble, i.e. not too proud to come to Jesus in faith. But just to be clear, there is no doubt that Jesus has a special place in His heart for those who are financially poor.

As for the rich, here again, commentators suggest Jesus may not be talking solely about the financially rich, but also those who are well-fed, popular, and seem to have everything going for them. It could mean those who are arrogant and haughty—the opposite of those who are spiritually poor. It is sometimes harder for people in all these positions to see clearly their own depravity and their need for saving faith in Christ. They have "already received [their] consolation" so "woe" to them (Luke 6:24).

Jesus makes a similar point when He says, "It is easier for a camel to go through the eye of a needle than for a rich person to enter the kingdom of God." He could be implying that rich people might not be as likely to turn toward Him. But it's also important to remember the verses that immediately follow. When the disciples ask Him who could be saved, He replies, "With man this is impossible, but with God all things are possible" (Matt. 19:26). He could be saying that no man can save himself, even with all the world's riches, which will do him no good after he dies. Human merit and human resources are not spiritual currency. Only through faith can one be saved, thus, "With God all things are possible."

Also consider the parable of the talents, where Jesus seems to reward those who end up with more than others. Is there an inconsistency in His attitude here, if we concede, for purposes of argument, that He is talking about the financially poor in the above-quoted passages? He surely speaks lovingly toward them elsewhere.

Not at all. In the parable of the talents, Jesus tells the story of a master with three servants. He gives each a specific amount of talents, or money. He gives one five talents, another two, and another one, according to their abilities. He is entrusting them with his property and counting on them to be responsible with it. The two with the five and two talents, respectively, put them to use and each double their holdings. The one who received only one hides it in the ground.

The master praises the first two as "good and faithful servants" and rewards them with more responsibilities. He rebukes the third servant as "wicked and slothful" and gives his talent to the one who already has ten, saying, "For to everyone who has will more be given, and he will have an abundance. But from the one who has not, even what he has will be taken way" (Matt. 25:29). He goes even further, casting the "worthless servant into the outer darkness."

This parable has little to do with the rich and poor per se. It is partly about the stewardship of one's resources and spiritual gifts. We should use, not squander, the gifts God has given us. More important, it is about the indispensability of faith. The master rewards the faithfulness of the two who wisely invest their resources and punishes the one who has little or no faith. As New Testament scholar William Hendriksen notes, the point of the parable is, "Let everyone be faithful in using the opportunities for service which the Lord has given him." We should make the best use of our gifts from God, in gratitude to Him. "Negligence is punished; diligence, rewarded."[46]

In the next chapter I'll discuss some more paradoxical biblical teachings that offer intriguing insights and meaningful lessons once you think them through.

CHAPTER 5

PARADOXES OF CHRISTIANITY, PART 2

THE PRODIGAL SON— AND HIS BROTHER

I n the parable of the prodigal son, a man's younger son squanders his inheritance while his older son dutifully remains home doing everything expected of him. When the younger son sees the error of his ways and returns home, his father forgives him. Protesting that this is grossly unfair, the older son refuses to come inside and join the party (Luke 15:11–32). The father lovingly assures his older son, "You are always with me, and all that is mine is yours." But the father also defends his actions, telling his son "to celebrate and be glad, for this your brother was, and is alive; he was lost, and is found" (Luke 15:31–32).

This seems unjust and contrary to biblical principles. The Bible teaches that children are to respect and obey their parents; it teaches the value of hard work, thrift, and the proper stewardship of our resources. It counsels against debauchery and stresses personal account-ability. But here we have the dissipating son getting away scot-free with all his misconduct while the older son's obedience seems completely unappreciated.

Yet as a reflection of God's salvation plan, the parable makes perfect sense. The father has unconditional love for his son, embracing him even before he knows the son will repent. (The son had already planned on repenting, but as far as the father knew, he was just returning home to beg for more money.) "What do you see here?" asks Pastor Timothy Keller. "You see a God of grace. Here is a Father who doesn't wait for repentance. Oh no. He doesn't say, 'You repent and then comes my Father's arms.' He gives you the Father's arms and *enables* the repen-tance. Don't you see? The repentance doesn't bring the Father's arms; the Father's arms bring the repentance. This is a God of grace. 'We love him not because we first loved him but because he loved us.' God doesn't just offer salvation; he goes and gets you. He pounces on you. He mugs you with his love. The Scripture says so."[1]

This is not to devalue our repentance, but rather to emphasize that God is the Prime Mover, even *in* repentance. Here Keller captures our God of grace. He's not to be seen as this angry, white-haired old scold. Though He does not take sin lightly, He is in fact a God of boundless love, and too often we fail to see Him that way. Christians and skeptics alike should try to get their minds and hearts wrapped around God's love instead of focusing on those areas where they think they've caught Him in a trap or acting callously. His love is paramount.

As for the older son who feels slighted, Jesus is telling us that he need not concern himself with the supposed unfairness of it all. He is clarify-ing that none of us is worthy; we can't earn our salvation. To think we can—which, in this parable, the older son clearly believes—is to betray our own pride, which is likely a greater obstacle to our own relationship with God than the other son's dissipation is for his relationship. The bottom line is this: don't fret over the other guy. Embrace, with humble gratitude, what He is doing for you.

STRENGTH IN WEAKNESS

Paul declares, "When I am weak, then I am strong" (2 Cor. 12:10). Similarly, the Book of Hebrews affirms that Gideon, Barak, Samson, Jephtah, David, Samuel, and the prophets "through faith conquered kingdoms...stopped the mouths of lions...[and] were made strong out of weakness" (11:32–34). The message is screaming out at us. In His incarnation, Christ set the example for us. Like Him, we must humble ourselves instead of trying to do everything by our own strength. We must surrender through faith to the unconquerable power of God. When we are down and out, in the spiritual doldrums, Christ can infuse us with spiritual strength if we'll just come to Him in faith. Through our weakness, Christ's strength and glory can be manifested through us, as it was for Paul.[2]

Some might find this teaching to be a copout, a crutch for weak people who don't have the gumption to do things for themselves. Well, when it comes to the question of saving ourselves by our own power, or reducing sin in our lives, we'll plead guilty. Recognizing the sad state of the human condition, Christians understand that we are members of the human family who need to rely on Christ for salvation and to eradicate our sinfulness. There is no shame in these admissions. Indeed, there is shame in holding on to the pride that impedes us from making them. To suggest that we can save ourselves is manifest folly that is wholly inconsistent with what we all observe.

Ironically, maybe those who have the humility and perspective to recognize their need for a savior are actually stronger than the proud, who are too weak to admit their own human limitations. Perhaps some skeptics are less independent than they think, deterred by peer pressure from pursuing a relationship with Christ.

Besides, becoming a Christian brings responsibilities. It's not a free ride. You don't simply lean on Jesus and thereafter get a free pass to sin. In fact, you acquire a higher calling, both to God and to your fellow man, and you become accountable to both. The atheist or agnostic, by contrast, might well use his unbelief as a crutch or even a shield to avoid

God's standards. He might use it to avoid looking at the sin in his own life and realizing he has to own up to it and rectify it. This isn't to suggest atheists can't be decent and moral people, in human terms. Many are. It's simply to say there is no shame in admitting we are weak. It's an essential step toward becoming stronger, which we accomplish by leaning on Christ.

JOY IN SUFFERING

Paul tells the Thessalonians, "You welcomed the message in the midst of severe suffering with the joy given by the Holy Spirit" (1 Thess. 1:6). He further explains, "For as we share abundantly in Christ's sufferings, so through Christ we share abundantly in comfort too" (2 Cor. 1:5). D. K. Lowery sums up the enigma: "One of the many paradoxes of the Christian life is that the grace of God is most keenly experienced not in the best but in the worst of times."[3]

I am not suggesting that Christians enjoy suffering and martyrdom. But Paul's suffering leads him to trust and focus on Christ alone,[4] which can provide an inner peace even during our struggles. The indwelling Holy Spirit gives joy to the believer.[5] Kistemaker and Hendriksen write, "The many sufferings that Christians have to endure for their faith are outweighed by the comfort that Christ extends to us."[6] Christian joy is not a denial of pain and suffering; instead, it reflects an awareness that our sufferings are temporary while our inheritance is eternal.[7] Furthermore, there is also joy in suffering because suffering produces character (Romans 5:3) and steadfastness (James 1:2).[8] As Paul exclaims, "I am filled with comfort. In all our affliction, I am overflowing with joy" (2 Cor. 7:4).

We sometimes hear from pop psychologists that suffering is a product of our imagination; that it's not real and that we have total control over it. But Pastor Mark Driscoll observes that the Bible treats suffering as something serious that we will all experience. Paul is not teaching about suffering in the abstract, but as one who has endured plenty of it.

Pastor Driscoll notes that Paul is exemplifying for us that as Christians, we must make our suffering, when we do experience it, purposeful. We must bear it in a way that allows God to do something good in us—make us more like Christ.

In other words, we must not use our suffering as an excuse to sin, but as an opportunity to grow spiritually. So many people have grown closer to Christ in their sufferings, and that is something in which they can rejoice. Driscoll quotes American missionary E. Stanley Jones, whose book *Conversion* happens to be in my library. "Don't bear trouble. Use it," advises Jones. "Take whatever happens, justice and injustice, pleasure and pain, compliment and criticism, take it up into the purpose of your life and make something out of it. Turn it into a testimony."[9]

"IT WAS AN HONOR FOR US TO SUFFER"

With that sage advice in mind, let me briefly share with you the story of two remarkable Christian women, Maryam Rostampour and Marziyeh Amirizadeh, who spoke at our church and described their harrowing tale of imprisonment by the Iranian regime because of their Christian faith. These two ladies personify the biblical admonition that we should gain joy through our suffering.

Both women were raised in Muslim homes in Iran. Having never embraced Islam, they became Christians as young adults. They met each other in 2005 while studying theology in Turkey, and when they returned to Iran, they evangelized together for several years, covertly distributing Bibles to some twenty thousand people and starting two secret house churches. In March 2009 they were arrested in Tehran for promoting Christianity, which is punishable by death. Charged with apostasy, antigovernment activity, and blasphemy, they were sentenced to execution by hanging. After enduring 259 days in Evin prison, the women were cleared of all charges and released in 2009 as a result of worldwide prayer and international pressure. They moved to the United States and wrote a book, *Captive in Iran*, describing their horrendous experiences.

In Evin prison, which the ladies explain, is notorious "for arresting, torturing, raping and executing innocent people,"[10] they experienced brutal and humiliating treatment, poisoning, and illness. They each faced solitary confinement and were interrogated every week for up to nine hours at a time. All the while, whether together or separated, they prayed for each other.

They were horrified during their first week and prayed to be released. But soon they came to see their imprisonment as an *opportunity* to witness to other prisoners, many of whom were prostitutes and addicts, "so hopeless, sad and disappointed."[11] Maryam and Marziyeh prayed for them and saw God work in their lives as they cried and confessed their sins. It became "like a church for us," says Marziyeh.[12] Maryam reveals that there was only one day out of the 259 during which she couldn't feel the presence of God. "That was the worst experience I ever had in my life," she says. "I was so sad. I didn't know what to do."[13]

That day, she was in a cell with a Muslim woman—a political prisoner—in a building where no loud noises were allowed. But she heard a voice inside her telling her to start singing. "I wanted to sing, but I couldn't find the words. [So] I started singing in tongues very loudly, and the woman in the cell with me was so scared she told me to quit singing, but I continued singing, and after one hour, I could feel the presence of the Holy Spirit all around me and in my cell."[14] Her Muslim cellmate, who also felt God's presence, asked if they could sing together in Farsi. "So I taught her some worship songs, and we started singing with each other, and after two hours, I could really feel the peace and joy, and God told me, 'I am with you every day, even if you don't feel my presence.'"[15]

At any time, the women could have secured their own release by simply renouncing their faith, but they emphatically refused. When a Muslim prisoner said they were "silly" for not renouncing Christianity, Marziyeh replied, "Our insistence on our faith is not out of stubbornness.... I have lived with God for many years.... He is my all. We are inseparable. My life has no value without him. I love God so much that denying him would be denying my own existence. How could I ever deny something that is in every cell of my body? I would rather spend the rest of my life in prison if that's what it takes to stay close to him. I would rather be killed than kill the spirit of Christ within me."[16]

Maryam and Marziyeh feel they were ultimately released because of God's grace. I find it moving that they were ambivalent about leaving the prison. Marziyeh relates in their book, "Though my body was free, my soul and spirit were still with our precious friends suffering terrible injustice inside Evin Prison. This thought made it impossible for me to enjoy our new situation. I felt strangely indifferent to our liberation."[17] They consider it an honor to have experienced a little of Christ's suffering by being imprisoned in His name. In their words, "It was an honor for both of us to suffer for our faith."[18]

They close their book with this: "We had no idea what the Lord had in mind for us. For all the heartache we have experienced on this journey, we wouldn't have missed it for anything. It has been our honor to serve Christ in this way, to take up our cross and follow Him faithfully anywhere He leads us."[19]

These women are a true inspiration for all Christians, modeling what it means to have authentic faith in Jesus Christ and to have a love for God that surpasses all understanding. We can talk in the abstract about taking joy in our suffering, but these ladies prove this isn't an unattainable ideal. They followed Christ's example of sacrifice and suffering; they lived that example, and they came away more fulfilled than they could have imagined had they not endured this experience. They truly understand the "joy" in suffering.

FEAR GOD, BUT SEEK INTIMACY WITH HIM

We surely grasp the importance of loving God, but what about the biblical teaching that we also "fear" Him? Scripture is pretty clear on the importance of fearing God. Job says, "He who withholds kindness from a friend forsakes the fear of the Almighty" (6:14). Psalms commands, "Serve the Lord with fear, and rejoice with trembling" (2:11). And Proverbs relates, "The fear of the Lord is the beginning of wisdom" (9:10); "the fear of the Lord prolongs life" (10:27); "the fear of the Lord is a foundation of life" (14:27); and "the fear of the Lord leads to life, and whoever has it rests satisfied" (19:23).

But there really is no inconsistency in the Bible's commands to love and fear God. This is more semantics than an actual paradox, because the fear mentioned in these passages includes a deep love, reverence, and devotion.[20] It is the reaction one should have in response to God's holiness (Exodus 3:5–6; Isaiah 8:13).[21] According to *Easton's Bible Dictionary*, "fear of the Lord" is used in the Old Testament as a designation of true piety. "It is a fear conjoined with love and hope, and is therefore not a slavish dread, but rather filial reverence."[22] *Holman Illustrated Bible Dictionary* draws an even stronger connection between "fear" and "love," explaining that "fear of the Lord" is "biblical shorthand for an entire life in love, worship, and obedience to God."[23]

The type of fear the Bible is describing also involves obedience (Gen. 22:12), loyalty, and faithfulness (2 Chr. 19:6–7). As John MacArthur comments, "This reverential awe and admiring, submissive fear is foundational for all spiritual knowledge and wisdom. While the unbeliever may make statements about life and truth, he does not have true or ultimate knowledge until he is in a redemptive relationship of reverential awe with God.... The fear of the Lord is a state of mind in which one's attitudes, will, feelings, deeds, and goals are exchanged for God's."[24]

The ultimate purpose of fearing God is that it leads us into a stronger relationship with Him. It is because God loves us that He wants us to be in that right relationship with Him, which involves our deep reverence for Him. So here's the paradox: cultivating an attitude of "fearing" God leads us into a relationship where we don't fear Him—in the conventional sense of the term—but love, honor, and worship Him.

BE LIKE A CHILD, BUT USE YOUR BRAINS

Jesus teaches that "unless you become like little children, you will not enter the kingdom of heaven" (Matt. 18:3). Does this validate the skeptics' presupposition that Christians abandon their intellect and accept biblical truth as a matter of blind faith? Not at all. Taken together with another directive from Jesus—to "love the Lord your God with all your heart, and with all your soul and with all your strength and with all your mind" (Matt. 22:37)—the command is rather analogous to His charge that His disciples be "as shrewd as serpents and as innocent as doves" (Matt. 10:16). Professors Benjamin B. DeVan and Thomas W. Smythe argue that "in its context, Jesus' command to 'turn and become like little children' is not an attack against reason or learning but an object lesson in humility."[25] It just means that the way to enter the kingdom is to receive God's gift readily and trustingly—even joyfully and appreciatively, as a child accepts a gift. And a child, of course, is not too proud to accept a gift.[26]

In addition to the command that we love God with all our minds, say DeVan and Smythe, "The Bible is saturated with language addressing the will, heart, and mind, or the cumulative mental capacities of a person. The Old Testament contains an entire book of practical 'sayings of the wise' (Proverbs) that urges, 'Get wisdom, get understanding…do not forsake wisdom and she will protect you; love her and she will watch over you…though it cost you all you have (Prov. 4:5–6).'"[27] Consider the context of Jesus' command that we love God with all our heart, soul, strength, and mind—it comes in reply to the question, "Which is the greatest commandment in the Law?" His charge that we use our minds in connection with our relationship with God is a direct refutation of the claim that we abandon our intellects in the faith process.

Another paradox is a corollary to this one. We are told to put our whole reliance on Jesus Christ—to surrender to Him—and yet we retain our individual, unique personalities. We don't surrender our individual personhood or uniqueness no matter how immersed we are in Christ. Additionally, the decision whether to trust Christ is individual to each of us. As the saying goes, "God has no grandchildren." If we want to be adopted as Christ's son or daughter, we must place our faith in Him. We can't get there by joining a church or relying on the faith of our parents. They can't do it for us and we can't do it for them, or for our own children. Individuality is essential to Christianity. We are individually accountable for our sins—and for our decision to accept or reject Christ's offer to wipe clean our sins. Our individuality persists throughout all of eternity. Quite different from the ideas of certain Eastern religions that we merge into an absolute or impersonal godhead, Christianity teaches that we retain our individual personhood as we relate to and commune with our personal, relational God.

IS THE BIBLE THE WORD OF GOD OR
WRITTEN BY MEN?

How can it be that the Bible is the Word of God when it was written by men? Jesus explicitly calls the Bible "the Word of God" (Matt. 15:6); Paul refers to the Scriptures as "the oracles of God" (Romans 3:2) and insists that "all Scripture is God-breathed" (2 Tim 3:16); the writer of Hebrews calls it "the Word of God" (4:12); and Peter calls it "the living and enduring word of God" (1 Peter 1:23).

From the words of the Bible, however, we also know that God gave us His Word through human agents. Peter says that in delivering prophecy, "Men spoke from God as they were carried along by the Holy Spirit" (2 Peter 1:21). Just as God sent His Son to us in human form and thereby revealed Himself through Christ, He also reveals Himself to us in Scripture through people, who were mostly writing in the context of their own historical setting. It is only natural that in the process of this communication there would be some difficulties. Dr. Norman Geisler quotes eighteenth-century writer Joseph Butler on this point: "He who believes the Scriptures to have proceeded from him who is the Author of nature, may well expect to find the same sort of difficulties in it as are found in the constitution of nature. [Hence], he who denies Scripture to have been from God, upon account of these difficulties, may for the very same reason deny the world to have been formed by him."[28]

But the existence of these "difficulties" does not mean errors were made in the writing of the Bible. To the contrary, the Bible is inerrant, meaning its original text was without error; even though human beings originally wrote it, they were writing under the power of the Holy Spirit. But biblical inspiration does not guarantee that later copies were without error, and indeed, a number of minor—and substantively insignificant—mistakes have been found in them, as we'll see in Chapter 9.

I view the human authorship of the Bible, especially the diversity of it, as probative of, rather than undermining, its inspired nature, as we'll see in Chapter 7. With many authors, we see many different historical and geographical contexts, the use of different languages, and messages communicated through the grid of different and distinct human personalities and with different styles.

As we contemplate this paradox of both divine and human authorship, we want to find the balance between the human component and the overarching divine influence. Obviously, if we believe all Scripture is inspired, then we believe God played the predominant role in creating it. But we can't take this so far as to deny all the human elements involved and treat the text as if it had simply been "downloaded" to human automatons without regard to their personalities or cultures.[29] As Dr. Geisler says, "Biblical Docetism...is a serious doctrinal deviation, for the Bible is truly a human book, and to deny this is no less a doctrinal deviation than to deny the humanity of Christ"[30]—a doctrine we explore fully in Chapter 6.

On the other hand, if the Bible tells us the Holy Spirit carried the writers along, we have to take that claim seriously indeed, and assume that the message comes directly from God, even if transmitted through various human beings. I believe that the Bible is wholly God's message, even if delivered through various human agents in their own styles, times, and environments. They wrote the words but God superintended their writing to communicate His inerrant and inspired message. We are not talking about human beings writing "inspired" works in the secular sense of that term; that is, these were not human authors doing their finest possible work. As Carl F. H. Henry notes, we aren't describing "holy men, or of human words at their profoundest, or of human thought at its purest. Rather, it is a matter solely of God speaking in His Word, supernaturally to and through chosen men, making his thoughts and message known to those who must otherwise have been strangers to them."[31]

Thus, the paradox is resolved; there was a merger between God's guiding hand and the individual words of the writers, with the product being one hundred percent inspired. God's influence and human agency were in total harmony as flipsides of the same coin.

GOD'S SOVEREIGNTY AND OUR PERSONAL RESPONSIBILITY

How is it possible that God is in control over His entire creation, and yet we retain our free will and are responsible for our actions? If God makes us do the things we do, how can we be held accountable for them? But if He doesn't, is He then not sovereign?

The biblical worldview, writes Dr. William Lane Craig, "involves a strong conception of divine sovereignty over the world and human affairs even as it presupposes human freedom and responsibility." These two streams of biblical teaching can be reconciled without compromising either.[32]

The Bible clearly teaches that God is sovereign. "Whatever the Lord pleases, he does, in heaven and on earth" (Psalms 135:6); "He does according to his will among the host of heaven and among the inhabitants of the earth" (Daniel 4:35). He does whatever He wills: "I know that you can do all things, and that no purpose of yours can be thwarted" (Job 4:2). And His will cannot be opposed: "Consider the work of God: who can make straight what he has made crooked?" (Ecc. 7:13).

Granted, there is a wide range of opinions as to how much control God exercises, but most Christians agree that God is sovereign. Most also concur that God's sovereignty does not nullify personal responsibility for one's actions.[33] The Bible is clear that humans are responsible for the moral choices they make and the actions they take before a sovereign God. The Lord will "repay each one according to his works," and this judgment will turn on whether we persevere in doing good or whether we obey the truth or yield to unrighteousness (Romans 2:6–8).[34]

God's control over each human being's fate, then, is rightly balanced with the moral responsibility each human has to respond appropriately to God.[35] "The very basis of prophetic preaching rested upon a belief that human action matters in a world governed by a sovereign God," writes Professor James O. Edlin. "The prophetic summons to repentance challenged people, 'Seek the Lord and live' (Amos 5:6). If they did not change, then God promised, 'my wrath will break out and burn like fire because of the evil you have done.'"[36] In his sermon at Pentecost, Peter illustrates the harmony between God's sovereignty and man's personal responsibility: "This Jesus, delivered up according to the definite plan and foreknowledge of God, you crucified and killed by the hands of lawless men" (Acts 2:23).[37]

In the context of this paradox I've often contemplated Judas' betrayal as being something he chose and for which he was held completely accountable. Yet ironically, it was also an outworking of God's divine will because He sent Jesus to die for us. I'm not saying God specifically chose Judas to bring about His plan—I don't know. But it was His will that His Son die for us—obviously. Jesus reinforced that He was in sync with that plan and wouldn't oppose it, as when He rebuked Peter for cutting off the ear of a soldier who came to arrest Him (Luke 22:51).

Reconciling these two seemingly competing forces is admittedly more difficult than some of the other paradoxes addressed in this chapter. There are certain things we can't fully understand, but we can get a pretty good idea. One explanation was offered by Luis Molina in the sixteenth century, and it's close to an idea I had formed independently. Simply stated, it is that as God is omniscient, He knows what any creature He creates will freely do in any set of circumstances. Therefore, in bringing about those circumstances, He is exercising His sovereignty while preserving the human actor's individual liberty.[38]

THE TRUTH WILL SET YOU FREE—OR WILL IT MAKE YOU OBEDIENT?

By giving us freedom, however, God isn't demonstrating that He is indifferent to the choices we make. Far from it. He exhorts us to be obedient to Him. But how does this obedience make us free?

Jesus says, "If you abide in my word, you are truly my disciples, and you will know the truth, and the truth will set you free" (John 8:31–32).

This is one of my favorite paradoxes, because I used to struggle with how growing closer to Jesus, Who holds us to such exacting standards, could make us free. Isn't obedience antithetical to freedom?

Without truth, or without regard for the truth of sin's consequences, we are free to sin. But if we find truth and it leads us not to sin, how is that freedom? After all, isn't sinning enjoyable? Isn't sinning freely part of what it means to be free? If I were truly free, I wouldn't be burdened by my sin-limiting conscience, would I? At least I would be free to ignore it.

One key, I think, to understanding this new freedom is found in John 8. "We are offspring of Abraham and have never been enslaved to anyone," a group declares to Jesus. "How is it that you say, 'You will become free'?" He responds, "Truly, truly, I say to you, everyone who practices sin is a slave to sin. The slave does not remain in the house forever; the son remains forever. So if the Son sets you free, you will be free indeed" (33–37).

When you can't resist the temptation to sin, you succumb to your passions or to external forces, meaning you are not really in control. That's not freedom. If you find yourself doing what you don't want to do, or even if you want to do it but know you shouldn't, you are, in a sense, in bondage to the sinful behavior. This is especially true of addictive behavior. On one level, the addict wants to escape the bonds of addiction, but he can't bring himself to do it.

To be out from under the controlling influence of sin is to be free. True liberation is found apart from sin; it is liberation from sin—when sin no longer controls our lives. When we are living licentiously or obsessed with the pursuit of money or any other idolatrous object, we are in bondage. Christianity is not our slave master; sin is.

Why is it that all human beings know the difference between right and wrong behavior—"the work of the law is written on their hearts, while their conscience also bears witness" (Romans 2:15)—yet we continue to sin, even when we anticipate negative consequences? According to Pastor Timothy Keller, "The Bible's explanation is *human hearts are sinful, but beyond that we're slaves to sin.* The Bible says that sin is not just an action; it's a power." It is a particularly destructive power "upon the faculty that put that action forth." So for example, says Keller, sinning with the mind "shrivels the rationality;" sinning with the heart "shrivels the emotions;" sinning with the will "destroys and dissolves your will-power and your self-control." He conveys this culminating insight: "Sin is the suicidal action of the self against itself. Sin destroys freedom. Sin is an enslaving power."[39]

I think this is particularly helpful, because we know that sin is more than just the sum of individual acts of misconduct we commit. We intuitively know that it is powerful—a dark force, spiritual in nature. When we are under its power we are spiritual slaves, but we know that when we try to resist it on our own power, we often fail. (Romans 7:18–19). And when we fail, it takes something out of us with its destructive force. Paul confirms that even he is not immune to sin's power: "Now if I do what I do not want, it is no longer I who do it, but sin that dwells within me" (Romans 7:20).

Thankfully, this is not the end of the story. Christianity frees us in Christ from the power and control of sin. As we've seen, at the moment of our conversion (when we are justified/declared righteous) we are freed not just from the penalty of sin, but from its power. We will still struggle with sin daily and often fail, but we are armed with the power of the Holy Spirit to resist it.

Paul describes another aspect of the Christian's newfound freedom: "There is therefore now no condemnation for those who are in Christ Jesus. For the law of the Spirit of life has set you free in Christ Jesus from the law of sin and death. For God has done what the law, weakened by the flesh, could not do. By sending his own Son in the likeness of sinful flesh and for sin, he condemned sin in the flesh, in order that the righteous requirement of the law might be fulfilled in us, who walk not according to the flesh but according to the Spirit" (Romans 8:1–4).

So the Christian is free from two things: the bondage of sin and the Law. He lives not by the Law but by the power of the Spirit. This doesn't mean his personal morality is irrelevant. To the contrary, as noted in the previous chapter, the Christian, while not technically under the Law, is motivated through love of God to imitate Christ in obedience. He will not be completely sin-free, but by relying on the Spirit, he can measurably reduce sin in his life.

Also remember that sin is that which separates us from God. We were made to be united with Him. We cannot possibly be free, much less fulfilled, if we remain apart from Him.

BE IN, NOT OF, THE WORLD

What about the supposed inconsistency between the ideas that God created the world, but as Christians, we should still be wary of it?

The Bible's acceptance of the material world sets it apart from other religions and philosophies.[40] For example, some Eastern religions hold that matter is an illusion or that we must strive to transcend the material plane of existence. Likewise, certain pagan philosophers like Plotinus considered matter the least good of all things,[41] while Plato held that matter was a formless chaos.[42]

In Christianity, the heresy that matter is evil was common in some of the early Christian churches. Gnostics were prevalent among the heretics in the second century. Like other early heretics and like Christian Scientists today, Gnostics believed matter to be an evil antagonist of God—to the point that they couldn't accept the actual incarnation of Christ.[43] Today, this idea still exists, leading some to pursue meditation or asceticism in the belief that physical satisfaction should be shunned.

In fact, Christian doctrine teaches that spirituality and salvation are not to be found by avoiding the material world.[44] As God completed each day of His creation activity, He declared, "It is good" (Gen. 1:4, 10, 12, 18, 21). At the end of the last day, "God saw everything that He had made, and behold, it was very good" (Gen. 1:31). Paul, in instructing his student Timothy to dispute the virtue of asceticism to the Ephesian Christians, made similar pronouncements: "Now the Spirit expressly says that in later times some will depart from the faith by devoting themselves to deceitful spirits and the teachings of demons, through the insincerity of liars whose consciences are seared, who forbid marriage and require abstinence from foods that God created to be received with thanksgiving by those who believe and know the truth. For everything created by God is good, and nothing is to be rejected if it is received with thanksgiving, for it is made holy by the word of God and prayer" (1 Tim.

4:1–4). Similarly, in his letter to the Romans Paul wrote, "I know and am persuaded in the Lord Jesus that nothing is unclean in itself" (Romans 14:14). So the Bible is consistent in affirming that everything God made is good. Even after the fall, all of creation is still good.

But aren't Christians often told they must be *in* the world but not *of* it? What does that mean? Jesus exclaims, "If the world hates you, know that it has hated me before it hated you. If you were of the world, the world would love you as its own; but because you are not of the world, but I chose you out of the world, therefore the world hates you" (John 15:18–19). Additionally, in His prayer to the Father He says, "All mine are yours, and yours are mine, and I am glorified in them. And I am no longer in the world, but they are in the world, and I am coming to you.... I have given them your word, and the world has hated them because they are not of the world, just as I am not of the world. I do not ask that you take them out of the world, but that you keep them from the evil one" (John 17:10–15).

John echoes Jesus' teachings: "Do not love the world or the things in the world. If anyone loves the world, the love of the Father is not in him. For all that is in the world—the desires of the flesh and the desires of the eyes and pride of life—is not from the Father but is from the world. And the world is passing away along with its desires, but whoever does the will of God abides forever" (1 John 2:15–17). Similarly, James writes, "You adulterous people! Do you not know that friendship with the world is enmity with God? Therefore whoever wishes to be a friend of the world makes himself an enemy of God" (James 4:4).

These are not indictments of God's material creation—material things aren't evil in and of themselves—but of Satan's influence on the world. The Bible tells us that Satan is in control of the world (1 John 5:19). It does not belong to him, but he presently controls it. So Christians should avoid the world's contamination, since believers are not to love that which organizes them against God.[45] This does not mean, however, that all Christians are under Satan's control. According to Daniel Akin, John's use of "the world" in this passage "represents human society under the power of evil and at war with God and his people."[46]

But more is involved than just avoiding being "of the world." As pastor Timothy Keller teaches, "It's not enough to say, as many people say, 'Christians should be in the world but not of the world. That's not good enough. Pharisees are in the world but not of the world, but they hate the world. They look down on it."[47] People are free to choose to be of the world influenced by Satan or to seek after Christ. And Jesus makes clear that He isn't asking the Father to take Christians "out of the world," but that He "keep them from the evil one." The point is that He is asking the Father to shield them not from the material world itself, but from the evil influences and temptations of Satan.

We are to avoid the carnal life and live the life of the Spirit. In his letter to the Colossians, Paul writes, "Put to death therefore what is earthly in you: sexual immorality, impurity, passion, evil desire, and covetousness, which is idolatry" (Col. 3:5). To say that everything God created is good does not negate the effects of the fall on human beings, who will always have to wrestle with their sinful nature while relying on the power of the Holy Spirit.

BECOMING MORE HOLY MAKES YOU MORE AWARE OF YOUR UNHOLINESS

Another interesting paradox emerges in the process of our sanctification. Once you place your faith in Christ and are justified by His righteousness, as noted above, you begin becoming more holy, by the power of the Holy Spirit working in you and by exercising the spiritual disciplines, such as Bible study, worship, and prayer. One might think this would cause the regenerated individual to become aware of his spiritual growth and feel elated that he is becoming holier. To the contrary, this growth in holiness, this indwelling of the Holy Spirit, will quicken one's sensitivity to his own sin, for "one of the marks of authentic spirituality is a heightened sensitivity to sin in one's own life."[48]

H. H. Rowley implies that this same process worked even among the Old Testament saints, if to a lesser degree. "With each fresh insight into the heart of God and each fresh emphasis on the conception of God," he says, "we find the same thing. It is the moral holiness of God which makes Isaiah conscious of the uncleanness of his own heart and makes him realize that these two cannot exist together."[49] Jesus promises

He will send the Holy Spirit for us and that He will convict the world concerning sin and righteousness and judgment (John 16:7–8). Rather than delighting in his progress, man will see his darkness like he never saw it before.[50] As Dr. Lloyd-Jones notes, the effect of the Holy Spirit working in us is that "he becomes more and more sensitive to sin and increasingly conscious of it, and so he comes to hate it more and more. The more sensitive we become to sin, the more we glorify Christ."[51]

While the power of the Holy Spirit to change our lives is real, some Christians deceive themselves into believing they're closer to the flame than they are, for John tells us, "If we say we have no sin, we deceive ourselves, and the truth is not in us" (1 John 1:8). It's a lifelong process and it will always be incomplete. "For I do not understand my own actions," says Paul. "For I do not what I want, but I do the very thing I hate" (Romans 7:15). Our greater awareness of our sinfulness could lead us into denial about the negativity we now witness in ourselves. So once we have acquired this "clarity," we must resist the temptation to close our eyes when God is showing us something "by the light of his word."[52] As Psalms proclaims, "Your word is a lamp to my feet and a light to my path" (119:105).

While it is discouraging that Paul—the Christian of Christians— could not wholly overcome his sinful nature, there is something immensely encouraging about that as well: if even Paul remained a sinner, we realize we must not be abnormal as Christians. It's also heartening to be assured that we are now empowered by the Holy Spirit to see our own sinfulness more clearly and to defeat it one day at a time.

GOD IS KNOWABLE, YET UNSEARCHABLE?

Unlike the gods of other religions, the God of the Bible is knowable to us, yet His wisdom is unsearchable. Jesus Christ came into our world so that we could know God (John 17:3). When Philip asks Jesus to show the Father to the disciples, "Jesus said to him, 'Have I been with you so long, and you still do not know me, Philip? Whoever has seen me has seen the Father" (John 14:9). Elsewhere Jesus says, "I and the Father are one" (John 10:30). The New Testament has many similar references.

Paul writes, "He is the image of the invisible God, the firstborn of all creation" (Col. 1:15). The writer of Hebrews says, "He is the radiance of the glory of God and the exact imprint of his nature" (1:3).

Paul tells us in Romans that since the creation of the world, God's invisible attributes have been clearly seen. They're invisible, yet visible, because He has revealed Himself to us. Paul also relates, however, that he was charged with preaching "the unsearchable riches of Christ" to the Gentiles (Eph. 3:8). He tells the Romans, "Oh, the depth of the riches and wisdom and knowledge of God! How unsearchable are his judgments and how inscrutable his ways! For who has known the mind of the Lord, or who has been his counselor" (Romans 11:33–34)? Similar references appear in the Book of Psalms—"Great is the Lord, and greatly to be praised, and his greatness is unsearchable" (145:3)—and in Isaiah—"His understanding is unsearchable" (40:28).

As finite creatures, even ones made in God's image, we can't possibly comprehend God entirely and can only marvel at Him in wonder and amazement. We can't begin to fathom all His complexities. But His infinite superiority does not make Him inaccessible or aloof from us. Not only can we know Him, we *must* know Him. Developing an intimate personal relationship with Him and loving Him should be our highest priorities. More than anything, Christianity is about cultivating a personal relationship with Jesus Christ.

WHY SHOULD WE PRAY?

Why does God exhort us to pray unceasingly (1 Thess. 5:17), even for those who persecute us (Matt. 5:44)? Not to be cynical, but what's the point of praying if God is in control and already knows how everything will turn out, which will be according to His sovereign will? God doesn't change His mind, right? So how is prayer going to change the course of events? Additionally, what's the point of verbalizing our concerns and needs to an omniscient God Who already knows them (Matt. 6:32), just as He knows every hair on our heads?

While this doesn't resolve the dilemma, the first reason we pray is out of obedience. God commands us to pray (1 Thess. 5:17; Col. 4:2).

Jesus encourages his disciples to pray and gives them the Lord's Prayer as a model for how to do it (Matt. 6:9–13). A lack of prayer demonstrates a lack of faith and trust in God's Word.[53]

Before we assume that prayer to an omniscient god is futile, understand that He not only tells us to pray persistently, but that we don't receive certain things because we don't ask for them (James 4:2). Jesus illustrates in a parable how persistent prayer will bring results (Luke 18:1–8). Even if we don't always recognize the results, God tells us prayer works: "The prayer of a righteous person has great power as it is working" (James 5:16; John 14:13–14).

Part of our misapprehension about prayer is that we have a narrow view of it—I certainly used to see it as little more than asking God for blessings and thanking Him for them. But it is so much more. Among many other things, we pray in adoration to God (Rev. 5:13); to confess sin (1 John 1:9); for God's protection (Num. 10:35); for His divine guidance (1 Samuel 14:36–41); for wisdom (1 Kings 3:1–15; 4:29–34); to praise God (Psalms 18:3; 103:1); that God will teach us to walk in His truth and guide our hearts toward a right relationship with Him (Psalms 86:11); to give thanks to God and to let our requests be known to Him (Philip. 4:6–7); to cry out in anguish to God in times of personal suffering (Job 6:8–10) or when we are depressed (Psalms 116:1–4); for physical strength (Neh. 6:9); for inner peace and for righteousness (Psalms 139:23–24); to have a forgiving spirit toward others (Matt. 6:14–15); and we pray for one another and for healing (James 5:16).

We must pray that God's will be done—not because there's any doubt that it will be, but to get ourselves into a right relationship with God and to align ourselves with His holy will. Prayer can be a means of discerning His will. Sometimes, in prayer, we have to be still and listen to God. We shouldn't be deterred from prayer just because we don't know what to discuss with God. The Bible tells us that on those occasions, the Holy Spirit will help us out (Romans 8:26).

It is perfectly proper for us to come to God in prayer with specific requests, but one of the main reasons we pray is to spend time with Him and build a relationship with Him. We were created to commune with God, and there's no more direct way to do it than prayer, other than reading and studying His Word. So even if God refuses to grant our specific petitions, the most important reason for prayer still remains: maintaining an ongoing conversation and building an intimate relationship with Him.

The Bible informs us that God listens to our prayers (1 Kings 8:52; Psalms 6:9); He does answer them. God has assured us that even when we don't receive the response we are requesting, our prayers are not in vain (Matt. 6:6; Romans 8:26–27). The fact that He answers prayers, and sometimes even alters the course of events in response to prayer, doesn't mean He changed His mind. God is unchangeable. Indeed, prayer is one of the ways God secures the outworking of His will.

The skeptic (me in a previous life) might reject the idea that an unchangeable God would respond to our prayers. He might even accuse God of egotism for, in effect, making us beg Him for things. But the truth is that prayer isn't some kind of cosmic game. God has designed a system whereby our prayers can be answered, not to satisfy His own selfish needs—He has none—but because the very process of prayer leads us into a stronger, more loving relationship with Him. In the words of Gary Newton, "Prayer unlocks the door to the storehouse of God's riches."[54]

Jesus prayed to the Father, and if prayer wasn't beneath Him, the God-man, how much more important is it for us? Just as we pray to strengthen and deepen our relationship with God, we also do so to become more Christ-like, as there is nothing more Christ-like than a praying person (Matt. 5:45). We pray for God's glory, of course, but when we do, it redounds to our benefit. And yes, prayer can be for our benefit, even though God knows the outcome in advance.[55]

Sometimes we neglect prayer because it can be difficult; even Paul called it a struggle. Voices wiser than mine have suggested part of the difficulty may stem from us being too self-centered in our prayers. Like with so many other things, if we get outside ourselves and develop a more serving attitude, we might find prayer more rewarding. We know that prayer is a spiritual discipline and that we must diligently exercise it. Perhaps if we reorient ourselves to some of the higher purposes of prayer—that we commune with God and conform ourselves to His will—we might realize what a privilege it is and more readily engage in it every day. If we think of prayer as what it actually is—a divine privilege to converse with the God of the universe—we will gain a profound appreciation for it and strengthen our prayer lives, which will inevitably lead to strengthening our faith and our relationship with God.

THE PARADOX OF FORGIVENESS

Doesn't our human sense of justice tell us that wrongdoers must be punished? How can God command us to forgive those who have deliberately, even persistently, wronged us, especially if they aren't repentant? As John MacArthur notes, vengeance is popular today, not forgiveness. Vengeance is often portrayed as a virtue reflecting self-esteem. But it's anything but a virtue, argues MacArthur. His own experience taught him that "nearly all the personal problems that drive people to seek pastoral counsel are related in some way to the issue of forgiveness." People are either struggling with their own guilt and seeking God's forgiveness, or withholding forgiveness from others who have wronged them. "Both tendencies," he observes, "are spiritually and emotionally debilitating." Both problems, says MacArthur, can be remedied only by a better understand of biblical teachings on the subject and an obedience to those teachings.[56]

Just as with prayer, God commands us to forgive (Eph. 4:32), so we should do so as a matter of obedience. We are to forgive, because we have been forgiven. It's so important that it is even part of the Lord's Prayer (Matt. 6:12). *Fine*, you say, *but that still doesn't satisfy my sense of fairness.* Well, in the scheme of things it isn't fair that Christ forgives us either, much less that He gave His life for us. But the gospel is all about forgiveness. "Forgiveness," as my church's associate pastor Brett Cheek says, "is the heart of God. It unleashes something divine." Jesus tells us, "If you forgive those who sin against you, your heavenly Father will forgive you. But if you refuse to forgive others, your Father will not forgive your sins" (Matt. 6:14–15). It was surely this principle John Wesley had in mind when John Ogelthorpe told him, "I never forgive." Wesley responded, "Then, Sir, I hope that you never sin."[57]

Forgiving others does not mean denying we have been hurt or down-playing our pain. This sort of dishonest denial, cautions Dr. Stanley, actually works against the forgiveness process.[58]

God's forgiveness leads to our eternal life with Him; it's no trifling matter. When we place our faith in Him our sins are forgiven and our slate is wiped clean. If He forgives us, how much more should we forgive our fellow man? God freely grants forgiveness, and we should just as freely grant it. Jesus doesn't merely tell us to forgive, but to forgive abundantly and repeatedly (Matt. 18:22; Luke 17:3–4).

We must forgive because an unforgiving spirit can poison our soul. It can eat us alive. When we forgive someone who has wronged us, we might feel they are getting something they don't deserve. But the unforgiving person is likely to be suffering from his unforgiving spirit more than the person he refuses to forgive, and he will benefit from forgiving more than the person who wronged him. Forgiveness is absolutely liberating, because until you give up whatever hold this unforgiving spirit has on you, you are in bondage to it.

We know this to be true from personal experience. An unforgiving spirit is haunting. Dr. Charles Stanley confirms Dr. MacArthur's experience. Some people, he says, aren't even aware that they suffer from an unforgiving spirit and that unforgiveness is the root of their problem. Consequently, they want to strike out at certain types of people or they lose their temper easily. They struggle over sins committed in the past, and they can't escape the pain of hating the ones they know they should love the most. They are the "real losers," more than the person they believe wronged them.[59]

Yes, the person you forgive may well not deserve it. But we don't deserve Christ's forgiveness either. Christianity, at its core, is about forgiveness and grace. We can hardly be Christ-like unless we cultivate a forgiving and gracious spirit. When we forgive someone else, we become more Christ-like in the process, just as we do when we pray—especially when we pray for our enemies.

Just as with God's counterintuitive salvation scheme, we must understand forgiveness in the context of God's grace. We must avoid thinking solely in human terms as to whether the person who wronged us deserves our forgiveness, and instead emulate Christ's model of grace. The person may not deserve forgiveness, but we must freely give it, and we will be rewarded in spirit.

If we reject God's directive that we forgive, the poison of our unforgiving spirit can be devastating to us emotionally, spiritually, and even to our health. It can separate us from our friends. But worst of all, it can and will separate us from God.[60] If we follow God's example and develop a forgiving spirit, we are doing the right thing, and it will benefit us. Do we want to receive that benefit, that liberating spirit, or would we prefer to remain mired in the negativity and destructiveness of our own pain?

ECCLESIASTES

The Book of Ecclesiastes, most likely written by Solomon, records a man's struggle to find meaning in life. The book's message could be considered paradoxical because it seems so overwhelmingly negative yet ultimately winds up being positive. The speaker, or preacher, spends almost the entire time demonstrating his consummate pessimism, challenging and undermining all that is good and even questioning the principles and pronouncements of the remainder of the Bible's wisdom literature, as if he is blasphemously mocking it. The book is so full of despair at times that one might wonder how it could have been included in the Bible.

The preacher may come off as a cynic who believes that life is meaningless, but there is a method to his madness, and he ultimately delivers a positive message. We gain insight into his viewpoint from his statement in 1:12–13: "I, the Preacher, have been king over Israel in Jerusalem. And I set my mind to seek and explore by wisdom concerning all that has been done under the heavens. It is a grievous task which God has given to the sons of men to be afflicted with." His statement is bolstered by his references to what he has seen in the Scriptures that follow that assertion.

He thoroughly investigated all aspects of life through his own efforts and discovered all was vanity. But we must recognize the implied qualifier. All life is vanity, but only to the extent that one lives apart from God. By sketching the utter hopelessness and meaninglessness of life apart from God, the preacher is emphasizing how essential it is for us to trust in God. In essence, nothing really matters without that trust. So his overall message is far from negative; it is that while life is indeed meaninglessness apart from God, a life of faith is anything but meaningless.

CONCLUSION

There are common threads running through almost all the paradoxes I have explored in these two chapters. In virtually every case, we see the theme of God's irrepressible love for us. Throughout, we learn that He freely bestows unmerited grace and blessings on mankind and teaches us that we must place our faith in Him, draw closer to Him, abide in Him, and commune with Him—though the messages are sometimes delivered mysteriously and seem counterintuitive.

These paradoxical teachings, as we've seen, are not limited to Jesus' parables, which by definition are paradoxical in nature. We see the same teaching method throughout Scripture—in Proverbs, Job, Ecclesiastes, and elsewhere. God chose to deliver His messages in this way because they resonate more. They teach us that by drawing closer to God, becoming more sanctified, and placing our trust in Him, things begin to make more sense and life has more meaning.

We also see in these messages and throughout the Bible that while God exhorts us to have faith in Him, we aren't always going to reap immediate rewards. Life often seems unfair, and even a strong faith is not guaranteed to produce bliss and prosperity in the short term. The Scriptures plainly demonstrate that our rewards may not be immediate, but we can always have inner peace and a sense of purpose, even throughout our struggles, if we have a faith-relationship with God through Jesus Christ. And though we may not receive these glories now, they do await us, and God will make good on that promise.

The writer of Hebrews, one of my favorite books in the Bible because of its emphasis on faith, makes this clear. In 11:32–40 he details many Old Testament heroes of faith who conquered kingdoms, enforced justice, and stopped the mouths of lions. But he also lists others, those who did not seem so blessed in this life, those who, because of their faith, "were stoned . . . sawn in two . . . killed with the sword . . . destitute, afflicted, mistreated . . . wandering about in deserts and mountains and in dens and caves of the earth." These people, he says, "the world was not worthy" of, and yet they suffered, sometimes because of their faith. But the writer concludes with this powerfully uplifting assurance: "These were all commended for their faith, yet none of them received what had been promised. God had planned something better for us so that only together with us would they be made perfect" (11:39–40).

This is followed by hopeful verses encouraging us to persevere in our struggles and to look to Jesus as the ultimate example of One Who suffered and Who is now glorified with the Father: "Let us run with endurance the race that is set before us, looking to Jesus, the founder and perfecter of our faith, who for the joy that was set before him endured the cross, despising the shame, and is now seated at the right hand of the throne of God. Consider him who endured from sinners such hostility against himself, so that you may not grow weary or faint-hearted" (12:1–3).

The paradoxical sections of Scripture also show us that while the Bible has endless riches for all of us to explore, it is not too difficult for the simple-minded and not too simple for the intelligent. The smartest of men can spend their entire lifetimes reading Scripture and never tire of it. Yet, repeatedly, the Bible affirms its own accessibility even to children. The Bible's words are so easy to understand that we are commanded to "teach them diligently to your children" (Deut. 6:7) and to "make them known to your children and your children's children" (Deut. 4:9).

John MacArthur quotes Clark Pinnock explaining that "Scripture is a 'light shining in a dark place (2 Peter 1:19). The 'Father of lights' has given His Word to be a lamp to our feet and a light to our path (Psalms 119:105). It is not inaccessible and hidden from us (Deut. 30:11–14). We are commanded to read and search it (John 5:39; Acts 17:11). It makes wise the simple, revives the soul, rejoices the heart, and enlightens the eyes (Psalms 19:7–8). Scripture is clear because it is God's. If it were not clear, it would fail in its intention."[61] While we may not understand every part, we'll grasp the essence of the message if we put our minds and hearts to it. When we don't at first understand, we must dig deeper and we will inevitably grow as a result.

The Bible is the great equalizer, because its message applies to every one of us regardless of intelligence—and besides, we see every day that intelligence hardly equates to wisdom. Furthermore, no matter how intelligent any of us may be, we are intellectually insignificant in comparison to our omniscient God. We must remember our place in relation to God, be humble before Him, and He will exalt us. In the words of Paul,

> For the foolishness of God is wiser than men, and the weakness of God is stronger than men. For consider your calling, brothers: not many of you were wise according to worldly standards, not many were powerful, not many were of noble birth. But God chose what is foolish in the world to shame the wise; God chose what is weak in the world to shame the strong; God chose what is low and despised in the world, even things that are not, to bring to nothing things that are, so that no human being might boast in the presence of God. And because of him you are in Christ Jesus, who became to us wisdom from God, righteousness and sanctification and redemption, so that, as it is written, "Let the one who boasts, boast in the Lord" (1 Cor. 25–30).

This method of teaching through paradoxes inspires me to explore the Scriptures and meditate on them. I hope it will stir the same reaction in you.

CHAPTER 6

JESUS CHRIST, FULLY HUMAN AND FULLY DIVINE

Christ's Humanity: From Stumbling Block to Foundational Pillar

"AND THE WORD BECAME FLESH"

Though the Bible teaches that Jesus is both man and God, I think we sometimes underappreciate His human side, which is so fundamentally important, and without which there would be no cross, no salvation, and no eternal life for believers. There would be no Christianity either, for Christianity does not teach that Jesus was 50 percent deity and 50 percent human; rather, that He was 100 percent God and 100 percent human.

In fact many, perhaps most, false teachings of various cults, from New Testament times to the present, can be traced to a misapprehension of this truth. Many believe that Christ was either deity or human (as an extraordinary prophet), but not both.

In *Basic Theology*, highly respected theologian Dr. Charles Ryrie notes that orthodox Christianity has considered Christ's dual nature definitive since the Council of Chalcedon in 451 AD.[1] That council declared, "Therefore, following the holy fathers, we all with one accord teach men to acknowledge one and the same Son, our Lord Jesus Christ, at once complete in Godhead and complete in manhood, truly God and truly man, consisting also of a reasonable soul and body; of one substance with the Father as regards His Godhead, and at the same time of one substance with us as regards His manhood."[2] Ryrie says, "More concisely one may describe the person of Christ incarnate as being full Deity and perfect humanity united without mixture, change, division, or separation in one person forever."[3] He continues, "This simply means that the attributes of both natures belong to the one Person without mixing the natures or dividing the Person. Practically speaking, it is the basis for Christ being seen to be weak, yet omnipotent; ignorant, yet omniscient; limited, yet infinite."[4]

I am emphasizing Christ's dual nature, especially His humanity, because my initial failure to grasp this concept, I think, created confusion and doubt for me. When we finally come to understand that Christ is as human as you and I, while at the same time being God, certain problematic passages in the New Testament radiate with clarity. I do not regret these doubts, because I believe my faith is stronger for having worked through them.

Back in my skeptical days I couldn't reconcile certain statements of Jesus with the idea that He is the Son of God. If He were truly God, and if He and the Father are one, why would He have accused God the Father of abandoning Him on the cross? "And at the ninth hour Jesus cried out in a loud voice, 'Eloi, Eloi, lama sabachthani?'"—which means, "My God, my God, why have you forsaken me" (Mark 15:34)? If He were truly One with the Father, He wouldn't need to be asking those questions, would He? In other words, if He were One in essence with God the Father, then how could He have been separated from the Father? If

He knows everything the Father knows, why would He have needed to ask Him anything?

My error was based in a misunderstanding of Jesus' humanity, which is a source of numerous Christian heresies. For example, second- and third-century Docetists claimed Jesus was pure spirit Who just appeared to be human. Denying Christ had a real physical body, they believed His humanity and suffering as well as His crucifixion and resurrection were illusory.[5] Gnosticism, as mentioned earlier, was a more convoluted set of beliefs based on the notion that a certain sect possessed secret, superior knowledge, and that the material world was evil. Gnostics believed Jesus was the absolute and transcendent God but was not incarnate in human flesh because the absolute God would not enter evil matter— Christ only *seemed* to be human.[6]

These and other heresies were no trifling matter, as Jesus' humanity is a crucial theological concept. Thus, the early Church and the Church fathers struggled to purge these ideas from accepted Christian doctrine. Gnostics were branded as heretics and have always been regarded as such by orthodox Christians.[7]

One Sunday my pastor Ron Watts preached on the ordinary human experiences of Jesus Christ. He understands our sufferings and everyday problems because He walked among us, He became one of us, and He experienced even the mundane things we experience, which makes Him that much more approachable for us. Jesus, said Ron, even understands what it's like to have His prayer go unanswered—or at least not to receive the answer He wanted. As the writer of Hebrews says, "For we do not have a high priest who is unable to sympathize with our weaknesses, but one who in every respect has been tempted as we are, yet without sin. Let us then with confidence draw near to the throne of grace to help in time of need" (4:15–16).

In *Life of Christ*, Archbishop Fulton Sheen puts it this way: "No man can love anything unless he can get his arms around it, and the cosmos is too big and too bulky. But once God became a Babe and was wrapped in swaddling clothes and laid in a manger, men could say, 'This is Emmanuel, this is God with us.'"[8] Like Pastor Watts, Sheen is saying that by taking on human form and enduring the same experiences we do—and then some—Jesus enabled us to identify with Him and form a personal relationship with Him. Christ's incarnation means that God is not just an abstract idea as unreachable to us as "the big and bulky cosmos." Through Him God became concrete and real. We could touch Him. Thomas did, Mary did. Others did. He was in swaddling clothes; He walked, He wept. He became someone we can wrap our arms around and love.

Within a few weeks of Ron's sermon, I serendipitously (or providentially) happened onto a similar line of thought in my research for this book. British preacher Charles Spurgeon, in a sermon delivered in 1876, declared,

> Jesus knows every experience, for he has passed through the same. Does not this thought already whisper comfort to your soul? My seeking friend, is it not a good omen that Jesus was heard in that he feared? Does not the fact that Jesus can sympathize with you raise some hope in your heart? It is true he never lived without the presence of God, as you have done, in consequence of personal sin; but for a grand reason, namely, because he stood in our stead, he was forsaken of God, and therefore was compelled to cry after him, even as you are doing, "My God, my God, why hast thou forsaken me? Why art thou so far from helping me?" Therefore he understands the grief which troubles your fainting heart, and enters into all your distresses while you are bewailing yourself and lamenting that you cry in the day time and the Lord hears not, and that in the night season you plead in vain. This reflection at the outset of our discourse should be as the note of a silver bell, soft, and restful to your wearied ear. Jesus foretells your success in seeking as the result of his own experience.[9]

You see, if Christ had not been fully human, the temptations He experienced in the wilderness would have only been for show. As the *Faith Life Bible* explains, "Jesus' temptations speak to the authenticity of the Incarnation; only people can experience temptation."[10] Yes, if Christ had not been human, his suffering—physical and spiritual—wouldn't have been real, and it had to be real for it to work on our behalf.

As Dr. Ryrie puts it, "The doctrine of the person of Christ is crucial to the Christian faith.... For if our Lord was not what He claimed to be, then His atonement was a deficient, not sufficient, payment for sin."[11]

To be sure, He was feeling excruciating physical pain when He uttered that cry. But more important—in fact, as important as any Christian truth I have been granted the grace to discover—is that His suffering involved inestimably more than physical pain, as horrible as that was. Please follow me here, because understanding this was essential for me—and might be for you—for I believe that when we finally understand that Christ, in fact, was capable of suffering and did in fact suffer, and why and to what extent this occurred, we will comprehend certain core truths of Christianity, and we will come to appreciate Jesus' incomparable love for us.

CHRIST'S SUFFERING HAD TO BE REAL

I must reluctantly confess that I used to wonder what made Jesus' death on the cross worse than the suffering many other people have experienced. No doubt, that level of physical pain is unimaginable, but surely many human beings through the ages have felt similarly unbearable physical pain, including Christian martyrs who were crucified for their faith. I don't think I fully understood at the time just how excruciating crucifixion was. It was such a horrible form of death that the Romans made it illegal to crucify their own citizens.[12] I also failed to take into account the sustained beatings to which Jesus was subjected. But the epiphany came for me when I realized that it wasn't *just* physical pain that Jesus experienced for the sake of our eternal salvation. We have to understand the whole story, not just its culmination.

The Son—the Second Person of the Trinity—has always existed with the Father and the Holy Spirit, before the creation of the world and mankind.[13] As noted in Chapter 4, however, He did not always have dual natures, but became human upon His incarnation. The Church has affirmed this eternality of Christ since the Council of Nicaea.[14] This is necessarily so if He is God, because if He lacks eternality He lacks deity.[15] It is not enough that He merely pre-existed creation, because some cults believe He was the first of the "created spirits."[16] He is eternal—He is and was and always has been. He was instrumentally involved in creation (John 1:3), and as the prophet Micah said of the prophesied Messiah, His "goings forth have been from of old, from everlasting" (Micah 5:2). The arguments for His eternality and for His deity are inseparable.[17]

In eternity past, the Persons of the Triune Godhead enjoyed infinite bliss through their infinite love.[18] Such was His love for us that before time began, before the creation of matter and human beings, and before Adam and Eve sinned, the Triune God planned to create us,[19] even though He knew we would sin and that Christ's suffering and death would be required to redeem us (Eph. 1:4; 1 Peter 1:20; Acts 2:23; 2 Tim. 1:9).[20] "At the cross we see the immensity of God's pain as He endured the sacrifice of Jesus," explains Christian author Ajith Fernando, "And God experienced that pain of the cross from the time He created the world, for the Bible describes Jesus as 'the Lamb that was slain from the creation of the world'"[21] (Rev. 13:8; 1 Peter 1:20).

For God's plan of salvation to work, the Second Person of the Godhead would have to humble Himself and take on human form. This would involve voluntarily refraining from using some of His divine attributes—which some theologians call the "kenosis," or "emptying"—in order to offer Himself in substitution for us.[22] Solely for our sake, then, because God didn't need to create us at all, Christ left His position of indescribable happiness and came to earth. As we read in Philippians, "Christ Jesus, Who, being in very nature God, did not consider equality with God something to be grasped, but made himself nothing, taking the very nature of a servant, being made in human likeness. And being found in appearance as a man, he humbled himself and became obedient to death—even death on a cross! Therefore God exalted him to the highest place and gave him the name that is above every name, that at the name of Jesus every knee should bow, in heaven and on earth and under the earth, and every tongue confess that Jesus Christ is Lord, to the glory of God the Father" (2:5–11).

As this passage makes clear, Christ's humiliation did not begin on the cross. He descended from heaven, became one with us, and began to suffer the indignities of humanity from the moment of His conception.

Imagine leaving your heavenly home to come to earth. Then imagine having to endure all the pain He did as He was scorned and rejected throughout His earthly life. Then consider His pain in the Garden of Gethsemane when He was preparing to be captured by the Roman soldiers and taken to His death.

God hates sin, and His perfect justice compels Him to deal with sin and His wrath that is incurred by that sin. The only way God's wrath and justice could be satisfied was by the sacrificial death of His sinless Son. This was critical for me to grasp: Jesus didn't come to earth as part of a symbolic exercise to satisfy God's sense of justice in some abstract way so that we could be saved. In order for justice to be administered, Christ's suffering *had* to be real; God's wrath *had* to be quenched; Jesus *had* to bear the entire force of that wrath in reality (Isaiah 53:4–6, 10).[23] "God died forsaken by God so that His people might claim God as their God and never be forsaken" (Heb. 13:5). As J. I. Packer writes, "The Cross propitiated God (i.e., quenched his wrath against us by expiating our sins and so removing them from his sight)."[24]

Immeasurable burdens were weighing on Jesus' heart as He fell face down in the Garden of Gethsemane and prayed, "My Father, if it is possible, may this cup be taken from me." In His humanity, He was momentarily asking the Father if He could spare Him from His wrath and from the excruciating pain of His separation. This was no mental lapse. He didn't momentarily forget that He couldn't be spared from fulfilling His very purpose in coming to earth—to suffer and die for our sins. He knew that He had to complete His mission on the cross, but the fullness of His humanity made His suffering nearly intolerable. Scripture describes what He was experiencing: "And, being in agony, he prayed more earnestly; and his sweat became like great drops of blood falling down to the ground" (Luke 22:44).

The *Bible Knowledge Commentary* states, "Christ died forsaken by God so that His people might claim God as their God and never be forsaken."[25] He endured abandonment so we'd never have to be abandoned; He endured loneliness so we'd never be alone.

Bishop Sheen puts Christ's suffering in perspective. "What Our Blessed Lord contemplated in this agony was not just the buffeting of soldiers," writes Sheen, "and the pinioning of His hands and feet to a bar of contradiction, but rather the awful burden of the world's sin, and the fact that the world was about to spurn His Father by rejecting Him, His Divine Son."[26] Just as quickly as He made His futile plea, however, Christ reverted to His servant-born obedience and answered His own question: "Yet not as I will, but as you will" (Matt. 26:39). Sheen encapsulates the enormity of Christ's act of humility that began with His birth and climaxed on the cross:

> It is hard for a human being to understand the humility that was involved in the Word becoming flesh. Imagine, if it were possible, a human person divesting himself of his body, and then sending his soul into the body of a serpent. A double humiliation would follow: first, accepting the limitations of a serpentine organism, knowing all the while his mind was superior, and that fangs could not adequately articulate thoughts no serpent ever possessed. The second humiliation would be to be forced as a result of this "emptying of self" to live in the companionship of serpents. But all this is nothing compared to the emptying of God, by which He took on the form of man and accepted the limitations of humanity, such as hunger and persecution; not trivial either was it for the Wisdom of God to condemn himself to association with poor fishermen who knew so little. But this humiliation which began in Nazareth when He was conceived in the Virgin Mary was only the first of many to counteract the pride of man, until the final humiliation of death on the Cross. If there were no Cross, there would have been no crib; if there had been no nails, there would have been no straw. But He could not *teach* the lesson of the Cross as payment for sin; He had to *take* it. God the Father did not spare His Son—so much did He love mankind. That was the secret wrapped in the swaddling bands.[27]

Now a clear answer emerges as to why Christ's suffering was so unique: He experienced humiliation, excruciating separation from the

Father, and unendurable suffering as the recipient of God's wrath, culminating in His absorption of all the past, present, and future sins of mankind. And He didn't have to do it!

What had begun as a major stumbling block to my faith had now become a foundational pillar reinforcing it. In the past I had balked at the idea that Jesus could be God and experience such limitations in His human form. I couldn't understand how He could be One with the Father while pleading with Him as if He were a different person. But now I understand that He is a different person of the Triune Godhead. If God were not triune, and if Jesus Christ were not simultaneously fully human and fully divine at the point of His incarnation, He could not have lived a sinless life, and His separation from the Father and His substitutionary endurance of the Father's wrath would not have been possible. He couldn't have truly suffered for us, He couldn't have become sin for us, the cross would have been meaningless, and the entire salvation scheme would become pointless. "If the redemption accomplished on the cross is to avail for humankind, it must be the work of the human Jesus," notes Millard Erickson. "But if it is to have the infinite value necessary to atone for the sins of all human beings in relationship to an infinite and perfectly holy God, then it must be the work of the divine Christ as well. If the death of the Savior is not the work of a unified God-man, it will be deficient at one point or the other."[28]

ELEVATING HUMANITY

Before leaving the subject of Christ's humanity I want to share another insight of Bishop Sheen's concerning Christ's incarnation—another benefit Christ bestowed upon us by taking on human form. Sheen writes, "By His reaching down to frail human nature and lifting it up to the incomparable prerogative of union with Himself, human nature became dignified. So real was this union that all of His acts and words, all of His agonies and tears, all of His thoughts and reasonings, resolves and emotions, while being properly human, were at the same time the acts and words, agonies and tears, thoughts and reasonings, resolves and emotions of the Eternal Son of God."[29]

Sheen is not only describing the wonder of Christ's dual nature here. He is telling us about something else that flows from it, apart from our salvation. We are corporeal beings; we are in the flesh. While we are also spiritual beings, we have always been most familiar with our tangible, physical, material existence. By taking on human form, Christ took on *our* form and thereby dignified our human existence in a way I hadn't previously considered. We were born in God's image and retained some glimmer of that image even after the fall, but Sheen is making a slightly different point. By taking on a human nature like ours, He lifted humanity to a different plane—"human nature became dignified." This is different from the glory we will share with Him in eternity. In the here and now our humanity got a boost. So not only did Christ demean Himself through His incarnation, but He elevated us as well.

Christ's Deity: The Son of God

"I AM WHO I AM"

As noted in Chapter 1, Christ asserted His deity on numerous occasions and in various ways. I am particularly fascinated by one of these assertions, made in a way that was undeniable, absolute, and provocative.

To understand the context, we must begin with the Old Testament account of God selecting Moses to lead Israel out of Egypt and into the promised land. Moses tells God he is inadequate to the task, asking, "Who am I that I should go to Pharaoh and bring the children of Israel out of Egypt?" (Exodus 3:11). After more objections, Moses asks God what he should say about God's identity if his people should challenge him.

From a human perspective, we might consider Moses' hesitation to assume such a formidable task a humble reaction. But from God's perspective, it could be just the opposite, because God is the one Who told him to do it. If God is directing Moses to do something—anything—who is Moses to challenge Him, even if the challenge concerns Moses' own abilities? Omniscient Jehovah obviously knows Moses is up to the job or He wouldn't have tasked him with it. But something more significant is about to play out in the narrative.

It's interesting that when Moses first demurs he asks God, "Who am I?" God essentially reverses this language after Moses asks Him how to respond if the Israelites ask who God is. God replies—in Hebrew— "Yahweh," which is translated, "I Am Who I Am." God says, "Say this to the people of Israel, 'I Am has sent me to you.'" He continues, "Say this to the people of Israel, 'The Lord, the God of your fathers, the God of Abraham, the God of Isaac, and the God of Jacob, has sent me to you.' This is my name forever, and thus I am to be remembered throughout all the generations" (Exodus 3:14–15).

God is making clear that His name—"I Am Who I Am"—is synonymous with "The Lord, the God of your fathers, the God of Abraham, the God of Isaac, and the God of Jacob," and that by these names He shall be known forever. God isn't just selecting an arbitrary name for Himself. Reflect for a moment on the profundity of His self-identification: I AM WHO I AM. How better to describe the indescribable? God is saying that He is pure essence. Who but God could devise such a name? The words signify God's dynamic, active, and eternal self-existence. *Nelson's Illustrated Bible Dictionary* explains this divine appellation:

> His "I am" expresses the fact that He is the infinite and original personal God who is behind everything and to whom everything must finally be traced. "I am who I am," signals the truth that nothing else defines who God is but God Himself. What He says and does is who He is. The inspired Scriptures are the infallible guide to understanding who God is by what He says about Himself and what He does. Yahweh is the all-powerful and sovereign God who alone defines Himself and establishes truth for His creatures and works for their salvation.[30]

As T. F. Torrance writes, "The very nature of God excludes the possibility of there being any other God beside himself. This is already evident in the unique self-naming of God to his covenant people Israel as 'I am who I am,' which also carries with it the sense of 'I will be who I will be,' for he is the ever-living completely self-sufficient and wholly self-grounded God in all that he is and does."[31]

"BEFORE ABRAHAM WAS BORN, I AM"

Significantly, Jesus uses a similar self-appellation. When the Pharisees challenge Him for essentially claiming to be a deity, He replies, "I tell you the truth, before Abraham was born, I AM" (John 8:58). This bold statement is ignored by the hard-nosed skeptics who deny that Jesus claimed to be God. They also overlook the violent reaction to Jesus' words by the Pharisees, who immediately recognize Jesus' assertion of deity and try to stone Him for blasphemy (John 8:59). Note that Jesus' answer contains a pun of sorts: He not only identifies Himself as Yahweh (I AM—the short form of I Am Who I Am), but also asserts that He was in existence before the patriarch Abraham, who had lived and died more than two thousand years before.

Jesus didn't say, "Before Abraham was born, I was." That also would have been true, but it wouldn't have told the entire story. By saying, "Before Abraham was born, I AM," Jesus is identifying Himself as Yahweh and asserting His existence from eternity past—way before Abraham and creation. If Jesus had said, "I was," it could have implied there was a time when He didn't exist. By using the present tense "I AM," however, He forecloses that inference. I AM, or Yahweh, is equivalent to saying, "I have always been and always will be." "This is," says John Piper, "the essential meaning of his Old Testament name Yahweh (or Jehovah). It is built on the verb 'to be.' . . . To be 'I am' is to be absolutely the first and the last. No 'before' and no 'after.' Simply 'I am.'"[32]

CHRIST'S OTHER "I AM" STATEMENTS

Christ's personal claims to deity are essential to Christianity. Some skeptics, however, deny His divinity even as they praise Christ as the greatest man who ever lived or as an extraordinary prophet who laid down the world's best moral teachings. As we saw in Chapter 1, Benjamin Franklin even allowed as much, while admitting strong doubts about Christ's deity.

But just as Christ's humanity is an essential component of the Christian faith, so too is His deity. Since becoming a Christian, one of my pet peeves has been the casual negligence with which people gloss over such a critical matter—as if it makes little difference, when in reality it makes *all* the difference.

Because Jesus asserted that He is God, we can't logically contend that He was the greatest exemplar of moral behavior in history without acknowledging that He is God. C. S. Lewis explains why this is so in a formulation now known as the "Trilemma": in short, Jesus is either the Lord, a Liar, or a Lunatic. Lewis writes,

> I am trying to prevent anyone saying the really foolish thing that people often say about Him: "I'm ready to accept Jesus as a great moral teacher, but I don't accept His claim to be God." That is the one thing we must not say. A man who was merely a man and said the sort of thing Jesus said would not be a great moral teacher. He would either be a lunatic—on a level with the man who says he is a poached egg—or else he would be the Devil of Hell. You must make your choice. Either this man was, and is, the Son of God: or else a madman or something worse. You can shut Him up for a fool, you can spit at Him and kill Him as a demon; or you can fall at His feet and call Him Lord and God. But let us not come with any patronizing nonsense about His being a great human teacher. He has not left that open to us. He did not intend to.[33]

Many writers end that quote at "the Devil of Hell," but I think the remaining lines resoundingly punctuate the argument. John Piper nicely sums up the importance of Jesus' "I AM" affirmations: "Nothing greater can any man say of himself. It is true, or it is blasphemy. Christ was God or godless."[34]

Jesus makes many other "I AM" statements in which He either directly asserts His deity, does so metaphorically, or describes His attributes or activities that derive from His divinity. Lest there be any remaining doubt that He was claiming to be One with Jehovah, Jesus exclaims, "Have courage, I am He! Do not be afraid!" (Matt. 14:27; Mark 6:50; John 6:20); "I am, and you will see the Son of Man sitting at the right hand of the Power and coming with the clouds of heaven" (Mark 14:62); "I, the one speaking to you, am he" (John 4:26); " I am the light of the world! The one who follows me will never walk in darkness, but will have the light of life" (John 8:12); "I am the one who testifies concerning myself, and the Father who sent me testifies concerning me" (John 8:18); "You are of this world; I am not of this world. I told you that you would die in your sins, for unless you believe that I am he you will die in your sins" (John 8:24). "Truly, truly I say to you, I am the door of the sheep" (John 10:7, 9); "I am the good shepherd. The good shepherd lays down his life for the sheep" (John 10:11, 14); "I am the resurrection and the life" (John 11:25); "From now on I am telling you before it happens, in order that when it happens you may believe that I am he" (John 13:19); "I am the way, and the truth, and the life" (John 14:6); "I am the true vine" (John 15:1, 5).

Hopefully that clears things up.

"FOLLOW ME"

In addition to Christ's "I AM" statements, He otherwise proclaims His deity and asserts divine prerogatives on numerous occasions. He claims to be one with the Father (John 5:17–18; 10:30; 12:44; 14:9; 19:7). He asserts the authority to answer prayer (John 14:14). He demonstrates His authority to forgive sin (Luke 5:20–24, 7:47–48). He adopts titles used for God in the Old Testament such as "I am the light of the world" (Psalms 27:1; Isaiah 60:20; John 8:12) and "I am the good shepherd" (John 10:11; Psalm 23; Ezek. 34:15). He considers Himself worthy to receive honor due to God only (Isaiah 42:8; John 17:1, 5).[35] He promises to provide spiritual comfort that only God could provide (Matthew 11:28). He and others assert His authority to judge mankind

(John 5:27; Matt. 25:31–33; Mark 8:38; Acts 17:31; Romans 2:16; 2 Cor. 5:10). He refers to Himself as Lord (John 13:13). He proclaims authority over our personal salvation (Mark 8:35–37; John 3:16). Finally, in the Book of Revelation, John quotes Christ, from his vision, making a clear claim to divinity: "Behold, I am coming soon...I am the Alpha and the Omega, the first and the last the beginning and the end.... I, Jesus, have sent my angel to testify to you about these things for the churches" (22:12–13, 16).[36]

Christ undeniably spoke with authority like no one before or since. He didn't simply say, "Follow my teachings," but "Follow me."[37] He boldly exclaimed, "All authority in heaven and on earth has been given to me" (Matt. 28:18).

The learned Christian writer G. Campbell Morgan expounded on this point in 1913:

> I propose to examine the claims which Christ made as to His own teaching. I take up the writings of other men, all of them valuable in greater or less degree—and it is always interesting to notice a man's estimate of the value of the things he says himself—and this I have observed; that the greatest human teachers have always been reticent as to the ultimate authority of their teaching. They have always admitted that there is room for interpretation, for question, for further investigation. That note is entirely absent from the teaching of Christ. There is no apology. He never said, "It is natural therefore to suppose; It may probably be; or consult the authorities."[38]

Christ left no doubt with this statement: "Heaven and earth will pass away, but my words will not pass away" (Matt. 24:35). His words, recorded in Matthew 7:24–27, are similarly definitive, declaring that everyone who hears and acts upon them would be like a wise man who built his house on a rock. But those who hear and don't act on His words will be foolish, like the man who built his house on sand. In his gospel, Mark has Jesus arguably going even further, warning, "Whosoever shall be ashamed of Me and of My words in this adulterous and sinful generation, the Son of Man also shall be ashamed of him, when He cometh in the glory of His Father with the holy angels" (8:38). No ordinary man could conceivably have made such statements! But nothing can beat His declaration in John 5:24: "Truly, truly, I say to you, whoever hears my word and believes him who sent me has eternal life. He does not come into judgment, but has passed from death to life."

In His final resurrection appearance recorded in Luke, Jesus makes a statement loaded with assertions of divine prerogative and with His unequivocal claim to be the very person (Christ, the Son of God) predicted in the Old Testament: "Then he said to them, 'These are my words that I spoke to you while I was still with you, that everything written about me in the Law of Moses and the Prophets and the Psalms must be fulfilled.' Then he opened their minds to understand the Scriptures, and said to them, 'Thus it is written, that the Christ should suffer and on the third day rise from the dead, and that repentance and forgiveness of sins should be proclaimed in his name to all nations, beginning from Jerusalem. You are witnesses of these things'" (24:44–48).

Citing some of these statements, G. Campbell Morgan observes, "I at once confess that it seems to my own heart that the mere reading of these passages brings us into an atmosphere in which we are conscious of the august sublimity of Christ's conception of the value of His own teaching. My own conviction is that there is not a single one of these passages that we can believe to be true if we deny the Deity of our Lord." Morgan adds this profound insight: "And if the statement be questioned, then take any of these claims, and put them into the lips of any other teacher, and it must at once be seen how entirely and absolutely they are out of place. They are words which claim a full and final authority for the One Who uttered them."[39]

"HIS WORDS CONSTITUTE THE VERY MEDIUM OF LIFE"

It's also significant that Christ claimed the unfettered right to interpret the sacred words of the Old Testament, to pronounce what they were intended to teach, and to expose existing errors in interpretation as if He were the final Authority—which He is. He does this six times in the Sermon on the Mount, where He introduces Old Testament quotes with words like, "You have heard that it was said," then follows the quotes with, "But I tell you," and proceeds to somehow modify or amplify the teaching.[40] Writing in 1902, Rev. Hugh McIntosh said, "He developed the principles, deepened the spirituality, broadened the application, and put new and unthought of meanings into parts of the ancient Scriptures—though never contrary to or condemnatory of the inspired Scriptures; and He put His own teaching in contrast as on a higher moral and spiritual plane than other ancient teaching. In short, He claimed the right to interpret, revise, use and reset the O.T. in His own unique way."[41]

He also preceded many of His pronouncements with the words, "Truly, truly," which many scholars believe is the functional equivalent of saying, "Thus says the Lord." Joachim Jeremias describes it as a consciousness of majesty expressed in a claim to divine omnipotence.[42]

In addition to expressly asserting His divine authority, Jesus demonstrates it, such as when He rises and rebukes the turbulent winds and sea, and causes a great calm, right on the heels of scolding His disciples for having "little faith" (Matt. 8:26). After purging a man of demons, Jesus tells him, "Return to your home, and declare how much God has done for you" (Luke 8:39). He even claims to be Lord of the Sabbath in response to critical Pharisees (Luke 6:1–11), which is so defiant that the Pharisees "were filled with fury and discussed with one another what they might do to Jesus" (Luke 6:11). Jesus also walks through the middle of the throngs preparing to stone Him and escapes (John 8:57–59). And, of course, He performs His miracles, which I discuss in Chapter 11.

One of my favorite passages on this topic is John 7:17, in which Christ says, "If anyone's will is to do God's will, he will know whether the teaching is from God or whether I am speaking on my own authority." Think about the implications of this. Christ is saying that we can't evaluate His authority or the soundness of His teaching through our own power. As G. Campbell Morgan notes, "Thus Christ said that the only way in which we can test His teaching is by obeying it; not by our own intellectual cleverness can we ever test the truth of His teaching; not by any philosophy or wit or wisdom of our own; but if we will do what He says, in doing, we shall come to certainty as to whether or not the thing spoken was speech from God."[43] Could a mere human being make such a claim with any kind of credibility?

Morgan explains that what Jesus is really saying is that if any man will resolve to organize his life around His Words—His teachings—then he will be strong enough in character to endure anything life can throw at him. Christ's teachings not only build character that enables us to persevere; they are the gateway to eternal life. "Not only is the foundation of character found in these words of His, they constitute the very medium of life," writes Morgan, "for if a man hears His word, it is the word which reveals the Father; and the man receiving it will believe the Father; and so the word will become the medium through which he will receive life."[44] This is a resounding confirmation of the point made in Chapter 1, that the Bible—the Word of God—can lead one to faith (and salvation). "So faith comes from hearing, and hearing through the word of Christ" (Romans 10:17). "From infancy, you have known the holy Scriptures, which are able to make you wise for salvation through faith in Christ Jesus" (2 Tim. 3:15).

"NO ONE EVER SPOKE LIKE THIS MAN"

Jesus speaks with unparalleled authority, and His audience instinctively acknowledges this authority without regarding His tone as audacious or presumptuous. They understand He is special. His words are uniquely received in acceptance of that authority. The Gospel of Matthew reports that after Jesus completes His Sermon on the Mount, "The crowds were astonished at his teaching, for he was teaching them as one who had authority, and not as their scribes" (7:28–29). When the chief priests and Pharisees ask the officers why they haven't brought Jesus back, they answer, "No one ever spoke like this man!" (John 7:45–46). When He teaches in the synagogue in His hometown, "They were astonished, and said, 'Where did this man get this wisdom and these mighty works?'" (Matt. 13:54; Mark 1:22, 6:2; Luke 4:32). When Jesus asks Peter who He is, Peter replies, "You are the Christ, the Son of the Living

God" (Matt. 16:16). Notably, Christ blesses him for believing (Matt. 16:17).

And there is certainly no doubt in the minds of the demons, who are powerless to resist awareness both of His deity and His authority, as when "the unclean spirits saw him, they fell down before him and cried out, 'You are the Son of God.' And he strictly ordered them not to make him known" (Mark 3:11).

Ajith Fernando's *The Supremacy of Christ* is an absolute treasure that was instrumental in my initial grounding in the New Testament and in fully comprehending Christ's deity. Before I read the book, I too felt there was a uniqueness in the way Jesus expressed Himself, so Fernando's section on "the attractiveness of Jesus' teaching" greatly resonated with me. There was more than an authoritative tone in Jesus' words. Reading them, you just can't escape the impression that He is the omnipotent God. This is why so many people become believers just by reading the gospels alone.

Fernando relates the story of a young English student using the gospels for his reading lesson. In the middle of one lesson, he got up and "paced up and down the room and said, 'These are not the words of man, these are the words of God.'"[45] Napoleon Bonaparte also recognized the uniqueness of Christ. "I know men and I tell you that Jesus Christ is no mere man," the French emperor exclaimed. "Between Him and every other person in the world there is no possible comparison. Alexander, Caesar, Charlemagne, and I have founded empires. But on what did we rest the creations of our genius? Upon force. Jesus Christ founded His empire upon love; and at this hour millions of men would die for Him."[46]

Fernando makes the additional, important point that the teachings of Christ were profound, yet simple. They were accessible to the ordinary man as well as to the intellectual, which distinguishes Jesus from the leaders of many other faiths. "The quality of ordinariness runs through much of the teaching of Jesus," observes Bishop Stephen Neill, "It is this perhaps which has given to his words their extraordinary power to move the hearts of men and women through almost twenty centuries."[47] R. T. France says, "One of the secrets of the appeal of the teaching of Jesus over so many centuries is its firm earthing in ordinary everyday life and in the unchanging features of human character."[48] Fernando, however, cautions us against assuming that the simplicity and accessibility of His teachings means their message is not profound. "There is a depth to Christ's teachings," notes Fernando, "the extent of which we can never plumb. However much you learn, there is more to learn."[49]

Anyone who has studied His teachings will vouch for this. The entirety of Scripture is robust with God's wisdom, which becomes more apparent every time we study it. "Oh the depth of the riches of the wisdom and knowledge of God! How unsearchable his judgments, and his paths beyond tracing out!" (Romans 11:33). "Who does great things and unsearchable, marvelous things without number?" (Job 5:9). "Can you find out the deep things of God? Can you find out the limit of the Almighty?" (Job 11:7). "How great are your works, O Lord! Your thoughts are very deep!" (Psalms 92:5). "Such knowledge is too wonderful for me; it is high; I cannot attain it;" (Psalms 139:6). "Even though a wise man claims to know, he cannot find it out" (Ecc. 8:17). "His understanding is unsearchable" (Isaiah 40:28). "Preach to the Gentiles the unsearchable riches of Christ" (Eph. 3:8). "Christ, in whom are hidden all the treasures of wisdom and knowledge" (Col. 2:3).

"FOR IN HIM THE WHOLE FULLNESS OF DEITY DWELLS BODILY"

New Testament writers also affirmed Christ's deity. For example, the Book of John begins, "In the beginning was the Word, and the Word was with God, and the Word was God. He was in the beginning with God. All things were made through him, and without him was not any thing made that was made. In him was life, and the life was the light of men. The light shines in the darkness, and the darkness has not overcome it" (1:1–5).

This passage, so rich with powerful theological information, has blown me away for years. G. Campbell Morgan confirms I am not alone. "John's Gospel opens with statements characterized by awe-inspiring sublimity," he writes, "and we are conscious of our inability to finally express their meaning. The suggestion of the opening statement is too mysterious, too high and too glorious for man's reaching, too profound for his fathoming."[50] That's true—but let's explore these words anyway.

Understand that "the Word" in this context is the Second Person of the Trinity, i.e., Christ. "The Word" as a New Testament designation of Christ occurs three other times: "And the Word became flesh and dwelt among us, and we have seen his glory, glory as the only Son from the Father, full of grace and truth" (John 14:1); "That which was from the beginning, which we have heard, which we have seen with our eyes, which we looked upon and have touched with our hands concerning the word of life" (1 John 1:1); and "He is clothed in a robe dipped in blood, and the name by which he is called is the Word of God" (Rev. 19:13).

John 1:1–4 tells us the Word is eternal, He made all things, and He is the creator, not a creature who was created; He is part of the Godhead but distinct from its other Persons ("the Word was *with God*"). Furthermore, He is life: life inheres in Him, He is the source of life, and He is the light of men—a source of goodness, hope, and salvation. Consider verse 9 as well: "The true light, which gives light to everyone, was coming into the world." Professor William Hendriksen explains that when life is manifested—as it was when the Word became flesh (the incarnation)—it is called light.[51]

The writer of Hebrews elegantly explains that in the old days God spoke through His prophets, but in the last days He has done so by His Son. "He is the radiance of the glory of God and the exact imprint of His nature, and he upholds the universe by the word of his power" (1:3). Note the powerful descriptions: "His Son," "the radiance of the glory of God," "the exact imprint of his nature." Wow. Christ is hardly a created being. He's hardly inferior to the Father. D. L. Allen argues that "Jesus is the effulgence of God's glory because he shares the same divine nature as the Father, yet he is distinct from the father in his person."[52]

The last clause is critical: "He upholds the universe by the word of his power." Here again is the stark contrast between the cavalier, mythical god envisioned by deists and others, and the superintending God of the Bible. Christ, as the Second Person of the Godhead, not only sustains the universe through his ongoing superintending stewardship, but he does so with the "Word of his power." Here we see "the Word" again. God breathed the universe into existence with His Word (Gen. 1:1–3) and He sustains it with that same power. The Word (Christ) sustains the universe through the power of His "word." According to D. L. Allen, "The Son's speaking is the expression of his providential will and has the force of a command that the universe obeys."[53] I find this immensely attractive because it is biblical confirmation that God's method of creating the universe was exactly what I imagined. As He is a spiritual being, I've always envisioned that he just "thought it" or "spoke it" into existence. The Bible, in Genesis and in Hebrews, confirms it.

Theologian Zane Hodges writes, "His Word is so powerful that all He has made is sustained by that Word."[54] D. L. Allen elaborates: "The Son sustains all things by his powerful word.... The basic meaning in this context is that of upholding, sustaining, and carrying to a proper goal."[55] Allen also points out that "upholding the universe" is significant theologically in that it indicates that the Son—Jesus—is distinct from creation and exists apart from it. He is not dependent on it; rather it is dependent on Him. This puts the lie to pantheism and all other worldviews that make God a part of nature. It also contradicts skeptics who posit that the God of the Bible doesn't care about His creation. For the act of sustaining expressed here "is a positive agency of moving creation to its designed goal. This is not a mere refraining from destruction."[56]

There are many other New Testament affirmations of Christ's deity (and humanity).[57] I have come to believe that the full deity and full humanity of Jesus Christ is not just fodder for theologians. Understanding it is immensely powerful for us ordinary Christians as well, and it's a vital key to understanding Christian doctrine in general. Jesus, the God-man, is the central focus of all Scripture whose presence is, in one way or another, on every page of the Bible, both Old Testament and New Testament. He is the unifying force of the Bible, and in the next chapter we examine just how unified Scripture is, something about which I've marveled in awe since I first began studying this divine book.

CHAPTER 7

THE AMAZING BIBLE, PART 1: UNITY

"THE WORD OF GOD STANDS FOREVER"

As we've shown, the Bible is not just another book. It is not just a book of great moral lessons, though it contains those in abundance. It is not just a book of beautiful writing, though it is full of wonderful prose and poetry. It is not just a book of history, though it includes authentic and reliable historical information. It is not just a book of wisdom, though it has the finest wisdom literature known to man. And it is not just a book of prophecy, though it includes hundreds of specific predictions that have come true.

It is not just one of the classics. It is like no other book ever written. It is the living Word of God with the power to transform hearts, to convert, to comfort, and to sustain. The Bible is truly divinely inspired, it is infallible, it is indestructible, and it is inerrant.[1] The Bible is unique in its unity, its circulation, its translation, its teachings, its influence on literature, its impact on civilization, and its durability.

147

Jesus affirms the infallibility of the Bible, declaring, "The Scripture cannot be broken" (John 10:35). Likewise the prophet Isaiah exclaims, "The Word of God stands forever," adding that "my word that goes out from my mouth: It will not return to me empty, but will accomplish what I desire and achieve the purpose for which I sent it" (Isaiah 40:8, 55:11). Paul describes Scripture as "the oracles of God" (Romans 3:2).[2]

Throughout history the Bible has been subject to attack—from anti-Christian Roman emperors to godless Communist despots to irreligious university professors—but has withstood all challenges. Christians who wouldn't forswear it have been persecuted and martyred throughout the ages. Among the thousands of examples, the Roman emperor Diocletian outlawed the Bible and decreed that any Christian caught with one would be executed. Maximian issued an edict that all Christian churches were to be destroyed and all copies of the Bible were to be burned.[3] In 1546, Peter Chapot brought a number of Bibles in the French language to France and sold them there, and as a result was tried, sentenced, and executed within days.[4] This martyrdom continued into the modern era, with particularly severe punishments meted out for Bible possession throughout much of the Islamic world.[5] The same goes for Communist nations; in Communist-era Romania, for example, the Baptist Ioan Clipa was repeatedly arrested by the secret police for distributing Bibles. He suffered a nervous breakdown and eventually committed suicide.[6]

French Enlightenment philosophe Voltaire predicted Christianity would cease to exist within one hundred years of his lifetime, at which point Bibles would only be found in museums. But the Bible endures. (Ironically, within fifty years of Voltaire's death in 1778, the Geneva Bible Society had purchased his home and used his printing press to make Bibles.)[7] It has been read by more people in more languages than any other book in history.[8] It has been translated into some 400 languages, and some parts of it have been translated into almost 2,500 languages; some of these languages were rendered in written form for the first time by earnest missionaries trying to spread the Word.[9] According to the United Bible Societies, their organizations distributed 633 million portions of Scripture throughout the globe in the year 2000 alone.[10] The Gideons International distributed 56 million Bibles internationally in

2001. Its website says the organization has placed 1.9 billion Bibles overall.[11]

Nineteenth-century Oxford professor M. Montiero-Williams, who spent forty-two years studying ancient Eastern books, made this stunning claim in comparing them to the Bible: "Pile them, if you will, on the left side of your study table; but place your own Holy Bible on the right side—all by itself, all alone—and with a wide gap between them. For…there is a gulf between it and the so-called sacred books of the East which severs the one from the other utterly, hopelessly and forever…a veritable gulf which cannot be bridged over by any science of religious thought."[12]

Through the ages, legions of critics have sought to undermine the Bible by exposing its supposed inaccuracies, inconsistencies, and errors, its allegedly unreliable transcriptions and preservations, and the ostensibly dubious authenticity of Jesus' recorded statements. As archaeological finds have verified names, places, and events described in the Bible and as its prophecies have been fulfilled, critics have resorted to new attacks, arguing for example that certain prophetic books couldn't have been written by their known authors because they lived *before* the prophecies occurred. Well, that's the point of a prophecy, isn't it? But many critics deny the very possibility of supernatural prophecies, so when confronted with them they resort to strained, unsupportable arguments. Similarly, they reject the Bible's account of miracles not because the eyewitness accounts are unreliable, but because they believe miracles are impossible. So yes, if you refuse to believe that biblical prophecies and miracles are even possible, you will also probably question the Bible's authenticity. But you'll have a lot of explaining to do.

A VOICE BEHIND THE VOICE

People have long believed in the divine inspiration and authority of the Bible, and the Book itself offers abundant evidence for it. For example, the Bible maintains a unified, continuous message across its sixty-six books, which were written over some 1,500 years by about forty authors.

If you read it enough you can't help but notice it has the same voice of authority throughout. I'm not saying each book has a similar style or that the authorial "voice" of each biblical writer is identical, as if they were scriveners merely transcribing dictation by the Holy Spirit. I'm saying that even through the medium of these unique, individual human beings writing in different historical time periods, in different geographical settings, and sometimes in different languages, there is a distinct voice behind the voice.

In my own reading of the Bible, just as I get the innate sense that there is divine authority behind Jesus' teachings, I can't help but feel the authority of the one God of the universe behind the entirety of Scripture. This is all the more impressive when you consider that other sacred books are the product of one man, and therefore present no problem of continuity that one would expect from a book written by such diverse and remote authors.[13] As Daniel Fuller observes, "In no other literature besides the Bible do some forty authors or editors, writing in a period of over a thousand years, in places and cultures as widely separated as Rome and Babylon, succeed in developing a body of literature that even at first inspection gives an indication of being a unity."[14]

The first inkling I had of this, as I reported in the first chapter, was when my friend introduced me to a reference Bible. But once you begin reading the Bible in earnest you hardly need a reference Bible to notice that major and minor themes, pronouncements, and teachings are sprinkled seamlessly throughout the Testaments to create an amazing, unified whole. I'm telling you that the Bible's interconnectedness is so striking to me that on that basis alone I would be a believer. It's hard enough for one person writing quickly to remain consistent. But to present such a consistency of message themes with this diverse authorship over such a long time period would be unimaginable without a sophisticated conspiracy, and even then, it would be nearly impossible to pull off.

Indeed, I will confess that I am convinced there *was* a conspiracy in the authorship of the Bible, but that it was a divine conspiracy, and that God Himself was the force behind the singular, remarkable integration that I witness each time I read it. I am certain that this alone could be as convincing a proof as many will ever need that this book was given to us by God. Evangelical author Chuck Missler's description of the Bible as "an integrated message system"[15] resonates with me. Similarly, Dr. Walter Elwell aptly describes the Bible as having "one heart beat" and as "an organic unity because an infinite God orchestrated its production."[16] But perhaps Dr. Colin Peckham puts it best:

> The Bible is a unique phenomenon, wholly unrivaled in the world of letters. It is a literary marvel, a moral miracle. It is not the product of one editor who chose his contributors, mapped out his course of study, gave each his assignment and then brought them all together in a neatly bound volume. Its writing is as diverse as can possibly be imagined.... The vast differences in every aspect of its production are obvious to even the most casual observer. The authors are so different and remote from one another that they would not have been acquainted nor could they have conspired together for either evil or good purposes.... What a dreadful muddle it would all be if there was no central controlling influence; but it all fits together like a hand in a glove. The unity is miraculous and marvelous.[17]

UNITY IN DIVERSITY

Granted, there is plenty of diversity amidst the unity, but in my view, this only adds to the book's credibility, just as the variances in the gospels suggest those accounts were not the product of a neatly crafted human conspiracy. As H. H. Rowley wrote in 1923, "It is unnecessary to close our eyes to the diversity in order to insist on the unity or to close our eyes to the unity in order to insist on the diversity."[18] Indeed, he admonishes, "It is important to remember the diversity." As for the unity, "It is not a static unity, but the dynamic unity of a process (of progressive revelation)."[19]

Progressive revelation is a key concept here. Some humanists tend to see humanity moving toward enlightenment or possibly even perfection.

But this is at odds with the biblical worldview. When we speak of progressive revelation to describe the unfolding of God's Word, we do not mean to suggest that man's spiritual development has increased over time or that humans are spiritually evolving to greater heights. "There is no automatic spiritual growth of mankind, and the Bible nowhere tells the story of such a growth," notes H. H. Rowley. "It does not tell how men by the exercise of their minds wrested the secrets of life and the universe from a reluctant Unknown, but how God laid hold of them and revealed Himself through them. If there is any truth in this, then a unity of the Bible is to be expected. If God was revealing Himself, then there should be some unity about the revelation, since it was the same Being Who was being revealed."[20]

But there was still diversity, says Rowley, because God revealed Himself to men of "limited spiritual capacity and could only reveal to each what he was capable of receiving."[21] Rowley argues that because God chose to reveal Himself through imperfect men, He was limited by the capacity He chose. The diversity in Scripture is not surprising, but inevitable. "It does not spring from any variation in God," Rowley claims, "but from the variety of the levels of the persons whom He used."[22] Then he gives us a zinger: "That is why the full revelation in human personality required the Incarnation."[23]

This is a perfect example of why I read theologians and pastors from past centuries: they often provide unique insights into God's timeless message. Rowley is saying there is yet another marvelous aspect of Christ's incarnation (beyond the glorious salvation of mankind and the elevation of humanity described in Chapter 6) that we might not have considered. His previous revelations through man resulted in variations of the message because the human beings delivering the message on God's behalf were all different and unique. This had its advantages, because this diversity of similar messages makes the point in a variety of ways and thus enhances our understanding. But in His final revelation through a human medium, He has given us a perfect, unchangeable medium—Jesus Christ—to deliver the perfect message. With the variety of writers in the Bible and the One God/Man in the incarnation, we have the best of all worlds, as recipients of God's revelation to us.

READING FOR THE BIG PICTURE

Paul emphasizes the importance of understanding and clearly communicating the unity of the biblical message. "If the trumpet does not sound a clear call, who will get ready for battle?" he asks the Corinthians. "Unless you speak intelligible words with your tongue, how will anyone know what you are saying?" (1 Cor. 14:8–9).

This theme is explored by pastor and author John Piper. In his foreword to Daniel Fuller's *The Unity of the Bible*, Piper describes his elation upon discovering the profound unity of the Bible, as expounded in Fuller's book. No book besides the Bible, writes Piper, has had a greater impact on his life. When he read it, "Everything began to change." Witness Piper's awe as he begins to discern the Bible's grand picture:

> The hallowing of God's name (Matthew 6:9) flamed up as the center of my prayers. God's passion for his glory (Isaiah 48:9–11) stopped seeming selfish and became the very fountain of grace that flings all wonders of love into being. God's law stopped being at odds with the gospel. It stopped being a job description for earning wages under a so-called covenant of works (which I never could find in the Bible) and became a precious doctor's prescription that flows from faith in the divine Physician (Romans 9:32). God's commitment to work with omnipotent power for those who wait for him (Isaiah 64:4) became my main weapon against worry. The discovery that "God is not served by human hands as though he needed anything" (Acts 17:25) stunned me with the thought that the apex of God's glory is not in being served but in serving (1 Peter 4:11). It has never ceased to be breathtaking that the God who made the galaxies is pursuing me with goodness and mercy all the days of my life (Psalm 23:6)—that he rejoices in doing me good with all his heart and with all his soul (Jeremiah 32:41).[24]

I have heightened my own awareness of the Bible's big picture by reading it, or certain books of it, at an accelerated pace. Instead of reading the Bible in a year, I once read it in two months. If you read a book of the Bible in a day or two, you will see the continuity of its themes in a way you haven't noticed before. Slow, thoughtful reading and meditation are also important, of course. But I've found that if you read the Bible or segments of it quickly, it will clearly show you how things connect, open your eyes to things you might not have noticed before, and enhance your overall understanding. It's an invaluable exercise.

"SAYING NOTHING BEYOND WHAT THE PROPHETS AND MOSES SAID WOULD HAPPEN"

Unlike the holy books of other religions, writes James Orr, the Bible is not "a miscellany of disjointed pieces, out of which it is impossible to extract any order, progress or arrangement."[25] The Zoroastrian and Buddhist scriptures as well as the Koran, says Orr, "are equally destitute of beginning, middle or end. They are for the most part, collections of heterogeneous materials, loosely placed together." This contrasts with the Bible, which "is not a collection of fragments, but has...an organic character." It is one connected story "from beginning to end; we see something growing before our eyes; there is a plan, purpose, progress; the end folds back on the beginning, and, when the whole is finished, we feel that here again, as in the primal creation, God has finished all his works, and behold, they are very good."[26]

It's worth noting that God didn't just speak the Bible through His human agents; He choreographed world events that would make their way into the Testaments. He's not a divine historian, He's the History Maker, the divine Author of Life who created us, made us a part of His story, and superintends history from its beginning to its triumphant conclusion. Many biblical stories weren't history when they were written; they were prophecies that became history after they came true. Of course, the Bible doesn't purport to be a comprehensive history, only a salvation history—a history concerning the grand sweep of man's redemption and salvation.

It is also much more than a book of salvation history. It is a special message from God to us revealing Who He is and His desire that we have a relationship with Him. It is a manual for how we should acquire wisdom, live moral lives, and love God and one another above all.

But much of the Bible's life instruction is presented in the context of orderly historical events, including David's cries to God in the Psalms, Solomon's wisdom in Proverbs, and Jesus' teachings in the gospels. We learn God's teaching in the historical context of the lives of others, especially the nation of Israel, and in our own lives as we interact with Him through prayer and through reading, studying, and meditating on His Word.

It is breathtaking to contemplate God's majesty in arranging events to play out exactly as He prescribed, in His sovereignty, yet preserving our free will. It is awe-inspiring to consider that He tells our redemptive story, teaches us about His nature, shows us how to approach Him, and instructs us how to live, through so many different people in so many different times and in so many different cultures and environments.

While it is doubtful that some of these writers, especially the Old Testament ones, were fully aware, if aware at all, as to how their contribution to revealed Scripture would relate to the whole, Paul and other New Testament writers do seem to be more aware of the unity of their message. This, in turn, should enhance our appreciation for the organic unity of the Bible as a whole.[27] For example, Paul tells the Ephesian church elders, "I have not hesitated to proclaim to you the whole [purpose] of God" (Acts 20:27). By "whole purpose of God," says Daniel Fuller, Paul means that he has taught God's entire message.[28] "Since Paul summarized his message as the whole purpose of God, it is clear that he regarded it as a unity."[29]

Paul underscores the unity of God's Word in a slightly different way in Acts 13:36, when he declares, "David had served God's purpose in his own generation."[30] That is, David, in his time, did what needed to be done toward fulfilling God's unfolding historical purpose, and by implication, so had others preceding David, and so would others in the future. Paul reinforces the notion of unity when he tells King Agrippa, "I am saying nothing beyond what the prophets and Moses said would happen" (Acts 26:22). Here again, we see Paul's constant awareness of the progressive, unified revelation. According to Fuller, in Galatians 1:8 Paul further indicates that he and his New Testament co-authors are acting in concert to communicate a unified message and that they are aware they're in unison. "Even if we or an angel from heaven should preach a gospel other than the one we preached to you, let him be eternally condemned," says Paul.

They not only know they are working together; they know they are doing so in obedience to higher authority and that disobedience would bring dire consequences. Jude, for his part, affirms his participation in this conspiracy by writing, "The faith that was once for all entrusted to the saints" (Jude 1:3).[31] In addition, at least some Old Testament figures and writers, especially the prophets, reveal their awareness that they and Israel were chosen as participants in God's plan. God directly tells Abram (who would become Abraham) that He is calling him out and that He will make a great nation out of him (Gen. 12:1–3). Likewise, the prophet Amos reports that God had told him, "You only [Israel] have I chosen of all the families of the earth" (Amos 3:2).[32]

CHARACTERS IN THE DIVINE STORY

Related to my reverence for the unity of Scripture, I have long been enamored with the speeches of the saints recorded in the Book of Acts. Chapter 7 provides the longest of the speeches, that of Stephen, who gives a history lesson on Israel and thereby points to the centrality of Scripture. In his speech he affirms his belief that the recorded events of the Old Testament are actual history. He reminds his audience that the "God of glory" appeared to *our father* Abraham. He reviews God's directive to Abraham to leave Mesopotamia and "go into the land that I will show you," and explains that Abraham first went to Haran and then on to Canaan after his father died. He reiterates God's promise of the land to Abraham and his descendants, even though he had no child at the time. He reviews God telling Abraham that his offspring would be wanderers in a land controlled by people who would enslave them for four hundred years, after which God would judge those slave masters. Stephen then gives a brief history of the patriarchs, the covenant of circumcision, and the story of Joseph, whom God saved despite his being betrayed by his brothers.

He continues rehearsing the history through the birth of Moses and his assumption of leadership of the nation of Israel, his leading the Israelites out of Egypt and his "performing wonders and signs," and the people's grumbling, groaning, and idolatry. He continues all the way through Israel's dispossession of the Canaanites and assumption of control of the promised land. He closes by condemning the people as "stiff-necked" and "uncircumcised in heart and ears," and as those who "always resist the Holy Spirit," as their fathers had. Just as Jesus had been punished for asserting the truth, the crowds cast Stephen out of the city and stone him to death. Just as Jesus commended Himself to the Father, Stephen calls out to Jesus, "Receive my spirit." And just as Jesus exhorted the Father to forgive His persecutors, Stephen asks Jesus, "Lord, do not hold this sin against them."

Stephen is not only emulating his Lord and Savior; he is not merely reciting Hebrew history for the sake of it; he is instructing his people on how essential their role is in God's plan. He explains that they are making the same mistakes over and over again—rejecting and disobeying God. He is giving them a lesson in human history as a backdrop for the larger lesson of salvation history, which began some two thousand years earlier and was continuing into the present.

Part of that lesson is that God was in charge in the past, despite the people's disobedience. He retained Moses as the people's leader even though they rejected him ("Who made you ruler and judge?") (Acts 7:35). And God is still in control in Stephen's time, as evidenced by Christ's conquering of death despite the people's rejection of Him. So Stephen is summarizing this history with the people who are every bit as intimately familiar with it as he is, because he wants to demonstrate to them that these stories are a prefiguring of what they are going through. Moses was a type of Christ, and the people in Moses' time were essentially the same as the people now. Martin Lloyd-Jones explains this further:

Follow the parallel. When Moses was sent to Egypt, he had a great struggle: he struggled with Pharaoh and his hosts and powers. And it was precisely the same with the Son of God when He came into the world.... Look at the world into which He came, a world that never understood Him, a world that was utterly opposed to Him. The whole organization of this world is against God, it is against Christ, and it is against each one of us. Look at it in its newspapers and in its films; look at it on the television; look at it in everything that is regarded as wonderful today. The Son of God came into a world like that. The whole mind and outlook of the world was the exact opposite of everything that He was and everything that He stood for.[33]

Moses liberated the people in his time—over their strenuous objections when they initially refused the command to go forward into the sea, but couldn't go back because pharaoh was on their tail. And Jesus was liberating them now. In the end, the stiff-necked people were utterly powerless to defeat God's pre-ordained deliverance. "He was rejected by the world, just as He was rejected by members of the Sanhedrin," says Lloyd-Jones. "But here is the message: in spite of man's rejection of Him, He is God's own appointed Savior."[34]

We see, then, in Stephen's recapitulation of Old Testament history, God's guiding hand moving world events according to His sovereign story line. We witness Stephen pleading with his people to wake up and realize they are the characters in this divine story, this unified story that is headed toward its conclusion despite what any of them, or any of us, do or say about it. It was a wake-up call, and the people failed to heed it.

"THE PEOPLE WERE CUT TO THE HEART"

Acts also records Peter's Sermon at Pentecost (Acts 2:14–36), in which he reviews for the "men of Israel" Christ's mighty works and wonders performed in their midst ("as you yourselves know"). Jesus,

Peter notes, was the One "delivered up according to the definite plan and foreknowledge of God," but Whom "God raised…up, loosing the pangs of death, because it was not possible for him to be held by it." In other words, he's saying, *Don't you dare deny what you saw with your own eyes—that Christ worked miracles and that He was crucified despite His innocence, but still conquered death, which was powerless to restrain Him, because God had always planned that He would die for our sins.*

Peter quotes David from Psalm 16 that God would not let His "Holy One see decay." Then he tells them "with confidence" that David must have been referring to Christ, Whom "he foresaw" and Whose resurrection he spoke about. "Let all the house of Israel therefore know for certain that God has made Him both Lord and Christ, this Jesus whom you crucified," Peter declares. Upon hearing this speech, the people "were cut to the heart," and they ask Peter what they should do. He tells them to "repent and be baptized every one of you in the name of Jesus Christ for the forgiveness of your sins and you will receive the gift of the Holy Spirit," whereupon three thousand people are converted. Just as with Stephen's speech, Peter is tying together the Old Covenant and New Covenant and tracing God's salvation history.

Later, when Peter and John are on trial before the Sanhedrin for healing a crippled man, Peter tells them in no uncertain terms that the healing had been done not in their power, but "by the name of Jesus Christ of Nazareth, whom you crucified, whom God raised from the dead…. This Jesus is the stone that was rejected by you, the builders, which has become the cornerstone. And there is salvation in no one else, for there is no other name under heaven given among men by which we must be saved" (Acts 4:10–12). Knowing that the man had been healed through Peter and John, the Sanhedrin are speechless and set them free, warning them not to speak of what they had seen and heard. But boldly, the pair tells these religious leaders that they—Peter and John—take their orders from God, not them.

All these speeches and sermons served as lessons demonstrating the unity of Scripture and God's purposeful direction of history toward the redemption of mankind.

"DID NOT OUR HEARTS BURN WITHIN US?"

One of my favorite stories in the Bible reinforces the unity of the Bible's message. In one of His resurrection appearances, Jesus approaches two men on the road leading to Emmaus, some seven miles from Jerusalem. They are kept from recognizing Him, and He asks them what they are discussing. They are amazed that He hasn't heard about the things "concerning Jesus of Nazareth," a mighty prophet whom they had hoped would redeem Israel but instead was crucified. Just that day, they tell Him, they heard Jesus had been put to death and buried three days earlier, but that morning women reported that his body was missing from the tomb and angels had told the women that Jesus was alive. After listening to the men, Jesus (Who still hadn't identified Himself to them) exclaims, "O foolish ones, and slow of heart to believe all that the prophets have spoken! Was it not necessary that the Christ should suffer these things and enter into his glory?" (Luke 24:25–26). Jesus is imparting the same lesson to them that Stephen and Peter had been preaching—that He hadn't come into the world to deliver Israel politically or militarily, but to save people from their sins.

But the most interesting part is still to come. The Scripture reads, "And beginning with Moses and all the prophets, he interpreted to them in all the Scriptures the things concerning himself" (Luke 24:27). After Jesus left, "They said to each other, 'Did not our hearts burn within us while he talked to us on the road, while he opened to us the Scriptures?'" (Luke 24:32). Just imagine this scene—what could top it as the most exhilarating, once-in-a-lifetime event? Christ in the flesh, back from the dead, taking men through the Scriptures and showing them how the Old Testament points to Him on every page, illuminating for them the unity of Scripture, centered in God Incarnate, Jesus of Nazareth, Whom Scripture says God chose before time began to save men from their sins through His sinless life and substitutionary, sacrificial death. Who wouldn't be blown away by the greatest biblical lesson of all time delivered by the greatest teacher ever?

As Ravi Zacharias says, "If one could only be face to face with Him from whom life comes, whom to know means Truth and to follow means direction, how delightful would be those moments when the most confounding questions of life are raised. We are not surprised when we read in the Gospel of Luke that the men who walked on the Emmaus Road, though unaware that they were walking with the risen Christ, said that their hearts burned within them as He opened up the past, the present and the future to them. When they realized who He was, a light for all of history had been turned on."[35] Note the way Ravi frames the event: Christ "opened up the past, the present and the future to them." Is it even possible to conceive of a more resounding affirmation of the unity of Scripture? And concerning "a light for all of history had been turned on"—what better way to describe the epiphany these men experienced, the same epiphany readers of the Bible will experience today when they come to grasp the unity and Christ-centeredness of Scripture?

Professor Oscar Cullman, one of Dr. Fuller's mentors, led him to the realization that the key to understanding Scripture is in grasping its essential unity.[36] Cullman, according to Dr. Larry Helyer, taught that the Bible is about one story, not many stories. "The unity of the Bible consists in the fact that a single redemptive history progressively unfolds from Genesis to Revelation. This story is God's self-revelation to human beings and clearly indicates his purpose and goal for all creation."[37] What Cullman was saying, then, is that "redemptive history" is just a small part of overall secular history, but "impacts forever all that transpires on the stage of world history." It consists of certain specific events "in which God intervenes or reveals Himself in history accompanied by an explanatory word by means of an inspired spokesperson—a prophet or apostle."[38] That is, the historical events described in the Bible actually occurred in history, but the Bible, as noted earlier, only covers those events that are relevant to God's salvation and redemption plan for humankind.

Biblical scholar Alfred Edersheim (1825–1899), a Jewish convert to Christianity, described the unity of Scripture in the context of God's progressive revelation as follows:

There is not merely harmony but also close connection between the various parts of Scripture. Each book illustrates the other, taking up its teaching and carrying it forward. Thus the unity of Scripture is not like that of a stately building, however ingenious its plan or vast its proportions; but rather, to use a Biblical illustration, like that of the light, which shineth more and more unto the perfect day. We mark throughout growth in its progress, as men were able to bear fuller communications, and prepared for their reception. The law, the types, the history, the prophecies, and the promises of the Old Testament all progressively unfold and develop the same truth, until it appears at last in its New Testament fullness. Though all testify of the same thing, not one of them could safely be left out, nor yet do we properly understand any one part unless we view it in its bearing and connection with the others.[39]

Dr. Helyer says that a belief in the unity of the Bible necessarily follows from the evangelical view that presupposes the inspiration and authority of Scripture. As the Holy Spirit "superintended the process of inscripturation for both Testaments," it's to be expected that the result would be "a unified, coherent message." Adds Helyer, "God does not speak out of both sides of his mouth."[40]

"THE WHOLE OLD TESTAMENT HISTORY IS FULL OF CHRIST"

Now, let's proceed to exploring the various ways the Bible is integrated as a unified, coherent message from God. My aim here is to enhance our appreciation for the Bible's oneness and thus its divine inspiration. Few other things have so bolstered my confidence that it is truly God's inspired Word, and that in its pages He tells the essential story of mankind, of which we are a vital part—his creation, his fall, his struggles with evil, and ultimately, his glorious redemption and salvation.

Though the Bible is unified in its central theme, there are a number of ways this unity manifests itself. So many Christians, myself included, describe the Bible as being fundamentally Christ-centered, meaning the

Old Testament points to Christ throughout, and He is the central figure in every aspect of Scripture. According to Bible scholar Warren Wiersbe, "Our Lord Jesus Christ is the key to the Bible, and it is impossible to understand the Old Testament apart from Him. As Graham Scroggie aptly puts it, 'Christ is predicted in the Old Testament, present in the Gospels, proclaimed in the Acts, possessed in the Epistles, and predominant in the Revelation.' The experiences of the Jewish nation in the Old Testament are links in the chain that leads to His birth at Bethlehem. Every type and symbol is a picture of Him. Look for Christ and the Old Testament will become a new book to you."[41]

As we've seen, Jesus Himself affirms this about the Old Testament to the men on the road to Emmaus. And in John's gospel He says, "You search the Scriptures because you think that in them you have eternal life; and it is they that bear witness about me, yet you refuse to come to me that you may have life" (5:39–40). He also validates the New Testament by promising that the Holy Spirit would superintend its authorship (John 14:26; 16:13). Alfred Edersheim describes the Christ-centeredness of Scripture this way: "For, properly understood, the Scripture is all full of Christ, and all intended to point to Christ as our only Savior. It is not only the law, which is a schoolmaster unto Christ, nor the types, which are shadows of Christ, nor yet the prophecies, which are predictions of Christ; but the whole Old Testament history is full of Christ. Even where *persons* are not, *events* may be types."[42]

"A REMARKABLE AND REASSURING COHERENCE AND CONSISTENCY"

In addition to its unifying redemptive history and its comprehensive Christ-centeredness, we can see the Bible's unity in its history, its recurring theological messages and themes, its abundant typology, its prophecies and their fulfillment, its structural unity, and what Dr. Helyer describes as its continuity/discontinuity.[43]

The Old Testament history begins with the creation of matter and the human race, and soon turns to God's focus on Abraham and His development of the nation of Israel through him. There is an unmistak-able continuity from that point revolving around the history of the chosen people, who are carefully preserved and protected by God right up to the birth of Jesus Christ, the Son of David. "The Bible proceeds according to a plan," notes Daniel Fuller. "Beginning with the creation of the world, it then relates and interprets a series of historical events that lead to the grand climax and goal of the world's history."[44]

Concerning theological unity, though God provides His biblical revelation progressively, a "permeating" theological continuity is present throughout Scripture.[45] A careful examination of it, according to Dr. Helyer, reveals that the attributes of God and His intentions for the universe are notably constant in both Testaments. "When one takes into account the progressive nature of redemptive history and the culturally conditioned backdrop against which God's saving activity unfolded, there remains a remarkable and reassuring coherence and consistency."[46]

I don't believe you have to be a Bible scholar to notice this. The more I've read the Bible, the more continuity I see in the doctrinal and moral messages. If you haven't observed this for yourself, try to develop a radar for it. You could also get a Bible concordance and look at the repeated themes of various topics interspersed throughout the Bible's pages. God's attributes and His nature are conspicuously revealed throughout the Bible, as are instructions for our developing a proper relationship with God.

We see His omnipotence and omniscience in His creation and in all His dealings with man. From the Bible's beginning to its end, His nature is consistently revealed. His compassion is illustrated in His deliverance of the Israelites from Egypt and in His tireless commissioning of proph-ets to rescue Israel from her sinful state and restore her to divine favor. His compassion culminates in His sending Christ as our savior. God's faithfulness is exhibited in every part of both Testaments. "Heathen Gods were fickle, of dubious morals and doubtful character," writes Dr. Peckham, "but all the Old Testament characters found God to be always the same."[47]

In the New Testament James affirms that with God there is "no variation or shadow due to change" (James 1:17). God is also shown throughout as utterly holy—His moral character is pure and changeless. Prophets did not say the same about Baal, Moloch, Ashteroth, or other pagan deities.[48] But there is no deviation from the prophets' uniformity in communicating this message, and God's holiness is itself a call for us to be holy, for we are to emulate God. Also permeating Scripture's pages is God's unswerving righteousness and His command that we be righteous. Further, nothing is clearer than His intolerance for idolatry and His uncompromising insistence that He is the one and only God. His hatred of oppression and evil is present throughout, as is His loathing of rebellion and His requirement of obedience. But just as evident are His patience, forgiveness, and lovingkindness.

The constant competing presence of evil is also readily observable throughout. Perhaps that can be said about other holy books, but when you read the Bible, you notice the unifying approach to what God considers good and what He considers evil, for goodness inheres in His nature and evil thrives apart from it. The goodness He possesses is unique, for He is the sole God of the universe, and that uniqueness overflows from the Bible's pages.

There is unity in the connectedness between God's nature and His moral pronouncements, because the latter proceed from the former. The more we read the Bible the more we understand God's nature and attributes, and consequently, the more we understand about what He desires for us—because we learn, above all, that He wants us to have an intimate relationship with Him, and faith is the only avenue toward that relationship. Building our faith helps us not only rely on Him, but also empowers us to overcome sin and to grow closer to our sinless, perfect God. So whether we are reading about God's nature or His moral precepts for us, we are concurrently learning about the other, because of their interrelationship. This is true for so many other themes in Scripture. No matter what part of the Bible we read, we learn something about other parts of the Bible in the sense that the same God superintends each letter, each verse, each chapter, each book, and Scripture as a whole.

Countless other themes are emphasized in the Bible. Brett Cheek, teaching and family pastor of my church, recently called our attention to the pervasive theme of God humbling the proud and lifting up the humble. Consider also these recurring themes: goodness, evil, man's fallen state, fearing God, honoring one's parents, prayer, faith, obedience, humility, God's sovereignty, moral living, wisdom, patience, justice, mercy, and numerous others. Indeed, Dr. Elwell points out that the Scriptures present a singular view regarding sin and salvation.[49] But lest we get caught up in the doctrinal themes, let's remember that there is more to the Bible than just mere doctrine and theology. As Dr. Walter Kaiser cautions, "This book has the power to grip a person and bring changes in his or her life if followed. This claim can be made for few other books in the world."[50]

"INDISSOLUBLY LINKED BUT DISTINCTIVE"

Typology, another unifying element, is when persons, events, or things in the Old Testament, while possessing true historical validity in themselves, also function as divinely appointed illustrations of what will come in the future—to be recorded in the New Testament.[51] As Augustine notes, "In the Old Testament the New Testament lies hidden; in the New Testament the Old Testament stands revealed."[52]

I previously mentioned one example of this—Moses' performance of miracles in deliverance of his people as a precursor of Christ's performance of miracles for similar redemptive activities. Similarly, in Romans 5:14 Paul identifies Adam as a type of Christ. The Bible is riddled with this kind of typology, both expressed and implied.

Joseph, for example, is a type of Christ. His character and experiences foreshadow the coming of the Messiah in that both Joseph and Christ are objects of special love by their fathers (Gen. 37:3; Matt. 3:17), are hated by their brothers (Gen. 37:4; John 15:24–25), are rejected as rulers over their brothers (Gen. 37:8; Matt. 21:37–39), are conspired against and placed in the pit of death (Gen. 37:18, 24; Matt. 26:3–4; 27:35–37), are sold for silver (Gen. 37:28; Matt. 26:14–15), become servants (Gen. 39:4; Phil. 2:7), are condemned though innocent (Gen. 39:11–20; Isaiah 53:9; Matt. 27:19, 24), are raised from humiliation to glory by the power of God (Gen. 41:38), are received finally by their brothers and recognized as a savior and deliverer (Gen. 45:1–15; Romans 11:1–27), and exalt their brothers to places of honor and safety (Gen. 45:16–18; Isaiah 65:17–25).[53]

Other examples include Adam, who foreshadows Jesus as the second Adam; the priesthood, which anticipates Jesus as our high priest; animal sacrifices, which prefigure Jesus as our blood sacrifice; the temple, which prefigures God dwelling among us in the person of Jesus; and shepherds reported in the Old Testament, which prefigure Christ as our Good Shepherd.[54]

The Passover (Exodus 12:1–51) is uncannily typical of Christ. It emphasizes salvation through blood, which importantly, involves two stages. The first was the shedding of the blood of the lamb. But if the Jewish people had done nothing further, their firstborn sons would all have died. They had to take the additional step of applying the spilled blood upon the lintel and the two door-posts of each home. In the same way, Christ shed His blood for us, but this will avail us nothing unless we appropriate that blood to ourselves by trusting Him for the remission of our sins.[55] Interestingly, Paul actually uses the phrase "passed over" concerning Christ's redemptive sacrifice on our behalf. "For all have sinned and fall short of the glory of God, and are justified by his grace as a gift, through the redemption that is in Christ Jesus, whom God put forward as a propitiation by his blood, to be received by faith. This was to show God's righteousness, because in his divine forbearance he had passed over former sins" (Romans 3:23–25).

Another example is the Old Testament Tabernacle and all its God-ordained furnishings, which are rich with Christian imagery. Presciently, the Tabernacle had only one door, which was unusual for such a large building. There is one way into God's presence. So it is that Christ tells us, "I am the way, the truth, and the life. No one comes to the Father except through me" (John 14:6); and "I am the door" (John 10:9).[56]

Additionally, God covered Adam and Eve with clothing after their fall (Gen. 3:21), which foreshadowed Christ's covering of our sin. Aaron's rod that budded is typical of Christ's resurrection (Num. 17: Heb. 9:4); the smitten rock in Exodus 17:5–7 is typical of Christ, Who was smitten and crucified and provided the water of salvation that completely satisfies.[57]

The Old Testament kinsman-redeemer was "a male relative who, according to various laws found in the Pentateuch (first five books of the Old Testament), had the privilege or responsibility to act for a relative who was in trouble, danger or need of vindication."[58] The kinsman-redeemer is an unmistakable type of Christ because it involved redemption by a substitute (Lev. 25:47–49). Christ is our kinsman-redeemer.[59]

We also observe the Bible's unity through prophecy and its fulfillment, which we'll illustrate in greater depth in the next chapter. Dr. Walter Kaiser observes, "If holy men of God spoke as they were moved by the Holy Spirit (2 Peter 1:21), then nowhere may we expect to find a greater case for the unity of the Bible than in the prophecies of the Bible."[60] Though the biblical prophets were separated by time and space, they spoke in harmony over the centuries in predicting future events. Along with the New Testament writers, they all cried out in one voice, "Prepare the way for the Lord; make straight…a highway for our God" (Isaiah 40:3).[61]

The Bible's unity can further be seen in Dr. Helyer's continuity/discontinuity concept. Although the two Testaments are "indissolubly" linked together, each one has distinctive features. Their continuity can be seen in the ideas, themes, practices, and concepts common to both Testaments. Some practices, themes, and features of the Old Testament, however, are discontinued and replaced by the New.[62] As Dr. Elwell clarifies, unity doesn't require unanimity. There can be differences, just as between Peter and Paul, and between Paul and Barnabas. These differences were not and are not irreconcilable, but reveal the struggle of the transition to a new religion. I think what he is saying is that the very diversity that exists and which is necessary to unfolding Scripture's progressive redemptive scheme, affirms the unity of its all-embracing central theme.

"I CALLED MY SON OUT OF EGYPT"

As I have discussed, there is a strong interrelationship between the Old Testament and New Testament. New Testament writers often referred to the Old Testament in their writings, as did Jesus. Entire books have been written about the presence of the Old Testament in the New. There are some 343 Old Testament quotations in the New Testament, and some 2,309 allusions and verbal parallels.[63] But as we've seen, these are not mere quotations. Often, New Testament writers demonstrate independence in interpreting the Old Testament in a "new" light based on God's progressive revelation.[64] It wasn't just Jesus who expanded on Old Testament passages.

But these interpretations were not inconsistent with the original. "In the Old Testament there is anticipation," explains Dr. Peckham. "In the New Testament there is realization. The Old witnesses to the New and the New confirms the Old. The New is the outgrowth of the Old. In the Old there are the shadows and types, and in the New, those shadows become realities."[65] Robert Morey agrees: "The Old Testament leaves us with unfilled prophecies, unexplained ceremonies, unsatisfied longings and an unfinished destiny. The New Testament fulfills, explains, satisfies and finishes all these things."[66]

"Christianity did not spring out of a vacuum," writes British Bible professor Steve Moyise, "but is in direct continuity with the religion enshrined in what Christians now call the Old Testament."[67] In fact, the New Testament expressly acknowledges its indebtedness to the Old Testament on its very first page, as Matthew begins with a genealogy that is given for the purpose of tying the Testaments together (Matt. 1:1–17).[68]

Theology professor Roger Nicole explains that the New Testament appeals to the Old Testament to "provide proof of statements made, confirmation of positions espoused, illustration of principles advanced, and answers to questions raised."[69] In addition, New Testament writers often affirm Old Testament thoughts, themes, and lessons implicitly. It is also fascinating to observe that New Testament writers, because of their heightened awareness of God's redemptive purposes, read the Old Testament with much greater insight than would have been possible for those living prior to God's unfolding revelation through Christ. They sometimes see dual applications to passages where that would have been impossible before the New Testament history transpired. For example, Matthew 2:15 quotes Hosea 11:1, "I called my son out of Egypt." Hosea is clearly referring to the nation of Israel, but Matthew focuses on the flight of Mary, Joseph, and the Christ child to Egypt and their later return to Palestine.[70] Similarly, Jesus Himself, as we've seen, highlights passages in the Old Testament that were pointing to Him, when they also had another meaning relevant to the Old Testament story they were describing.

The New Testament writers, in freely quoting the Old Testament, demonstrate the unity of Scripture in another important way, and it is analogous to the continuity/discontinuity idea above. They show the unity of Old Testament passages in their very diversity, as when they string a number of Old Testament citations in close proximity to enforce their point. For example, Paul, in Romans 3:10–18 makes a series of citations from the Books of Psalms and Isaiah (Psalms 14:1–3; 5:9; 140:3; 10:7; Isaiah 59:7–8; Psalms 36:1) to describe the various aspects of human wickedness. The cumulative effect is powerful, not just because of the number of instances cited, but because of their factual diversity.[71]

While we acknowledge the New Testament's abundant references to the Old Testament, we must also be aware that there is an interrelationship between the Testaments that goes in the other direction, and not just with predictive prophecy. The Old Testament is often future directed and points to the New Testament. From its very beginning as a nation, Israel had hopes for its future (Gen. 12:1–3; 49; Exodus 3:8; Num. 24; Deut. 33). This is only natural, as Israel was aware that God had singled it out as His chosen nation and would work through it to realize His grand plan. God actively intervened in Israel's affairs, and the prophets constantly warned the nation of the consequences of its obedience and disobedience. "The Old Testament looks forward to the future; and—according to the Christian faith—looks forward to the New Testament."[72]

"THE WHOLE HISTORY OF SALVATION MUST BE TAKEN INTO ACCOUNT"

The Bible's unity is not just present between the two Testaments, but within each of them. Dr. Elwell emphasizes how Old Testament books cite passages from other Old Testament books,[73] and of course, Jesus affirms the unity of the Old Testament (Luke 24:27). Note, for example, that numerous prophets, including Isaiah and Micah, predict the Babylonian captivity of Judah and its eventual restoration, as detailed in the next chapter. Dr. Fuller notes that several of the psalms relate how God has worked throughout Israel's history to redeem her despite her sins. Psalm 105, for example, recounts God's actions from Abraham to the Exodus, and Psalm 106, His dealings with Israel from the Exodus to the Exile.[74]

Similarly, the New Testament writings are tied together throughout, with Paul's confirmation of gospel history and theology, other epistles expressing common themes, and the speakers in Acts reaffirming the gospel message (as well as Old Testament truths). We just saw how the New Testament writers intentionally express a unified gospel message. Cullmann also addresses the interdependency of the various parts of Scripture with each other and to the Bible as a whole. "Whereas individual biblical passages afford only partial insights into salvation history, based, of course, on a total view, the canon offers a total survey including the whole salvation history from the creation," he says. "Now, through the *collection together* of various books of the Bible, the whole history of salvation must be taken into account in understanding any one of the books of the Bible."[75]

Professor Kaiser expands on the point. The four gospels, he says, are important to each other and to the whole Bible because they each present Jesus from a different point of view, but come together to present one unified gospel of Jesus Christ. The Gospel of John would be incomplete without the synoptics, but without John, there would be a deficiency in the presentation of Christ's deity. The five writers of the epistles, likewise, complement each other as part of the same "organically related truth." Paul stresses faith alone as the pathway to justification of sinners, but James emphasizes works as a byproduct of authentic faith. Peter emphasizes encouragement in the face of trials, John focuses on love and its relationship to eternal life in Christ, and Jude warns against apostasy. Kaiser summarizes, "The principle of a designed structure can be seen everywhere in Scripture and is a marked indicator of the Bible's organic nature."[76]

Additionally, Dr. Kaiser adds another category of biblical unity to those presented by Dr. Helyer, namely, structural unity. Like others, he notes that because the Bible consists of so many individual books written over such a long time, in different languages, by so many authors who mostly didn't know each other and were sometimes even from different continents, it's amazing that "any kind of coherence and ongoing strategy could be possible." But it was. The Bible, he says, "exhibits some strong general schemes that suggest a common archetypal plan and purpose in the story of redemption." He points out that each Testament is similarly structured in three parts—historic, didactic, and prophetic— "that tend to look to the past, present, and future." Surely, he argues, there is a diversity in the unity and a unity in the diversity. This unity from such a diverse group over such a period is "mind-boggling," he says. "There can be no real answer unless we also receive the claim of the writers that there was a supernatural aspect and a guiding mind at work in their writings as well."[77]

In the next chapter we turn to the subject of Bible prophecy, both Messianic prophecy (predictions concerning Christ) and other prophecy. Prophecy is not only an integral component of the Bible's unity, but in its own right, serves as one of the most powerful apologetics imaginable. As I mentioned in Chapter 1, I truly believe that my discovery of prophecy—particularly messianic prophecy—and its miraculous fulfillment is what finally tipped the balance of the scales for me in favor of the truth of Christianity. I continue to marvel at it and become more impressed the more I learn about it.

CHAPTER 8

✦✦✦✦✦✦✦✦✦✦✦✦

THE AMAZING BIBLE, PART 2: PROPHECY

"HOW MAY WE KNOW THAT THE LORD HAS NOT SPOKEN?"

Prophets are spokesmen of God's special revelation, and "prophecy," in the broad sense of the term, means "the message of a prophet."[1] The Bible clearly indicates that prophecy is a "medium of divine communication."[2] As stated in 2 Peter, "No prophecy was ever made by an act of human will, but men moved by the Holy Spirit spoke from God" (1:21). Both the Old and New Testaments affirm that language of the prophets that is recorded in Scripture possesses the authority of God.

Predictive prophecy—in which God enables a human messenger to foretell future events—is of paramount importance, but by no means encompasses the whole of prophecy.[3] The distinction is sometimes explained this way: prophets are not necessarily *foretellers*, but *forthtellers*, because they are speaking on God's behalf and declaring His truths.

There are many examples of Old Testament prophets advising and correcting kings and queens and political and religious leaders. For example, the prophet Nathan rebukes David for his adultery and murder, which leads David to repent (2 Samuel 12). An unnamed prophet opposes Jeroboam I for supporting pagan religion in Israel (1 Kings 13). The prophet Elijah confronts the prophets of Baal on Mount Carmel (1 Kings 18). Elijah condemns Ahab for murdering Naboth and taking his vineyard (1 Kings 21). Hanana scolds King Asa and gets imprisoned over it (2 Chron. 16). Jeremiah predicts the fall of Jerusalem and advises surrendering to the Babylonians, which leads to his imprisonment (Jer. 37–38). The prophet Amos denounces oppression and the corruption of religious and social leaders in the town of Bethel (Amos 7).[4]

One does not necessarily have to be called to a prophetic office to be a prophet. Examples of inspired prediction appear throughout the Bible's pages, even outside of books written by those specifically designated as prophets.[5] This is why Abram (Gen. 20:7), Aaron (Exodus 7:1), and Jeduthun (1 Chron. 25:3), for example, are all called prophets even though the Scriptures say nothing about their call to the office of prophet.[6]

In the Bible you'll notice a lot of diversity in prophecy. Prophets sometimes purport to speak on behalf of God Himself, as if directly channeling Him, such as when Isaiah refers to his own writings as "the book of the Lord" (Isaiah 34:16). At times prophets search diligently, attempting to make sense of their own predictions (1 Peter 1:10–11). Sometimes they aren't even aware when they are prophesying, and they occasionally admit ignorance about their own visions (Dan 8:27; Zech. 4:13).[7]

Scripture provides its own test to measure the authenticity of a prophet: "And if you say in your heart, 'How may we know the word that the LORD has not spoken?'—when a prophet speaks in the name of the LORD, if the word does not come to pass or come true, that is a word that the LORD has not spoken; the prophet has spoken it presumptuously. You need not be afraid of him" (Deut. 18:21–22). The prophet Jeremiah addresses the subject of false prophets: "And the LORD said to me: 'The prophets are prophesying lies in my name. I did not send them, nor did I command them or speak to them. They are prophesying to you a lying vision, worthless divination, and the deceit of their own minds'" (Jer. 14:14).

God says He will deal harshly with such people. It's no minor matter to falsely purport to speak on behalf of the God of the universe. That is presumptuousness and deceit of the highest order, for when people believe you are speaking in God's name, they accord you incredible authority, and if you are not really speaking on His behalf, you are leading them toward error. Paul calls one magician "the son of the devil" and an "enemy of righteousness" who is "full of all deceit and villainy" because he is "making crooked the straight paths of the Lord" (Acts 13:10). Elsewhere he declares, "Even if we, or an angel from heaven, should preach to you a gospel contrary to that which we preached to you let him be accursed" (Gal. 1:8). As the Bible stresses repeatedly, there is only one gospel; it is the gospel of salvation by the grace of God apart from any human works (Gal. 2:21; 3:11; cf. Romans 4:5; Titus 3:5–7; Eph. 2:8–9).

"WHEN IT COMES TO PASS, YOU MAY BELIEVE"

Predictive prophecy constitutes a significant portion of biblical prophecy. J. Barton Payne calculates, "Of the entire Bible's 31,124 verses, 8,352 contain predictive material, or 27 percent of the whole."[8] Biblical prediction serves numerous functions. It can motivate us to holiness; in Peter's words, "We have the prophetic word made more sure [by Christ], to which you do well to pay attention" (2 Peter 1:19). Additionally, Jesus tells us that prophecy can enhance our faith: "Now I have told you before it comes to pass, that when it comes to pass, you may believe" (John 14:29). For example, David forecast his victory over Goliath, "that all the earth may know that there is a God in Israel" (1 Sam. 17:46).[9]

Overall, the fulfillment of predictive prophecy serves as an amazing apologetic for the truth of the Christian faith and demonstrates God's faithfulness and dependability. As Bible prophecy expert John Walvoord relates, about half the Bible's predictive prophecies have already been fulfilled, giving us a firm basis to expect the other prophecies to come true in time.[10] And the Bible stresses the importance of heeding its prophetic words, as when John writes at the beginning of Revelation, "Blessed is the one who reads aloud the words of this prophecy, and blessed are those who hear, and who keep what is written in it" (1:3).[11]

I personally find fulfilled predictive prophecy so probative as to the authenticity of Christianity that I'd love to devote chapters upon chapters detailing it. But for our purposes here, I'll limit the discussion to some of the most fascinating prophecies and their fulfillments, which will hopefully whet your appetite to explore more for yourself.

ABRAHAMIC COVENANT

The Abrahamic Covenant laid out in Genesis is important for understanding the Old Testament and the entire Bible. God calls Abram (12:1), who lives in Ur of the Chaldeans (some 220 miles southeast of modern Baghdad), to leave his country and "go to the land I will show you." God makes a series of promises to Abram in subsequent verses and chapters: to make him into a great nation; to bless him; to make his name great; to bless those who bless him and curse those who curse him; and that all peoples on earth will be blessed through him (12:2–3). Abram ultimately arrives in Canaan, and God promises that he will be given the land of Canaan and will have countless offspring (13:14–17). In Chapter 15, God solemnizes these promises into a formal covenant, assuring Abram that the covenant will be everlasting: "I will establish my covenant as an everlasting covenant between me and you and your descendants after you for the generations to come, to be your God and the God of your descendants after you" (17:7).

The Bible shows that some of these promises of the Covenant have already been fulfilled. Abram, through God's miracle, has a son by the aged and barren Sarah (Gen. 21:2). God makes Abraham into a great nation by giving him his promised descendants, who become the Jewish nation. And God fulfills His promise to make Abraham's name great;

as Dr. Lewis Sperry Chafer notes, "No name is more honored outside of Christ's than Abraham's."[12] Indeed, the world's three major monotheistic religions—Judaism, Christianity, and Islam—all regard him as an archetypal patriarch.

But by far the most important promise of the covenant is that God has graciously made His blessing available to all families of the earth through saving faith in His Son, Jesus Christ (Gal. 3:16; Acts 3:25–26), a descendant of Abraham (Matt. 1:1, 17; Luke 3:34). In addition, the Scriptures, which have led many to Christ and thereby blessed them, were produced and preserved primarily by Jews—the nation of Abraham. Furthermore, God delivered the promised land to Israel after the exodus and wilderness wanderings (Deut. 31:7–8; 32:45–52; Joshua 1:1–5, 10–11), though modern Israel has not occupied the entirety of the allotted land—yet.

In summary, the Abrahamic Covenant is a series of unconditional promises given by God to Abraham and his patriarchal descendants. The promises, which involve seed, land, and blessing, apply variously to Abraham personally, to Israel, and to the Church. The Covenant can be viewed as a unifying biblical theme with the common thread being God's unlimited, unqualified grace and love for the beings He created in His own image. The ultimate outworking of God's covenant with Abraham, of which all believers have become heirs, is God's gift of eternal life through faith in Jesus Christ, His Son.

SOJOURNERS AND SLAVES

God tells Abram in Genesis 15:13–16, "Know for certain that your offspring will be sojourners in a land that is not theirs and will be servants there, and they will be afflicted for four hundred years. But I will bring judgment on the nation that they serve, and afterward they shall come out with great possessions. As for you, you shall go to your fathers in peace; you shall be buried in a good old age. And they shall come back here in the fourth generation, for the iniquity of the Amorites is not yet complete."

Accordingly, Exodus confirms that the Israelites lived in Egypt 430 years, and it records God's ten plagues upon Egypt and Israel's exodus from Egypt with great possessions (Exodus 7:14–12:29, 12:35–36, 40). Abraham lived to the age of 175 and "died in a good old age" (Gen. 25:7–8). Joseph ordered his own bones to be taken to Canaan (Gen. 50:24–25), and Hebrews 11:22 describes Joseph mentioning the exodus and giving directions concerning his bones as a matter of faith.

THE FALL OF ISRAEL AND THE PUNISHMENT OF ASSYRIA

Israel was a united kingdom for 120 years, from approximately 1051 BC to 931 BC. In the latter year the kingdom divided into the Northern Kingdom (Israel, with its capital Samaria) and the Southern Kingdom (Judah, with its capital Jerusalem). Numerous prophets predicted that the Northern Kingdom, because of its sinfulness and disobedience, would be destroyed (Hosea 1:4–6; Isaiah 9:8–10:4; Amos 3:11–12; Micah 3–7). The prophecy was fulfilled in 734–722 BC, when the Assyrian Empire invaded and subsumed the Northern Kingdom (2 Kings 15:29; 17:3–6). The Southern Kingdom, which was more obedient to God, remained intact but would later be conquered by the Babylonian Empire, which was also prophesied, as detailed below.

While God had raised up Assyria for the task of punishing the Northern Kingdom, that was not a reflection of Assyria's righteousness, as God often uses unlikely instruments to accomplish His will.[13] The Assyrian king also thought he could easily conquer Jerusalem in the Southern Kingdom, but God vowed to punish his arrogance by destroying his army through disease and fire, leaving so few trees standing that even a child could count them (Isaiah 10:10–19).

The Bible records the fulfillment of this prophecy. In 701 BC, 185,000 Assyrian soldiers surrounding Jerusalem were killed (Isaiah 37:36–37; 2 Kings 19:35). Secular sources corroborate that a disaster befell this army. In *The Histories* (ca. 450 BC), Herodotus relates that Sennacherib's army of "Arabians and Assyrians" was destroyed when field mice devoured their weapons and "great multitudes fell, as they had no arms with which to defend themselves."[14] While he quibbles with some of Herodotus' details, Jewish historian Josephus, in his *Antiquities of the Jews*, tells of a similar catastrophe befalling the Assyrian army. Josephus seems to endorse the account of the Babylonian historian Berossus, who reported that 185,000 soldiers were lost when a plague destroyed an Assyrian army led by Sennacherib's general Rabshakeh:

> Now when Sennacherib was returning from his Egyptian war to Jerusalem, he found his army under Rabshakeh his general in danger, for God had sent a pestilential distemper upon his army; and on the very first night of the siege, a hundred fourscore and five thousand, with their captains and generals, were destroyed. So the king was in a great dread, and in a terrible agony at this calamity; and being in great fear for his whole army, he fled with the rest of his forces to his own kingdom, and to his city Ninevah; and when he abode there a little while, he was treacherously assaulted, and died by the hands of his elder sons, Adrammelech and Seraser, and was slain in his own temple, which was called Araske. Now these sons of his were driven away, on account of the murder of their father, by the citizens, and went into Armenia, while Assarachoddas took the kingdom of Sennacherib. And this proved to be the conclusion of this Assyrian expedition against the people of Jerusalem.

Assyrian accounts (recorded in the Taylor Prism, kept in the British Museum) deny any such calamity, claiming the siege of Jerusalem was so successful that King Hezekiah was forced to pay tribute—and that when he did, Sennacherib and his troops left the city in triumph. But we can expect the biblical writers to be the more trustworthy chroniclers, since ancient kings often tried to cover up their defeats. As Bible commentator Gary V. Smith notes, "For political reasons, Sennacherib's Prism does not mention how this battle ended, although one is left with the false impression that the Assyrians were successful against Judah."[15] In any event, whether or not Sennacherib was falsifying history, we have in his Taylor Prism—his own account—secular validation of the biblical report that he laid siege to Jerusalem and that he shut up Hezekiah "like a caged bird."[16]

As for the fate of Sennacherib, Isaiah predicted that the Assyrian king would die by the sword in his own land (Isaiah 37:7; 2 Kings 19:7), which was fulfilled when Sennacherib's sons Adrammelech and Sharezer "struck him down with the sword and escaped into the land of Ararat" (Isaiah 37:38; 2 Kings 19:37), as also confirmed by Josephus. According to the *Baker Encyclopedia of the Bible*, "The nonbiblical Babylonian Chronicles also refer to the assassination but do not name the sons."[17] Similarly, the *International Standard Bible Encyclopedia* reports that "the Babylonian Chronicle says that Sennacherib 'was slain by his son in a revolt,' where the Old Testament speaks of both the sons as assassins. The Chronicle, however, may refer to the actual murder by one son and the Old Testament to the complicity of both."[18]

JUDAH WOULD BE EXILED TO BABYLON AND LATER RELEASED FROM CAPTIVITY

After the fall of the Northern Kingdom (Israel) around 722 BC, the Southern Kingdom (Judah) held on until Babylon invaded and began taking the Jews into captivity in 605 BC. Numerous prophets, including Jeremiah (Jer. 25:11–12; 29:10), Isaiah (44:24–28), and Micah, predicted the Babylonian Captivity (or Babylonian Exile) of Judah and the nation's eventual return to the land. Micah prophesied, "Now why do you cry aloud? Is there no king in you? Has your counselor perished, that pain seized you like a woman in labor? Writhe and groan, O daughter of Zion, like a woman in labor, for now you shall go out from the city and dwell in the open country; you shall go to Babylon. There you shall be rescued; there the Lord will redeem you from the hand of your enemies" (Micah 4:9–10). This prophecy is particularly impressive because at the time it was made, Babylon was far from the most powerful empire and, in fact, was under the rule of Assyria.[19]

CYRUS

Isaiah's prophecy about Judah and its capital Jerusalem (Isaiah 44:24–28) is one of the most amazing prophecies in the Bible. He predicted that the Babylonian Exile would end with the Jews' return to Judah and the restoration of their ruins. He also foretold that "Cyrus" would authorize the rebuilding of the temple in Jerusalem, which the Babylonians had destroyed. Isaiah named Cyrus in this prophecy one hundred years before Cyrus, King of the Medo-Persian Empire, was born. At the time the prophecy was made, the people of Judah were not even in captivity, the city of Jerusalem was intact, and the temple was standing.[20]

A year after conquering Jerusalem in 538 BC, Cyrus freed Judah and allowed the Jewish people to return to their land and rebuild their temple, as recorded in the Book of Ezra: "Thus says Cyrus king of Persia: The Lord, the God of heaven, has given me all the kingdoms of the earth, and he has charged me to build him a house at Jerusalem, which is in Judah. Whoever is among you of all his people, may his God be with him, and let him go up to Jerusalem, which is in Judah, and rebuild the house of the LORD, the God of Israel—he is the God who is in Jerusalem. And let each survivor, in whatever place he sojourns, be assisted by the men of his place with silver and gold, with goods and with beasts, besides freewill offerings for the house of God that is in Jerusalem" (1:2–4).

In Chapter 45 Isaiah again mentions Cyrus, calling him God's "anointed"—the one whom God would stir up in righteousness to free His people.

BETHLEHEM

One of the most outstanding prophecies in the Bible involves the Messiah's preexistence and human birth in the town of Bethlehem as specifically named by the prophet Micah, who prophesied during the reigns of the Judean kings Jotham (750–735 BC), Ahaz (735–715 BC), and Hezekiah (715–687 BC): "But you, O Bethlehem Ephrathah, who are too little to be among the clans of Judah, from you shall come forth for me one who is to be ruler in Israel, whose coming forth is from of old, from ancient days" (Micah 5:2).

JUDAS

Matthew tells of Judas' apparent remorse for betraying Christ and his attempt to return the thirty pieces of silver to the chief priests and elders. They wouldn't take the money so he threw it into the temple, left, and then hanged himself. Because it was unlawful for the chief priests to accept the "blood money," they used it to purchase the potter's field as a burial place for strangers (Matt. 27:3–10). The Old Testament prophet Zechariah, who began his prophetic ministry in 520 BC, prophesied, "So I took the thirty pieces of silver and threw them into the house of the LORD, to the potter'" (Zech. 11:13).

THE REBUILDING OF JERUSALEM AND THE RE-GATHERING OF ISRAEL TO THE LAND

Some two and a half millennia ago, the prophet Jeremiah made this prediction: "Behold, the days are coming, declares the LORD, when the city shall be rebuilt for the LORD from the Tower of Hananel to the Corner Gate. And the measuring line shall go out farther, straight to the hill Gareb, and shall then turn to Goah. The whole valley of the dead bodies and the ashes, and all the fields as far as the brook Kidron, to the corner of the Horse Gate toward the east, shall be sacred to the LORD. It shall not be plucked up or overthrown anymore forever" (Jer. 31:38–40). Some believe this prophecy has been fulfilled in Israel's miraculous return to the land after almost two thousand years and the rebuilding of modern Jerusalem in the precise area described in this prophecy. Today, as John Walvoord states, there are lovely apartments and streets where garbage heaps and dead bodies were before.[21]

Moses and other prophets predicted that the Jews would be dispersed from their homeland twice and scattered "among all peoples, from one end of the earth to the other." The Jews were warned, "Among these nations you shall find no respite," and "night and day you shall be in dread and have no assurance of your life" (Deut. 28:64–68; Jer. 25:11). And in fact, the Jews were exiled by the Babylonians and allowed to return by Cyrus, then carried off again in 70 AD when the Roman emperor Titus destroyed the city of Jerusalem and scattered the people.

Similar to a prophecy by Ezekiel (37:21–28), Isaiah prophesied that God would re-gather the Jews to their homeland "from the four corners of the earth" (Isaiah 11:11–13). Like Jeremiah's prediction above, many scholars believe Isaiah's prophecy was fulfilled with the rebirth of Israel in 1948.[22] David Ben-Gurion, Israel's principal founder, certainly believed so. On May 14, 1948, when he announced to the world that the new Jewish homeland would be called "Israel," he cited the book of Ezekiel as his authority.[23] Other scholars such as John Walvoord believe this prophecy of the Jews being re-gathered to their land refers to a time after Christ's second coming,[24] and not to an already fulfilled prophecy of 1948, though Walvoord does believe Jeremiah's prophecy concerning the rebuilding of Jerusalem has been fulfilled, as noted.

Either way, it is remarkable that the Jews were twice dispersed, first for seventy years as predicted (Jer. 25:11), and a second time for almost two thousand years, yet retained their national identity and have now returned, as a nation, not to some other geographical location, but to their very promised land. Maybe there will be a more comprehensive return to the land in the future, but who could argue that the reestablishment of Jewish national civilization in the Holy Land has at least set the groundwork for a more complete restoration?

Josh McDowell puts this into perspective by noting that for almost two thousand years the Jewish people lived all around the world and were persecuted from every side, culminating in the slaughter of some 6 million Jews in the Holocaust. The odds against Israel being reborn after such persecution and dispersion were astronomical, yet it happened—and the country has somehow withstood outright military invasions by its neighbors as well as constant attacks by sundry terrorist organizations.

I remember the goose bumps I felt when I first read the following passage some twenty years ago in McDowell's *Evidence That Demands a Verdict*: "Through all of this, the nation neither perished nor lost its national identity. History has demonstrated that any people who leave their homeland will, after about five generations, lose their national identity by being absorbed into the new culture, but the Jews remained a distinct entity. Not only have they survived, but the nations that persecuted them—Moab, Ammon, Edom, Philistia, and many others—have either been destroyed or completely lost their individual identity."[25] Pastor Tony Evans notes, similarly, that other than the Jewish people, no nation in human history that was vanquished from its land for fifty years or more ever returned to that land still speaking the same language.[26]

I will add a personal observation to this. I have long sensed God's divine hand protecting the nation of Israel, as witnessed by its astonishing return to the land and its improbable victories in the wars of 1948, 1967, and 1973. These facts, coupled with the virtually uninterrupted unrest in the Middle East, serve as further compelling proof to me that the Bible is the Word of God. No nation could survive the type of hardship and dispersion Israel has repeatedly experienced without the intervention of the God of the Bible. Bible scholar A. C. Gaebelein explains this eloquently:

> Massacred by thousands, yet springing up again from their undying stock, the Jews appear at all times and in all regions. Their perpetuity, their national immortality, is at once the most curious problem to the political inquirer; to the religious man a subject of profound and awful admiration. Herder called the Jews "the enigma of history". What human mind could have ever foreseen that this peculiar people, dwelling in a peculiar land, was to be scattered among all nations, suffer there as no other nation ever suffered, and yet be kept and thus marked out still as the covenant people of a God,

whose gifts and callings are without repentance. Here indeed is an argument for the Word of God which no [unbeliever] can answer. Jehovah has predicted the history of His earthly people. "Though I make a full end of all nations whither I have scattered thee, yet will I not make a full end of thee" (Jer. 30:11).[27]

THE DEMISE OF EDOM

The prophets Jeremiah, Ezekiel, and Obadiah independently predicted that the lush, fertile land of Edom would become a barren and desolate wasteland because it had mistreated Judah. "Behold, I will make you small among the nations: you shall be utterly despised," the Edomites were told by Obadiah, who predicted Edom would be totally destroyed (Obadiah 2, 8). "Edom shall become a horror. Everyone who passes by it will be horrified and will hiss because of all its disasters.... no man shall dwell there, no man shall sojourn in her" (Jer. 49:15–20; Ezek. 25:12–14). And indeed, the Edomites disappeared from history after Jerusalem was destroyed in 70 AD,[28] marking the obliteration of one of Israel's enemies.[29] Dr. Hugh Ross observes that the former land of Edom, which is part of Jordan today, is now bleak and desolate.[30]

THE DESTRUCTION OF TYRE

Ezekiel predicted the destruction of Tyre, in Phoenicia, because its inhabitants rejoiced in Judah's demise, thinking it would benefit them economically: "Therefore thus says the Lord GOD: Behold, I am against you, O Tyre, and will bring up many nations against you, as the sea brings up its waves. They shall destroy the walls of Tyre and break down her towers, and I will scrape her soil from her and make her a bare rock" (Ezek. 26:3–4). In 332 BC Alexander the Great annihilated Tyre and scraped the debris into the sea to make a causeway to the island fortress.

"The bare ground where Tyre once stood is testimony today of the literal fulfillment of this prophecy," John Walvoord writes. "Tyre never regained power after this attack."[31]

THE DESTRUCTION OF NINEVEH

Jonah described Nineveh as a great and populous city, the flourishing capital of the Assyrian empire (Jonah 3:3; 4:11). Despite Nineveh's impressive size and seemingly impregnable walls (40–50 feet high), numerous prophets predicted Nineveh's wholesale destruction: Nahum (Nahum 1–3), Ezekiel (Ezek. 32:22–23), Zephaniah (Zeph. 2:13–15), and Zechariah (Zech. 10:11), as well as Isaiah, who prophesied it one hundred years before it occurred (Isaiah 10:12–19; 14:24–25; 30:31–33; 31:8–9). In 612 BC Nineveh was utterly smashed and transformed into a mere pile of sand, never to be rebuilt. It was so thoroughly devastated that its location was unknown for centuries, until archaeologists finally found it in 1845.[32]

JOSHUA AND JERICHO

After conquering Jericho, Joshua predicted that the person who would rebuild the city would be cursed before the Lord: "At the cost of his firstborn son will he lay the foundation; at the cost of his youngest will he set up its gates" (Joshua 6:26). Some seven hundred years later,[33] in the time of Ahab, Hiel of Bethel rebuilt the city, and as he built the foundations he lost his firstborn son Abiram. He also lost his youngest son Segub when he set up the city's gates (1 Kings 16:34).

JOSIAH AND THE BONES OF THE PRIESTS

1 Kings 13:1–3 records that a man of God came from Judah to Bethel and, as King Jeroboam was standing by the altar, prophesied that

someone named Josiah, a future king of the house of David, would sacrifice the bones of the pagan priests on King Jeroboam's altar. This prophecy was fulfilled some three hundred years later (2 Kings 23:15–17) through King Josiah. So we see that Cyrus is not the only person predicted by name more than a century in advance.

THE INCREDIBLE PROPHECIES OF DANIEL

The Book of Daniel is filled with stunning prophecies. Here are a few of the most notable:

Daniel Chapter 5:
Belshazzar's Feast and Babylon's Fall

King Nabonidus ruled the Neo-Babylonian Empire from 556 BC until 539 BC, when the Medo-Persians conquered Babylon and overthrew him. But Daniel 5 identifies Belshazzar as the Babylonian king during part of this time period, which critics often cited as a historical error of the Bible. But they stopped gloating in the nineteenth century when archaeologists discovered the Nabonidus Cylinders, which were clay tablets with inscriptions by Nabonidus himself. As the cylinders made clear, Belshazzar was Nabonidus' son who was appointed as co-regent when Nabonidus left Babylon to live in a desert oasis.[34]

At one point, the Medes and Persians had conquered all of the Babylonian Empire except for the capital Babylon, the greatest city of the ancient world. Immensely fortified and built to withstand a sustained siege, the city had thick walls that were impervious to battering rams.[35] Belshazzar and his colleagues were confident the city was impregnable even when the enemy surrounded it.

The Babylonians held a banquet to assure the people that their god Bel was superior and that they would ultimately triumph over their attackers (Daniel 5). At the feast Belshazzar and others drank from Jehovah's vessels that had been looted from the Jerusalem Temple, thus insulting the God of Israel.[36] A supernatural event then occurred—the fingers of a human hand appeared and wrote on the plaster of the wall, near the lampstand in the royal palace. After various sorcerers, diviners, and astrologers proved incapable of interpreting the writing, the king summoned Daniel, an exiled Israelite employed as a court advisor. Daniel told the king that the inscription meant, "God has numbered the days of your reign and brought it to an end" (5:26). He had "been weighed on the scales and found wanting" (5:27), and his kingdom "is divided and given to the Medes and Persians" (5:28). That very night, Belshazzar was slain and Darius the Mede took over the kingdom (5:30).

The Medo-Persians resorted to an interesting trick to finally seize Babylon. According to scholar Renald Showers, ancient historians related that King Cyrus of Medo-Persia diverted the Euphrates River from its normal channel under the city to make it shallow enough that his soldiers could walk underneath the city walls. (Cyrus, says Showers, appointed Darius the Mede to rule over the Chaldeans, which explains the above reference in Daniel 5:30 to Darius as king).[37] It is truly amazing that Daniel foresaw this unlikely turn of events—occurrences that demonstrate the active hand of God. Through this miracle, God showed His glory and vindicated Himself against a depraved empire that was defiling His name.

Daniel Chapters 2 and 7: The World Empires

There are striking parallels between the remarkable prophecies of Chapters 2 and 7 in the Book of Daniel. Chapter 2 centers on a dream seen by Babylonian King Nebuchadnezzar. His crew of magicians and sorcerers could not interpret it, but Daniel could, without the king even telling him what he'd seen. Daniel told the king he'd had a vision of a large, dazzling statue. The head was pure gold, the chest and arms were silver, the lower body and thighs were bronze, the legs were iron, and the feet partly iron and partly baked clay. Daniel said, "A rock was cut out, but not by human hands," and "it struck the statue on its feet of iron and clay and smashed them." The whole statue then broke up into fine pieces and blew away and disappeared. The rock that smashed the statue grew into a huge mountain filling the whole earth.

Daniel told Nebuchadnezzar that he represented the head of gold, because he had great dominion and glory. The upper part of the body (silver) was a separate kingdom that would be inferior to Babylon because it would be split and thus less unified.[38] It would be followed by a third kingdom (bronze) that would rule over the whole earth. In Chapter 8 of Daniel, these kingdoms are identified as Medo-Persia (silver) and Greece (bronze), respectively. The fourth kingdom was unidentified, but was strong as iron, because iron breaks to pieces and shatters all things. Interpreters agree that this was the Roman Empire. Daniel explained that the feet and toes were represented as part iron and part clay because this was a divided kingdom, which would simultaneously have the strength of iron but the weakness of clay. This symbolized that the kingdom would be partly strong and partly brittle. Daniel said that the crushing rock represented a kingdom set up by God that would crush all the worldly kingdoms—"not by human hands"—and would continue to rule. Scholars have interpreted this as Christ's future kingdom.

Chapter 7 of Daniel involves a similar dream, except that it was seen by Daniel directly and contained different imagery, though it corresponds to the imagery of Chapter 2. Daniel saw the four winds of heaven stir the sea into chaos, which probably represented the world of nations in turmoil. Daniel then saw four great beasts come up from the sea in succession. They represented four great Gentile kingdoms—"the same ones depicted in Chapter 2. The first beast looked like a lion with the wings of an eagle. This signified Babylon, as the Bible elsewhere portrays Nebuchadnezzar as a lion (Jer. 50:17) and an eagle (Ezek. 17:3, 12), animals that represent the swift and dominating way that Babylon conquered other nations. In the dream, the lion's wings were plucked off, it stood on its back feet like a human, and it acquired a human heart, which some interpret as Nebuchadnezzar becoming more humane after God punished and humbled him.[39]

The second beast was a bear, symbolizing the Medo-Persian Empire. A bear is more massive but slower than a lion, and so it was with Medo-Persia, which would grow larger but conquer nations at a slower pace than the Babylonians. The bear was on its side with one side higher than the other, which signified that the Persians would be dominant over the Medes in their joint empire. The bear had three ribs in its mouth, which some believe represented three significant kingdoms that Medo-Persia would conquer—Lydia, Babylon, and Egypt.

The third beast was a leopard with four wings and four heads. This represented Greece—as in Nebuchadnezzar's dream. Leopards move quickly, as do wings, so this imagery represented the speed with which Alexander the Great conquered the world. After his death in 323 BC, Alexander's empire was divided into four parts, each run by one of his generals: Cassander (Macedonia and Greece), Lysimachus (Thrace), Seleucus (Babylonia and Syria), and Ptolemy (Egypt).[40] The four heads of the leopard represented that fourfold division.

The fourth beast was not identified, but again, scholars believe it symbolizes the Roman Empire. It was so powerful and terrifying that it could not be fairly represented by any living animal. Ten horns then grew out of the beast's head, and then an eleventh one among them, which uprooted three of the other ten. These horns represented kings and kingdoms. The eleventh horn is believed to represent the Antichrist of future prophecy. The Romans, of course, became world rulers around 146 BC following the Greeks.

Daniel, Chapter 11:
Prophecy of Kings

Bible prophecy scholar John Walvoord states that Daniel 11:2–35 contains the most detailed prophecy in Scripture—so detailed that the interpreter, if he believes the passages were written before the events occurred, can't help but conclude that God is omniscient. This section contains over one hundred specific prophecies, all of which have been fulfilled.

According to Walvoord, no one questioned the authenticity of the Book of Daniel for at least eight hundred years after it was written in the sixth century BC. But in the third century AD the atheistic philosopher Porphyry concluded that the prophecies of Daniel 11:2–35 were so minutely accurate that they must have been written by someone after the events occurred. He speculated that the book was written in the Maccabean period, about 175 BC. Porphyry stood alone in his skepticism until the modern era, when a proliferating clique of critical scholars adopted Porphyry's position and began arguing that the dazzling prophecies must be a second-century forgery. Unfortunately for them, the discovery of the Dead Sea Scrolls in the mid-twentieth century included fragments from Daniel that were hundreds of years older than the earliest known manuscript at the time. This, according to Walvoord, "served to undermine the liberal position because it brought the book of Daniel back to the second century B.C. but in comparatively modern Hebrew instead of ancient Hebrew."[41] This would mean that a couple of centuries had to have elapsed between this copy and the original, which, says Walvoord, would put this copy back into Daniel's lifetime, or at least before the prophesied events.[42]

Norman Geisler agrees with Walvoord that the Book of Daniel was written by Daniel himself in the sixth century BC. The prophecies, he says, were presented as prophetic. They were described as things the wisest men in the kingdom could not divine, which would have been senseless to report had they already occurred. Additionally, Daniel makes a clear distinction between the present and the future, which proves he was consciously writing prophecy, not history. Geisler confirms that it wasn't until the rise of modern anti-supernaturalism that the sixth-century date for Daniel was questioned. The skepticism wasn't based on some archaeological or historical discovery, he notes, but simply on certain scholars' presupposition against supernaturalism.

Furthermore, Jesus referred to Daniel as a prophet (Matt. 24:15), and as Dr. Geisler points out, Jewish historian Josephus (37–100 AD) attested to the early date. He listed Daniel among *the Prophets* (the second section of the Jewish Old Testament), not among *the Writings* (the third and last section). "At that date, then," writes Geisler, "Daniel was considered a prophet, not a historian." Geisler notes that the discovery of the Dead Sea manuscript from the Book of Daniel in the second century was a copy. Similar to Walvoord, Geisler concludes, "Since this was only a copy, it would place the book earlier." Even a late date of around 170 BC, according to Geisler, would still validate some of Daniel's most sensational predictions, such as the seventy-weeks prophecy in Chapter 9,[43] which we'll turn to later.

Daniel 11:2–35 presents a prophecy of the years following the reign of Cyrus the Great. Verse 2 mentions three more Persian kings who ruled before Persia invaded Greece in 480 BC. Scholars believe verse 3 prophesies the march of Alexander the Great in the 330s, and verse 4, the division of his empire among his four generals following his death. Verses 5–9 detail the wars between two of those succeeding rulers, the Ptolemies of Egypt and the Seleucids of Syria, from the 320s to the death of Seleucus III in 223. The prophet focuses on only two of the four successor empires because they had important relationships to Israel; Palestine was located between them and was first controlled by the Ptolemies and then by the Seleucids.[44]

Observe the detail about Alexander's empire in 11:3–4: "Then a mighty king will appear, who will rule with great power and do as he pleases. After he has appeared, his empire will be broken up and parceled out towards the four winds of heaven. It will not go to his descendants, nor will it have the power he exercised, because the empire will be uprooted and given to others." If these words were written before the events occurred, as conservative scholars firmly believe, this is astoundingly detailed prophecy.

In 11:5–6 the prophecy gets even more specific: "The king of the South will become strong, but one of his commanders will become even stronger than he and will rule his own kingdom with great power. After some years, they will become allies. The daughter of the king of the South will go to the king of the North to make an alliance, but she will not retain her power, and he and his power will not last. In those days she will be handed over, together with her royal escort and her father and the one who supported her." This is referring to Syria (North) and Egypt (South). Historically, Ptolemy I Soter (323–285 BC) was the king of the South. The one stronger than he was Seleucus Nicator (312–281 BC). It is believed that Seleucus left Antigonus in Babylon and was briefly associated with Ptolemy I in Egypt. Then they united to defeat Antigonus, making way for Seleucus to control the vast territory from Asia Minor to India militarily. He thus became stronger than Ptolemy, who ruled Egypt.[45]

The prophecy continues with the same precise detail. Verses 10–19 predict the years of Antiochus III. Verse 20 describes his successor, Seleucus IV, and verses 21–35 detail the career of Antiochus IV (Epiphanes), who attempted to eradicate Judaism and convert the Jews to Hellenic paganism.[46]

Concerning these prophecies, Leon Wood writes in his *A Commentary on Daniel*, "The detail of this history as presented provides one of the most remarkable predictive portions of all Scripture."[47] Old Testament scholar Gleason Archer adds, "There is only one alternative left. The author of Daniel knew of the whole future course of history from Cyrus the Great to the Roman Empire through direct revelation from God. No other theory fits the objective data of the text or the known facts of history."[48]

Daniel Chapter 9:24–27:
The Seventy Sevens

The Chapter 9 prophecies are fascinating for many reasons, especially the prediction of the precise date of Jesus' death. The passage reads,

> Seventy "sevens" are decreed for your people and your holy city to finish transgression, to put an end to sin, to atone for wickedness, to bring in everlasting righteousness, to seal up vision and prophecy, and to anoint the most holy. Know and understand this: From the issuing of the decree to restore and rebuild Jerusalem until the Anointed One, the ruler, comes, there will be seven "sevens," and sixty-two "sevens." It will be rebuilt with streets and a trench, but in times of trouble. After the sixty-two "sevens," the Anointed One will be cut off and will have nothing. The people of the ruler who will

come will destroy the city and the sanctuary. The end will come like a flood: War will continue until the end, and desolations have been decreed. He will confirm a covenant with many for one "seven." In the middle of the "seven" he will put an end to sacrifice and offering. And on a wing of the temple he will set up an abomination that causes desolation, until the end that is decreed is poured out on him.[49]

Daniel was told that God's program would be completed in seventy *sevens*. He was to understand a *seven* as seven years, so that seventy *sevens* would be 490 years. At the end of the 490 years God would complete the transgression of Israel—i.e., Israel's sin of disobedience would be brought to an end at Christ's second coming, when Israel would repent and turn to Him as its Messiah and Savior. Then Israel would be restored to the land and blessed.

The 490-year period, as the text suggests, would be broken into three sections. Daniel 9:25 tells us that the seventy *sevens* would begin with the issuing of the decree to restore and rebuild Jerusalem. This is different from Cyrus' decree to rebuild the temple in Jerusalem; conservative scholars believe the decree foretold by Daniel was issued on March 5, 444 BC by Artaxerxes Longimanus (Neh. 2:1–8), whereby he granted the Jews permission to rebuild Jerusalem's city walls. So from the time this decree was issued until the "anointed one"—the ruler—comes, there will be seven *sevens* and another sixty-two *sevens*. This most likely means that the city walls would be rebuilt in about 49 years (seven *sevens*) and then, in an additional sixty-two *sevens* (434 years)—making a total of sixty-nine *sevens* (483 years)—the Anointed One (Christ) would come. This second period ended on the day of Christ's Triumphal Entry. At the end of that period (the 483 years), Christ would be "cut off" or put to death. Therefore, these first two periods—the seven *sevens* and the sixty-two *sevens*—were to run consecutively. Some believe they ran from the date of Artaxerxes' decree in 444 BC to March 30, 33 AD—*the precise day* when Christ made His Triumphal Entry.[50] Even if Daniel was written around 175 BC, as some critics insist, that would still have been some two hundred years before Christ's death.

Daniel 9:26 says that Christ would not be cut off during the seventieth *seven*, but only after the seven *sevens* and sixty-two *sevens* had run their course. This suggests an interval between the sixty-ninth and seventieth *sevens*. Christ's crucifixion was in that interval, as was the sacking of Jerusalem and the destruction of its temple by Titus in 70 AD. In fact, the entire present Church Age is still in the interval between the sixty-ninth and seventieth *sevens*.

The final or seventieth *seven* would begin after the Rapture of the Church—not necessarily immediately after, but sometime after—and would end with Christ's return to earth. This seven-year period is known as the Great Tribulation or the Time of Jacob's Trouble. I'll not examine this further, as it is prophecy yet to be fulfilled.[51]

MESSIANIC PROPHECIES

In Chapter 1, I mentioned a number of messianic prophecies—predictions about Jesus Christ—but I want to include more here, in summary form, to give you an idea of the abundance of these predictions and their remarkable accuracy.

Jesus, Satan, Death, and Redemption

One of the first prophecies in the Bible is a messianic prophecy. God tells the serpent, "I will put enmity between you and the woman, and between your offspring and her offspring; he shall bruise your head, and you shall bruise his heel" (Gen. 3:15). This prophecy is referring to one of the woman's descendants—Jesus Christ (Gal. 4:4). Though God had pronounced judgment on mankind because of his sin, He was also providing a plan of redemption through Jesus Christ, which He hereby revealed in this prophecy. He cursed the devil and the serpent and prophesied that there would always be enmity between the devil and the woman's descendants. Satan would strike Christ's heel—in the sense that He would die on the cross—but Christ would crush Satan's head, because through that very cross He would conquer death (Heb. 2:14). As John says, "The reason the Son of God appeared was to destroy the devil's work" (1 John 3:8).[52]

Jesus' Birth, Genetic Line, and Ministry

Christ would be of the seed of Abraham (Gen. 22:18, fulfilled in Matt. 1:1 and Gal. 3:16). He would also be in the line of Isaac (Gen. 21:12, fulfilled in Luke 3:23, 34), Jacob (Num. 24:17, fulfilled in Luke 3:23, 34), and Jesse (Isaiah 11:1, fulfilled in Luke 3:23, 32). He would be of the tribe of Judah (Gen. 49:10, fulfilled in Luke 3:23, 33). Christ would be born in Bethlehem (Micah 5:2), and would be born of a virgin (Isaiah 7:14, fulfilled in Matt. 1:18, 24–25; Luke 1:26–35). He would be God and man (Isaiah 9:6, fulfilled throughout the New Testament). He would be preceded and announced by one like Elijah who would live in the wilderness (Malachi 3:1, 4:5, fulfilled in Matt. 3:3; 11:10; John 1:23; Luke 1:17). He would be presented with gifts (Psalms 72:10, fulfilled in Matt. 2:1). Children would be killed (Jer. 31:15, fulfilled by Herod in Matt. 2:16). He would be of extraordinary character—holy, righteous, good, faithful, innocent, zealous, meek, forgiving, patient, loving, and full of justice (Isaiah 9:6–7; 11:1–5; 52:13–53:12, fulfilled in everything He did). His ministry would begin in Galilee (Isaiah 9:1, fulfilled in Matt. 4:12–13, 17) and reach its peak in Jerusalem when He would ride in on a donkey, then appear boldly in the temple (Zech. 9:9; Hag. 2:7; Mal. 3:1, fulfilled in Luke 19:35–37).

His miraculous ministry was also predicted. He would heal the blind, deaf, and lame (Isaiah 35:5–6). He would teach people using parables (Psalms 78:2, fulfilled in Matt. 9:35, 32, 33; 11:4–6; Mark 7:33–35; John 5:5–9; 9:6–11; 11:43, 44, 47). He would enter the temple (Mal. 3:1; fulfilled in Matt. 21:12). He would be rejected by His own people (the Jews) and would be a stumbling block to them (Psalms 118:22, fulfilled in 1 Peter 2:7; Romans 9:32–33). He would be a light to the Gentiles (Isa. 60:3, fulfilled in Acts 13:47–48). He would be betrayed by a friend for thirty pieces of silver and the silver would be thrown on the temple floor, then used to buy a potter's field (Psalms 41:9; 55:12–14; Zech. 11:12–13, fulfilled in Matt. 10:4; 27:3, 5, 7).[53]

Jesus' Death and Resurrection

The Old Testament predicted that when the shepherd (Jesus) was struck, the sheep (His followers) would be scattered (Zech. 13:7, fulfilled in Mark 14:50). He would be oppressed and falsely accused by malicious witnesses, but would not defend Himself (Isaiah 53:7; Psalms 35:11, 38:13, fulfilled in Matt. 26:59, 60).

Isaiah 53 and Psalm 22 are probably the most amazing descriptions of Christ's character, His work, His rejection and abandonment by the human beings He came to save, His suffering, His being forsaken by God, and His physical beating. The two passages graphically depict His execution on the cross in minute detail that would have been impossible to predict absent supernatural illumination.

You must read them one after the other, along with a few additional passages, to capture the miracle of these fulfilled prophecies. He would be forsaken by His disciples (Zech. 13:7; fulfilled in Mark 14:50). He would be hated by mankind, mocked, beaten, whipped, and crushed for the transgressions of mankind, whose iniquities He would bear, and make intercession for our transgressions, though He had done no violence (Psalms 22:7–8; Isaiah 53:2–12, fulfilled in Matt. 26:67, 27:26, 29; John 19:11). They would disrobe Him and gamble away His clothing (Psalms 22:17–18, fulfilled in John 19:23–24). He would be executed along with criminals (Isaiah 53:12, fulfilled in Matt. 27:38; Mark 15:27).

His hands and feet would be pierced for our transgressions (Isaiah 53:5; Psalms 22:16, fulfilled in Luke 23:33; John 20:25). He would plaintively cry out to God, asking why He had forsaken Him (Psalms 22:1, fulfilled in Matt. 27:46). His strength would be drained from Him, He would be extremely thirsty, His tongue would stick to the roof of His Mouth and His heart would be broken with grief (Psalms 22:14–15; John 19:28). He would be offered gall and vinegar (Psalms 69:21, fulfilled in Matt. 27:34). He would plead for mercy for His accusers (Isaiah 53:12, fulfilled in Luke 23:24). His friends would stand far away (Psalms 38:11, fulfilled in Luke 23:49). People would shake their heads (Psalms 109:25, fulfilled in Matt. 27:39). He would be stared upon (Psalms 22:17, fulfilled in Luke 23:35). He would commend Himself to God (Psalms 31:5, fulfilled in Luke 23:46).

His bones would not be broken (Psalms 34:20, fulfilled in John 19:33). His side would be pierced (Zech. 12:10, fulfilled in John 19:34). There would be darkness over the land (Amos 8:9, fulfilled in Matt. 27:45). He would be with a rich man in His death but assigned a grave with the wicked (Isaiah 53:9, fulfilled in Matt. 27:57–60). Though it would be the will of God to crush Him, He would ultimately be satisfied because He would have caused many to be accounted righteous by bearing their iniquities (Isaiah 53:10–12). Upon His return He would be given a portion among the great (Isaiah 53:12) and would be resurrected from the dead (Psalms 16:10; 30:3; 41:10; 118:17; Hosea 6:2, fulfilled in Matt. 28:6; Acts 2:31). Finally, He would ascend (Psalms 68:18; fulfilled in Acts 1:9) and would sit at the right hand of God (Psalms 110:1, fulfilled in Heb. 1:3; Mark 16:19; Acts 2:34–35).[54]

Christ's Nature

The Old Testament brims with predictions of the nature of Jesus Christ. He would be the Son of God (Psalms 2:7; 1 Chr. 17:11–14; 2 Samuel 7:12–16, fulfilled in Matt. 3:17, 16:16; Mark 9:7; Luke 9:35; 22:70; Acts 13:30–33; John 1:34, 49). He would be One who pre-existed His birth (Micah 5:2, Psalms 102:25; Prov. 8:22–23; Isaiah 9:6–7, 41:4; 44:6; 48:12, fulfilled in Col. 1:17, John 17:5, 24; Rev. 1:1–2; 1:17; 2:8; 8:58; 22:13). He would be called "Lord" (Psalms 110:1; Jer. 23:6, fulfilled in Luke 2:11; Matt. 22:43–45). He would be called Immanuel (Isaiah 7:14, fulfilled in Matt. 1:23). He would be a prophet (Deut. 18:18, fulfilled in Matt. 21:11), a priest (Psalms 110:4, fulfilled in Heb. 3:1), a judge (Isaiah 33:22, fulfilled in John 5:30), and a king (Psalms 2:6, fulfilled in Matt. 27:37). He would receive a special anointing by the Holy Spirit (Isaiah 11:12, fulfilled in Matt. 3:16). And He would have zeal for God's house—the temple (Psalms 69:9, fulfilled in John 2:15–16).[55]

Applying Mathematics to the Equation

Peter Stoner, a professor of mathematics and science, chose just eight of the roughly three hundred messianic prophecies and calculated the probability of these occurring to one man. What are the odds that a certain human being would fulfill prophecies that he would be born in Bethlehem, preceded by one who would announce his coming, enter Jerusalem as a king riding a donkey, be betrayed by a friend for thirty pieces of silver, that this silver would be thrown into the temple and used to buy a potter's field, and that this man would be put on trial and refuse to defend himself, though innocent, and then be crucified with thieves?

In his book *Science Speaks*, Stoner reveals his results: "We find that the chance that any man might have lived down to the present time and fulfilled all eight prophecies is 1 in 10^{17} (10 to the 17th power)." This, Stoner says, is about the same odds as if you covered the whole state of Texas with stacks of silver dollars two feet high, then marked one of the coins and had a blindfolded person pick the right coin. "Now these prophecies were either given by inspiration of God or the prophets just wrote them as they thought they should be," concludes Stoner. "In such a case the prophets had just one chance in 10^{17} of having them come true in any man, but they all came true in Christ. This means that the fulfillment of these eight prophecies alone proves that God inspired the writing of those prophecies to a definiteness which lacks only one chance in 10^{17} of being absolute."[56]

Stoner also calculates the odds of forty-eight of the prophecies all occurring to one man, yielding a result of 1 in 10^{157}. A silver dollar is too big to illustrate these odds, so Stoner uses something else. The electron, he says, is so small it would take 2.5 times 10^{15} of them laid side by side to make a one-inch long, single-file line. "If we were going to count the electrons in this line one inch long, and counted 250 each minute, and if we counted day and night, it would take us 19,000,000 years to count just the one-inch line of electrons. If we had a cubic inch of these electrons and we tried to count them it would take us, counting steadily 250 each minute, 19,000,000 times 19,000,000 times 19,000,000 years or 6.9 times 10^{21} years."[57] Stoner's work was deemed to be scientifically sound by members of the American Scientific Affiliation.[58]

The abundance of astonishingly accurate prophecies detailed in this chapter illustrate beyond a reasonable doubt that divine inspiration was behind the writing of the Bible. As I mentioned before, the messianic prophecies alone tipped my scales in favor of believing in the truth of Christianity. But I also admitted to you that I had no bias against the supernatural. For those who do, there is more proof. In the next two chapters I turn to that proof—evidence for the historical reliability of the Bible. After all, if the Bible isn't reliable, then we can't rely on the prophecies it contains. But fear not, for as we shall see, it is more reliable, by far, than any other ancient writing whose accuracy we routinely accept.

CHAPTER 9

◇◇◇◇◇◇◇◇◇◇◇◇

THE AMAZING BIBLE, PART 3: RELIABILITY AND INTERNAL EVIDENCE

The evidence for the unity of the Bible and its divinely made and fulfilled prophecies is so powerful that a firm foundation of faith can be firmly planted on it. Some people, however, will need more—and understandably so. Happily, there is additional, substantial evidence that the Bible is historically reliable and was not forged by clever men through the ages. There is also plenty of external evidence—non-Christian sources substantiating the existence of Jesus and archaeological evidence corroborating historical events recorded in the Bible. When compared to any other ancient document or book, by any fair measure, the Bible acquits itself—objectively—as more historically reliable. In this chapter and the next we'll examine this evidence.

TWELVE POINTS THAT SHOW
CHRISTIANITY IS TRUE

As we point to the Bible as evidence for the truth of Christianity—in its prophecies, its unity, the miracles, and in Jesus' assertions of His deity—we need to assure ourselves that the Bible itself is reliable. As I noted in Chapter 1, Dr. Norman Geisler and Dr. Frank Turek build their twelve-point case for the truth of Christianity first by demonstrating that "truth" actually exists and that anything that is contradictory to truth is false.[1] You would think that would be obvious, but in this so-called postmodern age, the very idea of truth is under attack. Next, Geisler and Turek offer proofs for the existence of a theistic God and for the possibility of miracles, and then they demonstrate that miracles performed in connection with a truth claim confirm the truth of God, through a messenger of God. (I discuss the subjects of truth, miracles, postmodernism, and Christ's resurrection in Chapter 11.)

Having established these matters, Geisler and Turek show that New Testament documents are reliable, which I intend to demonstrate in this chapter and the next. That is crucial because from there, they make the case that Jesus claimed to be God (which I showed in Chapter 6), that Jesus proved His assertions of deity by performing miracles (Chapter 11) and fulfilling prophecies (Chapter 9), and that therefore, Jesus is God.[2] Geisler and Turek then reason that because Jesus is God, anything He claims is true, must be true. As Jesus clearly affirms that the Bible is the Word of God—both Old Testament and New Testament—which I show in this chapter and elsewhere in this book, the Bible is in fact the Word of God. Finally, if the Bible is the Word of God, argue Geisler and Turek, anything that is opposed to any biblical truth is false.[3]

Anticipating a challenge from critics, Geisler and Turek demonstrate that their apologetic proofs are not a form of circular reasoning—sometimes called "begging the question." They assert, "It is not begging the question to use the Bible to prove the Bible" when you prove that the Bible is a historically reliable document.[4]

So in this chapter and those following we'll examine the historical reliability of the Bible, we'll confirm that the New Testament credibly records that Jesus lived a sinless and miraculous life, that He performed miracles—including the greatest miracle of all, His resurrection from the dead, which He predicted and which is the lynchpin of Christianity's truth claims—and that the miracles He performed were not random demonstrations of His divine power, but an outworking of His message and purpose. We will also document His affirmation that the Bible is the Word of God.

THE QUEST FOR THE HISTORICAL JESUS

Before examining the evidence itself, we must look at some developments in our culture concerning the quest for the historical Jesus and attacks on the New Testament, as well as modern trends in critical scholarship, all of which tend to undermine the public's confidence in the historical reliability of the Bible. There has been renewed interest of late in studying the historical Jesus. Was He real? If so, what was He like? Various theories have been popularized to suggest that Jesus isn't Who the Bible claims He is and that the gospels are inaccurate, unreliable, religiously biased, and largely mythological accounts.

"Some scholars think that the Gospels are poor records, dominated not by historical concerns, but written as religious propaganda for the purpose of communicating a particular message," notes scholar Gary Habermas. "Many such critical surveys have sought to reinterpret the story of Jesus in manners that emphasize non-traditional roles, viewing him as a political revolutionary, or as a Jewish prophet, or even as a magician."[5] Many of these modern inquiries are not simply challenging the traditional view of Who Jesus was, but are advancing the idea of a completely new Jesus.[6]

Perhaps the most notorious example is Dan Brown's book and the subsequent movie *The Da Vinci Code*, which depicts Christianity as having been founded on myths and legends.[7] One of the book's characters, for instance, exclaims, "What I mean, is that almost everything our fathers taught us about Christ is false."[8] *The Da Vinci Code* did have the effect, intended or not, of spreading doubts about the New Testament's authenticity and reliability. I witnessed it first-hand among friends and acquaintances.

According to apologetics professor Dr. R. B. Rudge, "The idea that the canonical Gospels are historically unreliable is a common theme that runs throughout the *Da Vinci Code*." The book asserts that more than eighty gospels were considered for inclusion in the New Testament, says Rudge, and only a few made it. It portrays early Christianity as a power struggle—a time when competing Christianities were vying for prominence, and the one that prevailed at the Council of Nicaea (325 AD) is the one we have today. The book suggests that until that council, Jesus was viewed by His followers as a mortal prophet, not as divine. *The Da Vinci Code*'s implication, Rudge explains, is that "when we read the canonical Gospels, we are not reading the best material on Jesus. Rather we are merely reading the perspective of the 'winners' of the 4th century A.D. theological battle."[9]

The evidence tells a different story. Christians did affirm Jesus' deity prior to the Council of Nicaea, argues Rudge, citing the gospels, the Pauline epistles, the early Church fathers, and even a non-Christian source—Pliny the Younger, who served as governor of Bithynia in Asia Minor. In a letter to Emperor Trajan about how to deal with Christians within his jurisdiction, Pliny wrote, "They [the Christians] were in the habit of meeting on a certain fixed day before it was light, when they sang in alternative verses a hymn to Christ, as to a god."[10] Indeed, we've already examined the scriptural evidence for Christ's deity in Chapter 6, and it's hard to deny that the Bible, written in the first century AD, some 250 years prior to the Council of Nicaea, portrays Him as divine.

"THERE WEREN'T [MULTIPLE] CHRISTIANITIES"

Along these lines, Lee Strobel asks New Testament historian Craig Evans, "Is it true that the earliest Christianity was a fluid melting pot of different perspectives about Jesus?" Evans replies, "It's not true at all. This is the product of a modern agenda—a politically correct, multicultural agenda motivated by sympathy for marginalized groups. The question is: What really did happen in the first century? What are the facts?"[11] The facts are, says Evans, that the early Christians did have disagreements, "but there weren't 'Christianities.' There wasn't one Christianity that thought Jesus was the Messiah and another Christianity that didn't; another Christianity that thought he was divine and another Christianity that disagreed; and another Christianity that thought he died on the cross as a payment for sin and another Christianity that scoffed at that. This is nonsense."[12]

Evans explains that the disagreements in early Christianity concerned issues such as circumcision and whether Christians could eat meat sacrificed to idols. But these critical scholars are claiming something altogether different, he says. "They're trying to smuggle into the first century a mystical, Gnostic understanding of God and the Christian life, even though first century Christians had never heard of these things."[13] Evans emphatically states that Christianity's core message, "That Jesus is the Messiah, he's God's Son, he fulfills the Scriptures, he died on the cross and thereby saved humanity, he rose from the dead—those core issues were not open for discussion."[14]

The evidence shows—as we'll see below—that theories that the gospels are historically unreliable are themselves fictitious. Evans agrees: "There's every reason to conclude that the Gospels have fairly and accurately reported the essential elements of Jesus' teachings, life, death, and resurrection. They're early enough, they're rooted into the right streams that go back to Jesus and the original people, there's continuity, there's proximity, there's verification of certain distinct points with archaeology and other documents, and there's the inner logic. That's what pulls it all together."[15]

STEALING FROM THE GREEKS?

In a somewhat similar attack, some liberal critics claim that early Christianity was heavily influenced by Platonism, Stoicism, pagan mystery religions, or other ideas prevalent during New Testament times. If this is true, the conviction that the New Testament is inspired by God would likely be dealt a serious blow. It would be hard to square the notion that the New Testament was inspired by God with the idea that the New Testament writers derived their essential beliefs from paganism.

Ronald Nash devotes an entire book to this subject, *The Gospel and the Greeks: Did the New Testament Borrow from Pagan Thought?* Nash answers the question, unequivocally, in the negative. Although most Bible scholars and classical studies experts now regard this as a dead issue, Nash wrote a book about it anyway because the theory is still touted by scholars of history and philosophy. Additionally, there has been a renewed interest in ancient Gnosticism, and some New Testament critics believe they've caught a second wind with their theory that Christianity is a syncretic mix of other religions and belief systems.[16]

Nash systematically refutes one of the critics' core arguments—that Paul strongly borrowed from the traditions of Platonic dualism and the Hellenistic philosophy of Stoicism. "Does Paul quoting a Stoic writer in Acts 17:28 demonstrate anything more than a passing acquaintance with Stoicism?" asks Nash. "It must be remembered that Paul was an educated man speaking to Stoics. What better way to gain their attention than to show that he had some acquaintance with their writers and could quote them with appreciation?"[17] Critics claim other New Testament writers such as Peter also borrowed from Stoicism, but Nash concludes that such references only show "that Christian writers utilized language and imagery of their time in a new and qualitatively different way. They do not prove that the New Testament appropriated any Stoic ideas."[18] Nash also rejects the popular theory that John borrowed the concept of *logos*, prominently featured in his gospel, from Hellenistic thought.

There's no question that as the New Testament was written in Greek, it uses words found in pagan writings. But, says Gordon Clark, "the point in question is not the use of words but the occurrence of ideas.... One cannot forbid Christian writers to use common words on pain of becoming pagans."[19] Nor does the existence of some parallels between the New Testament and pagan literature prove dependence. The New Testament writers were not living in a vacuum, but that doesn't mean Christianity was some artificial construct created from other sources. Indeed, a cursory knowledge of Christian doctrine will tell you just how unique Christianity is.

British scholar T. W. Manson argues that the early Church did not first develop its doctrine of Christ and then later look around for some historical events to which it could be pegged. Rather, the early Christians' ideas about Christ's deity, incarnation, atonement, and resurrection began with their own experience—their own history. "The Church," says Manson, "began with the picture and tried to find a frame for it rather than the Church first built an elaborate frame and then painted the portrait to suit.... The first Christians were Christians in the sense that they knew in their hearts that they owed their life to Christ, and that he had done for them something that they could not do for themselves and something that no other man, no institution, could do for them."[20] Thus, explains Manson, "The Church is built on the *fact* and not on a theory. The theories that we meet in the New Testament and in later doctrines are attempts to explain the fact. The fact is not an invention to suit the theories."[21]

As we'll see in the next chapter, archaeological finds also undermine the theory that Christianity borrowed from pagan religions.

"A CUMULATIVE CASE EMERGES"

Professor Craig Blomberg, one of the foremost authorities on the New Testament documents, notes that the origins of Jesus and Christianity continue to fascinate the public and that bookstores are full of titles on these issues. Responsible scholars have written some of these books, but some are pure fiction "foisted on the unsuspecting reader as the latest 'true discovery' about the beginnings of Christianity." He says there are three categories of these types of books that fall outside the mainstream of serious, biblical scholarship: those "based on no genuine historical evidence of any kind"; those that involve "the distortion of newly discovered evidence"; and those from "fully credentialed New Testament scholars on the theological 'far left' who do bona fide research, but present their opinions as if they reflected a consensus of scholarship" when in fact they don't.

The most famous recent example of the third category, Blomberg notes, is the Jesus Seminar, a group of "mostly New Testament scholars (though many had not specialized in historical-Jesus research)," who started with some two hundred members and shrunk to less than fifty. The clique garnered media attention with its semiannual conferences in the late eighties and nineties. By method of group vote, these scholars concluded that only 18 percent of Jesus' sayings and 16 percent of His actions in the four gospels and the apocryphal Gospel of Thomas came close to representing what He actually said or did.[22]

But the conclusions of these critical scholars were tainted by their anti-supernatural presuppositions, which made it impossible for them to examine the evidence objectively. They even candidly admitted that they approached their study with the bias that "miracles cannot happen, so that all of the supernatural events of the Gospels are rejected from the outset, and that Jesus never talked about himself, or about the future, or about final judgment (a topic unworthy of an enlightened teacher)." Blomberg points out that these further restrictive biases precluded the idea that Jesus could have considered Himself to be divine or to have predicted the future accurately and inerrantly.[23]

How's that for a scientific, academically rigorous approach? They simply agreed in advance that Jesus couldn't possibly have performed miracles, didn't claim to be God, didn't prophesy, and didn't talk of hell. Therefore, He didn't—not because He actually didn't, but because these "scholars" chose to view Him as one who wouldn't have said or done such things. So by pseudo-academic fiat, they gutted the gospels and the divinity of Christ. I remember learning about the Jesus Seminar back in my seeking days and thinking how disturbing its findings could be for those unfamiliar with the sophistry underlying their arguments.

Blomberg reports that while there are some promising trends for the historical Jesus in modern New Testament scholarship, "outside of distinctively evangelical circles, even in mainstream, centrist New Testament scholarship, it is still by no means believed that any substantial majority of the Gospels or Acts is historically accurate."[24] Blomberg, of course, dissents from these conclusions and believes that the evidence supports "a substantial measure of confidence in the historical trustworthiness" of all four of the gospel accounts—Matthew, Mark, Luke, and John—and the Book of Acts, which relates the history of the early Church. Blomberg insists that in examining the evidence he has labored

to avoid the error committed by the Jesus Seminar of presupposing conclusions. If we just apply the same standards used by classical historians
to evaluate the historical reliability of works from the ancient Jewish,
Greek, and Roman worlds, Blomberg says, "a cumulative case emerges
which suggests that the Gospels and Acts are very historically reliable."[25]

The Bible is in fact historically reliable—demonstrably so, as I'll
show in this chapter—in that the New Testament documents are authentic and the New Testament writers are credible.[26] This is a matter of
evidence. If we can show that the New Testament documents are authentic—that they have been carried down to us as originally written, and
that they contain accurate reports by New Testament writers—then we
will have gone a long way toward making a strong evidentiary case for
Christianity's truth claims. It would mean we have in the New Testament
a compilation of writings that have been accurately transcribed and
transmitted to us as they were written, close to the historical events they
describe, and that they were written by men on whose credibility we can
rely.

THE AUTHENTICITY OF THE
NEW TESTAMENT DOCUMENTS

Let's first look at the authenticity of the New Testament documents
and then examine the reliability of the writers. To measure the accuracy
of the Bible by the same standards historians use to evaluate the reliability of historical works, we should apply three types of tests: bibliographical, internal evidence, and external evidence.[27] The internal and
external evidence tests assess the reliability of the writers, while the
bibliographical test measures the authenticity of the documents.

The bibliographical test examines the textual transmission by which
the documents ultimately reach us. This is useful for determining how
reliable the copies are, since we don't have the original documents.[28] The
process involves dating the original New Testament writings, determining how much time elapsed between the actual events and the original
writings that recorded those events, ascertaining the number and examining the accuracy of the extant manuscript copies we have, determining

how much of a time gap exists between the original writing and the oldest copies we have, and finally comparing this evidence with similar evidence for manuscripts of other writings from ancient secular history.[29]

DATING OF THE ORIGINAL WRITINGS

From ancient times until about five hundred years ago, there was no way of duplicating books and other writings except by hand, one copy at a time. Most things, such as letters, didn't need to be copied. But people did want copies of great works of literature, and so hundreds of handwritten copies were made of ancient manuscripts deemed worthy of reading and preserving. The original writings, called "autographs," were copied, and copies were made from the copies. This process sometimes continued through several centuries. The autographs of these ancient books, including the Bible, perished long ago, and today we only have copies of copies, usually many times removed from the originals, and which inevitably contain errors.

The autographs for the New Testament, according to Scottish theologian and Church historian Philip Schaff, probably perished before the close of the first century, or soon after they were copied and distributed. The apostles and evangelists, says Schaff, "did not write on Babylonian bricks, or Sinaitic rocks, or Egyptian walls, or stones, or tablets of wood or brass, but on paper, with reed-pen and ink."[30] The paper in common use at the time was made of brittle and perishable Egyptian papyrus. Interestingly, John refers to his writing tools in 2 John 12: "Though I have much to write to you, I would rather not use paper and ink. Instead I hope to come to you and talk face to face, so that our joy may be complete." He says the same in 3 John 13. Paul alludes to ink as well in 2 Corinthians 3:3.

As there are no remaining autographs of the New Testament books or the classical Greek and Roman writings, scholars use textual criticism to study copies of them and determine the exact words the authors actually wrote. Textual criticism takes the existing manuscripts of a book, studies the differences between them, and then attempts by established principles to determine the exact wording of the original. It is less subjective than literary criticism, which attempts to identify the sources underlying an author's work to find out where he got his information.[31] According to Professor Blomberg, textual criticism allows us to reconstruct what the original authors of the New Testament first wrote with a high degree of accuracy.[32]

Dr. Geisler and Frank Turek, in *I Don't Have Enough Faith to Be an Atheist*, argue that most of the New Testament books were written before 70 AD—within forty years of Jesus' death.[33] Among the reasons they cite for their dating is that Jerusalem and the Jewish temple—as predicted by Jesus—were ransacked and destroyed by the Romans in 70 AD, yet not one of the New Testament writings mentions this monumentally significant tragedy. More than that, these writings mention Jerusalem and the temple as if they are still intact at the time of the writings.[34]

Dr. Geisler notes elsewhere that most scholars—both conservative and critical—believe the New Testament was completed by 100 AD. Paul, who lived at the same time as the eyewitnesses, wrote around ten of his New Testament epistles somewhere between 50 and 60 AD.[35] Relying on written documents and eyewitness accounts, Paul's colleague Luke wrote one of the gospel accounts and the Book of Acts, completing them around 62 AD (Luke 1:1–4). Many believe that Mark's gospel, which was probably written before 60 AD, is essentially the account of Peter, who was a disciple of Jesus and an eyewitness to the events recorded in that account. Matthew, also a disciple and eyewitness, is believed to have written his gospel account before 60 AD as well. John was another eyewitness, and though there is debate about when he wrote his gospel account, it was no later than 100 AD. Professor Blomberg agrees, saying that most conservative scholars date all three synoptic gospels and Acts in the 60s AD and John in the 90s.[36]

Geisler and Turek in fact argue, based largely on the research of classical scholar and historian Colin Hemer, that the Gospel of Luke was written at or before 60 AD, because if Acts was written by 62 AD, Luke had to have been written sometime earlier. Indeed, in the first verse of Acts, Luke refers to his former book, which must have been the Gospel of Luke.[37] They reason that if Luke was written by 60 AD, then Mark must have been written in the mid-to-late 50s and perhaps earlier—because Luke notes that he obtained his facts from eyewitness sources (Luke 1:1–4), and most scholars believe the Gospel of Mark was among those sources.[38]

Thus, whether we use liberal or conservative dating, the gospels and Acts were written in the first century.[39] As Christ probably lived until roughly 30–33 AD, we have in the New Testament all these eyewitness accounts written between twenty and fifty years after the events they record,[40] though some scholars narrow the range to between fifteen and forty years.[41] By ancient standards, this is an extraordinarily short time frame, especially considering that the first-century Roman Empire largely comprised oral cultures in which important information was circulated mostly by word of mouth. And even though Jewish men had a higher literacy rate than most, they still relied on rote memorization in their educational disciplines. In this environment, it is altogether likely that many men would have committed the gospel accounts to memory.[42] Furthermore, many scholars are convinced that the gospel writers were relying on earlier written sources.[43]

Professor Blomberg adds another important point that lends credence to the dating and reliability of the gospel story. "Particularly telling," he writes, "are those references to 'the Jesus tradition' in the New Testament epistles that predate the composition of the Gospels." While Paul doesn't extensively quote Jesus in his letters, he does allude to many events from His life, and refers to "a broad cross section of Jesus' individual teachings and larger sermons." "These references," says Blomberg, "demonstrate that accurate information about Jesus was circulating by word of mouth long before the first written accounts of his life were penned."[44]

MANUSCRIPT EVIDENCE

New Testament professor Mark Strauss says the evidence indicates that the early Church carefully transmitted the words and deeds of Jesus.[45] Dr. Geisler agrees, declaring, "The New Testament documents are copied accurately—the New Testament has more manuscripts, earlier manuscripts, and more accurately copied manuscripts than any other book from the ancient world."[46]

The evidence, however, is changing all the time based on new discoveries. Geisler recounts that when he began writing on this topic in the sixties, there were about 5,000 Greek New Testament manuscripts. By 1986 the number had climbed to 5,366, in 1999 there were 5,656, and now there are around 5,800. The number of New Testament translations into languages of nearby countries—Syriac, Arabic, Ethiopic, Latin, Coptic, and others—totals about 19,300. When added to the 5,800 Greek manuscripts, there are some 25,000 New Testament manuscripts, a figure that dwarfs the number of manuscripts of any other ancient book.[47]

In comparison, the number of existing manuscript copies of most books from the ancient world, with the exception of Homer's *Iliad* and *Demosthenes*, averages between ten and twenty. "All told, the New Testament is represented by approximately one thousand times as many manuscripts as the average classical author's writings," write evangelical scholars Ed Komoszewski, M. James Sawyer, and Daniel B. Wallace.[48] Craig Blomberg adds, "By contrast [with other ancient books], the textual evidence for the New Testament from the first centuries after it was written is staggering. Scholars of almost every theological stripe agree that Christian scribes copied the New Testament with extraordinary care, matched only by the accuracy of the Jewish scribes copying the Hebrew Scriptures (the Christian Old Testament)."[49] Professor Strauss concurs, noting that Paul's use of the Greek terms for "received" and "passed on" are technical terms in Judaism for the careful handing down of tradition (1 Cor. 11:23; 15:1–2).[50]

Homer's *Iliad* is second to the Bible in the number of existing manuscripts among ancient books. Scholars have long listed the number of *Iliad* copies at 643, but large numbers of Greek papyri manuscripts of the work (dating to 300–150 BC) were recently discovered, bringing the number of manuscripts to almost 1,800. However, it's important to note that the time gap between the original *Iliad* and the first known manuscript is between 350 and 400 years. And among non-biblical ancient books, the *Iliad* is the exception, both in having more manuscript copies and in having a shorter gap between the time of writing and the date of the first manuscript. Most other ancient works have more than a thousand-year gap between the original and the first copy. Bible scholar John A. T. Robinson says of the New Testament, "The wealth of manuscripts, and above all the narrow interval of time between the writing and the earliest extant copies, make it by far the best attested text of any ancient writing in the world."[51]

The earliest undisputed New Testament manuscript fragment is the John Rylands Fragment (117–138 AD), which contains five verses from John 18. That would mean, notes Geisler, a gap of less than fifty years between the original—scholars believe John was written by 90 AD—and this fragment. A longer series of texts, the Bodmer Papyri (circa 200 AD), contains most of the books of John and Luke as well as 1 Peter, 2 Peter, and Jude, which means there's a gap of between 100 and 140 years for these. Most of the New Testament is included in the Chester Beatty Papyri (circa 250 AD), which is 150-plus years from the time the New Testament writings were completed.[52] The Codex Vaticanus (325–350 AD) contains all of the New Testament except for the latter part of Hebrews, Philemon, the Pastoral Letters, and Revelation,[53] and most of the Greek Old Testament. The Codex Sinaiticus (340 AD) is the oldest copy of the entire New Testament and also contains much of the Old Testament.[54] The Sinaiticus and Vaticanus Codices, then, date only about 250 years after the original autographs.[55]

All in all, according to Komoszewski, Sawyer, and Wallace, "The wealth of material that is available for determining the wording of the original New Testament is staggering: more than fifty-seven hundred Greek New Testament manuscripts, as many as twenty thousand versions, and more than one million quotations by patristic writers (early church fathers). In comparison with the average ancient Greek author, the New Testament copies are well over a thousand times more plentiful. If the average-sized manuscript were two and one-half inches thick, all the copies of the works of an average Greek author would stack up four feet high, while the copies of the New Testament would stack up to over a mile high!"[56] Philip Schaff adds, "The large number of various readings is a positive advantage in ascertaining the true text. The word of the wise man may be applied here: 'In the multitude of counselors there is safety' (Prov. 11:14). The original reading is sure to be preserved in one or more of these sources. Hence we need not, as in the case of the ancient classics, resort to subjective conjectural criticism, which never leads to absolute certainty. The very multitude of readings is the best guarantee of the essential integrity of the New Testament."[57]

In his interview of New Testament scholar Bruce Metzger, Lee Strobel emphasizes the importance of having a large number of manuscript copies. Strobel says he was skeptical when he first discovered there were no surviving autographs of the New Testament. If all we have are "copies of copies," he asks, "how can I have any confidence that the New Testament we have today bears any resemblance whatsoever to what was originally written?" Metzger replies that this isn't unique to the Bible, but is true of all ancient documents: "But what the New Testament has in its favor, especially when compared with other ancient writings, is the unprecedented multiplicity of copies that have survived." The reason this is so important, explains Metzger, is that "the more often you have copies that agree with each other, especially if they emerge from different geographical areas, the more you can cross-check them to figure out what the original document was like. The only way they'd agree would be where they went back genealogically in a family tree that represents the descent of the manuscripts."[58]

ACCURACY OF THE WRITINGS

In comparing New Testament documents with other ancient documents, an examination of their relative accuracy is also relevant. Interestingly, there are so few manuscripts for many ancient books as to make any such comparison unfeasible. But as for those few ancient books for which sufficient manuscripts exist, their accuracy pales in comparison to that of the New Testament. Bruce Metzger found that manuscripts for the ancient Indian work *Mahabharata* were about 90 percent accurate. When there were only 643 known copies of the *Iliad*, he found that its manuscripts were about 95 percent accurate. The New Testament manuscripts, by contrast, were 99.5 percent accurate.[59]

Admittedly, there have been a number of "variants"—that is, differences in wording—in the New Testament manuscripts, which are not necessarily errors, but different readings from the standard texts.[60] "The vast majority of variants," says Geisler, "are grammatical in nature and have no bearing on the substance of the message. Only a small fraction of the variants bear on the meaning of the text, and none affect any major doctrine of the Christian faith."[61]

More than half the textual variants involve spelling differences and obvious scriveners' errors that are easily detectable and don't affect anything significant in the text, say Komoszewski, Sawyer, and Wallace. The next largest group involves synonyms and the like, but nothing of major consequence. Some potentially meaningful variants turn out not to be significant, as they "have no plausibility when it comes to reflecting the wording of the original because the manuscripts in which they are found have a poor pedigree." Ultimately, only about 1 percent of all the textual variants (please note that by this I mean 1 percent of the variants, not 1 percent of the entire text) are both "meaningful and viable," and few of these, if any, affect much of a theological nature.[62] Komoszewski, Sawyer, and Wallace conclude that "any uncertainty over the wording of the original New Testament does not have an impact on major teachings of the New Testament. They certainly do not affect the deity of Christ. There is simply no room for uncertainty about what the New Testament originally taught."[63]

Indeed, Blomberg writes that "even the most liberal members of the Jesus Seminar" agree "that there is no historical evidence whatsoever to support the claims of some modern-day Mormons or Muslims that the text of the New Testament became so corrupted over the centuries that we have no way of being sure what the original contained."[64]

Numerous scholars state it slightly differently but come to essentially the same conclusion.[65] A. T. Robinson argues, "The real concern is with a thousandth part of the entire text." Geisler notes that this means the reconstructed text of the New Testament "is 99.9 percent free of any real concern."[66] Philip Schaff says of the many variants known in his day, only 400 affected the sense, and of those only 50 were of real significance, "and even of these fifty not one affects an article of faith or a precept of duty which is not abundantly sustained by other and undoubted passages, or by the whole tenor of Scripture teaching."[67] Westcott and Hort estimate that only one-sixtieth of the variations were more than trivial, which means the text is 98.33 percent pure. Ezra Abbott concludes the text is 99.75 percent pure.[68] Richard Bentley, "the ablest and boldest of classical critics of England" according to Philip Schaff, "affirms that even the worst of [manuscripts] does not pervert or set aside 'one article of faith or moral precept.'"[69]

Concerning the New Testament, the words of British paleographer and biblical and classical scholar Sir Fredric Kenyon still ring true today: "The interval between the dates of the original composition and the earliest extant evidence becomes so small as to be in fact negligible, and the last foundation for any doubt that the Scriptures have come down substantially as they were written has now been removed. Both the authenticity and the general integrity of the books of the New Testament may be regarded as finally established."[70]

CORROBORATION BY EARLY CHURCH FATHERS

Here's another astonishing fact: the early Church fathers—Origen, Clement, Tertullian, Irenaeus, Ignatius, Polycarp, etc.—prolifically cited the New Testament in their writings. Just a few of the early fathers alone account for 36,000 New Testament citations, but the number of such citations from all the Church fathers exceeds one million. "So extensive are these citations," say Komoszewski, Sawyer, and Wallace, "that if all other sources for our knowledge of the text of the New Testament were destroyed, they would be sufficient alone for the reconstruction of practically the entire New Testament."[71] And as Sir Fredric Kenyon observes, "The number of manuscripts of the New Testament, of early translations from it, and of quotations from it in the oldest writers of the Church, is so large that it is practically certain that the true reading of every doubtful passage is preserved in some one or other of these ancient authorities. This can be said of no other book in the ancient world."[72]

THE RELIABILITY OF THE
NEW TESTAMENT WRITINGS

On the equally important question of the reliability of the New Testament writers, Dr. Geisler says there were more writers, earlier writers, and more accurate writers than for any other book from the ancient world.[73] What is involved, he says, is the unquestioned integrity of the witnesses in both number and nature, the apparent sanity and accuracy of the writers, and the corroboration of their testimony by external sources.[74]

New Testament professor Mark Strauss notes that some scholars erroneously contend that eyewitnesses to the events of Jesus had little to do with passing along the tradition. This assertion flies in the face of the strong evidence that the apostles were the central guardians and transmitters of the gospel accounts. Throughout the pages of the New Testament, notes Strauss, eyewitness testimony is highly esteemed (John 19:35, 21:24; Acts 1:21–22, 10:39, 41; 1 Cor. 15:6; 1 Peter 5:1; 2 Peter 1:16; 1 John 1:1–3; Romans 6:17; and 1 Cor. 7:10, 12).[75]

Indeed, the New Testament, relatively speaking, has a large number of writers—nine—including Matthew, Mark, Luke, John, Paul, Peter, James, Jude, and the writer of Hebrews.[76] Just think about their credentials: Matthew, John, Paul, and Peter were apostles; Mark, Luke, and the writer of Hebrews were associates of the apostles; James was the brother of Jesus; and Jude was the brother of James and probably the half-brother of Jesus.[77] As noted earlier, some of them—Matthew, Peter (through Mark), and John—were direct witnesses of Christ's life, His miracles, and His teachings. Luke and Paul relied heavily on eyewitness and written accounts, while Jesus' death was witnessed by John (John 19:26, 27), Jesus' mother, the soldiers, the crowd, and many other women standing nearby (John 19:25; Mark 15:40–41). The resurrection—the most critical historical event upon which Christianity is based—was witnessed by more than five hundred people, when Jesus appeared to them in His physical body, making numerous appearances before both small and large groups (John 20:1, 20:24, 26–29; Matt. 28:2, 16–20; Luke 23:55, 24:10, 13–32, 34; 1 Cor. 15:6, 7a; and Acts 1:4–12).[78]

Christian apologist Dan Story also examines the New Testament's reliability based on the quality of witnesses, which he calls their primary source value. He concurs with Dr. Geisler that the gospels were written either by eyewitnesses to the events in Christ's life (Matthew and John) or by men who knew and interviewed eyewitnesses (Mark and Luke). As I pointed out in Chapter 2, the New Testament authors repeatedly insist they are accurately reporting their historical accounts and that first-hand, eyewitness testimony enhances the credibility of their chronicles. Moreover, the writers address their readers as those who have seen and heard the events they are describing (Acts 2:22, 26:24–28). Story, along with many others, points out that the writers are addressing people who observed Christ's miracles and had every opportunity to refute the accounts, "yet, in the case of the birth, ministry, death and resurrection of Jesus, not a single piece of contrary historical evidence surfaced during the first century to claim these events were false."[79] The fact that Christianity's enemies couldn't refute the gospel accounts is persuasive evidence of their historical reliability.

Christian apologist J. P. Moreland notes that the existence of so many witnesses means the writers wouldn't have invited challenges from contradictory witnesses unless they were telling the truth. The apostles, Moreland notes, began evangelizing in the very area where Jesus had ministered. "If the early portrait of him was untrue, how could the apostles have succeeded there? Why would they have begun there in the first place?"[80] Norman Geisler and Frank Turek, in *I Don't Have Enough Faith to Be an Atheist*, note that the New Testament writers refer to more than thirty people whose historical existence has been confirmed. Such references would have destroyed their credibility had they included well-known people in fabricated stories, Geisler and Turek say. They would have been exposed as flagrant liars had they invented stories about Pilate, Caiaphas, Festus, Felix, and others.[81]

Moreland adds the compelling argument that if the New Testament image of Jesus had not been based on bona fide eyewitness testimony, it is hard to imagine how a consistent tradition about Him could have been formed and written. It would have resulted in competing Christologies and, essentially, chaos and disunity in the message of the early Church.

If there hadn't been strong and widespread eyewitness corroboration, various stories would have sprung up everywhere, diluting the religion from its infancy. "Eyewitness apostolic control over the tradition is the best explanation," writes Moreland, "for the emergence of a consistent, written portrait of Jesus."[82] Indeed, while there are some differences in emphases in the various gospel accounts, what intellectually honest person can read all four books and deny that they put forward a consistent image of Jesus as fully divine and fully human?

Renowned Bible scholar F. F. Bruce confirms the "primary source value" of the New Testament accounts. "The earliest preachers of the gospel," writes Bruce, "knew the value of...first-hand testimony, and appealed to it time and again. 'We are witnesses of these things,' was their constant and confident assertion."[83] Bruce also affirms that "had there been any tendency to depart from the facts in any material respect, the possible presence of hostile witnesses in the audience would have served as a further corrective."[84]

"THEY HAD VERY LITTLE TO GAIN AND MUCH TO LOSE"

Another factor adding probative value to the New Testament accounts, as we've discussed with the Bible in general, is that the authors unhesitatingly cast themselves in an unfavorable light, such as the reports of Peter humiliatingly denying Jesus three times, and the self-absorbed disciples vying over who would be the greatest in the kingdom. It's obviously quite unlikely that the writers would have invented these embarrassing details. Nor did the writers sanitize Jesus' harsh words or conceal the slanderous allegations leveled against Him, such as that His power was derived from Satan. The writers didn't omit Jesus' anger or disappointment, His anguish on the cross, or His request that the Father remove the cup from Him. Had they been conspiring to ignite a new religious movement, it's far more likely they would have cherry-picked the details of His life to make Him more appealing. But the fact that the writers included so many "negative" elements, says Dan Story, "is compelling evidence for the authenticity and integrity of their writings and witness."[85]

J. P. Moreland argues that such evidence militates strongly in favor of the New Testament writers' reliability. They were, he said, "able and willing to tell the truth. They had very little to gain and much to lose for their efforts." He points out that they were Jewish theists who knew that changing the religion of Israel in this way would have subjected them to the risk of damnation. "There is no adequate motive for their labors other than a sincere desire to proclaim what they believed to be the truth," argues Moreland.[86]

Professor Blomberg also assesses Jesus' "hard sayings and missing topics." He says the reliability of the New Testament is bolstered, not undermined, by some of Jesus' hard sayings. For example, Jesus says, "If anyone comes to me and does not hate father and mother, wife and children, brothers and sisters—yes, even life itself—such a person cannot be my disciple" (Luke 14:26). This, states Blomberg, would have "scandalized" Jewish audiences who obeyed the commandment to honor father and mother, which Jesus also endorses elsewhere (Mark 7:10). Jesus obviously didn't mean this command literally, and more likely meant they had to love God indescribably more than they loved their own family, which is closer to what Matthew has Him saying (Matt. 10:37). But if these accounts had been fabricated to put Jesus in the best or most defensible light, they could have easily omitted the statement altogether.[87]

Other examples are when Jesus seems to lack power because of the "unbelief" of the people in Nazareth (Mark 6:5–6) or have limited knowledge (Mark 13:32).[88] As I discussed in Chapter 6, Christian theology holds that Christ voluntarily surrendered use of certain of His divine attributes during His incarnation, which makes these passages wholly understandable—in fact, they happen, ironically, to fortify my own faith. But if the gospel writers were creating a neat, tight story, they probably would have omitted such potentially confounding passages.

There is also the question of "missing topics"—controversial issues that the gospels don't record Jesus as addressing. The Book of Acts details certain disagreements in the early Church such as whether circumcision is required of believers and differences over speaking in tongues. The gospel writers could have eliminated these problems if they had simply put words into Jesus' mouth about them, but they apparently were too committed to truth to invent facts, even for the purpose of reducing tension and thereby promoting the Church's growth. This too enhances the reliability of the accounts.[89]

Perhaps the most compelling evidence of all is that the New Testament writers abandoned their long-held religious beliefs and practices, and under severe pressure and shunning, adopted an entirely new belief system, then held fast to these convictions under life-threatening persecution.[90] This was probably most significant for Paul, who had been one of Christianity's greatest persecutors and who became its most ardent evangelist following his conversion on the Damascus Road. New Testament professor Mark Strauss adds, compellingly, "It pushes the limits of credulity, to argue that the same early Christians who taught the greatest ethical system in the world, passionately proclaimed the truth of their message, and suffered and died for their faith were at the same time dishonest schemers and propagators of a great fraud."[91]

"THESE THINGS ARE WRITTEN THAT
YOU MAY BELIEVE"

Moreland also dismisses the argument that the gospel accounts can't be relied on for historical accuracy because they were written by those promoting a message, i.e., Christianity. The theological dimension of the books is in no way incompatible with their historicity, especially since the theological message is grounded in Jesus' actual history.[92] If He wasn't God, if He hadn't become man, if He hadn't lived a sinless life, if He hadn't fulfilled the Old Testament prophecies about Himself, if He hadn't engaged in sublime teaching, if He hadn't ushered in a New Covenant, if He hadn't performed miracles, if He hadn't predicted His own death, if He hadn't been crucified, if He hadn't been resurrected and appeared before many witnesses, if He hadn't asserted His deity, if He hadn't forgiven sins, if He hadn't offered eternal life through faith in

Him—if He hadn't done each and every one of these things, there would be no theological message for the writers to have communicated.

In studying archaeological evidence, which I discuss in the next chapter, I came across a fascinating quote bearing on this subject from Sir William Ramsay, who came away convinced of the accuracy of Luke's historical account in Acts after engaging in archaeological studies. Ramsay writes, "There was then, and there still is a strange and quite widespread prepossession that an early Christian, like Paul, must have been wholly occupied with the religious propaganda, so that he could see nothing, hear nothing, feel nothing, and observe nothing except the chance of converting some heathen individual or group of persons. This prepossession, that Christian authors lie outside the pale of real literature and that early Christians were not to be estimated as men, has been the enemy for me to attack ever since I began to look into the Christian authors with unprejudiced eyes. It may be true of some smaller figures and narrower minds. It is not true of the greater men."[93]

Craig Blomberg notes that in attacking the credibility of the New Testament writers as more theologically than historically motivated, some critics focus on the Gospel of John, arguing that it is more theological than the historically oriented Synoptics, and citing John 20:31, "But these [things] are written that you may believe that Jesus is the Messiah, the Son of God, and that by believing you may have life in his name." This statement could suggest to some that John is interested more in spreading the faith than in historical accuracy. I think the opposite is the case. Ask yourself, why would he even want to spread the faith if he hadn't witnessed the glories of Christ? It certainly was bringing John no glory and would eventually lead to hardship and imprisonment. Plus, if he were telling lies, he could not expect to be widely believed since others were alive who could contradict his account. It's also noteworthy that this statement in John 20:31 is one of the only interpretive theological statements in any of the gospels, which shows just how focused the gospel writers were on historical facts rather than on hammering home theological points.

Additionally, John was writing his accounts later than the other gospel writers and surely assumed his audience would have already been familiar with the historical material. John stresses that he is telling the truth and links his truthfulness to his credibility: "He who saw it has borne witness—his testimony is true, and he knows that he is telling the truth—that you may also believe" (John 19:35). He adds, "This is the disciple who is bearing witness about these things, and who has written these things, and we know that his testimony is true" (John 21:24). John also makes clear that he firmly believes he is writing with the guidance and inspiration of the Holy Spirit (John 14:26).[94]

Some critics argue that the ancients were less interested in historical accuracy than we are today, but Moreland rejects the charge. He notes that ancient Greek and Roman historians emphasized the importance of eyewitnesses and accurate reporting.[95] Even when some of them couldn't remember speeches they were citing because they hadn't taken verbatim notes, they proclaimed their intention to recreate a faithful proximity of the communications. Although some believe that Herodotus, one of the great historians of antiquity, embellished or fabricated some of his accounts, even if that's true, it doesn't taint the Greek and Roman commitment to historical accuracy in general.

More important, even if other ancients weren't committed to historical accuracy, that wouldn't mean the Hebrew gospel writers weren't, especially considering why they were writing their accounts in the first place—to spread the "good news," which wouldn't have been news at all unless true. If Jesus had not done everything they reported Him as doing, they'd have had no incentive to write about Him, much less to risk their lives promoting faith in Him. In addition, we have the testimony of the New Testament writers themselves concerning their own commitment to accuracy, as I detailed in Chapter 2.

Blomberg concedes that conventions for history and biography in our modern era are much more exacting than they were in ancient times, but insists that the ancients nevertheless were committed to substantive accuracy. "In cultures that had yet to create any symbol corresponding to our quotation mark, or to feel any need for one, it was perfectly appropriate to rephrase someone else's language in one's own words, so long as one was faithful to the 'gist' or intention of the original speaker."[96] The emphasis would also be different in a modern biography than a gospel account of Jesus' life; whereas a modern biography would almost certainly include details about a person's upbringing and not focus so much on his death, the gospel accounts weren't written as comprehensive biographies any more than the Old Testament historical books were. These are books of salvation history, and only those facts relevant to Jesus' mission were included in the record.

Also corroborating the accuracy of the gospel accounts are the sermons from early Christianity recorded in the Book of Acts that I discussed earlier.[97] These discourses include important biographical details of Jesus' life that parallel the gospel accounts, especially Mark.[98] Paul similarly relies on details from Jesus' life in support of his moral teachings (Romans 15:3, 8; 2 Cor. 8:9; Philip. 2:6–11).[99]

MASS HALLUCINATION?

Dr. Geisler raises, and then refutes, claims that the apostles were delusional. Mass hallucination is not plausible, he says, because hallucination usually occurs when there is a readiness to believe in something, and the apostles were initially inclined to disbelieve the resurrection reports. Additionally, the apostles had known Jesus closely for years, so recognition was not an issue. Furthermore, Jesus had many conversations with different groups of people at different times, which makes this theory highly unlikely. The various numbers of witnesses at different times reporting the same thing, some of whom saw Christ numerous times, also argues against the theory.

Moreover, Jesus performed "many proofs" and "signs" in His resurrection appearances to demonstrate He was Who He said He was and to convince the disciples (John 20:30; Acts 1:3). Finally, there is no specific evidence or even a suggestion that they were subject to any hallucination or group self-deception.[100] Besides, hallucinations don't usually occur in mass. There is also the matter of the empty tomb, which the Jews didn't dispute, as I discuss in Chapter 11. If all this were a product of a mass hallucination, the Jews could have squashed Christianity at the very beginning by retrieving the body.

APPLYING THE RULES OF EVIDENCE

Dan Story further examines the reliability of the New Testament by applying fundamental principles of the law of evidence, which is particularly intriguing to me as a lawyer whose favorite course in law school happened to be Evidence. These rules are the ancient documents rules, the parol evidence rule, the hearsay rule, and the principle of cross-examination.[101]

The common law ancient documents rule presumes a document is truthful unless it is self-contradictory, inaccurate, or there is internal evidence of text tampering. The one challenging the document generally shoulders the burden of proof.[102] Unsolved problems or lack of clarity in the document don't necessarily invalidate it as erroneous or unreliable. Biblical textual criticism, says Story, has resulted in historical research resolving allegedly problematic passages in favor of the Bible's reliability. There are a number of excellent books dealing with difficult areas or "hard sayings" in the Bible, and careful examination of the overwhelming number of these passages yields satisfactory answers.[103]

The parol evidence rule provides that external, oral testimony or tradition will not be admitted into evidence to add to, subtract from, vary, or contradict an executed written instrument such as a will or a contract. This means the document, absent any applicable exceptions, will stand on its own. Dan Story explains that as applied to the examination of the reliability of Scripture, we should first try to use Scripture to help us interpret other Scripture. "In other words," Story says, "we give Scripture a fair hearing" just as we would with any other document. We don't bring our presuppositions into the mix, but allow the document to sink or swim on its own.

The hearsay rule precludes a witness from testifying as to what others may have said and, generally speaking, requires the witness to have firsthand knowledge of the matter to which he is testifying. As applied to the New Testament documents, this rule lends credence to New Testament authors who say they were eyewitnesses to the events they recorded.

The cross-examination principle holds that the more the testimony holds up once it is subjected to rigorous cross examination, the more credible we deem it to be, which, incidentally, is one reason for the hearsay rule, i.e., it excludes testimony from witnesses that can't be subjected to cross-examination. One particularly pertinent area where this applies to vindicate the New Testament is the testimony of the resurrection. Law professor and historian John Warwick Montgomery, who rigorously applied all these evidentiary rules to an examination of the Bible, finds that witnesses who were challenged to confirm having witnessed Jesus' resurrected body did so "in the very teeth of opposition, among hostile cross-examiners who would certainly have destroyed the case of Christianity" had such accounts been contradicted by the facts.[104]

Josh McDowell summarizes Montgomery's approach to New Testament examination as giving the document the benefit of the doubt, which is another way of saying the burden of proof is on the critic or challenger. So, Montgomery writes, "One must listen to the claims of the document under analysis, and not assume fraud or error unless the author disqualified himself by contradictions or known factual inaccuracies."[105] Applying this approach and similar ones, McDowell argues that we can't just assume that what appears to be a difficult passage constitutes a valid argument against it. We must be sure we correctly understand the passage using accepted rules of interpretation. It is common knowledge, writes McDowell, that countless problem areas have been fully resolved, sometimes, for example, through an archaeological find.

One example involves the biblical record of Assyrian king Sargon in Isaiah 20. Critics had declared, "There is no such king. The Bible has confused this man with Shalmaneser who initiated the siege of Samaria." But in the 1840s, Sargon's palace was uncovered at the village of Khorsabad, a few miles from ancient Nineveh in what is today Iraq. Among the battle descriptions found in the palace was the record of the exact military campaign against Ashdod that is referred to by Isaiah.[106] Likewise, Babylonian king Nebuchadnezzar, whose boasts about rebuilding Babylon were recorded in Daniel 4:30, was also unknown apart from the Bible until relatively modern excavations confirmed Daniel's account.[107]

A WORD ON ALLEGED INCONSISTENCIES AND CONTRADICTIONS

Many people are truly bothered by the alleged contradictions and inconsistencies in the Bible, as noted above. Critics have written extensively in attempts to discredit the Bible, and its defenders have responded by explaining certain difficult passages. Most alleged contradictions could very well result from our demanding more historical precision than the gospels ever intended to provide.[108] Furthermore, what appear at first to be inconsistencies are often fully explained on more careful examination. For example, today we might attribute a certain statement to the president when technically it has been delivered through his spokesman. So we should not assume a contradiction between Luke's account that the Gentile centurion requested, through Jewish intermediaries, a miracle from Jesus (Luke 7:6), and Matthew's version reporting that the centurion made the request personally (Matt. 8:5).

There are more problematic examples, but we should know that Bible students have always been aware of these issues. They have not been discovered by some new, sophisticated techniques that would have caused waves of unbelief had they been available long ago. The early Church fathers addressed these very issues, and Augustine even wrote a fifth-century commentary, *Harmony of the Gospels*, that discussed many of them. "Too often skeptics make it sound as if we know something today that our predecessors did not that *now* makes belief in the historical reliability of Scripture untenable," says Blomberg. "That claim is simply false."[109]

Bible scholar Dr. Gleason Archer has studied these issues in depth. In the *New International Encyclopedia of Bible Difficulties*, which analyzes hundreds of "problem passages," he avers,

> As I have dealt with one apparent discrepancy after another and have studied the alleged contradictions between the biblical record and the evidence of linguistics, archaeology, or science, my confidence in the trustworthiness of Scripture has

been repeatedly verified and strengthened by the discovery that almost every problem in Scripture that has ever been discovered by man, from ancient times until now, has been dealt with in a completely satisfactory manner by the biblical text itself—or else by objective archaeological information. The deductions that may be validly drawn from ancient Egyptian, Sumerian, or Akkadian documents all harmonize with the biblical record; and no properly trained evangelical scholar has anything to fear from the hostile arguments and challenges of humanistic rationalists or detractors of any and every persuasion. There is a good and sufficient answer in Scripture itself to refute every charge that has ever been leveled against it. But this is only to be expected from the kind of book the Bible asserts itself to be, the inscripturation of the infallible, inerrant Word of the Living God.[110]

Josh McDowell, in affirming that apparent contradictions have often been resolved in the Bible's favor, relates a story about his associate who was perplexed by seemingly conflicting accounts of the death of Judas Iscariot—the Book of Matthew says Judas hanged himself, while Acts reports that he fell headlong into a field and "his body burst open and all his intestines spilled out." The associate reasoned that the two accounts could only be reconciled if Judas hanged himself off the side of a cliff and the rope gave way and he fell into a field below. A few years later, Josh's friend visited the Holy Land and discovered that the traditional site of Judas' death happens to be a field at the bottom of a cliff outside Jerusalem.[111]

McDowell also offers a helpful summary of principles for understanding apparent discrepancies in the Bible.[112] Please consider these if you run across a difficult passage:

1. The unexplained is not necessarily unexplainable.
2. Fallible interpretations do not mean fallible revelation.
3. Understand the context of the passage.

4. Interpret difficult passages in light of clear ones.

5. Don't base teaching on obscure passages.

6. The Bible is a human book with human characteristics.

7. Just because a report is incomplete does not mean it is false.

8. New Testament citations of the Old Testament need not always be exact.

9. The Bible does not necessarily approve of all it records. (McDowell is saying here that just because the Bible sometimes records gruesome or unpleasant events doesn't mean that God, or the Bible writers, caused or approved of them.)

10. The Bible uses nontechnical, everyday language.

11. The Bible may use round numbers as well as exact numbers.

12. Note when the Bible uses different literary devices.

13. An error in a copy does not equate to an error in the original. (Biblical inerrancy, as I noted before, means that there were no errors in the autographs of Scripture, not that there were no errors in the copies).

14. General statements don't necessarily mean universal promises.

15. Later revelation supersedes previous revelation.[113]

At the very least, I want you to be aware of the abundance of scholarship that exists from conservative Christian scholars on every possible aspect of all these questions, from all the claimed difficulties in the Old Testament, to the alleged inconsistencies in the synoptic gospels—Mathew, Mark, and Luke—to the supposed problems in the Gospel of John, to the "hard sayings" of Jesus, to the alleged distortion of the gospel by Paul and how different his message supposedly is from that of Christ Himself and the gospel writers.

What you'll find is that almost all these alleged problems are not problems at all, and that there are not different versions of Christianity. There are some legitimate questions that deserve our attention, but these have legitimate answers. Far from the anti-intellectual stereotype attributed to Christians in our culture, there exists among us robust scholarship and thoughtful commentary across the board. If you encounter any of these difficulties on your own or through interaction with nonbelievers, I humbly suggest you explore some of the excellent resources covering these issues, including the following books:

- *New International Encyclopedia of Bible Difficulties* by Gleason Archer
- *Hard Sayings of the Bible* by Walter Kaiser Jr.
- *When Critics Ask* by Norman Geisler and Tom Howe, now sold under the title *The Big Book of Bible Difficulties*
- *Making Sense of the New Testament: Three Crucial Questions* by Craig Blomberg

JESUS' PROMISES ABOUT THE NEW TESTAMENT

In addition to vouching for the Old Testament as the inspired Word of God (see below), Jesus promises the same for the New Testament—a promise the New Testament writers claim to fulfill in their writings (John 20:31; 1 John 1:1). Jesus says that the Holy Spirit would help the New Testament writers to remember what He'd taught them and teach "all truth" (John 14:26; 16:13).[114]

RELIABILITY OF THE OLD TESTAMENT

The type of evidence that underlies the reliability of the New Testament serves the same purpose for the Old Testament: there is strong manuscript evidence, archaeological corroboration, and a reporting of history that Old Testament writers would have been unlikely to have created out of whole cloth.[115]

If the Hebrews were fabricating their own history, would they include so many self-damning stories, chronicling their consistent disobedience to God, Who had singled them out as the chosen people, entrusted the Law to them, and was present with them for instruction and guidance? Would they have revealed their leader, Moses, as lacking the self-confidence to speak God's Word to his people? Would they have included the account of his murdering an Egyptian? Would they have exposed King Saul as a petty paranoid? While portraying David as a man after God's heart, would they have tainted his reputation by describing his despicable adultery and his committing murder? How about his son Solomon, who on the one hand they describe as the world's wisest person, and on the other reveal to be something of a hypocrite?

In asserting that the Old Testament is both relevant and trustworthy, Old Testament scholar Walter Kaiser Jr. observes, "In every part of the Old Testament the writers claim the divine origin of their writings." See, for example, Exodus 31:18 and Deuteronomy 5:22; Moses' description of the Ten Commandments as "Stone tablets inscribed by the finger of God"; and the repeated use of the phrase, "The Spirit of the Lord spoke through His prophets, His word was on their tongues" (2 Samuel 23:2). Moreover, notes Kaiser, "The 39 books of the Old Testament were immediately received as authoritative and canonical." It is a myth that the Old Testament canon was not settled prior to the rabbinical council in Jamnia in 90 AD.[116]

Kaiser also argues, "The writers of the Old Testament were aware that they were writing not only for their generation but also for those who would come later. Peter acknowledges this in the New Testament, 'It was revealed to the (prophets of the Old Testament) that they were not serving themselves but you (people of Peter's generation and us).'"[117] Kaiser adds that the historical chronology found in the histories of the kings of Israel and Judah has been thoroughly validated. He cites the work of renowned archaeologist and Old Testament scholar Edwin Thiele, whose doctoral dissertation at the University of Chicago documents the Old Testament's historical authenticity.[118]

Writing in the 1920s about the historical validity of the Old Testament, H. H. Rowley had a few words for pseudo-sophisticated scoffers who had begun to rear their heads in his time. He wrote,

If we wish to be scientific, however, we must not be content with an irrational doubt that merely relieves us of what we do not find it convenient to accept. That is as unscientific as an unquestioning credulity. "There is no serious reason to doubt that a body of Israelites was once in Egypt and later came forth. This event was too deeply stamped in the memory and tradition of Israel to be totally groundless. There is no reason to doubt that Moses went into Egypt from the desert to bring them forth. No rational explanation of the creation of such a tradition can be offered, if it contained no truth. There is no reason to doubt that the deliverance of the Israelites was not affected by their own activity and power, but by forces beyond their control and beyond the control of Moses. No people would have invented the story that it and its leader were passive in the supreme moment of peril, if they were not. There is no reason to doubt that Moses promised deliverance in the name of Yahweh, and that after deliverance the people committed themselves to this God in a sacred covenant. If this is denied, we are left without any clue to much in the Old Testament that finds its simple explanation in terms of this. If all this story is denied any historicity, we have not only to explain how and why it came to be invented, but what was the true origin of that which is explained in this story, and why the true origin was wholly suppressed, leaving itself to be recreated out of nothing today. The way of the skeptic is much harder than the way of faith, and an unreasoning prejudice can lay no claim to be called scientific.[119]

RELIABILITY OF OLD TESTAMENT MANUSCRIPTS

Serious Old Testament criticism only arose in the late nineteenth century, as there were very few extant early Hebrew manuscripts. But the discovery of the Dead Sea Scrolls in 1947–1956 changed that. There are now more than 3,000 Hebrew manuscripts of the Old Testament,

8,000 of the Latin Vulgate, more than 1,500 of the Septuagint, and some
sixty-five copies of the Syriac Peshitta.[120] Let's take a look at how the
Old Testament has stood up to the test in terms of the transmission of
the manuscripts, textual criticism, and the primary sources.

TRANSMISSION OF THE
OLD TESTAMENT MANUSCRIPTS

Scholars assume that while some Old Testament material may have
been passed down from generation to generation orally, eventually it
was written down to preserve its accuracy. Certain biblical passages
speak to how highly the Hebrews regarded the Scriptures and believed
in their veracity (Exodus 17:14–16; 24:3–4, 7). God's Word was held in
such honor and deference that the stone tablets of the Ten Commandments were stored in the Ark of the Covenant (Exodus 25:16, 21; Heb.
9:4), and the Book of the Law was held in the tabernacle next to the ark
(Deut. 31:24–26). Moses ordered his people to teach God's laws and
statutes to their children (Deut. 4:9), and the Law was safeguarded by
the priests, who were instructed to teach the people (Deut. 33:10). They
were charged with reading it to the people every seven years to ensure
they would remember it (Deut. 31:9–11) and under strict orders not to
add or subtract from it (Deut. 31:9–11),[121] similar to Jesus' later admo-
nitions.

While certain Old Testament passages allude to written portions of
prophetic oracles and recorded histories, there is no mention of a collection of scriptural books until Daniel 9:2. Later writers, however, do refer
to earlier biblical books (2 Kings 14:6; 2 Chron. 25:4, 35:12; Ezra 3:2,
6:18; Neh. 8:1).[122]

No original manuscripts (autographs) remain because, as with the
New Testament, they were most likely written on papyrus or leather
scrolls that would have deteriorated in the damp climate, as opposed to
the dry climate of Egypt, which was more favorable for preservation.[123]
As Josh McDowell states, the main reason we have fewer Old Testament

manuscripts is a combination of antiquity and destructibility.[124] When the scrolls began to wear, the scribes would have scrupulously copied them and then reverently buried the originals, because they contained the sacred name of God.[125] There exist no manuscript copies dated before 400 BC.

To understand the practices of the ancient scribes, experts look at internal evidence from the Bible and to similar practices in the ancient Near East at the time the Old Testament books were being written. These both suggest the scribes were strongly committed to preserving the text. The fact that so many copies have survived intact demonstrates the scribes' commitment to safeguarding them.[126]

Old Testament scholar Gleason Archer says that we have objective evidence that any errors in transmission have not corrupted the substance of God's Old Testament revelation. He explains that a careful study of the variants (different readings) of the earliest manuscripts shows that not one affects a single scriptural doctrine. This is verifiable, he says, by comparing the variant versions found in the Hebrew manuscripts that exist anywhere—Dead Sea Scrolls or otherwise—and seeing that there are no significant alterations. "The vast majority of them are so inconsequential as to leave the meaning of each clause doctrinally unaffected."[127]

Such a record of accuracy, says Archer, distinguishes the Old Testament from any other pre-Christian works of literature. The *ESV Study Bible* says there are some significant variants, but they constitute less than 1 percent of the text and none of these affect any point of doctrine. Moreover, the variants are not hidden away and accessible only to scholars, but are indicated in the footnotes of the ESV and other modern English translations. According to the *ESV Study Bible*, "As a general assessment it is safe to say that the OT text that is the basis of modern English translations is remarkably trustworthy."[128]

Walter Kaiser agrees. "The Text of the Old Testament books was uniquely preserved when compared with other ancient writings," he says, adding, "The present literary form of the books comes to us from ancient times and in the final shape in which we presently possess them."[129]

THE DEAD SEA SCROLLS

As I mentioned, the discovery of the Dead Sea Scrolls was enormously significant because they included copies of the Old Testament dating from more than a century before the birth of Christ. Prior to this discovery, the oldest complete Hebrew manuscripts we had were dated from 900 AD and later. One of the Dead Sea scrolls was a complete copy of the Hebrew text of Isaiah dated around 125 BC. A comparison of that text with the previously oldest manuscript—the Masoretic Text, dated 916 AD—revealed extraordinary accuracy. For example, the Christ-centered chapter 53 of Isaiah contains 166 words and only seventeen letters of those words were at all in question. Ten were spelling differences, four were minor stylistic differences, and the remaining three involved the addition of the word "light" in verse 11, which has little effect on the meaning.[130] Gleason Archer says that though the two copies of Isaiah discovered in Qumran Cave 1 near the Dead Sea in 1947 pre-dated by a thousand years any copies we had, they were identical in more than 95 percent of the text, and the 5 percent of variants mainly consisted of spelling errors and obvious slips of the pen.[131]

Josh McDowell summarizes, "The thousands of Hebrew manuscripts, with their confirmation by the Septuagint and the Samaritan Pentateuch, and the numerous other cross-checks from outside and inside the text, provide overwhelming support for the reliability of the Old Testament text. Hence it is appropriate to conclude with [Sir Frederic] Kenyon's statement 'The Christian can take the whole Bible in his hand and say without fear or hesitation that he holds in it the true word of God, handed down without essential loss from generation to generation throughout the centuries.'"[132]

JESUS VALIDATES THE OLD TESTAMENT

Jesus affirms the authenticity of the Hebrew canon and instructs His disciples to honor it (Matt. 5:17–18). He and His disciples use the phrase "it is written" more than ninety times, signifying their unqualified affirmation of the Bible's authority.[133] In fact, He declares it to be imperishable: "Do not think that I have come to abolish the Law or the Prophets; I have not come to abolish them but to fulfill them. For truly, I say to you, until heaven and earth pass away, not an iota, not a dot, will pass from the Law until all is accomplished" (Matt. 5:17–18). He declares it to be inspired: "How is it then that David, speaking by the Spirit, calls him 'Lord'?" (Matt. 22:43). He says the Bible is unbreakable: "The Scripture cannot be broken" (John 10:35). He affirms the Old Testament as the Word of God (Matt. 15:3, 6; 5:17–18). He pronounces that it is supreme over tradition (Matt. 15:3, 6), and that, in effect, it is inerrant (Matt. 22:29).[134] He affirms Scripture's total truthfulness: "Thy word is truth" (John 17:17).

Further, by affirming as historically true a number of Old Testament events, He confirms the reliability of the Old Testament and its historicity in places where critics insist it is purely allegorical. He verifies the creation of Adam and Eve, the story of Jonah and the great fish, the flood, the slaying of Abel, the miracles of Elijah, and others.[135] By affirming the creation account, Norman Geisler argues, Jesus endorsed the scientific accuracy of the Old Testament.[136]

Having established the reliability of the Old and New Testaments by examining the manuscript evidence and the internal evidence of these writings, we turn in the next chapter to an examination of the external evidence—non-Christian sources and archaeology, which will further prove their reliability.

◇◇◇◇◇◇◇◇◇◇◇◇◇◇◇◇◇◇

CHAPTER 10

THE AMAZING BIBLE, PART 4: RELIABILITY AND EXTERNAL EVIDENCE

T he primary types of external evidence for the truth of Christianity and the Bible, and for proof that Jesus was a real-life historical figure, are non-biblical writers, including both secular and Christian sources, as well as archaeological discoveries. The evidence corroborating the Bible's authenticity in all these categories is plenteous.

NON-BIBLICAL CHRISTIAN EVIDENCE

Although it's hard to believe, some critics deny that Jesus existed at all. These contentions contradict abundant evidence from early Christian writers, even apart from the authors of the New Testament. Eusebius of Caesarea, in his *Ecclesiastical History*, recorded the writings of Papias, the Bishop of Heirapolis (130 AD), in which Papias relates sayings of the apostle John, whom he refers to as "the Elder." It is significant that Eusebius reports that Irenaeus, a second-century Church father and Bishop of Lyons, identifies Papias as a "hearer" of John's. Papias quotes John stating, "Mark having been the interpreter of Peter, wrote down accurately all that he (Peter) mentioned whether sayings or doings of Christ."[1] In the same book, Papias says that "Matthew composed his history in the Hebrew dialect."[2]

Irenaeus was a student of Polycarp, whom Irenaeus identifies as a disciple of John and an opponent of Gnosticism.[3] "So firm is the ground upon which these Gospels rest," Irenaeus writes, "that the very heretics themselves bear witness to them, and, starting from these (documents), each one of them endeavours to establish his own particular doctrine."[4] According to the *International Standard Bible Encyclopedia*, "Polycarp's traditional connection with John on the one hand and Irenaeus on the other makes Irenaeus' testimony to the apostolic authorship of the Fourth Gospel [John] a particularly weighty piece of evidence."[5]

Polycarp was martyred in 156 AD, at the age of eighty-six, for his relentless Christian faith. Josh McDowell rightly notes that Polycarp's martyrdom is powerful proof of his firm belief in the reliability of Scripture. When given the chance to renounce his faith and save his own life, he defiantly replied, "Eighty and six years have I served Him, and He hath done me no wrong. How can I speak evil of my king who saved me?"[6] Polycarp and Ignatius, who both wrote around 115 AD, referred to verses in the synoptic gospels as the words of Christ.[7]

There are plenty of other references by early Christians that help to verify the life of Christ and His teachings. Clement of Rome (95 AD) refers to the "Gospel," quotes portions found in all three synoptic gospels, and refers to them as the words of Jesus.[8] Likewise, Barnabas (ca. 135 AD) refers to the text of Matthew 22:14 as "Scripture" and quotes a portion that appears in all three synoptics as the apostles' "Gospel."[9]

NON-CHRISTIAN SOURCES

Jewish historian Josephus, close to the end of the first century, referred twice to Jesus in his *Jewish Antiquities*. In one section he writes, "James, the brother of Jesus who was called the Christ."[10] The modern translation of this work has Josephus affirming that Jesus was the Messiah, that He was resurrected on the third day, and that He might have been God. But this rendition is in doubt because Christians, not Jews, preserved the book, and many scholars believe they doctored the text to enhance its impact. Craig Blomberg, however, cites a growing scholarly consensus that while the passage was probably edited, Josephus did say that Jesus' followers reported seeing Jesus alive after His death on the cross and that He was *perhaps* the Messiah.[11] Even if later scribes altered the text, Josephus still provides "admissible testimony on the death of Jesus."[12]

There are also numerous references to Jesus from Greek and Roman historians. Julius Africanus quotes the first-century Greek historian Thallus, who speaks of the darkness that spread during Jesus' crucifixion.[13] And as noted in Chapter 9, the early second-century Roman legate Pliny the Younger wrote Emperor Trajan to ask his counsel on how to handle Christians who would not worship the emperor and who sang hymns "to Christ as if to a god."[14]

Roman historian Tacitus, writing in the early second century, reported that following Pilate's execution of Christ, the "pernicious superstition [Christianity] broke out afresh in Judea."[15] Around the same time, Roman historian Suetonius referred to Jews being expelled from Rome during the reign of Claudius because of a riot that had been incited by Chrestus. Interpreting Chrestus as a corrupted reference to Christ, most scholars regard this passage as evidence of internal tension in the Jewish community at the time due to evangelizing by Jewish Christians.[16]

Other examples abound. Mara bar Serapion, a Greek writer of the late first century, referred to Jesus as a "wise king" of the Jews.[17] Greek rhetorician Lucian of Samosata (c. 125–180 AD), in his *The Death of Peregrinus*, mocked Christians as those who come "after him whom they still worship—the man who was crucified in Palestine for introducing this new cult into the world."[18] Third-century Christian theologian Origen cites Celsus, one of Christianity's pagan critics, who acknowledged Jesus' existence and the reports concerning His divinity and resurrection, albeit while ridiculing and challenging them.[19]

Based on all these sources, it is somewhat ludicrous for anyone to deny that Jesus existed, and serious scholars don't. But some suggestively question why more wasn't written about such an influential figure. Professor Blomberg persuasively responds that in those days few could have predicted that Jesus would end up having the impact He has had on history. Moreover, before the twentieth century, historical writing focused mostly on rulers, military generals, officeholders, and the wealthy, but Jesus was none of those. Blomberg comments, in fact, that "we could argue that it is surprising that these non-Christian references to Jesus survived."[20]

EVIDENCE FROM ARCHAEOLOGY

Biblical archaeology is the scientific study, by excavation, examination, and publication, of the evidences of cultures and civilizations from the biblical period. Most Old Testament archaeology occurs in the land that encompassed ancient Israel, but it also takes place in the regions of the ancient empires in the Nile and Mesopotamian valleys. New Testament archaeology, by contrast, centers on a larger area comparable to the Roman Empire.[21] It encompasses the eastern Mediterranean, roughly tracing the spread of Christianity outward from the Holy Land, particularly the journeys of Paul. The primary areas of interest, then, are the modern states of Israel, Jordan, and Syria, followed by Turkey, Greece, and Italy.[22]

Little was known of Old Testament times before the advent of modern archaeology in the early nineteenth century. That's because Alexander the Great imposed the Greek language and customs on the vast lands he conquered, thus destroying the languages, cultures, and historical records of Old Testament–era civilizations such as ancient Egypt, Persia, Canaan, and Babylon. Greek historians, however, preserved substantial background material on the New Testament period.[23]

Fortunately for us, ancient civilizations left a rich historical record to be unearthed through archaeology. Ancient towns and cities were typically built near a water source or along trade routes. This made the homes, commonly built of sun-baked brick, vulnerable to floods, earthquakes, and enemy attacks. Once destroyed, towns were usually rebuilt directly over the rubble. As this process continued over time, a mound of earth would develop with layers of remnants of previous inhabitants—their buildings, tools, and pottery. These sites are called *tells*, which is Arabic for mounds. In excavating these tells, the archaeologist generally finds large stationary objects first, such as houses, monuments, tombs, and fortresses. Smaller artifacts usually follow, such as jewelry, tools, weapons, and cooking utensils. These remains help researchers validate or supplement what the Bible records.[24]

While the archaeological record can't confirm everything in the Bible, it does fill in many gaps and increase our knowledge of the life and customs of the people in those times. After all, writes Walter Kaiser, the "real role of archaeology is not to 'prove' the Bible, for that kind of 'proof' is available only in certain deductive sciences such as mathematics and logic." Instead, its role is threefold: to supply cultural, epigraphic, and artifactual materials that provide the background for Bible interpretation; to anchor recorded biblical events in the history and geography of the time; and to increase our confidence in God's revelation when the truth of the Bible is tied to historical events.[25]

"Over the last century or so, archaeology has strengthened the case for biblical reliability," says Kaiser. "Missing individuals, peoples, places and obscure customs, historical and political settings have been helpfully identified."[26] We know from archaeology, for example, that at the time of Abraham (2000 BC), there were many thriving cities throughout the ancient Near East. Sir Charles Leonard Woolley, in excavating Ur, the city where Abraham began his journey, discovered that the patriarch was surrounded by idolatry when God called him to begin a new nation. Archaeologists also believe they might have discovered Peter's house in Capernaum, referred to in Matthew 8:14.[27]

Hammurabi's Code—a Babylonian law code written on black stone and clay that was discovered in 1901—revealed some similarities in the intellectual and cultural heritage of the Hebrews and Babylonians. But it also confirmed that the Law of Moses neither borrowed from, nor was dependent on, the Babylonian laws that preceded it by some three centuries. The respective bodies of law had radically different origins and moral bases.[28]

NEW TESTAMENT ARCHAEOLOGY

More artifacts have been discovered to support the Old Testament than the New Testament because the Old Testament spans a much longer time period (2500 BC to 400 BC) than the New Testament (7 BC to 100 AD). Additionally, Old Testament civilizations used more permanent materials such as stone, and the older remains are buried deeper, all of which has given these artifacts a better chance to survive.[29] Nevertheless, there have been some remarkable archaeological finds corroborating the New Testament record.

In addition to confirming the historical existence of some one hundred biblical figures and dozens of biblical cities, archaeology has substantiated more than sixty historical details in the Gospel of John and eighty in the Book of Acts.[30] Hundreds of archaeological finds have confirmed the existence of specific people and events that were recorded in Luke's gospel and the Book of Acts, and were originally assumed to be incorrect. Luke's reliability as a historian is thus considered impeccable. "The Acts of the Apostles is now generally agreed in scholarly circles to be the work of Luke, to belong to the first century, and to involve the labors of a careful historian who was substantially accurate in his use of sources," notes Bible scholar and theologian Merrill Unger. "Attempts to impugn Luke's reliability have constantly been made, but most of these have been rendered futile by light from the monuments of antiquity and the archaeologist's spade."[31]

Luke's reliability is crucial in light of his authorship of Acts—the history of the early Church—as well as his gospel account. It is another reason to take him at his word when Luke begins his gospel by declaring his determination to provide an accurate historical account (1:1–4). Archaeology has demonstrated that Luke did, in fact, use the correct names for official titles, such as referring to rulers of Thessalonica as "politarchs" (Acts 17:8)[32] and calling Gallio the "Pro-consul of Achaea." He also correctly calls the Ephesian proconsul a "temple warden," among other examples.[33]

Scholars used to be skeptical of Luke's reference to "Lysanias the tetrarch of Abilene" as governing when John the Baptist began his ministry, but archaeological finds have vindicated him. The veracity of other New Testament references to Caesar and Herod has also been confirmed.[34] In addition, Luke's implication in Acts 14:6 that Iconium was in Phrygia had been disputed until an inscribed monument was discovered that validated Luke's account.[35] In *The Book of Acts in the Setting of Hellenistic History,* historian and classical scholar Colin Hemer conducts a detailed, critical study of Luke's historical references in Acts, concluding that Luke was indeed meticulous and reliable as a historian.[36]

Luke's accurate renditions of the titles of government officials, says New Testament professor Mark Strauss, are the equivalent of someone accurately distinguishing specific titles of our day such as "supervisor, councilor, mayor, governor, senator, representative, speaker of the house, vice president and president." Those who could identify these titles today would have significant knowledge of the workings of government, as Luke must have had in his day. In addition to being demonstrably attentive to historical detail, Luke, according to Strauss, has a keen sense of the Zeitgeist—the spirit of the times. He cites the example of Luke 3:2, where Luke identifies both Annas and Caiaphas as high priests in Israel, even though technically only Caiaphas served in that official capacity. But Luke obviously knew that Caiaphas' father-in-law Annas, a former high priest, remained the moving force in the priesthood.[37]

Norman Geisler and Frank Turek confirm that Hemer identifies eighty-four facts in the last sixteen chapters of Acts that have now been confirmed by historical and archaeological research.[38] Dr. Geisler writes elsewhere, "In all, Luke names thirty-two countries, fifty-four cities and nine islands without an error."[39]

A particularly fascinating discovery concerns Luke's disputed account of a riot breaking out in Jerusalem after Paul took a Gentile into the temple (Acts 21:28). As it turns out, two inscriptions were found in 1871 and 1935, respectively, that read, "No foreigner may enter within the barrier which surrounds the temple and enclosure. Anyone who is caught doing so will be personally responsible for his ensuing death."[40] Also disputed was Luke's account of a separate riot at Ephesus, wherein Luke refers to a civic assembly occurring in a theater (Acts 19:23–29). When the theater was excavated, it was discovered that it could hold 25,000 people and was the regular meeting place of the civic assembly.[41]

After exhaustively examining the references in Acts to trials, punishment, city government, and citizenship, Roman historian A. N. Sherwin-White found that without exception the "narrative agrees with the evidence of the earlier period." Concerning the authenticity of Luke's account in Acts, he writes, "Any attempt to reject its basic historicity even in matters of detail must now appear absurd."[42]

Sir William Ramsay, the famed archaeologist of Asia Minor, was the first to discover that the archaeological data confirms the New Testament, not the theories of critical scholars. When he embarked on an archaeological mission in the late 1800s he accepted the dogma of the Tubingen school that the Book of Acts was written later than conservative scholars claimed and was generally unreliable. He came away, however, thoroughly convinced of the essential reliability of the New Testament.[43] "I began with a mind unfavorable to it [Acts]," wrote Ramsay, "for the ingenuity and apparent completeness of the Tübingen theory had at one time quite convinced me. It did not lie then in my line of life to investigate the subject minutely; but more recently I found myself often brought into contact with the book of Acts as an authority for the topography, antiquities, and society of Asia Minor. It was gradually borne in upon me that in various details the narrative showed marvelous truth."[44] Elsewhere Ramsay declared, "The present writer takes the view that Luke's history is unsurpassed in respect of trustworthiness." He was "describing what reasons and arguments changed the mind of one [himself] who began under the impression that the history was written long after the events and that it was untrustworthy as a whole."[45]

Another interesting find was made at Delphi, where an inscription was discovered that helps date the arrival of the proconsul Gallio at Corinth (mentioned above) in the summer of 51 AD, which would mean that Paul visited there in 50 AD—a fact that helps date that portion of his journey (Acts 18:11–17).[46] Further digs in sites along Paul's journeys—Corinth, Athens, Philippi, and Ephesus—help anchor his accounts in history.[47] Paul's claim to being a free Roman citizen was corroborated by archaeological discoveries confirming that Tarsians had been granted citizenship status.[48] Discovery of the huge temple of Artemis (Diana) in

Ephesus also supports Paul's account of his evangelical activities in that area (Acts 19).[49] Furthermore, in the Book of Romans, Paul refers to Erastus as the city treasurer of Corinth (16:23). Accordingly, when Corinth was excavated in 1929 a pavement was found with the inscription, "Erastus, curator of public buildings, laid this pavement at his own expense." Bible scholar F. F. Bruce concludes that this is the man to whom Paul referred.[50]

Archaeological finds have similarly shored up the authenticity of the gospels. As Colin Peckham notes, "New Testament scholarship has often been plagued with extremism [from critics] but archaeological research has brought balance and a more accurate understanding to the whole scene."[51] For example, there was no record of the court where Pilate tried Jesus (John 19:13), but discoveries have revealed that the trial took place in the court of the Tower of Antonia, which was the Roman military headquarters in Jerusalem. The name of Pilate was also found on a stone in the Roman theater at Caesarea.[52] Additionally, in 1990, archaeologists working in Jerusalem's Peace Forest accidentally discovered an ossuary (a bone chest) with inscriptions "Caiaphas" and "Joseph, son of Caiaphas." The Bible records that Caiaphas was the high priest in Jerusalem the year that Jesus died, having served between 18 AD and 36 AD and who, along with Pilate, was involved in the trials and crucifixion of Jesus.[53] This means that we very likely have the bones of the man who presided at Jesus' trial and whom the gospel writers viewed as the primary priestly foe of Jesus, and who showed his willingness to sacrifice Jesus in order to achieve peace and tranquility in Israel.[54] All of these finds have helped authenticate John's gospel as historically accurate, as have many other discoveries, such as the Well of Jacob (John 4:12),[55] the Pool of Bethesda with five porches (5:1–4), and the Pool of Siloam (9:7), to which Jesus sent a blind man.[56]

Jesus predicted the temple would be destroyed (Matt 24:1ff.; Mark 13:1ff.; Luke 21:5ff.), and His prophecy was fulfilled within a generation (in 70 AD) following a Jewish revolt against Nero's Rome. Archaeological finds have confirmed the thorough devastation, including evidence of thick layers of ash, Roman catapult balls from below the Convent of the Sisters of Zion, and the skeletal remains of a woman. According to Edwin Yamauchi, the huge ashlars that were toppled from the parapet of the Royal Stoa crashed with such impact that they buckled the road pavement below the temple platform.[57] Not one synagogue of the early Roman period survived the attack.[58]

For years, critical scholars often placed the Gospel of John in the second half of the second century, which would mean it was not a legitimate, eyewitness account. But their pessimism was dealt a fatal blow with the discovery of the John Rylands fragment (mentioned in Chapter 9), published in 1935, which contains five verses from John dated between 100 and 150 AD.[59]

As we saw in Chapter 9, critics have also claimed that Christianity isn't so unique—that it was strongly influenced by mysterious Eastern religions. Archaeological finds in Palestine, Syria, and Egypt, however, have undermined these charges as well. While Jewish synagogues, Christian churches, and heathen temples have been uncovered, no evidence has been found of these mystery sects.[60]

OLD TESTAMENT ARCHAEOLOGY

As with the New Testament, archaeological finds have helped illuminate and validate the Old Testament and its historicity. Joseph Holden and Norman Geisler, in *The Popular Handbook of Archaeology and the Bible*, present an impressive table of dozens of Old Testament persons confirmed by archaeology, from King Ahab to King Uzziah, which should convince any objective reader of the value of biblical archaeology and the reliability of the Old Testament as history.

There are many other valuable resources chronicling Old Testament archaeological discoveries. The following is a sampling of some of the more interesting and relevant ones.

Egyptian Pharaoh Shishak

1 Kings 14:25–26 describes an attack on Israel by Egyptian Pharaoh Shishak at the end of the tenth century BC. Megiddo was one of the cities he captured, and excavators uncovered an inscribed pillar (known

as a "stele") at the site that contains two common titles for Shishak. These pillars were often set up by pharaohs to claim a conquered area as a subject state.[61]

Black Stele

Advocates of "higher criticism" were confident that the Pentateuch—the first five books of the Bible—couldn't have been written by Moses because they believed writing did not yet exist in his time. Therefore, they alleged, these books must have been assembled centuries after Moses died and fraudulently ascribed to him. But in 1901 a black stele containing Hammurabi's Code was discovered, as noted above, with writing that preceded Moses by at least three hundred years.[62]

Ebla Tablets

In the 1970s, archaeologists in Syria discovered documents written on clay tablets in the ancient kingdom of Ebla, which existed a thousand years before Moses. The documents, written in about 2300 BC, not only verify the existence of early writing, but corroborate names of persons and places described in the first five Old Testament books. Critics had assumed, for example, that "Canaan" was incorrectly used in Genesis, but the word is found in the Ebla Tablets. Likewise, the word for "the deep" appearing in Genesis 1:2—*tehom*—was once believed to have originated long after Genesis was written, but this term too appears in the tablets.[63]

Mesopotamian Roots

The Bible teaches that Israel derives its ancestry from Mesopotamia (Gen. 11:27–12:4), the place from which God called Abram (later Abraham) to leave and eventually go to Canaan. Archaeological discoveries seem to vindicate the biblical record.[64] J. A. Thompson, in *The Bible and*

Archaeology, writes, "There is good evidence that the area was occupied by Semites at an early date. It is not at all unlikely, therefore, that a Semite like Abraham should come from southern Mesopotamia, although we may not be able to tell the precise Semitic group from which he came."[65]

Patriarchal Names and Towns

Researchers have confirmed that personal names such as Abraham, Isaac, and Jacob were current names in the areas referred to in the Bible. The Amorites, for example, routinely used the names Jacob and Isaac. We also have contemporary evidence about towns mentioned in the biblical records such as Ur and Nahor. We find these names exactly in these areas of Mesopotamia where the biblical records place the homes of the patriarchs, writes Austrian Old Testament scholar J. A. Thompson. He adds, "We may conjecture that a good deal of contact took place between Palestine and these lands to insure a continuity of culture."[66]

Single Language and Babel

According to both Norman Geisler and Josh McDowell, there is now considerable evidence that there was at one time a single language on earth, as the Bible suggests. Not only are there references in Sumerian literature to this, but also, say Geisler and McDowell, archaeology has revealed that an ancient king of Ur named Ur-Nammu, who ruled from 2044 to 2007 BC, was ordered to build a great temple tower, or "ziggurat," in honor of the moon god Nannat. One clay tablet shows him honoring the gods in beginning the construction of the tower, and another shows the tower was thrown down because it offended the gods, and the people were scattered and their speech was made strange. If true, this story has striking similarities to the Genesis record. Additionally, numerous modern philologists believe in a common origin for all the world's languages.[67]

Enuma Elish

~~~~~~~~~~~~~~~~~~~~

While uncovering the famous library of Assyrian King Ashurbani-pal, archaeologists discovered a collection of cuneiform tablets telling a story of creation. The original written form of this Babylonian epic is dated in the third millennium BC, a thousand years before Genesis. This, of course, delighted critics, who lurched to the conclusion that Genesis copied the Babylonian account, known as the Enuma Elish.

There are similarities between the two accounts, but a more thoughtful examination, says Dr. Eugene Merrill, reveals that the differences are far more pronounced.[68] The Genesis creation story, of course, involves a monotheistic God, whereas the Enuma Elish describes a pantheon of gods. While the God of the Bible is omnipotent and loving, the gods of the Mesopotamian myths are petty and vengeful. Perhaps most important, the Bible teaches that God created the universe out of nothing, while Enuma Elish tells that creation came from something pre-existing and evil. Another important point is that scholars have established that mythical stories tend to become more mythical over time, rather than the other way around. Yet the Genesis account is simpler, more historical, more believable, and altogether less fantastic than the Enuma Elish.[69]

The Epic of Gilgamesh and the Flood

~~~~~~

Just as with the creation accounts, critics have long argued that the Bible's flood story was borrowed from an earlier myth—in this case, the Mesopotamian Epic of Gilgamesh. Joseph Holden and Norman Geisler, however, offer five main arguments for the originality of the Genesis story:

1. The religions are so radically different. The polytheistic gods of the Mesopotamian culture are arbitrary, selfish, and constantly at war with one another, while the God of the Bible loves His creation.

2. The mythical gods create man because they need him to give offerings, but the Bible teaches that man needs God, not the other way around.

3. The mythical religions teach that man begins as dysfunctional and progresses in a positive direction, whereas the Bible teaches the fall of mankind.

4. The reasons given for the flood in the mythical account, unlike the Genesis account, had nothing to do with man's moral state, but were more a matter of the gods being disturbed by man's annoying noises and overpopulation.

5. As with the creation stories, scholars believe myths tend to become more mythical over time, but the Genesis story is less mythical, more natural, and simpler.[70]

Sodom and Gomorrah

While many critics used to believe the biblical story of the destruction of Sodom and Gomorrah was fictitious, modern evidence has revealed that the five cities mentioned in the Bible were actually centers of commerce in the geographical area where Sodom and Gomorrah stood. An archaeological survey reported by W. Rast and T. Schaub in 1973 pointed out parallels between sites and findings from the Ghor (valley or plain) southeast of the Dead Sea, and information known about the Cities of the Plain from Genesis 14–19. In that survey, five relatively similar sites were located that all dated to the end of the Early Bronze Age—late in the third millennium BC (about the time of Abraham). There is now evidence that violent earthquakes occurred in the area, throwing layers of earth high into the air and resulting in heavy amounts of bitumen.[71]

One of the sites, Numeira, which some believe to have been Gomorrah (and there is a linguistic connection in the names as well), was destroyed twice, the first time by fire. In the Bible, Sodom and Gomorrah were involved in a recorded event—Genesis Chapter 14—before they were famously destroyed in Chapters 18 and 19. Chapter 14 describes a battle wherein Sodom and Gomorrah led a coalition of western kings against armies of the eastern kings. The eastern kings, after defeating the western armies, plundered Sodom and Gomorrah and took prisoners, including Abraham's nephew Lot, and it was apparently common for ancient kings to burn cities they had vanquished. The evidence isn't conclusive, of course, but it is consistent with what easily could have occurred. Bryant G. Wood first suggested this scenario in *Bible and Spade* magazine in 1983.

There is abundant evidence for the final destruction of Numeira, particularly in the residential area. There is a great amount of ash where residential rooms were severely impacted with debris, which indicates burning. An excavation in 1981, following those in earlier years, revealed that "the entire area was covered by the ashy debris of the final destruction of the town, up to .4 meters in depth. The ash contained fragments of wooden beams that had supported the roofs of the dwellings and lay immediately over the latest occupational layer within each room, sealing the material beneath it. Not infrequently there was mudbrick detritus over the ash, which had resulted from the collapse of the mudbrick superstructures after the final conflagration."[72]

The Bible states that Sodom and Gomorrah were finally destroyed by a fire initiated by God and refers to fire and brimstone raining down on the cities. According to William Shea, "All of the natural elements necessary to produce such a destruction (geological fault line, petroleum, salt) are present in the area for God to have used if He chose."[73]

Tel Dan Stele and Merneptah Stele

Critics have long disputed the historicity of King David. But in 1993, Avraham Biran of Hebrew Union College discovered a ninth-century-BC Aramaic inscription at Tel Dan in northern Israel confirming that Israel had a dynastic founder named David ("House of David") who ruled before the eighth century.[74] It is the first extra-biblical reference to Israel's King David. This find was bolstered by other ones, such as the Mesha Stele, which also contains the phrase "House of David."[75] A separate inscription, known as the Merneptah Stele, contains the earliest extra-biblical mention of the name "Israel," in the context of an Egyptian pharaoh boasting of a victory over Israel around 1230 BC. This find shows that the Israelites were already in the promised land at that time.[76]

The Hittites

The Hittites, whose rule extended to Syria and Lebanon, are mentioned in the Bible some fifty times. But very little was known about them before modern times, and some critics thought they never existed. Around 1900, however, archaeologists discovered the ancient Hittites' large capital city of Hattusa about ninety miles east of Ankara, Turkey.[77]

Canaanite Gods

Archaeologists discovered hundreds of stories on clay tablets among the ruins of the ancient city of Ugarit, in modern Syria, about the Canaanite gods and goddesses that figured so prominently in the Old Testament accounts of idolatry. (Num. 25; 1 Kings 11; Jer. 23; Hosea 13).[78]

Pool at Gibeon

In 1956, six miles north of Jerusalem, excavators discovered a largely intact pool in Gibeon that was dated prior to 1000 BC. This corresponds to the biblical description of the great water pool at Gibeon (Samuel 2:13; Jer. 41:12).[79]

Samaria

Excavations have uncovered large parts of Samaria, the capital of ancient Israel's Northern Kingdom, and determined it to be extravagant, prosperous, and strong, which corresponds to biblical accounts (1 Kings 16:24; 2 Kings 6:22; 2 Chron. 18).[80]

Hazor

The Bible describes Hazor as "the head" city of the Israelites, as it was the biggest city in ancient Israel. Archaeologists have found that it spanned two hundred acres, which would justify the biblical description (Joshua 11).[81]

The Cyrus Cylinder

Archaeologists found a nine-inch-long clay cylinder from ancient Babylon, dating to 539 BC, telling of King Cyrus of Persia's conquest of Babylon and his critical decree to let Babylonian captives return to their lands and restore their temples. This is similar to his decree that the Jews would be freed and allowed to rebuild Jerusalem, as detailed in Chapter 8. This discovery doesn't verify the decree on the Jews, but it implies a pattern that lends credence to the biblical record.[82]

There are so many exciting archaeological discoveries that vindicate the biblical record, and I have only begun to scratch the surface here. There are several books and other publications solely devoted to archaeology and the Bible that go much further. But I trust I've shared enough to demonstrate that this is an exciting field that has done much to strengthen our assurance that in its recording of historical events, the Bible is accurate and authentic. In the next chapter we will examine the subject of truth—what it is and how it has come under assault—as well as proofs for God's existence and miracles, including the greatest miracle of all: the resurrection of Jesus Christ, the Son of God.

CHAPTER 11

TRUTH, MIRACLES, AND THE RESURRECTION OF CHRIST

DOES TRUTH EXIST?

U ntil recently, it would have seemed absurd to discuss whether truth exists. But with the advent of the postmodern era and with the culture's concomitant assaults on the very concept of truth, the subject has become an integral part of apologetics. Indeed, Norman Geisler and Frank Turek's proof for Christianity originally contained ten points, but as they presented their case around the country, they encountered so much resistance to the very idea of truth that they added two points to address the subject.

Postmodernism—which originated in aesthetics, architecture, and philosophy—is difficult to define. As apologist Amy Orr-Ewing observes, a postmodern perspective questions "the possibility of clear meaning or truth," and it "approaches art, science, literature, and philosophy with a pessimistic, disillusioned outlook."[1]

Understanding postmodernism is important for successful evangelizing; in order to reach people, we have to speak the same "language" as
they do. We will have great difficulty trying to convince people of Christianity's truth claims if they deny that truth even exists and we are unable
to convince them otherwise. So in this chapter I address the subject of
truth, the postmodern challenges to truth, the philosophical proofs for
the existence of God, the possibility of miracles, and finally, the miraculous resurrection of Jesus Christ.

Many Christian apologists now address the subject of postmodernism seriously. Ravi Zacharias eloquently discusses truth and postmodernism in his writings and lectures, while Geisler and Turek, as noted,
have added truth to their twelve-point proof for Christianity. Stated
affirmatively, Geisler and Turek say, "Truth about reality is knowable."[2]
The subject is hardly frivolous, for the Bible itself not only affirms truth
and its embodiment in Jesus Christ—"the Way, the Truth, and the
Life"—but the entirety of the Christian religion depends on the reality
of objective truth. As Dr. Carl F. H. Henry writes in the six-volume
treatise *God, Revelation and Authority*, truth is "Christianity's most
enduring asset."[3]

The Bible plainly states that God is sovereign and has absolute
authority over His creation (1 Samuel 2:6; Psalms 24:1, 50:10, 135:6).
This means all the Bible's revelations and the entirety of its moral teachings are absolutely true and right. Truth and ethics don't blow in the
wind; they are unchanging and timeless (Romans 2:13; Exodus 20).[4]
Note that Paul tells the Philippians to meditate on whatever things are
true. Furthermore, according to Paul, truth stands over against falsehood
(Eph. 4:25), has its norm in God (Romans 3:4), goes hand in hand with
goodness, righteousness, and holiness (Eph. 4:24, 5:9), is climaxed in
gospel-truth (Eph. 1:13, 4:21; Col. 1:5–6), and belongs to the armor of
the Christian soldier (Eph. 6:14).[5]

In 1 Corinthians, Paul writes a particularly arresting passage that
emphasizes the indispensability of historical truth to Christianity: "If
Christ has not been raised, our preaching is useless and so is your faith.
More than that, we are then found to be false witnesses about God, for
we have testified about God that he raised Christ from the dead. But he

did not raise him if in fact the dead are not raised. For if the dead are not raised, then Christ has not been raised either. And if Christ has not been raised, your faith is futile; for you are still in your sins. Then those who have fallen asleep in Christ are lost. If only for this life we have hope in Christ, we are of all people most to be pitied" (15:14–19). Notice how vigorously Paul asserts the historical, factual truth of the resurrection; in his view, if it didn't actually happen, then the entire foundation of Christianity crumbles and anyone who adheres to it is a pathetic fool.

Overall, the existence of objective truth is essential to Christianity because the reality of its truth claims is essential. If Christianity is not objectively true, and if Christ is not "the Truth," then Christianity is a sham. Unfortunately, the challenge of proving Christianity's truth claims becomes more difficult when the concept of truth itself is under attack. But thankfully, as we shall see, attacking the concept of truth is logically self-defeating.

CONFUSION LEADS TO BEWILDERMENT

Christian philosopher Francis Schaeffer was ahead of his time in recognizing the dangers of postmodernism and moral relativism. Writing in 1982, he noted that people were looking at truth differently. Young people in Christian homes were trained in the "old framework of truth," he observed, but when they entered society at large they became confused and overwhelmed by the newer alternatives. This confusion spread throughout our entire culture, affecting not only children but pastors, Christian educators, evangelists, and even missionaries. With alarm Schaeffer wrote, "So this change in the concept of the way we come to knowledge and truth is the most crucial problem, as I understand it, facing Christianity today."[6]

Dr. Carl F. H. Henry echoes that lament. "No fact of contemporary Western life is more evident than its growing distrust of final truth and its implacable questioning of any sure word," he argues. "The prevalent mood, as Langdon Gilkey tells us, is 'skeptical about all formulations of ultimate coherence or ultimate meaning, speculative as well as theological,' and 'doubts the possibility both of philosophical knowing and religious faith.'"[7]

People used to unquestioningly share the same presuppositions about the existence of absolutes and absolute truths. "They took it for granted that if anything was true, the opposite was false," Schaeffer contends. But there has been a radical change in the very concept of truth. "Wherever you look today, the new concept holds the field.... On every side you can feel the stranglehold of this new methodology...the way we approach truth and knowing."[8] Sadly, however, many people aren't even aware they are succumbing to this intellectual and moral nihilism.

I personally have found this to be true, having encountered people who maintain that two mutually contradicting propositions can both be true, or that the competing truth claims of various religions can all be reconciled in a mythical world where faux tolerance and blinding pluralism are the supreme values. They often defend their outlook as an expression of individualism, with arguments such as, "I don't feel comfortable when you talk about 'truth' per se. What is true for you may not be true for me."

PREMODERNISM, MODERNISM, AND POSTMODERNISM

Many historians and sociologists recognize three main historical periods—the premodern, modern, and postmodern.[9] The premodern period was a time when people believed in the rationality and order of the universe. There was little, if any, secularization, and people's everyday reality typically had a supernatural component, usually manifested in a belief in some kind of god.[10] A prime example of premodernism was the era of Christendom in Western culture prior to the modern era.[11] While there was no clean break between the premodern and modern periods, premodern thought was first shaken by the Renaissance period, which included both Christian and non-Christian elements, and later by the Reformation, which destabilized Christendom and split it into Catholic and Protestant camps.[12]

The modern era, which followed the Reformation in the seventeenth century, is generally associated with the Enlightenment, which was characterized by an emphasis on human reason.[13] Whereas the Reformation challenged certain Roman Catholic doctrines and papal practices, modernists challenged Christianity itself and attacked the authority of divine revelation.[14] They agreed with the premoderns that objective reality and objective truth exist in the material world, but pushed aside the supernatural. Everything could be explained by rational thought and modern science; nothing was outside their grasp.

Ultimately, however, modernism was distinguished from premodernism by the concept of humanism. Whereas God had traditionally been considered central and supreme, with the advent of humanism, the human being became the center of reality. Alongside humanism, naturalism and materialism were also in ascendance,[15] and these spawned some of the most influential theories of the nineteenth and twentieth centuries—Darwinian evolution would purport to explain the development of biological systems; human behavior would be understood through Freudian psychology; and Marxism would interpret historical and economic events in the context of the material world. If nothing else, these ideologies shared a self-important arrogance in providing all-encompassing explanations for the questions they claimed to answer.[16]

In the mid-to-late 1900s, modernism was eclipsed by postmodernism and its assault on the concept of truth. Postmodernism, which found a bastion of support in academia, involves what Jean-Francois Lyotard calls an "incredulity towards metanarratives"[17]—that is, it rejects overarching stories of humankind into which all the more particular narratives fit. It denies the modernist metanarratives of progress and history, including, for example, Marx's theory that history inevitably progresses in a certain direction. It also rejects the biblical metanarrative of salvation history: creation–the Fall–redemption–new creation.[18] Amy Orr-Ewing points out the fallacy of this approach of rejecting metanarratives: "The fundamental problem with this challenge to the Bible—this suspicion of authority and rejection of metanarrative—is that it is essentially inconsistent. That is, we soon discover when probing this denial of overarching stories that an exception is made for the overarching idea that there are no overarching ideas! Postmodern skeptics critique all worldviews except their own."[19]

Postmodern challenges to truth sometimes find expression in the rise of literary theories such as deconstructionism, which essentially posits that it's not the author who determines the meaning of a text, but each individual reader who decides for himself what the meaning is. French philosopher Jacques Derrida famously "deconstructed" texts to deny them any authority, and these methods have been used on the Bible.[20] Instead of the world having inherent meaning through God's work and through the life, death, and resurrection of Jesus Christ, each person decides for himself what the meaning is. A postmodernist approach says the Bible is true to the extent it is found meaningful or spiritually inspiring for the individual believer, but not in any kind of objective sense, because objectivity is brushed aside in favor of radical subjectivity. Postmodern ideas have now moved from literature to philosophy, effectively making the whole world, in the words of one professor, "a kind of deconstructed text."[21] Postmodernism, according to its adherents, left modernism and Enlightenment thinking behind.

Enlightenment ideas, for all their faults, proclaimed the objectivity of truth and the universality of reason. Postmodernism, in full flower, says there is no truth, that truth is a completely deconstructed concept that alights on the shifting sands of relativism. Along these lines, Richard Rorty developed the idea of philosophical pragmatism, which holds that truth is determined by whether it works for us. It's not permanent or objective, it's just a function of its utilitarian value to us, analogous to Derrida's ideas on the truthfulness and authority of texts. According to Rorty, words refer only to other words, not to anything "extralinguistic" (that is, not included within the realm of language or linguistics). He further argues that statements find their justification not in an objective truth, but in "solidarity" with a community that defines truth.[22]

Adherents of postmodernism dismiss the elevation of science and reason as modernist myths and cultural inventions of the powerful and the dominant. Truth for them is a mere political tool by which the powerful control the powerless. Similarly, rationality is a white male construct, and progress merely serves the interests of the dominant culture.

I encountered postmodern ideas in a college criminology class back in the early seventies. The primary textbook for the course was *The Social Reality of Crime*, which essentially argued that the concept of crime is a construct used by society's powerful and privileged to control others. Criminals weren't actually dangerous outlaws; rather, society's powerbrokers defined crime in such a way as to criminalize those it wanted to subjugate. My professor was a delightful man, but with all due respect, these types of postmodern ideas have always struck me as unadulterated psychobabble.

It should be noted that while postmodern theories characterize the current era and have deeply impacted our culture and our scholastic life, they are by no means the subject of universal acclaim. To the contrary, a large majority of Americans still profess Christianity, while millions of others believe in other religions or adhere to various modernist theories that are antithetical to the postmodern worldview.

POSTMODERNISM: THE LOGICAL EXTENSION OF MODERNISM?

Postmodernism and modernism share certain orientations, such as their general rejection of a theistic worldview. Postmodern thinkers—Rorty, Derrida, Foucault, Lyotard, and Baudrillard—all reject God, which squares with late forms of modernism that even abandoned deism as they progressed into agnosticism or atheism.[23] Both modernism and postmodernism also largely embrace philosophical naturalism, which assumes that supernaturalism is fictitious and that the material universe is all that exists.

But the two belief systems diverge on the issue of objective reality, as we've noted. Douglas Groothuis argues, however, that postmodernism, while different from modernism and rejecting certain aspects of it, "is, in many ways, modernism gone to seed, carried to its logical conclusion and inevitable demise."[24] That is, postmodernism is, at least in part, a reaction against the rationalist idea that all truth must be scientifically proven. While rationality and scientific inquiry are valid means of taining objective truth, says Groothuis, their adherents went too far, exaggerating their theories to the point of falsehood. "It was believed that human reason could be completely objective," states Groothuis, "that scientific study defines the limits of knowledge (scientism), and that progress is inevitable when science and reason are our tools."[25]

But Groothuis also observes that postmodernism wasn't just a reaction to the exaggerated elements of modernism—the near deification of reason and science—but also a reaction to the *false* elements in modernism that essentially denied objective truth outside the realm of naturalism. The ideas of God and spirituality became empty words devoid of objective referents. Thus, modernist thinking laid the groundwork for attacks on the Bible. From there, the relativizing of moral values was inevitable, argues Groothuis. So while modernism flourished, much of the cultural elite embraced moral relativism—the notion that morals are devised by cultures, not laid down by God—and postmodernism has popularized it even further.[26]

Christians who downplay the dangerous appeal of postmodernism should consider polling done by George Barna, who reported way back in 1994 that 72 percent of respondents agreed with the statement, "There is no such thing as absolute truth; two people could define truth in totally conflicting ways, but both could be correct."[27] Barna's more recent polling found that only 9 percent of all American adults have a biblical worldview, and only 19 percent of so-called born again Christians actually possess what Barna describes as a Christian worldview.[28]

"IT BEGAN IN THE GARDEN OF EDEN"

The first inklings of postmodernism are sometimes attributed to German skeptic Friedrich Nietzsche. Proclaiming "the death of God," Nietzsche criticized Enlightenment philosophers for retaining Christian moral principles and Christianity's belief in an orderly, rational universe even as they expunged God from their belief systems.[29] I believe Nietzsche was on to something here, for modern anti-theists such as Richard Dawkins and the late Christopher Hitchens often argued that man can be moral on his own without having to borrow from Christianity, which they blamed, along with other religions, for much of the evil and violence throughout world history.

Ravi Zacharias argues that postmodernism began in the Garden of Eden, when the tempter asked, "Has God really said this?" This is when man first ignored God's word and took it upon himself to become the authority.[30] And Pontius Pilate certainly foreshadowed postmodern thought when he asked Jesus, "What is truth?"

"EVERYONE SUBSCRIBES TO A CORRESPONDENCE VIEW OF TRUTH"

Ultimately, postmodernism leads to intellectual chaos and, if its roots are planted deeply enough, moral anarchy. By asserting the right of individuals to define their own "truth," it undermines objective truth and the very basis of reality.[31] Francis Schaeffer observes that "when a man is lost, he is lost against all that there is, including what he is." Every such lost person lives in the real world and must somehow reconcile his internal presuppositions to the external world he experiences. "He may let the pendulum swing back and forth between them," Schaeffer states, "but he cannot live in both places at once."[32] Alister McGrath, paraphrasing Schaeffer, says that man "lives with a foot in each of two worlds—the real, external world characterized by its depth and complexity, and an internal world of thought, shaped by a longing for understanding, love, and significance. If these two worlds stand in tension with each other, an individual cannot live meaningfully. There must be a correspondence between our experience of the external world and our internal world."[33]

Regardless of how prevalent we believe the postmodern influence to be, it has undoubtedly done great damage to our intellectual heritage by eroding the concept of truth. Today, we've even lost confidence that statements of fact are more than mere opinions.[34] So we must return to the questions that modern apologetics now needs to address: What is truth? Is truth about reality knowable? Is truth absolute?

The correspondence theory of truth holds that what one thinks is true is indeed true when it matches what is real. In other words, truth corresponds to reality,[35] and things that fail to correspond to reality are false. As Dr. Geisler says, "Truth tells it like it is, it corresponds to the facts; it matches its object. False is what does not tell it like it is, correspond to the facts, or match its object."[36] Efforts to deny the correspondence theory of truth are self-defeating because one cannot deny it without using it—those who deny it assume their view corresponds to reality. So, in a sense, everyone holds to a correspondence view of truth, whether or not they realize it.[37]

The fact that we can't always identify the truth with absolute certainty doesn't mean an absolutely certain truth does not exist. If one courtroom witness says he saw the defendant shoot another man, and another witness says the defendant did not shoot the man, that discrepancy does not alter the objective reality—whatever it is—as to whether the defendant shot the victim. He either did or he didn't, even if others may never know for sure.

Here's a related example: recently I was explaining to my daughter that I believe Christ is the Son of God, and that some people don't believe that is true. Either I am right or the people who disagree with me are right, but our respective beliefs have no effect on what the truth actually is. If Jesus is the Son of God, He is whether or not I, you, or anyone else in the world believes Him to be so. One's opinion, no matter how sincerely he holds it, does not alter objective reality. It's meaningless to say that it can be true for me that Jesus is the Son of God but not for you. He either is or He isn't.

THE LAW OF NONCONTRADICTION

An important corollary to the proposition that truth is knowable and that it corresponds to the facts is what is known as the law of noncontradiction. The second of Geisler's and Turek's twelve-point proof, this proposition simply asserts that the opposite of true is false. Thus, if A is true, the opposite of A is false. If you argue, "That's not right, they can both be true at the same time," then you are necessarily asserting that by disagreeing with you, I am wrong. So you are proving exactly what you purport to disprove.

PLURALISM, EXCLUSIVITY, AND "TOLERANCE"

Pluralism holds that all religions can be true, so it is intolerant and unenlightened to claim that only one is true. According to this outlook, the only thing we can say absolutely is that pluralism is true—i.e., all religions are equally valid.

Note that we are not talking about whether to allow freedom of religion—of course we should. We are not talking about whether to treat people of other faiths with love and respect—of course we should. We are talking about whether religions whose teachings flatly contradict each other can all be true. And contrary to the tenets of pluralism, of course they cannot.

Prominent *New York Times* columnist Tom Friedman once wrote that we all worship the same God through our different histories, languages, and cultures.[38] I'm amazed by this intellectual laziness; if Christianity's major truth claims are true, then the major truth claims of other religions must be false whenever they contradict Christianity's claims. This does not mean that if Christianity is true, *all* truth claims of other religions are necessarily false, since other religions surely have valid truth claims that don't conflict with Christianity's claims.

If, as I have argued in this book, Jesus is in fact the Son of God and other religions say He is not, then those other religions, to the extent they deny Christ's deity, are false. If someone claims that Christ was merely a great prophet, as we discussed in Chapter 6, that claim cannot possibly be reconciled with Christianity's truth claim that He is God. Likewise, the New Age idea that we all are on a path to the same God, through different means or different routes, is incompatible with Christ's assertion that "I am the Way, the Truth, and the Life. No one comes to the Father except through Me" (John 14:6).

Christianity's truth claims are unique, but Christianity's claim to uniqueness is not. That is, Christianity has exclusive truth claims, but all other religions do as well. Muslims claim Christ was a great prophet but was not God. So they are exclusive about that and about many of their other beliefs. Buddhists and Hindus broke away from one another because they disagree with certain aspects of each other's respective creeds, meaning they each have an element of exclusivity. Adherents of some other religions believe God is impersonal, meaning they deny the Christian contention that He is personal. No religion other than Christianity believes that God is Triune, therefore all other religions have the exclusive belief that God is not triune. Some religions and belief systems maintain that man is inherently good by nature, but Christianity teaches that man, though born in God's image, is fallen. None of these contradictory claims can be reconciled.

So please understand that the question of whether Christianity can be squared with other religions that don't accept its truth claims is an entirely different question from whether Christianity's truth claims are true. As Christianity holds that Jesus is the Son of God and the God of the Bible is Triune while other religions don't, these other religions can't be squared with Christianity, whether or not, in fact, Jesus is the Son of God or God is Triune. So when people argue that the various contradictory religions are all essentially the same, they cannot possibly be right.

Though Christianity does assert exclusive truth claims, it is not intolerant of other faiths; it does not command the mistreatment of non-Christians or the infringement of their religious freedom. Some Christians may be disrespectful at times, as we are all human, but nothing in the gospels encourages the mistreatment of nonbelievers.

Nor is Christianity unloving simply because it teaches that Jesus is the only way. Though perhaps come Calvinists would object to this—and I have great respect for them—I believe that everyone is on an equal footing in Christianity. One may be born into a Christian family, but that doesn't make him a Christian—he has to personally accept Christ. That being said, everyone is invited and welcome. Christ, the Good Shepherd, doesn't want to lose any sheep. God rejoices more over finding one lost sheep than over the ninety-nine He still has (Luke 15:4). He is ecstatic at the return of the prodigal son and lovingly embraces him. Christ says that He is the only way to God, but we are all welcome, no matter what gender we are, what race, what ethnicity, or what culture. "Seek me," He says, "and you shall find me."

PROOFS FOR GOD'S EXISTENCE

As noted earlier, I can't cover every issue in this book to the extent I would like, so I've emphasized those areas that involved obstacles to my own faith or that particularly attracted me to Christianity. For many years I didn't fully embrace the God of the Bible but I never doubted His existence, and I always intuitively understood that someone or something must have created the material universe; otherwise it just existed on its own, apart from God, the uncaused Cause—which is impossible. It is much more difficult to believe that matter always existed than that someone created it. Something cannot come from nothing without a cause. The most reasonable conclusion is that God created the universe, even though we finite creatures can't completely comprehend an infinite and eternal God.[39]

This brings us to point three of Geisler's and Turek's twelve-point proof: "It is true that a theistic God exists." Incorporating the various "proofs for God's existence," this point does not claim to demonstrate that the God of the Bible exists, only that a theistic God exists. Theism holds that an infinite, personal God created the universe and miraculously intervenes in it from time to time—that God is both transcendent over the universe and operating within it.[40] Thus defined, Christians, Jews, and Muslims all believe in a theistic God.

The Christian apologist, of course, does not make his case simply by demonstrating that God is a theistic God. He must also present evidence that this theistic God is the Christian God, which is what much of this book attempts to demonstrate. While I don't want to make light of the importance of these proofs for the existence of a theistic God or disparage those who doubt the existence of God, I doubt that abstract proofs for God's existence are going to lead many to the faith, or even if they do, that I'm the person to make that case persuasively. I can't imagine many people reasoning their way to believing in God's existence if they are predisposed against believing, because I don't believe these skeptical predispositions are primarily grounded in reason. I am not saying the predispositions are necessarily irrational, only that they are ultimately based on something other than reason.

Some argue that while these proofs are rationally sound and even persuasive, the most you can expect from them is to show that there is nothing irrational about accepting the arguments.[41] Even most thinkers who advance these arguments don't claim they constitute absolute proof for God's existence. As Dr. Geisler and Frank Turek explain, "As limited human beings, we do not possess the type of knowledge that will provide us with absolute proof of God's existence or nonexistence. Outside of the knowledge of our own existence (I know I exist because I have to exist in order to ponder the question), we deal in the realm of probability. Whatever we've concluded about the existence of God, it's always possible that the opposite conclusion is true."[42] Yet I believe, along with Geisler and Turek, that the evidence demonstrates beyond a reasonable doubt that God does exist, as I have endeavored to demonstrate in these pages.

Though there are other proofs, such as the ontological argument, I will focus on three of them: the cosmological, teleological, and moral arguments.

THE COSMOLOGICAL ARGUMENT

The cosmological argument is a law involving causation. Briefly stated it is:

1. Everything that begins had a cause.
2. The universe had a beginning.
3. Therefore, the universe had a cause.[43]

This invites a question: If God was the "first cause" of the universe, who "caused" God? Let's examine that.

The first premise is considered self-evident because something cannot come from nothing. Put differently, being cannot come from non-being. Even a ten-year-old knows that, right? We personally observe that everything in the physical universe was caused by something, e.g. a tree depends on a seed from another tree, as well as water, minerals, and sunshine.[44]

The second premise is now supported on scientific and philosophical grounds.[45] Most scientists accept the Big Bang theory, which tells us that the universe had a beginning. (Many Christians, incidentally, believe in the scientific evidence for the Big Bang, which is consistent with the biblical account of creation, but reject the naturalistic speculations about how the bang occurred.) Additionally, the Second Law of Thermodynamics informs us that the universe has a finite amount of energy and that it is decreasing. Entropy is moving the universe irreversibly toward a state of maximum disorder and minimum energy, which means it cannot be eternal. Because maximum entropy has not yet been realized, the universe could not have been here forever.[46] Moreover, the universe is expanding, which means it had a beginning point when nothing existed. But again, nothing cannot produce something.

Dr. Norman Geisler sets out the philosophical basis for the second premise (the universe had a beginning):

1. An infinite number of moments cannot be traversed.
2. As such, today could never have arrived if there were an infinite number of moments preceding today.
3. Today has in fact come.
4. Thus, there could only have been a finite number of moments prior to today, which means time had a beginning. Because everything with a beginning must have been caused, the temporal world had a Beginner.[47]

Stated another way, unless a first cause (God) exists, the universe would have to be eternal because there would be an infinite series of causes and effects that would never lead to a first cause or starting point. As evidence from science and philosophy demonstrate that the universe is not eternal, however, it is impossible that an infinite series of causes and effects preceded it. It had to have begun at some point in time. And because no contingent being can create itself, the first cause must have been uncaused or self-existent and must transcend the material universe. To explain the existence of a contingent, temporally finite universe, there has to be a non-contingent being who is wholly independent of the physical universe and who created it.[48] As one writer put it, "If God needed a cause then God is not God."[49]

THE TELEOLOGICAL ARGUMENT

The teleological argument is based on the order and design we observe in nature. These cannot possibly have resulted from random processes and chance—an intelligent designer (Being) had to have caused them. The teleological argument maintains:

1. Every design had a designer.
2. The universe has a highly complex design.
3. Therefore, the universe had a Designer.[50]

There is abundant and various evidence in support of this argument involving things we've learned from astronomy and biology, some of which I discuss in Chapter 12.

THE MORAL ARGUMENT

The moral argument (the moral law) states:

1. Every law has a lawgiver.
2. There is a moral law.
3. Therefore, there is a moral lawgiver.[51]

The first premise is self-evident: every law must have a lawgiver or it wouldn't be a law. The second premise assumes our experience teaches us that all people have a fundamental sense of right and wrong that corresponds to an objective moral standard beyond humanity. If there is a moral law, there surely must be a moral lawgiver. As noted earlier, a prominent group of atheist intellectuals known as the "new atheists" strongly disputes that the existence of moral law necessarily implies a moral lawgiver. They seem to believe that mortals somehow bootstrapped their way into possessing moral consciences. While people can certainly invent their own moral codes, unless there is an objective standard beyond humanity, then everything is just a matter of human opinion. Without God, there's no way to justify that Hitler was evil, or that the behavior of Mother Teresa was better than Hitler's.

One of the chief stumbling blocks to faith is the existence of evil and suffering in the world. Why would an all-powerful, all-loving God permit that? I mentioned this issue previously and will explore it more in Chapter 13, but for now note that this reason for doubt can be turned on itself. Human beings would arguably have no concept of evil, especially in any kind of universal sense, unless a moral standard exists apart from us—that is, uncreated by us. "[As an atheist] my argument against God was that the universe seemed so cruel and unjust," writes C. S. Lewis, who was an atheist before transforming into one of Christianity's most effective apologists. "But how had I got this idea of just and unjust? A man does not call a line crooked unless he has some idea of a straight line. What was I comparing this universe with when I called it unjust?"[52]

Without a moral absolute that is independent of human consciousness, there would be no point of reference and no basis for determining right or wrong. All moral standards, if they existed at all, would be relative, and there would be no authority behind our moral judgments. But anthropological and sociological research shows there is a universal standard of behavior in people that transcends cultures and races. There is a universal recognition of evil and an intrinsic sense of right and wrong. This is not to say there are no variations in moral codes among peoples. The basics, however, are often quite similar.[53]

MIRACLES

We now turn to the idea of miracles. I must confess at the outset that the subject of miracles as an important part of the apologetic arsenal has always baffled me; I believe life itself is a miracle and that the miraculous is self-evident through our own observation. As Paul declares in Romans,

"For what can be known about God is plain to them, because God has shown it to them. For his invisible attributes, namely, his eternal power and divine nature, have been clearly perceived, ever since the creation of the world, in the things that have been made. So they are without excuse" (1:19–20). I believed this, by the way, before I discovered that passage.

If God created everything out of nothing, which I firmly believe, then the discussion of the possibility of miracles is moot before it begins. But because some liberal critics harbor an anti-supernatural bias that rejects the possibility of miracles outright, and because this presupposition infects much modern biblical criticism, I want to address it briefly. Proving that miracles are possible, after all, is an integral part of Dr. Geisler's and Frank Turek's twelve-point proof and is a subject treated seriously by most of the great Christian apologists today.

We must believe that miracles are possible if we are to believe in Christianity; for if miracles are impossible, the Bible can't be God's Word, Jesus can't be God's Son, Christ's resurrection couldn't have happened, and His redemptive plan for our salvation is non-existent.[54] As Christian philosopher William Lane Craig writes in *Reasonable Faith*, "We must first deal with whether such divine action is possible in the first place...the problem of miracles." Christianity, he says, is a religion of miracles: God's incarnation, His virgin birth, the various miracles He performed, and of course, His miraculous resurrection.[55]

But I must reiterate that this subject has never been a stumbling block for me, and I've never quite understood why it causes so many problems for some people, given the manifest miracles of creation and life that we all witness and experience. And I doubt that anyone who lacks faith principally because he refuses to believe in miracles would be persuaded by philosophical arguments showing that they could occur. William Lane Craig, after thoroughly discussing the subject of miracles, acknowledges that "the material shared in this chapter...does not, I must confess, admit of much practical application in evangelism. I've never encountered a non-Christian who rejected the gospel because of an overt objection to miracles." But Craig insists the subject is nonetheless "extremely important" precisely because biblical critics' skepticism necessitates a defense of miracles. He also senses that some doubters have "covert problems" with miracles—they may not develop a formal argument against miracles, but they still find it hard to believe that the miracles described in the gospels actually occurred.[56]

I believe part of the problem is human pride, exacerbated by modern man's scientific and technological advancements. If we think man was puffed up during the Enlightenment, when reason often attempted to relegate faith to the backseat or outside the car altogether, our postmodern world is even more hostile to such notions as miracles, which are often dismissed as glorified superstition.

How do we define a miracle? Antony Flew, formerly a renowned atheist, defines miracles as "something which would never have happened had nature...been left to its own devices."[57] Examining miracles in light of the natural law, Dr. Geisler expands on this idea. "Natural law," he writes, "describes naturally caused regularities; a miracle is a supernaturally caused singularity." Further, "Natural law can be understood as the usual, orderly, and general way that the world operates." Thus, "a miracle is an unusual, irregular, specific way in which God acts within the world."[58] More specifically, it is "a divine intervention in the natural world that produces an event that would not have resulted from purely natural causes."[59]

Though we often use the term miracle loosely, for example, to describe astounding coincidences, these are not miracles because they are not supernatural acts of God.[60] Miracles include God's parting of the Red Sea, Jesus' healings, His turning water into wine, His walking on water, and His resurrection.

Once again, it is not just nonbelievers who reject the possibility of miracles. For example, holding to an anti-supernatural presupposition, liberal Christian theologians have virtually redacted those portions of Scripture that include the supernatural. They also twist themselves into pretzels to deny that certain books were written by biblical authors at the time they were said to have been written. Prominent among these are the Books of Daniel and Isaiah, the latter of which critics conveniently attribute to two or sometimes three different authors because they refuse to accept that Isaiah, who lived before the events he prophesied came to pass, actually penned those prophecies.

ANTI-SUPERNATURALISTS NEED MORE FAITH
THAN CHRISTIANS

Much like Darwinists, liberal critics insist they will go wherever the facts take them, but their presuppositions won't allow them to go in certain directions, and they take gigantic leaps of faith as they avoid the pathway of truth. This is why Norman Geisler and Frank Turek titled their book *I Don't Have Enough Faith to Be an Atheist*. Whether it's the naturalists' belief, against the best known evidence, that the complexity of creation does not point to an intelligent designer, their nearly blind faith in innumerable non-existent "missing links" (transitional evolutionary forms), their unsupportable idea that the fossil record really supports their worldview, or their willingness to accept that matter was created from non-matter or that life sprang from non-life, they need more faith than Christians. I am not the slightest bit discouraged by the ridicule that the cultural elite will heap upon these arguments, for truth is not defined by popular opinion, especially in an age that is hostile to the very concept of truth (Psalms 14:1; Prov. 1:7, 14:8, 14:12; 1 Cor. 1:20).

DAVID HUME

Modern skepticism about miracles began during the Enlightenment in the seventeenth century. Deists, who didn't believe God was actively involved in the world after creating it, led the charge against the belief that miracles are possible. Dutch philosopher Benedict de Spinoza and Scottish philosopher David Hume played central roles. Hume argues, essentially, that it's impossible to prove that a miracle occurred because even if there were strong proof of it, that explanation would be eclipsed by the laws of nature, which are unchangeable and do not permit miracles to happen. "A miracle is a violation of the laws of nature," he maintains, "and as a firm and unalterable experience has established these laws, the proofs against a miracle, from the very nature of the fact, is as entire as any argument from experience can possibly be imagined.... No testimony is sufficient to establish a miracle, unless the testimony be of such a kind, that its falsehood would be more miraculous, than the fact, which it endeavors to establish."

Hume says that if someone told him "that he saw a dead man restored to life," he would question which is more probable: that the witness is deceiving us or himself, or that the resurrection actually occurred? Because experience teaches that the first explanation is more probable than the second, he must reject the truth of the resurrection.[61] Dr. Geisler and Frank Turek summarize this argument as follows:

1. Natural law involves regular occurrences.
2. Miracles involve rare occurrences.
3. The evidence for the regular is always greater than for the rare.
4. Wise people always base their belief on the greater evidence.
5. Therefore, wise persons should never believe in miracles.[62]

Geisler and Turek identify point three as Hume's false premise because the evidence for regular events is *not* always greater than the evidence for the rare. They cite examples of rare events that we believe or know happened, such as the Big Bang theory, the origin of life on earth, and the entire history of the earth, all of which are unrepeated.[63]

To me, Hume's argument seems circular, i.e, that he would not believe his lying eyes even if he witnessed a miracle himself because he possesses a fixed, intransigent bias against the supernatural. All his life experiences tell him that things must operate according to natural law, and therefore supernatural events don't occur. Hume, in effect, is ruling out miracles precisely because they are miracles. Miracles, however, almost have to be rare; if they were commonplace they would hardly get our attention and they wouldn't serve their intended effect as signs pointing to God.

Ultimately, Hume simply devised a clever, circular philosophical explanation to justify his anti-supernatural bias. I don't think it's any more complicated than that even after reading his entire essay on miracles. Simply put, the argument against Hume is this: if you believe in

God—at least the God of the Bible—you can believe in miracles because the existence of the universe and life are obvious miracles (Romans 1). Even more to the point, if you can believe that the universe (matter) came from nothing, or that matter always existed, you can surely believe in miracles, which takes far less faith.

MIRACLES CONFIRM MESSAGES FROM GOD

The main purpose of miracles is to confirm a message from God. They are always connected with a truth claim in His name.[64] Miracles, by definition, come from God, and He doesn't perform them simply to amuse Himself. This is made clear throughout the Bible. Nicodemus asks Jesus, "Rabbi, we know that you are a teacher come from God; for no one can do these signs [miracles] that you do unless God is with him" (John 3:2). Peter declares, "Men of Israel, hear these words: Jesus of Nazareth, a Man attested by God to you by miracles, wonders, and signs which God did through Him in your midst, as you yourselves know" (Acts 2:22). The writer of Hebrews says, "How shall we escape if we neglect such a great salvation? It was declared at first by the Lord, and it was attested to us by those who heard, while God also bore witness by signs and wonders and various miracles and by gifts of the Holy Spirit distributed according to his will" (Heb. 2:3–4).[65] Paul exclaims, "The things that mark an apostle—signs, wonders and miracles—were done among you with great perseverance" (2 Cor. 12:12). And John relates, "Truly Jesus did many other signs in the presence of his disciples, which are not written in this book; but these are written that you may believe that Jesus is the Christ, the Son of God, and that believing you may have life through His name" (John 20:30–31).[66]

Now consider the following statement by Hume: "It is no miracle that a man, seemingly in good health, should die on a sudden: because such a kind of death, though more unusual than any other, has yet been frequently observed to happen. But it is a miracle, that a dead man should come to life; because that has never been observed in any age or country."[67] He later adds, "A wise man, therefore, proportions his belief to the evidence."[68]

With all due respect to Mr. Hume, "that a dead man came to life" was observed by many witnesses who testified to the resurrection of Jesus Christ. The powerful evidence of this having occurred far exceeds evidence to the contrary. So now we turn to an examination of the miracle upon which the truth of Christianity most depends: the resurrection of Jesus Christ.

THE MIRACLE OF THE RESURRECTION

Entire books have been written on Jesus' resurrection, which is central to Christianity's truth claims, but I will simply highlight the essentials. J. P. Moreland observes, "It is the foundation upon which the Christian faith is built. Without the resurrection, there would have been no Christian faith, and the most dynamic movement in history would never have come to be."[69] But the idea, as noted earlier, was first suggested by Paul, who declared, "And if Christ has not been raised, then our preaching is in vain and your faith is in vain" (1 Cor. 15:14). Furthermore, on the day of Pentecost, Peter stressed the significance of the resurrection and cited the prophecy predicting it in Psalm 16: "God raised him up, losing the pangs of death, because it was not possible for him to be held by it.... Brothers, I may say to you with confidence about the patriarch David that he both died and was buried, and his tomb is with us to this day. Being therefore a prophet, and knowing that God had sworn with an oath to him that he would set one of his descendants on his throne, he foresaw and spoke about the resurrection of the Christ, that he was not abandoned to Hades, nor did his flesh see corruption. This Jesus God raised up, and of that we are all witnesses" (Acts 2:24, 29–32).

Scripture frequently emphasizes the essentiality of the resurrection to the Christian faith. It explains that the resurrection is critical for us to have eternal life (John 11:25–27); to demonstrate Christ's power over death (Acts 2:24; Romans 6:9), to forgive our sins (Acts 13:37–38; 1 Cor. 15:17); for our justification (Romans 4:23–25; Acts 13:39); to unite us with Jesus in His resurrection (Romans 6:5–8); to provide us with future glory (Romans 8:18); to adopt us into God's family (Romans 8:23); to

conquer death (1 Cor. 15:26, 54–57; Luke 20:36); to give us new heavenly and imperishable bodies (1 Cor. 15:42–48); and thus to give us
immortality (1 Cor. 15:53).[70]

THE FACT OF CHRIST'S DEATH

Before delving into the evidence supporting Jesus' bodily resurrection, we have to examine the evidence that He actually died prior to His
reported resurrection appearances. This responds to critics who, while
attacking the historicity of the gospels, make the bizarre claim that Jesus
was a real person Who was nailed to the cross, but that He did not die
on it.[71] Norman Geisler notes that the evidence for Christ's death is
greater than that for almost any other event in the ancient world.[72] The
nature of His wounds—from whipping, crucifixion, and the spear thrust
in His side—ensured His death (Mark 15; John 18); His mother, friends,
and closest disciples witnessed His passing (Mark 15:40; John 19:25–26;
Luke 22:54); the Romans, who were expert executioners, pronounced
Him dead (John 19:33), and Pilate double-checked to ensure it (Mark
15:45); the Jews never disputed that Jesus' dead body was buried in the
tomb of Sanhedrin member Joseph of Arimathea (John 19:38); non-
Christian writers from the first and second centuries—Josephus, Tacitus,
Thallus, Lician, Phelgon, the Jewish Talmud—recorded Jesus' death;
and modern medical authorities, having examined the evidence, have
verified His demise.[73] Additionally, early Church fathers such as Polycarp
and Ignatius confirmed the death of Jesus on the cross.[74]

As further proof, Josh McDowell cites an article from the *Journal
of the American Medical Association* with this striking finding: "Clearly,
the weight of historical and medical evidence indicates that Jesus was
dead before the wound to His side was inflicted and supports the traditional view that the spear, thrust between His ribs, probably perforated
not only the right lung, but also the pericardium and heart and thereby
ensured His death. Accordingly, interpretations based on the assumption
that Jesus did not die on the cross appear to be at odds with modern
medical knowledge."[75]

British New Testament scholar Michael Green notes that eyewitnesses testified that blood and water came out from Jesus' pierced side, but had He been alive when He was thrust, say experts, blood would have gushed out with every heartbeat. But the witnesses saw "semi-solid dark red clot seeping out, distinct and separate from the accompanying watery serum. This is evidence of massive clotting of the blood in the main arteries, and is exceptionally strong medical proof of death." This is even more probative when you consider that the witnesses living in those days couldn't conceivably have realized the medical significance of what they were reporting.[76]

In addition, Jesus Himself declared He was dying when He committed His spirit into the Father's hands (Luke 23:46), and John, who was an eyewitness to the crucifixion, verified Jesus' exclamation (John 19:30). The assembled crowds were also witnesses to this (Luke 23:47–49). The Roman soldiers were so sure He had died that they thought it unnecessary to break His legs (John 19:33), which was the customary practice to hasten death on the cross.

After His death, Jesus was wrapped in some one hundred pounds of cloth and spices and placed in a sealed and heavily guarded tomb for three days (Matt. 27:60; John 19:39–40). If He hadn't died beforehand, those conditions in themselves would have been fatal.[77] And Dr. Geisler remarks that even if Jesus had survived that unbearable ordeal, He would have appeared more like a "resuscitated wretch than a triumphant Savior."[78] He cites liberal scholar David Strauss as admitting that it is "impossible" that a man in the condition Jesus would have been in "could have given to his disciples the impression that he was a conqueror over death, the prince of life, an impression which lay at the bottom of their ministry." Instead, he says, it would have "weakened the impression which he had made upon them in life and in death." It could not, argues Strauss, "have elevated their reverence into worship."[79]

Indeed, the evidence is so overwhelming that even most critical scholars agree, according to New Testament researcher Gary Habermas, that Jesus died by crucifixion, He was buried, and His death initially caused His disciples to despair and lose hope.[80]

THE EMPTY TOMB

While many critical scholars concede the empty tomb as a historical fact, according to Habermas, not all do.[81] So let's briefly examine the evidence for the tomb being left empty after Jesus' resurrection. The New Testament has numerous citations verifying the empty tomb (Matt. 28:11–15; Mark 16:1–8; Luke 24:1–12; John 20:11–18), and various speeches in Acts presuppose that the tomb was empty, as does 1 Corinthians 15:3–8.[82]

Moreover, many scholars agree it is highly probable that the resurrection was preached in Jerusalem just a few weeks after the crucifixion, which would never have happened if the tomb had not been empty. The body of Jesus could have been produced, especially since the location of the tomb of Joseph of Arimathea—a well-respected member of the Sanhedrin—was well known.[83] "Without having a reliable testimony for the emptiness of Jesus' tomb," German theologian Wolfhart Pannenberg observes, "the early Christian community could not have survived in Jerusalem proclaiming the resurrection of Christ."[84]

Furthermore, according to J. P. Moreland, in New Testament times the tombs of prophets and holy people served as sites of religious worship, and there were at least fifty such sites in Palestine, yet there is no evidence this practice was associated with Jesus' tomb.[85] The early speeches of Acts made no reference to the empty tomb, most likely because believers and unbelievers agreed it was empty, so there was no reason to mention it. Also, Matthew 28:11–15 relates that the Jews proposed an alternative theory for the empty tomb ("tell the people the disciples stole the body"), which proves they didn't dispute that it was in fact empty. And there are no known conflicting burial accounts of Jesus.[86]

What about this theory that Jesus' disciples stole the body? According to Habermas, it is entirely implausible and no New Testament scholar, to his knowledge—not even those who dispute the supernatural aspects of Christianity—considers it "as remotely possible." The disciples had nothing to gain by staging some elaborate hoax in order to start a new religion; in fact, they all faced ridicule, hardship, persecution, and many suffered martyrs' deaths. Additionally, as mentioned earlier, we are talking about Jewish theists here. The pre-Christ religion of the disciples would inform them that this would be lying against Israel's God and risking damnation. And finally, if they were going to make a story up, why would they do so about a Messiah who didn't fit the description of what they anticipated the Messiah would be, i.e, one who would deliver the Jews politically from Gentile oppression?[87]

THE RESURRECTION EVIDENCE

Habermas states that while many critical scholars in the nineteenth century disputed the resurrection on naturalistic grounds, few liberal critics take that position anymore. He says contemporary critical scholars basically agree with these nine key facts concerning the resurrection of Jesus:

1. The disciples believed they had encounters with the risen Jesus.
2. The disciples were transformed from doubters who lacked the courage to identify with Jesus to bold declarants of His death and resurrection.
3. Jesus' tomb was empty.
4. The resurrection message was central to the teaching of the early Church, especially in Jerusalem, where Jesus was both crucified and buried.
5. Jewish leaders could not disprove the disciples' message (Acts 1–5).
6. Accounts of the resurrection were crucial to the Church's birth and its rapid spread.
7. Sunday became the primary day of worship.
8. James was transformed from skeptic to believer because he was convinced he had encountered the resurrected Christ.
9. Paul, just a few years later, was converted as a result of an encounter with one whom he believed to be the risen Christ.[88]

What about the claim that the transformation of Jesus' disciples is no different from the experiences of adherents of other religions or even of certain political theories? "In the case of Jesus' disciples," says Gary Habermas, "one grand distinction makes all the difference in the world. Like other examples of religious or political faith, the disciples believed and followed their leader's teachings. But unlike all others, the disciples had more than just their beliefs—they had seen the resurrected Jesus. This is a crucial distinction; their faith was true precisely because of the resurrection."[89]

Habermas follows up with this question: "Which is more likely—that an ideology we believe in is true or that we and a number of others saw a friend several times during the last month? If eternity rested on the consequences, would we rather base our assurance on the truth of a particular religious or political view, or would we rather that the consequences followed from repeated cases of seeing someone?"[90] Unless you are David Hume, if you and your friends actually saw someone—some of you seeing him several times, often with more than one person present—you would probably believe that personal experience rather than placing your faith in the veracity of some ideological belief. But in the case of Jesus' disciples, they not only witnessed the resurrected Christ, they heard His unique teachings. Jesus was the only founder of a major world religion who had miracles reported of Him in reliable sources—as we've shown—within a few decades, and during the lifetime of many of the eyewitnesses.[91]

THE RESURRECTION APPEARANCES

Jesus made twelve resurrection appearances. All of these occurred in the immediate forty days following His crucifixion except for the last appearance, when He came to Paul on the road to Damascus. His first appearance—to Mary Magdalene (John 20:10–18)—is especially significant because, had this been a concocted story, it is highly unlikely that He would have appeared first to a woman, as a woman's testimony wasn't considered as reliable as a man's. Next Jesus appeared to the other women with Mary Magdalene (Matt. 28:1–10). These women saw Jesus, clasped His feet, worshipped Him, heard Him speak, and saw the empty tomb.

He also appeared to Peter (1 Cor. 15:5), who saw and heard Jesus, and saw the empty tomb and grave clothes. Jesus appeared to the men on the road to Emmaus (Mark 16:12; Luke 24:13–35), and He ate with them, explained the Scriptures to them, and they saw Him, though they did not at first recognize Him. He appeared to ten of His disciples (Luke 24:36–49), who not only heard and touched Him, but saw Him eating fish, which proves the physical/material nature of His resurrection body. He appeared to eleven disciples, and though Thomas wasn't there and initially doubted the account, he later was allowed to see and touch His wounds. He also appeared to seven disciples who were fishing in Galilee (John 21). They all saw Him, heard Him, and ate breakfast with Him. He appeared again to His disciples by the Sea of Tiberias (John 21:1).

Then Jesus appeared to commission His apostles (Matt. 28:16–20). Perhaps the most noteworthy appearance was when He showed Himself to more than five hundred people at once (1 Cor. 15:6). Paul was believed to have written about this large appearance around 55–56 AD—only twenty-some years after the resurrection, meaning many of the eyewitnesses would have still been alive—and he challenged his readers to dare contradict his account. Jesus also appeared to James (1 Cor. 15:7), who along with Jesus' other brothers, was not a believer prior to His resurrection (John 7:5). Jesus' final appearance during the first forty days following His crucifixion was at His ascension and before all His apostles. "He presented himself alive to them after his suffering by many proofs," Luke relates, "appearing to them during forty days and speaking about the kingdom of God." Jesus' last appearance was to Paul (1 Cor. 15:8)—not in a vision, as is sometimes mistakenly believed, but physically.[92]

To sum up, the evidence that Jesus Christ died an excruciating death on the cross, was buried in a tomb, that the tomb was later empty, and that He was resurrected from the dead in a physical body is powerful and overwhelming—and much more convincing than any contrary indications.

In the next chapter we look at some of the scientific evidence pointing toward the truth of the Christian worldview. Contrary to conventional wisdom, science and Christianity are perfectly compatible and mutually supportive, as we shall see.

CHAPTER 12

<><><><><><><><><><><><><><>

SCIENCE MAKES
THE CASE—
FOR CHRISTIANITY

D r. Geisler quipped in a lecture, "Atheists used to ridicule Christians for saying that God made something out of nothing, but now they say that nothing created something out of nothing." That's the irony of scientific advances for you. Some skeptics used to argue—as absurd as it seemed to most of us—that some form of matter always existed, so life ultimately sprang from non-living matter. But as indicated, scientific discoveries have demonstrated that matter could not have always existed, so it had to have a beginning. Thus, even if Darwinists could scientifically demonstrate that macroevolution accounts for living matter springing from non-living matter and for human beings evolving from simple life forms, they still couldn't get around the intractable, insuperable problem of showing how matter sprang from absolutely nothing.

Yet some persistent skeptics maintain that a naturalist explanation for matter springing from nothing—or nonmatter—is possible, and they point to the Big Bang theory for support. But isn't it a stretch to say that any kind of cosmic super-explosion from absolutely nothing could result in the beginning of the universe? The Big Bang is much more compatible with the Bible's creation account—that God created the heavens and earth out of nothing (ex nihilo).

Naturalists are perplexed by the emerging scientific evidence showing that the universe had a beginning. They are precluded from arguing that unlimited time existed in the past to accommodate some of their cosmological or biological theories. The "new atheists" are thereby reduced to arguing a number of fantastic positions. Some refuse to address the origin of matter or the origin of life altogether, insisting the burden of proof is on the theist to prove that God exists. Others employ a linguistic dodge, arguing that anything beyond an ordinary naturalistic explanation is nonscientific and therefore not worth discussing.

But some have ventured onto new turf and devised resourceful—albeit incredible—theories to explain the universe's origin. Some have suggested the existence of a multiverse—the bizarre idea that multiple universes exist simultaneously, each one the result of random events, and out of these countless parallel universes, ours happens to have life. Others speculate that aliens from another universe deposited life here—without, of course, explaining how they were created or who created them.

Notice that these theories posited by proud scientists are wholly bereft of scientific evidence. They are based solely on their naturalist philosophy that precludes belief in a designer or creator God.[1] "The fine-tuning of the universe provides *prima facie* evidence of deistic design," says cosmologist Edward Harrison. "Take your choice: blind chance that requires multitudes of universes, or design that requires only one.... Many scientists, when they admit their views, incline toward the teleological or design argument."[2] Similarly, American physicist, radio astronomer, and Nobel laureate in physics Arno Penzias notes that "some people are uncomfortable with the purposefully created world. To come up with things that contradict purpose, they tend to speculate about things they haven't seen."[3]

Having virtually deified science—arrogantly stretching it beyond its limits into the realm of philosophy, religion, and metaphysics, and treating Charles Darwin as a saint of their naturalist faith—they have no way to explain what can best be explained by supernatural intervention. It's instructive that Darwin himself never really gave serious attention to the question of how life began.[4] But to get a feel for the hubris of some Darwinists today, you need look no further than this statement by anti-God evangelist Richard Dawkins: "Today the theory of evolution is about as much open to doubt as the theory that the earth goes round the sun.... It is absolutely safe to say that if you meet somebody who claims not to believe in evolution, that person is ignorant, stupid or insane (or wicked, but I'd rather not consider that)."[5]

As I've indicated, I've always believed that God created the universe, because nothing else comes close to making sense. Furthermore, I never accepted Darwinism, and I find wholly incredible the idea that man and apes (and other creatures) share a common ancestor and that all life is ancestrally related from the first single-celled creature. I believe far fewer people would accept these improbable theories if our cultural and academic elite didn't relentlessly drill them into us from childhood while heaping ridicule on those showing the slightest skepticism of the dominant orthodoxies.

I wasn't always so confident in my own beliefs. Though I was instinctively suspicious of macroevolution, I used to assume I must be wrong because almost everyone else seemed to believe it. But once I started studying the subject in greater depth, I realized that much of the conventional wisdom is based on misinformation and ideologically-driven pedagogy. The evidence for macroevolution—one species evolving into another—and for the universe having evolved from nothing, is shockingly tenuous in many respects, considering its near universal acceptance. I humbly submit that scientists who readily accept Darwinian explanations for these questions are not doing so primarily with their scientific hats on—it is their anti-supernaturalist presuppositions that are driving their thinking.

If you are serious about approaching these subjects objectively and allowing the facts to take you wherever they lead, then you don't get to end your inquiry by pointing out that so-called Christian "creationists" believe in a young earth, which many argue is so contrary to science that we need discuss these issues no further. Not all "Bible-believing Christians"—a term that would be considered redundant in a more rational world—believe in a young earth, and of those who do, many are hardly science deniers; they don't base their beliefs simply on blind faith. They subscribe to different scientific theories, even if one might find those outside the mainstream of scientific consensus, or they question the unprovable assumptions used in dating techniques or other generally accepted scientific theories. Nevertheless, even if "young earthers" are embarrassingly wrong, Darwinists are not exempted from explaining all the gaps, errors, misinformation, fraud, and inadequacies associated with Darwinism.

INTELLIGENT DESIGN

Contrary to what you've probably been led to believe, adherents of the modern intelligent design movement are not glorified biblical creationists—that's a dishonest smear. The movement's proponents emphatically insist they apply the standard that anti-supernaturalists falsely claim to employ—they let science and the evidence lead them wherever it happens to go. And in their informed and thoughtful view, the evidence overwhelmingly points to intelligent design, from the irreducible complexity of the cell to the wonders of DNA to the anthropic principle (the fine tuning of the universe)—all of which, along with many other scientific matters, I'll address in this chapter.

The movement's critics claim intelligent design is unscientific by definition because it can't be tested by the scientific method. Well, neither can atheism, but do these same critics deem that fatal to the plausibility of atheism? The question is not whether intelligent design is technically "science," but instead, in the words of British mathematician and philosopher of science John Lennox, "Is there any scientific evidence for the involvement of intelligence in the origin of nature and its laws of operation?" Lennox adds, "Certainly, those scientists who argue on the basis of their science that atheism is the only intellectually respectable position scarcely have grounds to object to others using scientific evidence to support the opposing metaphysical position of theism."[6]

Along the same lines, J. P. Moreland makes a keen observation about the axiom, "Only what can be known by science or quantified and empirically tested is rational and true." Moreland argues that the statement is self-refuting because it is not a statement *of* science, but a philosophical statement *about* science.[7] There is no way to quantify and empirically test the statement, so are we to assume it is false? In other words, according to Moreland, "The aims, methodologies, and presuppositions *of* science, cannot be validated *by* science. To attempt to have science validate itself is tantamount to pulling oneself up by one's own bootstraps."[8]

In fact, Moreland claims that no definition of science is agreed upon by a majority of philosophers of science. Various definitive characteristics of science have been proposed—repeatability, observability, empirical testability—but none has emerged as a consensus. There are valid examples of science that don't have these characteristics, such as magnetic fields, which cannot be observed—only their effects can be. There are examples of "nonscience," however, in which some of these characteristics are present. So, in Moreland's view, there isn't an adequate definition of science that covers all cases. This is not to denigrate science, but to recognize that it can't be fit into a tidy compartment.[9]

Old Testament professor C. John Collins agrees. In *Science and Faith: Friends or Foes?* he writes, "Philosophers do not agree on whether there is something like a 'scientific method' that unites all the different sciences; and they also don't agree on what is the essence of science that would allow you to define it." Many of them also disagree on the connection between "science" and "knowledge."[10]

What about the claim that scientists (and others) who believe in God have no model of the universe that leads to testable predictions? To the contrary, writes John Lennox, "The hypothesis of creation is testable. Arno Penzias, who was awarded a Nobel Prize for discovering the microwave background, makes precisely this point: 'The best data we have are exactly what I would have predicted, had I nothing to go on but the five books of Moses, the Psalms and the Bible as a whole.'"[11]

"WE HAVE A PRIOR COMMITMENT TO MATERIALISM"

Contrary to popular belief, just because one is a Christian or open to Christianity or theism does not mean he is uninterested in truth or in science. If this were true, why did a 1996 survey conducted by two scientists show that the percentage of university scientists who believe not only in God, but in a personal God Who answers prayer—a theistic God—has remained fairly steady at about 40 percent since 1916?[12] Indeed, many high level scientists are committed Christians. The difference between the two groups, according to Lennox, is not based as much on science as on their respective worldviews, with believers having a Christian worldview and nonbelievers a naturalistic worldview.[13] The bottom line is that Christian faith and science are perfectly compatible.

Some anti-supernaturalists falsely maintain that science is the only field interested in truth and rationality.[14] And some of them, in their heart of hearts, know they are not open-minded and have doggedly fixed presuppositions against the supernatural. As Harvard evolutionary geneticist Richard Lewontin memorably puts it,

> We take the side of science *in spite* of the patent absurdity of some of its constructs, *in spite* of its failure to fulfill many of its exaggerated promises of health and life, *in spite* of the tolerance of the scientific community for unsubstantiated just-so stories, because we have a prior commitment to materialism. It is not that the methods and institutions of science somehow compel us to accept a material explanation of the phenomenal world but, on the contrary, that we are forced by our *a priori* adherence to material causes to create an apparatus of investigation and a set of concepts that produce material explanations, no matter how counter-intuitive, no matter how mystifying to the uninitiated. Moreover, that materialism is absolute for we cannot allow a divine foot in the door.[15]

Since this book is a broad survey of apologetics, I can barely scratch the surface of many of these scientific issues. But I hope to introduce you to some new evidence and ideas, since we are often exposed to only one side of these arguments. In the remainder of this chapter, I will briefly cover some of the interesting scientific insights in the Bible, the overall harmony of science and Scripture, the erroneous assumptions our society has accepted concerning the so-called "missing links" and the fossil record, and scientific questions bearing on evolution, including the origin of life, the complexity of the cell, and the marvels of DNA. I'll also discuss the anthropic principle, which explains how finely tuned myriad conditions have to be for life to exist on earth, and some of the other scientific evidence for design in the universe.

SCIENTIFIC THINKING AROSE IN ONE CULTURE

With today's stifling prejudice against the supernatural, it is almost shocking to recall that for more than two millennia, leading Western thinkers from Plato to Newton accepted that the natural world exhibits evidence of a design from an intelligent mind—a creator God. Indeed, it is also almost forgotten that in the recent past Christianity was not viewed as hostile to science—because it wasn't, just as it isn't today.

Even the Galileo affair, argue Nancy Pearcey and Charles Thaxton in *The Soul of Science*, was not a simple confrontation between science and religion as is commonly perceived. The often-overlooked context of this incident is that several early scientists were at odds with ecclesiastical politics while holding fervently to their personal religious beliefs. Pearcey and Thaxton cite Giorgio de Santillana, who argues in *The Crime of Galileo* that "the major part of the Church intellectuals were on the side of Galileo, while the clearest opposition to him came from secular ideas (i.e., from the academic philosophers)." Pearcey and Thaxton conclude, "The truth is that, on the whole, the Catholic church had no argument with Galileo's theories as science. Their objection had to do with Galileo's attack on Aristotelian philosophy—and all the metaphysical, spiritual, and social consequences they associated with it. As philosopher of science Philipp Frank explains, the reason Galileo's attack on Aristotle was treated so seriously was that to many people at the time Aristotle's philosophy was 'regarded as necessary for the formulation of religious and moral laws.'"[16]

Historically, scientific advancements were not a function of being liberated from religion.[17] Indeed, science did not flourish on its own. Science writer Loren Eiseley notes that scientific development is not "natural" to mankind. "Several great civilizations have arisen and vanished without the benefit of a scientific philosophy," he observes. Noting Eiseley's remarks, Pearcey and Thaxton explain that scientific thinking arose in one culture—Western Europe—and in no other. There is a reason for that.

Eiseley acknowledges that man is naturally curious, but argues that the discipline of science and scientific advancement requires more. It is "an *invented* cultural institution not present in all societies, and not one that can be counted upon to arise from human instinct." Science, he says, "demands some kind of unique soil in which to flourish." "What is that unique soil?" ask Pearcey and Thaxon. Eiseley identifies it—reluctantly—as the Christian faith. "It is the Christian world which finally gave birth in a clear, articulate fashion to the experimental method of science itself," he confesses.[18]

Pearcey and Thaxton observe that Eiseley is not a lone wolf in crediting Christianity for the rise of science. Science historians, they say, have developed a new respect for the intellectual and cultural advances of the Middle Ages, an epoch often viewed—incorrectly—as being characterized by religious obscurantism and little else. "Today, a wide range of scholars recognize that Christianity provided both intellectual presuppositions and moral sanction for the development of modern science."[19]

The predominant Christian worldview fostered scientific thought thanks to the Christian belief that God created the world with natural laws and orderliness, and that these are discoverable by man. "Centuries of meditation will produce no empirical knowledge, let alone science," states Professor Rodney Stark. "But to the extent that religion inspires efforts to comprehend God's handiwork, knowledge will be forthcoming, and science arises.... And that's precisely how not only the Scholastic scientists but also those who took part in the great achievements of the sixteenth and seventeenth centuries saw themselves—as in the pursuit of the secrets of the creation."[20]

In the late nineteenth century, however, many scientists began to abandon the notion that an intelligent designer was behind creation. Materialism, which holds that all existing phenomena—including human consciousness—stem from physical matter, entered the scene with Darwin's theory of evolution by natural selection and other alternative theories of the origin of life, the solar system, and the universe, which all depicted nature as self-existing apart from any intelligent design.[21] At this time the Christian faith lost its hold as a shared, public commitment and began to retreat to the area of private, individual belief.[22]

In *Evolution: A Theory in Crisis*, Australian scientist Dr. Michael Denton captures the devastating impact Darwinism has had on the modern world. "Darwinian theory broke man's link with God and set him adrift in a cosmos without purpose or end," he writes. "No other intellectual revolution in modern times (with the possible exception of the Copernican) so profoundly affected the way men viewed themselves and their place in the universe." Concerning evolutionary theory's destructive impact on Christianity, Denton comments that "the suggestion that life and man are the result of chance is incompatible with the biblical assertion of their being the direct result of intelligent creative activity.... Chance and design are antithetical concepts, and the decline in religious belief can probably be attributed more to the propagation and advocacy by the intellectual and scientific community of the Darwinian version of evolution than to any other single factor."[23]

"THE UNIVERSE AND LIFE APPEAR DESIGNED BECAUSE THEY WERE"

Today, evidence for intelligent design has made a significant comeback, to the point that even unapologetic Darwinists have to acknowledge it, if only grudgingly and indirectly. Richard Dawkins has said, "Biology is the study of complicated things that give the appearance of having been designed for a purpose,"[24]—but he apparently believes that natural selection can explain the complexity we observe in all living things. One wonders what it would take to crack his impregnable fortress of anti-supernatural bias. I think it understates the case to say that some of these complex things or organisms merely have the appearance of intelligent design. Some things, such as the cell and DNA (discussed below), work so magnificently that it's hard to imagine they weren't the product of intelligent design.

Dawkins notwithstanding, today's leading intelligent design advocates—and there are more than a handful of them—argue that discoveries over the last fifty years in biology, physics, astronomy, and cosmology suggest that life and the universe show signs of real, not merely apparent, design. Moreover, they affirmatively dispute the validity of the Darwinian mechanism for explaining the complexity and manifest design of living organisms.

Increasing numbers of scientists and philosophers subscribe to this view.[25] They do not necessarily believe the earth is young, and they don't base their scientific conclusions on the Bible or on Christian presuppositions. They genuinely believe this is where the science takes us—that intelligent design is "empirically detectable" wholly apart from the Bible and the Christian worldview.[26] This is not to deny some of them are Christians; I'm simply stating that they base their conclusions concerning design on the scientific evidence and not on any religious teachings.

Darwinists need to accept that one can be skeptical of their sweeping theories or even reject them outright without being hostile to science. In fact, the scientific evidence appears to be taking us in that direction. But many Christians also believe that science has its limitations and that scientists should acknowledge that their expertise doesn't speak to the realms of philosophy, religion, and metaphysics.

I would also respectfully observe that while some naturalists ridicule Christians for our supposed blind faith, many naturalists are far more close-minded to new ideas than any Christian I've ever met. Peter Atkins, for example, maintains, "There is no reason to suppose that science cannot deal with every aspect of existence."[27] But if this were true, says John Lennox, "it would at once spell the end of many academic disciplines, such as philosophy, ethics, literature, poetry, art, and music.... Science can tell you that if you add strychnine to someone's drink, it will kill her, but it cannot tell you whether it is morally right or wrong to put strychnine into your grandmother's tea in order to get your hands on her property."[28]

SCIENCE AND THE BIBLE

The Bible, written long before the advent of modern science, contains certain scientific information that couldn't have been known at the time. Evangelist Ray Comfort has catalogued a number of these instances that point to the Bible's supernatural origin:

- Around 1500 BC it was generally believed that the earth sat on something, but the Bible speaks about it floating in space: "He...hangs the earth on nothing" (Job 26:7).
- The Bible talks of the earth as being round or spherical before that was known: "It is he that sits upon the circle of the earth" (Isaiah 40:22).
- Three different passages suggest the earth is wearing out, consistent with entropy, or the Second Law of Thermodynamics. "For the heavens vanish like smoke, and the earth will wear out like a garment" (Isaiah 51:6; Psalms 102:25; Heb. 1:11).
- In Genesis 6, God gave Noah precise dimensions for the ark that were later used in shipbuilding. According to Comfort, by 1900 every large ship on the high seas was inclined toward the proportions of the ark, which was verified by "Lloyd's Register of Shipping" in the *World Almanac*.[29]

The Bible also contains some interesting information about medicine and hygiene that was far ahead of the relevant scientific discoveries. There are many dietary laws prescribed in the Old Testament which, for

many centuries, were believed to serve no other purpose than facilitating
ceremonial functions or distinguishing the people of Israel from surrounding pagan cultures. But modern medicine reveals that the laws are
also important for health and hygiene. Rules for washing following
contact with the dead or sick (Lev. 13–15; Num. 19), properly disposing
of excrement and blood (Lev. 17:13; Dt. 23:12–13), and quarantining
gravely sick people and anything they touch (Lev. 13) have proven effective at containing diseases.[30]

THE ORIGIN OF THE UNIVERSE

Josh McDowell observes that once we reject the idea that the universe is just an illusion, we are left with three possible ways it could have
begun:

1. The universe is not eternal but began out of nothing with
   no preexistent cause.
2. The universe is eternal in its existence, though it could
   have changed form at various times.
3. The universe is not eternal, but came into existence by
   something or someone other than itself.[31]

The first and third alternatives involve a universe that is not eternal
and the second one a universe that is eternal. As noted in the previous
chapter, something cannot come from nothing, which rules out the first
alternative—few would argue otherwise. How about the second alternative? Here again, based on what we know about the material universe, it
would seem highly unlikely, if not impossible, that the universe is eternal.

Only option 3 makes scientific sense—and it also happens to jibe
with the Bible.[32] As we've seen, the First Law of Thermodynamics states
that the total amount of matter and energy in the universe remains constant. The Second Law of Thermodynamics (also known as entropy)
holds that the amount of available energy in the universe decreases in
time. Given enough time, no more available energy would remain in the
universe, so we know that an infinite amount of time could not have

preceded the present. Since we still have available energy right now, this leads, inescapably, to the conclusion that the universe had a beginning in time.

The Theory of General Relativity—which shows that the universe is expanding and demonstrates the interdependence between time, space, and matter—points to the universe having a beginning. Moreover, scientific discoveries, beginning with astronomer Edwin Hubble's observations in 1927, corroborate that the universe is actually expanding. Evidence for this lies with our knowledge that the greater distance a galaxy is from us, the more light emanating from it is shifted toward the red end of the spectrum. Hubble observed this "red shift" in the light from every observable galaxy.[33] This indicates the universe is expanding, and since expansion cannot continue indefinitely, the universe must have had a beginning.[34]

Hubble's discovery ultimately led to what is now known as the Big Bang theory, which holds that the universe began from a large explosion around fifteen billion years ago and has continued to expand since. This Big Bang originated from a state of enormous density in which all mass, energy, space, and time were contained in a single mathematical point with no dimensions. These ideas suggest the universe exploded into existence out of nothing a finite time ago.[35]

The Big Bang theory was further supported by the discovery of cosmic background radiation. That is a kind of afterglow from the Big Bang explosion—light and heat from the initial explosion that can't be seen but can still be detected.[36] Scientists believe the Big Bang caused slight variations in temperature of the cosmic background radiation, which would allow matter to consolidate through gravity into galaxies. As Frank Turek marvels, the NASA COBE satellite "not only found the ripples, but scientists were amazed at their precision. The ripples show that the explosion and expansion of the universe was precisely tweaked to cause just enough matter to congregate to allow galaxy formation, but not enough to cause the universe to collapse back on itself."[37]

Moreover, the Second Law of Thermodynamics also points to an intelligent and powerful designer. We've learned that complexity increases in systems only when there is an external energy source, a proper energy conversion mechanism, and a design. We know from the

Second Law of Thermodynamics that at the time of its origin, the universe must have possessed an enormous amount of useable energy that has been decreasing since.

This indicates there must have been an external energy source for the universe, that it was capable of converting that energy into a usable form, and that some sort of intelligent plan was being followed. Thus whatever caused the universe must have had great energy that it was capable of converting, which means it was extremely powerful.[38] Astronomer Robert Jastrow, a professed agnostic, affirms this point in his discussion of the Big Bang. "Now we see how the astronomical evidence leads to a biblical view of the origin of the world," he says. "The details differ, but the essential elements in the astronomical and biblical accounts of Genesis are the same: the chain of events leading to man commenced suddenly and sharply at a definite moment in time, in a flash of light and energy."[39]

THE ORIGIN OF LIFE

Though Darwinists have no credible explanation for the origin of the universe or for the transformation of nonliving matter into living beings, they generally argue that random chance over time resulted in the origin and evolution of life. The rough equation is supposedly this: chemicals + time + random chance = life.[40] Based on rather vague evidence, our science textbooks teach that there was a primordial soup where chemicals existed on, around, and under the earth's surface, and then somehow life spontaneously occurred. Granted, the theories are far more complex than that, but they all end up suggesting spontaneous generation of one sort or another.

Consider this: advances in microbiology have shown the amazing complexity of a single cell. In every living cell, thousands of organic machines transport matter back and forth. Michael Denton explains what we'd witness if we magnified a cell a billion times, to the size of a giant airship covering all of New York City: "We would then see an object of unparalleled complexity and adaptive design. On the surface of the cell we would see millions of openings, like the portholes of a vast space ship, opening and closing to allow a continual stream of materials to flow in and out. If we were to enter one of these openings we would find ourselves in a world of supreme technology and bewildering complexity."[41]

It's one thing for cells to be this complex, but think about how much more profound this is considering their minute size. In *Darwin's Black Box*, Michael Behe argues that biochemical systems by their very nature are irreducibly complex, comprising "a single system composed of several well-matched interacting parts that contribute to basic function, wherein removal of any one of the parts causes the system to effectively cease functioning."[42]

Now reflect on this admission from Charles Darwin himself: "If it could be demonstrated that any complex organ existed which could not possibly have been formed by numerous, successive, slight modifications, my theory would absolutely break down."[43] What Darwin knew, and what Behe demonstrated, is that irreducibly complex machines cannot be produced by the slight incremental changes postulated by Darwin's theory of evolution. Any protosystem that lacks even one of the parts that contributes to "basic function" would be nonfunctional, thus preventing natural selection from operating on it to produce an improved form. In other words, irreducibly complex systems, and thus biochemical systems, must be produced all at once. This leads to the reasonable conclusion that irreducibly complex biochemical systems came into existence through intelligent design.[44]

Some naturalists claim to have refuted Behe's theory, but their arguments require preposterous leaps of faith. For example, they conjure "possible scenarios" for the evolution of an amazingly complex molecular machine called the bacterial flagellum: first, "a secretory system arose" that was "based around the SMC rod and pore-forming complex." Then, there was an "association of an ion pump" and "to this structure improved secretion," and so on. In other words, these theorists speculate that this cell just put its minute self together bit by bit over time.

Writing in "Evolution News and Views," a biology graduate student with the pseudonym Jonathan M. challenges these arguments, claiming they trivialize

the sheer complexity and sophistication of the flagellar system—both its assembly apparatus, and its state-of-the-art

design motif. Actually the process by which the bacterial
flagellum is self-assembled within the cell is so sophisticated
that I have long struggled to convey it in an accessible way to
lay-persons. Its core concepts are notoriously difficult to grasp
for those not accustomed to thinking about the system or for
those encountering it for the first time. But, at the same time,
the mechanistic basis of flagellar assembly is so breath-tak-
ingly elegant and mesmerizing that the sheer engineering
brilliance of the flagellar motor—and, indeed, the magnitude
of the challenge it brings to Darwinism—cannot be properly
appreciated without at minimum a cursory knowledge of its
underpinning operations.[45]

To imagine that the minute cell, as complex as it is, gradually evolved,
is truly hard to fathom. The alternative—that it was a result of intelligent
design—is much more plausible, unless you have a fixed anti-supernatural bias. Behe's critics notwithstanding, biochemist Dr. Fazale Rana
argues in his book *The Cell's Design* that irreducible complexity "is but
one of a vivid ensemble of biochemical features that individually and
collectively point to intelligent design. The cell's design," argues Rana,
"goes beyond irreducible complexity and communicates a vast range of
amazing properties that characterize life's chemistry.... A magnificent
gallery of awe-inspiring characteristics signify a Master's brilliance at
work."[46]

Rana is just taking the argument a step further; he's saying that
whereas Behe's approach shows that Darwinism couldn't produce an
irreducibly complex organism, there is also positive evidence for intelligent design in the biochemical features that reflect the creator's signa-
ture.[47] Note that this is not a "god of the gaps" argument. That is,
intelligent design proponents are not just devising ingenious theories to
fit their presuppositions; they are not arguing from what we do not
know, but from what we do know. Only intelligence can account for the
vast amounts of information found in the genome (more on DNA below)
and the integrated machinery of the cell.

With the discovery of such enormous biochemical complexity, arguments relying on randomness have lost their persuasiveness. Complexity

of life, however, is not the naturalist's only problem; he also has to overcome the near insuperable barrier of limited time—and here, the random chance explanation was dealt a devastating blow by the Big Bang evidence, which shows that time had a beginning. Chance is now hard to defend scientifically, and in fact, many of the Darwinists' beliefs are no longer based on hard science but on articles of faith.[48]

Even if modern science hadn't revealed the complexity of the cell and other life forms, Darwinists would still be obliged to demonstrate how life can be produced from non-life. But they cannot do that, even with all the modern science available to them, so they are reduced to basing their arguments on their blind faith that conditions must have been vastly different then.[49]

DNA

Other scientific advancements have lent additional credibility to intelligent design theory. Take DNA—Professor Walter Bradley suggests its discovery was perhaps the most impressive scientific achievement of the twentieth century. DNA is a tiny molecule that contains genetic codes with instructions for building and replicating all life forms. "That such a remarkable information storage system exists, and that the DNA molecules have somehow come to be encoded with the precise information needed for life," says Bradley, "is the climax to an amazing testimony from science of God's providential care for us in His creation." He notes that for the accidental origin of the cytochrome-C molecule to have the required sequencing of the various amino acids has a probability of just 1 in 10^{60}.[50]

DNA contains information in a long sequence of four different chemical "letters" that produces information somewhat analogous to Morse Code.[51] The characteristics of living organisms, such as eye color, are specified by information in this code contained in the DNA. The code has also been compared to a complete set of engineering drawings, with a copy found in the nucleus of every cell in the body. Adult humans have trillions of cells and thus trillions of copies of the genetic code in their bodies.[52] "The incredible specified complexity of life becomes obvious when one considers the message found in the DNA of a one-celled amoeba (a creature so small, several hundred could be lined up in an inch)," say Dr. Geisler and Frank Turek. They note that even Richard Dawkins admits "that the message found in just the cell nucleus of a tiny amoeba is more than all thirty volumes of the Encyclopedia Britannica combined, and the entire amoeba has as much information in its DNA as 1,000 complete sets of an encyclopedia." And these "encyclopedias" are not composed of "random letters but of letters in a very specific order—just like real encyclopedias."[53]

John Lennox argues that the design inference from DNA is much stronger than from other classical design arguments that are based on analogy. Lennox quotes science philosopher Dr. Stephen Meyer, who explains why this is so: "'The DNA does not imply the need for an intelligent designer because it has some similarities to a software program or to a human language. It implies the need for an intelligent designer because…it possesses an identical feature (namely, information content) that intelligently designed human texts and computer languages possess.' We are not, therefore, arguing from analogy; we are making an inference to the best explanation."[54]

Some light was shed on this topic by Alan Turing, a founder of computer science. In the mid-1930s Turing determined that the way to solve complex problems through computation was to treat them as a series of simple operations. Using this method, each operation would have an input comprising a string of numbers or characters that would be operated on by a finite control that alters the input to produce an output string. This formulation is known as a Turing machine. The output of the first operation would become the input of the second and continue in that manner.

As Fazale Rana explains, Turing machines were thought to be a purely conceptual idea that did not exist in the real world.[55] But in 1994, Leonard Adelman launched so-called DNA computing when he discovered that the cellular processes operating on DNA—the proteins responsible for DNA replication, repair, and transcription—function as Turing machines.[56] Researchers have now discovered a number of advantages to DNA computers.[57] They can speed the process by performing many operations simultaneously, and are capable of storing a vast quantity of information. "Theoretically," says Rana, "one gram of DNA can house as much information as nearly one trillion CDs. And DNA computers operate, in principle, near theoretical capacities with regard to efficiency."[58]

This, says Rana, "provides a double analogy for intelligent design." These biochemical Turing machines, he explains, highlight the informational aspects of DNA, but they also serve as "a remarkably profound type of Watchmaker analogy"—the idea that human experience teaches us that machines and motors don't just happen randomly in nature. The simplest of machines and motors "require thoughtful design and manufacture" and therefore represent a strong argument for the existence of God.[59] Rana notes, however, that the analogy in this case "is between the conceptual Turing machines in the human mind and the concrete biochemical Turing machines inside the cell."

MATHEMATICS

Further complicating matters for Darwinists is applied mathematics. David Foster researched the probability of the development of DNA for one of the most primitive single cells from random processes. He concluded that "the DNA of the T4 bacteriophage has an improbability of 10 to the 78,000th power. In a universe only 10 to the 18th power seconds old, it is obvious that life could not have evolved by random chance."[60] "But what if the universe is older than David Foster says it is?" asks Christian author and pastor Joe Coffee. "The consensus of today's naturalists claims the universe is 13.7 billion years old. That's less than 10 to the 42nd power seconds old and, according to the mathematics of the Big Bang, still not nearly enough time to explain the complexities of DNA and the origin of life."[61]

GENETIC LIMITATIONS

Naturalists have been bombarded from all angles, including by the science of genetics. Geneticists have determined that many changes can be engineered within a species, but there are limits to such changes. While you could engineer a bigger dog, you can't make one with wings—because genetic boundaries preclude it.[62] This casts further doubt on Darwinist theories of species evolving into other species (macroevolution).

THE FOSSIL RECORD

In addition to admitting the potential problem of irreducible complexity, Darwin also recognized the threat to his theory posed by the fossil record. He believed that evolution happens so gradually that it can't be noticed, a theory he expected the fossil record to validate. But he confessed, "Geology assuredly does not reveal any such finely graduated organic chain; and this, perhaps is the most obvious and gravest objection which can be urged against my theory. The explanation lies, as I believe, in the extreme imperfection of the geological record."[63]

In other words, *If only we had better geological evidence we could prove my theory.* This is why Darwinists and their followers have forever groped for a missing link or missing links (transitional forms). But since it would take more than one missing link just to demonstrate the evolution of man from his supposed ape-like ancestors, imagine the number of missing links needed to trace complex human life, with its incredible intelligence and creativity, back to the primordial soup.[64]

Evolutionary theory argues that all life forms evolved from other life forms, so there ought to be all kinds of transitional or intermediate forms linking the well-defined and distinct groups of plants and animals found in nature. But there are gaps all over the place. Once again, the scientific evidence not only doesn't support the evolutionary theory, it affirmatively supports the notion of a supernatural creation.

One major challenge to Darwinism is the Cambrian explosion, sometimes referred to as biology's big bang, in which almost all the major groups of animals that we know to exist began to appear in the fossil record abruptly and fully formed in strata from the Cambrian period (around 500–600 million years ago).[65] Paleontologists James Valentine, Stanley Awramik, Philip Signor, and Peter Sadler write, "The most single spectacular phenomenon evident in the fossil record is the abrupt appearance and diversification of many living and extinct phyla" at the beginning of the Cambrian period. These four researchers concluded that the explosion was even more abrupt and extensive than they had thought earlier.[66] It's as if God refused to cooperate with the Darwinists and created each species "after its kind," just as the Bible says.

Jonathan Wells concurs that the Cambrian explosion is problematic for Darwinists, but even worse, he argues, is "the fact that phyla and classes appeared right at the start." But how can this be when, according to Wells, Darwin claimed that phylum- and class-level differences emerge only after a long history of divergence from lower categories such as species, genera, families, and orders? The problem is that the major animal groups "appear in the fossil record as Athena did from the head of Zeus—full blown and raring to go," writes evolutionary theorist Jeffrey Schwartz.[67]

If the Cambrian explosion issue isn't fatal for the naturalist, he has another problem to deal with: according to Michael Denton, almost all (99 percent) of an organism's biology inheres in its soft anatomy, and fossils can tell us nothing about that.[68] But that is no deterrent to the stubborn Darwinists.

THE MISSING LINK?

Darwinian theory holds that the origin of the human species is similar to the origin of every other species. Human beings are modified descendants of an ancestor they shared with other animals, and their distinctiveness resulted from natural selection acting on small variations. This gave rise to two inferences that were highly controversial, according to Jonathan Wells: that human beings are just animals, and that "they are not the preordained goal of a directed process."[69]

I am always amused by those who glibly assert that Darwinism can be squared with biblical Christianity, which clearly teaches that man is a distinct and special creature made in the image and likeness of God, and that animal species were created by God, neither of which allow for the Darwinian process. Sure, biblical Christianity can accommodate microevolution, involving evolution within a species, but how anyone can believe it is compatible with macroevolution—from species to species—is beyond me, unless you dilute the term "biblical Christianity."

To Darwin's knowledge, there was no existing fossil evidence for human evolution, there was no evidence for natural selection, and the origin of variations was not yet known. But that didn't stop his theory from becoming an unquestionable dogma that even seeped into mainstream culture, gaining popular expression in the archetypical drawings showing a knuckle-dragging ape evolving progressively into an upright human being. As Dr. Wells trenchantly observes, such drawings, which are now in countless textbooks, museum exhibits, and the like, "constitute the ultimate icon of evolution, because they symbolize the implications of Darwin's theory for the ultimate meaning of human existence."[70]

In the twentieth century it appeared that the evidence supported the naturalists. Numerous fossil discoveries were thought to supply the transitional links in the evolutionary chain leading to human beings; experiments on peppered moths and other organisms appeared to provide the missing evidence for natural selection; and geneticists believed they had discovered the raw materials for evolution in DNA mutations. But none of these developments ultimately panned out for the Darwinists, writes Dr. Wells, as the moth experiments were flawed, the "oscillating natural selection observed in Darwin's finches produces no long-term evolution," and "the morphological mutations in four-winged fruit flies produce cripples not raw materials for evolution."

According to Dr. Wells, "Interpretations of the fossil evidence for human evolution are heavily influenced by personal beliefs and prejudices."[71] Darwinists will not be denied and go to great lengths to reconstruct the record based on "Hail Mary" missing link discoveries that are later revealed to be frauds or egregious mistakes. As Geisler and Turek observe, they've built entire missing links from fossil remains as minimal as a single tooth.[72] Dr. Wells cites Henry Gee, chief science writer for *Nature*, who argues, "To take a line of fossils and claim that they represent a lineage is not a scientific hypothesis that can be tested, but an assertion that carries the same validity as a bedtime story—amusing, perhaps even instructive, but not scientific."[73]

Yet their desperate quest continues. As recently as 2009, for example, Mayor Bloomberg of New York held a special ceremony to laud the recently discovered fossil Ida, said to be the "missing link" between humans and other primates. Those claims were shortly retracted. Denyse O'Leary, writing in "Evolution News and Views," tells us that "Sediba, another supposed ancestor, fared no better in 2013. A science writer at *Wired*, not known for intelligent-design sympathies, derides the ceaseless buzz as 'ancestor worship.'"[74] Dr. Daniel Janosik, who has studied the fossil record of man extensively, concludes that most of the so-called missing links that have been discovered are either some ancestral form of ape or could be some aberrant forms of man that were isolated from the centers of civilization. Further examination and research remains to be done on certain specimens, but Janosik believes "that in the end we will find that these questionable specimens are either fully ape or fully man, and not anywhere in between."[75]

THE ANTHROPIC PRINCIPLE

Developments in physics and cosmology have given new credence to the notion that the universe was intelligently designed. Starting in the 1960s, physicists began to explain that the universe appears to have been fine-tuned for the existence of life. Our existence in the universe depends on numerous cosmological factors that were calibrated precisely so as to accommodate our lives, such that if a single variable were slightly off, we wouldn't exist. There is an extreme improbability that this many variables could line up so perfectly by mere chance, which leads many to argue that it can only be explained by intelligent design.[76] "The impression of design is overwhelming," exclaims British physicist Paul Davies.[77] As English astronomer Sir Fred Hoyle notes, "A commonsense interpretation of the facts suggests that a superintellect has monkeyed with physics, as well as chemistry and biology, and that there are no blind forces worth speaking about in nature."[78]

For example, if there were even slight alterations in the expansion rate of the universe or the strength of its gravitational attraction, life on earth would be impossible.[79] (It is important to emphasize that the expansion rate of the universe was an initial condition of creation. It existed from the very beginning, which means that no cosmological evolutionary process can account for it.)

Consider the following: protons—positively charged sub-atomic particles—are 1,836 times larger than electrons. If they were slightly larger or smaller we would not exist because atoms could not form the molecules required for our existence. If the positive charge of the protons did not balance the electrons, which are of a different size, we also would not exist.[80]

The unique properties of water are also essential to earth's habitability. All life forms require water, which is unique among substances in that its solid form (ice) is less dense than its liquid form, which causes ice to float. Without this floating property earth would freeze beyond the point of accommodating human life.

The earth's atmosphere is also delicately balanced with the right proportion of many different gases that prevent an excessive greenhouse effect on the one hand and cosmic radiation on the other.[81] Our atmosphere contains 21 percent oxygen. If it were slightly more (25 percent) fires would erupt, or slightly less (15 percent), human beings would suffocate.[82]

The earth also absorbs just the right amount of light and reflects the rest—otherwise we would suffer either from an excess greenhouse effect or we would freeze.[83]

The earth's magnetic field is just the right strength to prevent cosmic radiation, but not so strong that it invites deadly electromagnetic storms. The earth is also perfectly placed in the solar system because if we were much closer to the sun it would boil, but if we were much further away its water would freeze. The placement of our solar system in the galaxy is also just right because if it were too close to the center of the galaxy, or to any of the spiral arms on the edge of the galaxy, or to any cluster of stars, cosmic radiation would destroy the earth.[84]

The color of the sun is also important for our ability to live on this planet—other colors would diminish photosynthesis, which is a natural biochemical process vital to earth's habitability.[85]

There are countless other examples of this fine-tuning:

- The centrifugal force of planetary movements precisely balances the gravitation forces, permitting planets to be held in orbit around the sun.
- Our galaxy includes around 100 billion stars, with an average distance between them of 30 trillion miles. If that distance were altered slightly, it would create erratic orbits and extreme temperature variations on earth.
- A slight variation in the speed of light would preclude life on earth.
- Jupiter's constant state of orbit prevents space materials from bombarding earth.
- The thickness of the earth's crust is just right to support life. If it were thinner, volcanic and tectonic activity would be deadly. If it were thicker, too much oxygen would transfer to the crust to support life.
- If the earth's rotation were longer than twenty-four hours the variations in temperature between day and night would be too great to support life. But if the rotation were shorter, atmospheric wind velocities would be too extreme.
- If the earth's axis were tilted slightly more, temperature differences would make life impossible.
- More seismic activity on earth would lead to many more human deaths, and if there were less activity, nutrients on the ocean floors and river runoff would fail to cycle back to land via tectonic uplift.[86]

I've only mentioned a fraction of the abundant scientific evidence today that points to a creator—such an abundance, in fact, that I'm amazed this information isn't more widely disseminated. It is inexcusable that these groundbreaking discoveries are largely absent from public education textbooks and from academic teachings, presumably because of the bias against a theistic worldview.

HUMAN CONSCIOUSNESS

Before leaving the subject of science, I want to mention one other marvel that involves science to be sure, but might well transcend the subject as well, for science cannot explain the phenomenon of human consciousness that we all experience but can't completely comprehend.

It has always been obvious to me that there is something unique about the human mind and its interrelationship with the body. While the brain is part of our body, we have the sense that it transcends it as well—that our consciousness exists apart from the body and that it cannot be explained on solely physical or material terms. Though we don't fully understand this, many of us have a sure sense that there is a spiritual component present. We can't imagine that our unique transcendent existence and our individual personality are temporal or that they evolved from some random selection process.

These ideas convinced me that there is apologetic value in the existence of human consciousness, and I was gratified to come across a chapter in Douglas Groothuis' *Christian Apologetics* on this subject. Groothuis says that human beings, being made in God's image, are moral and personal creatures who "exercise a sentient, logical and linguistic supremacy over the rest of creation (Psalm 8). This means that humans possess a unique awareness of themselves, creation and God (consciousness), are uniquely able to relate concepts rationally within their awareness (cognition), and can communicate their rational awareness through signs, both written and spoken (language)."[87] Christians, he continues, believe that these particular human capacities cannot be accounted for by any nontheistic worldview. So human beings are not merely evolved animals possessing only natural properties. Of course, they cannot be lifted to divinity either, as they are finite creatures, even though created in the image of the infinite God.

Groothuis observes that consciousness is a mystery to materialist philosophers. They have it, but have no clue how or why. One such materialist—Colin McGinn—concedes, "The bond between mind and the brain is a deep mystery, a mystery that human intelligence will never unravel."[88] This has to be deeply troubling to materialists, who seem to believe that everything can be explained in terms of physics, chemistry, and biology.[89] Dr. Hugh Ross puts it this way: "The human spirit manifests itself, at least in part, by humans' unique consciousness. While no reputable scholar disputes that human beings are uniquely conscious beings, many scholars hesitate or refuse to give God credit for that conscious nature. Some of this generation's most brilliant researchers have tried valiantly to find within matter, energy, and the natural biochemical processes of our space and time dimensions a hypothesis for the origin and operation of human consciousness, but none of their efforts has come close to succeeding. In fact, their findings only help build the case for a supernatural origin."[90]

Groothuis confirms what I realized instinctively: consciousness simply cannot be explained on purely physical terms. There has to be something more. He argues that there is a difference *in kind* between mental and physical states that has ontological implications, meaning that it bears on the very type of beings we are. "Even if some device could register every material property and process of the human brain," writes Groothuis, "it could not capture the consciousness itself." Just because the brain influences consciousness and other physical things does not mean consciousness itself is physical, "any more than a wooden oar that [moves] water turns the water into wood."[91]

The materialist will doubtlessly argue, however, that because certain brain functions correlate with specific sections of the brain, consciousness must also be physical.[92] Groothuis replies that while science may show these relationships are existentially inseparable, "It would not show that they are ontologically identical." In other words, brain functions and consciousness can be connected, interrelated, and mutually influential, but they are two separate things. A human being "is made up of two substances: mind and body, neither of which is reducible to the other."[93] The Christian worldview doesn't purport to explain every aspect of the interrelationship between mind and body—and thus doesn't obviate brain research. But it does provide a "metaphysical foundation" for the correlation between brain and mind.

J. P. Moreland agrees, noting that "it is hard to see how finite consciousness could result from the rearrangement of brute matter." This assumes a "commonsense understanding of conscious states such as sensations, thoughts, beliefs, desires, and volitions."[94] Mental states, argues Moreland, have features that distinguish them from physical ones. There is a qualitative feel to experiencing mental states, such as pain, and many mental states are intentionality directed toward an object. Internal and private to individual persons, these states lack certain physical features like spatial extension and location, and thus can't be described with physical language. One reason the existence of these mental states—in the aggregate, referred to as consciousness—serve as a proof for God's existence is that to believe they just randomly evolved is tantamount to believing that something came from nothing, which is absurd.

The idea that the mind emerged from nothing constitutes a "radical discontinuity" that "seems like a rupture in the natural world.... Both the sheer existence of conscious states and the precise mental content that constitutes them is outside the pale of evolutionary explanation."[95] The evolutionists' claim that consciousness simply evolved appears to be without any basis in evidence, scientific or otherwise. The notion that physical-chemical reactions in the brain could lead to consciousness seems to be pure wishful thinking by those with an anti-supernatural bias.

Groothuis explains it in a slightly different way. Materialists, he says, cannot explain the sensations that make up our subjective feelings or the experience of being conscious. These things may be associated with material states, but they are not material—they are experiential. As Howard Robinson puts it, "The notion of having something as an object of experience is not, prima facie, a physical notion; it does not figure in any physical science."[96] The same principle, says Groothuis, applies to propositional attitudes—that is, "the cognitive orientation one takes toward a proposition." A computer, he notes, has no cognitive orientation toward the codes; though it computes, it doesn't think or experience anything. "Belief, disbelief, suspension of belief and confusion—as well as hoping, fearing, wishing and so on—are propositional attitudes *about* things in the world. They are directed at something." Groothuis argues that materialists have utterly failed to explain this phenomenon, which he calls "intentionality."[97] I was reminded of this recently by an article I read about computers being programmed to compose music. No matter how sophisticated they compose, computers will never be consciously aware of their own "genius" or that they even exist.

Propositions, which Groothuis says are "at the heart of all human language," don't fit neatly into a material universe because they are not material in nature. Even truth itself presents a problem for the materialist because it is a proposition that corresponds with its referent. "The relationships required for truth cannot occur in a (solely) materialistic world," notes Groothuis, "because beliefs and propositions are not reducible to material states."[98]

The materialist is also impotent to explain the existence of love in material terms. It is inconceivable that love—or any other human emotion—is just a physical reaction to material influences, such as a burp or sneeze.[99] If love is just a collection of one's individual material states, how can people who have completely different collections of material states love each other?

Furthermore, the materialist has trouble explaining free will—though researchers at the University of California at Davis think they have found the answer. After conducting a study that monitored subjects' brain activities while they sat in front of a screen and received cues to look either left or right, the scientists concluded that free will—that is, our ability to make autonomous choices—may be an illusion resulting from so-called "neural noise" in the brain.[100] That theory may strike many people as bizarre, but it's no more fantastic than Richard Dawkins' argument that the universe just "appears" to be designed. Rejecting supernaturalism, as many scientists do, leads to these kinds of strange theories on human consciousness and other topics, which are often much less plausible than assigning a role to God.

Finally, the materialist cannot conceivably explain our ability to reason and our capacity to understand the world, but the Christian worldview can—and does. Darwinism certainly doesn't offer any guidance because these abilities surely didn't evolve due to their survival value. Even Darwin, says Groothuis, had difficulty squaring his rational abilities with his naturalist theories. Darwin wrote, "With me the horrid doubt always arises whether the convictions of man's mind, which has been developed from the mind of the lower animals, are of any value or at all trustworthy. Would any one trust in the convictions of a monkey's mind, if there are any convictions in such a mind?"[101] Indeed, if our thoughts were just material in nature, they would resemble a reflex action like a muscle twinge. "But," asks C. S. Lewis, "can glorified muscle twinges weigh evidence and reach warranted conclusions?"[102]

Groothuis makes a compelling case that neither consciousness nor reason can be explained by materialism (or pantheism), but are perfectly understandable as products of Christian theism.[103] It's ironic that it is one of God's greatest gifts to man—his intelligence—that leads some to get puffed up to the point that they think He doesn't exist or they don't need Him. The marvel we call the human brain is powerful evidence that God exists. But our consciousness, our awareness, and our sense of being are even stronger proof that we are more than the combination of molecules of which we are physically made. The best explanation for our cognitive faculties and the qualities they produce is that the God of the Bible created human beings in His image and likeness, which includes the characteristics of rationality, personality, uniqueness, consciousness, love, and subjective experiences. The qualities that distinguish us from other creatures—the ones that mark us as God's special creatures—are the very ones the skeptics fail to recognize as being particularly special.

In the final chapter I will discuss evil as well as pain and suffering, which are problematic issues for so many people and which stand as obstacles to their faith.

CHAPTER 13

✧✧✧✧✧✧✧✧✧✧✧✧✧

PAIN AND SUFFERING

I don't think anything was a greater obstacle to my faith than the question of why an omnipotent, omnibenevolent God, which the God of the Bible most certainly is, would permit such evil as exists in the world. This conundrum has kept many people from turning to God and caused many who were with Him to turn away. If God is good why is there evil? If God permits evil why do we insist He is good?

As I explained earlier, the pervasiveness of evil in the world is something that once caused me to have doubts about Christianity, but became something that helps me to *overcome* doubt. Ironically, it reminds me that we are morally oriented beings, and that is only possible, in my view, if a moral God created us. Furthermore, it reinforces the authority of the Bible, because only the Bible captures the true state of the human condition.

Atheists and other critics often argue that an all-powerful, all-loving God would not permit evil, pain, and suffering of the type we witness daily, and therefore God does not exist. But as Alister McGrath comments, this is a self-defeating argument because, by invoking a moral argument to disprove God, they are essentially proving Him. After all, to ascribe moral aspects to suffering presupposes an absolute moral framework. Put differently, we all recognize human suffering as an undeniable, objective fact, but to attach morality to it requires an external reference outside ourselves. That reference can only come from God. Ravi Zacharias agrees, arguing that the reality of evil does not disprove God's existence because evil only exists if an absolute moral law exists—and if an absolute moral law exists, then God exists.

We have already noted that skeptics deny the moral argument for God, claiming that man, having evolved from the primordial soup, could have developed his own conscience and moral compass. But does their argument really stand up to scrutiny? If we are the product of random chance, does it make sense that we would have an innate sense of morality, conscience, guilt, and the recognition of a distinction between good and evil?[1] The more reasonable position is that human beings were created as moral beings.

"THEY DON'T BELIEVE IN GOD, BUT THEY HATE HIM"

Let's assume for the sake of argument that the God of the Bible does exist. Isn't it obvious that we are judging God just by asking why He allows suffering? The skeptic may deny this too, because he can't judge someone he claims not to believe in. Well, in theory that's true, but as my friend Frank Turek says of some of the atheists he's debated, "They don't believe in God, but they hate Him."

In other words, deep down they know He exists, even if their knowledge is buried under pride or denial. Similarly, our reflexive instinct to presume to judge God on moral grounds may well reveal that we know He exists and that He defines objective morality—that is, it inheres in His nature. We may not realize it, but we could be registering bewilderment at God because we know He is not only God, but that God is morally perfect and wouldn't do anything immoral. It could be a rebellion of sorts on our part, a symptom of our frustration over our own moral and intellectual limitations.

But as Ravi notes, God gave us the moral law, which sanctifies each and every human life and leads us, inevitably, to think in a moral frame of reference. "We can't shake it off," Ravi contends. So when we ask why God permits suffering that we wouldn't permit if we were in charge of the universe, we are both presuming to judge Him and revealing our own dismay that He would stray from the very standards that only He could have established, which is ludicrous.

People have been asking these questions about evil and suffering for thousands of years. Many of them are addressed in the Book of Job, from which we learn that people tend to have a simplistic view of God. When Job—and all of us by extension—interrogate God as to why He permits suffering when He could prevent it, we are attempting to reduce Him to human terms and subject Him to our moral judgment. If not outraged, we are certainly perplexed that He doesn't seem to abide by His own rules, which, again, is absurd. We insist that He act in accordance with our concepts and standards of justice and fairness.

Along these lines, British atheist Bertrand Russell employs a proof to argue against God's existence: if God exists, He willed a moral law. If He willed that law arbitrarily, He is not essentially good. But if He did not will it arbitrarily He willed it according to some external standard, which would mean that He is not ultimate—He is not the God we have perceived Him to be.

This riddle makes God too small and reduces Him to our terms. God does not will His moral law arbitrarily, and we intuitively know that or we wouldn't be so confused in the first place. God, in His very nature, defines morality—He is the standard. He is absolutely moral, just as He is the absolute truth, and His moral will is neither arbitrary nor subject to any standard outside Himself. Just because we don't fully comprehend our infinite God doesn't mean He acts arbitrarily. It is not a copout to concede that human beings are incapable of fully understanding every aspect of life and the outworkings of good and evil in a fallen world.

We know that God, as a perfectly moral being, wouldn't will evil, so unless we draw from that the illogical conclusion that He doesn't exist, we need to ponder why He might permit evil to occur. There is nothing wrong with believing Christians pondering these questions—as the Bible writers themselves did. After all, God did create us as moral, intellectual creatures in His image, so it's only natural for us to wonder why things don't seem quite right about this issue.

The Bible teaches that God doesn't act whimsically or arbitrarily, and He wouldn't create evil or allow suffering for any nefarious purpose. He is not capable of sinister motives. Our questioning of God's actions should be aimed at getting ourselves right with God rather than judging Him, because we surely accept that He sets the standard—that He *is* the standard. So we might begin by asking what is wrong with *us*? What part of the picture are we not seeing?

"A PRIVATION OF A GOOD THING"

It might be helpful to examine more closely what we mean by the term "evil." Rejecting the dualist idea that evil co-exists with good, the biblical worldview discounts the notion that God created evil. Rather, He created freedom, and with freedom comes the possibility of evil. As Dr. Geisler explains, God makes evil possible but free creatures make it actual.

Geisler illustrates the confusion with this fallacious syllogism: God is the creator of everything. Evil is something. Therefore, God is the creator of evil. The first premise is correct because denying that God creates everything suggests dualism—that evil exists as a separate entity empowered on its own or by someone or something else apart from God. The second premise, however, is flawed because evil is not a thing or a substance; it is a lack or privation of the goodness that God made. So Dr. Geisler's corrected formulation reads like this: God created every substance. Evil is not a substance but a privation of a substance. Therefore God did not create evil.[2]

Something is only a privation if it is supposed to be part of something and is not. So a book without a brain is not a privation because a book is not supposed to have a brain. Don't infer from this that evil is not real;

it most certainly is. But instead of being its own separate entity, it is a corruption of another entity.[3]

OTHER OPTIONS?

Why, then, does God allow evil to exist? I've read and thought a great deal about this question, and I think the best answer is a rather simple one. God permits evil to exist for the same reason He allowed it to arise in the first place: because He can't destroy evil without eradicating free will, which is necessary for a moral universe. Let's examine this more closely.

God didn't have to create us at all, nor did He have to create the universe. But since He did, why did He create us the way He did and place us in a world that allows evil and suffering? Is ours the best possible world God could have made?[4] I have to believe so, in keeping with my idea of a perfect and perfectly loving God.

What other options did He have once He decided to create human beings? Ravi Zacharias says that scholars through the years have posited four possible alternatives:

1. He could have not created at all.
2. He could have created human beings but given them no free will.
3. He could have created an amoral world where there was no such thing as good or evil.
4. He could have created the world we live in, where good and evil exist and we have the possibility of choosing either.

The first option doesn't require much discussion, except to repeat that He could have chosen not to create us, being in a perfect Triune relationship without us, but He chose to anyway, despite all the anguish it would entail. As to the second option, what would be the point of creating a world full of androids? They certainly couldn't have given and received love in any genuine sense. And what would be the point of the third option, creating an amoral world? If you remove morals altogether, you remove goodness. Only option four permitted God to make us in His image—beings with free will who are capable of love and spirituality. As Ravi says, of the four choices, our world is the only one where love is genuinely possible.

To make us capable of love God had to give us free will, and in granting that, He opened up the possibility of evil and suffering. "For God to prevent evil, He would have had to make humanity other than it is," i.e, without free will, says theologian Millard Erickson. "Evil was a necessary accompaniment of God's plan to make people fully human."[5] We are not God; we are creatures and we are imperfect, though made in His image.

OUR SUFFERING IS NOT WITHOUT RECOVERY

There are also some mitigating aspects to the existence of evil that we should consider. One thing that provides me some peace of mind is that God knows that our suffering, no matter how real and excruciating, is finite and temporal, and that without diminishing the reality and awfulness of it, it is nothing in comparison with the eternal glory we will share with Him in the afterlife (2 Cor. 4:16). Ravi notes that in the purview of God, an act that involves human suffering is not an act "without recovery." God is the Author of Life and has the power to restore it to one who has lost it. The recovery is even greater than the life lived in the flesh.[6] As Paul says, "For to me, to live is Christ and to die is gain" (Philip. 1:21). While it's much easier to say this in the abstract than to say it while we are actually in pain, it helps to keep the long view in mind when we consider these questions.

At times God may have good reasons to allow evil—reasons we may not see at the time. He allowed Lazarus to die so that He could demonstrate His power over death by bringing him back to life.[7] Additionally, as I summarized in Chapter 3, the convoluted story of Joseph exemplifies how God wove a tapestry of good out of multiple threads of evil. I also believe this is one of the central messages of Job. As it turns out, in permitting Job's suffering, God drew Job closer to Himself and also created critical lessons for legions of Bible readers through the ages.

As seen with Job, sometimes our suffering leads us to seek a closer relationship with God, and nothing is more important than that, for God ultimately created us, I believe, for His glory and to form a voluntary, loving relationship with Him. God is always with us through our darkest moments (Psalm 23). Romans tells us that "suffering produces perseverance; perseverance, character; and character, hope. And hope does not put us to shame, because God's love has been poured out into our hearts through the Holy Spirit, who has been given to us" (5:3–5).

WHY NOT GIVE US AN ESSAY ON EVIL?

Let's take a further look at the enigmatic Book of Job, which has so much to say about why God permits evil and suffering and why He allows bad things to happen to good people.

God's answer is not what we would expect and might even seem like a dodge at first glance. But properly understood, it is a complete and satisfying explanation. I think part of the beauty of the book is that it shows just how limited we humans are. That is, our initial failure to understand God's approach to the question is tied to the limitations inherent in humanity—limitations that He reveals to us in His response to Job's question. We can't put God in a box; we can't bring Him down to our level, which is precisely what we do when we demand that He answer the question on our terms or submit to some outside moral standard apart from Himself. In the end, His answer is majestic, exciting, and uplifting because it gives us hope and reaffirms our basis for trusting Him, even if it isn't what we initially anticipated.

We tend to expect God, who created us in His image as beings capable of rational thought, to provide a clear, logical, direct answer to the disturbing question of why an omnipotent, omnibenevolent God would allow human suffering. Instead of giving us the cryptic Book of Job, why didn't God just give us an essay providing straightforward answers to these questions? Why do such important matters have to be shrouded in mystery?

When God finally begins to answer Job's question, instead of giving a pat answer to the "why" question, He tells us Who He is. He begins by showing Job just how inadequate and inferior we human beings are in comparison to Him.

God takes Job (and us) on a tour of His creation, from the heights of cosmology down to some of the most minute and fascinating details of animal life on earth, revealing to us that He is the divine administrator of the universe and that we don't have the first notion of the magnitude of its complexity. No matter how far we advance in science or technology, we'll never be able to approach God's creative powers as demonstrated in the beauty and intricacy of His simplest life forms. God's created cosmology and biology render us in awe of His greatness—even more so than Paul tells us in Romans. In effect, God's reply to Job cuts him, and us, down to size, treating us as philosophical neophytes who are so utterly diminutive relative to God as to make our questioning of His moral standards absurd.

As He takes Job on this tour, God asks him whether he is competent to pass judgment on His workings. God doesn't merely show His creative power concerning material and living things, He also reveals aspects of His moral character, demonstrating that He is completely sovereign, down to every hair on our heads and the actions of every one of His creatures, including the evil ones, represented by Behemoth and Leviathan. He shows that even they are ultimately under His thumb. In describing some of the attributes of His creatures, which might otherwise seem random, God demonstrates that He is mindful of their suffering and that He always balances matters, in the long run, in favor of good for His people (Romans 8:28).

In showing us the advantages and disadvantages certain animals possess, God is imparting the lesson that His divinely designed benefits for these creatures exceed their burdens. For example, while the ostrich is awkward and can't fly, it can outrace the "majestic steed." God may be showing us here that He superintends everything, that He cares, and that He is perfectly fair and just even if we don't see it from our limited perspective.[8]

By illustrating His incomparable power in creating the universe, God shows us an infinite superiority that not only extends to His administration of the universe, but also to the moral law in His providential dealings with men. This sovereign tour on which God takes Job preemptively refutes the argument that God is operating under the principle that might makes right. He does not act arbitrarily or capriciously. The universe He created and controls has both material and moral order. God makes this point Himself in Chapter 40. He lets Job know in no uncertain terms that he (Job) is no more able to exercise jurisdiction in the moral realm than he is able to control nature.

God shows that He created everything, including forces hostile to Himself, which are symbolized by the sea, but that He subdued these forces, which, as noted, signals that He is sovereign over everything, including those things that have turned evil. This point is also underscored in God's demonstrated control over Satan, whom He permitted to test Job.

But we mustn't conclude that because God is sovereign over evil yet permits it to exist, that He is indifferent to it, or that He lets it run amok. No, there is a limit to evil's sway. Evil is subject to God's superior, infinite power. It neither controls nor limits Him, and it does not detract from His greatness. Nothing in His creation is powerful enough to reduce or compromise His power. He will be victorious over evil in the end—in His time and in His way.

IT'S NOT KNOWING ABOUT GOD, BUT *KNOWING* GOD

Let's revisit Bertrand Russell's suggestion that God is either not good because He allows evil to exist when He could prevent it, or He is not "ultimate" because He follows a moral law outside Himself. In the final analysis, Russell's argument fails because it is rooted in a gross misapprehension of God's nature. In His response to Job, according to Dr. Tom Howe, God passes between the horns of Russell's dilemma. God is not arbitrary, for He is the ultimate source of moral law. In fact, we may identify evil as that which is contrary to God's nature. God is God;

He is ultimate because He is ultimate. His whirlwind speeches (Job 38:1–42:6) make this point emphatically. His perfect nature means that He is both absolute and absolutely moral.

As imperfect beings, we cannot completely understand everything. Divine rewards and punishments still occur, but they are not always on a temporal timetable—at least not one that we can discern from our limited perspective. In this fallen world, forces interrupt the normal cause and effect sequence, and thus the (relatively) righteous sometimes suffer and evil people sometimes prosper. As noted earlier, we must be mindful of the long view. In the end, God will administer perfect justice, as He did, foremost, on the cross.[9]

What God teaches Job is that even he—a relatively righteous man—did not really know God. He knew *about* God; he tried to appease God through sacrifices out of fear of His wrath. But he didn't really *know* Him. Through his sufferings, Job learns that the most important thing in life is to have a relationship with God. While he enjoyed prosperity and good health, it didn't seem so important to develop and strengthen that relationship. And although at one point it appeared that God had gratuitously allowed a relatively innocent Job to suffer, He actually blessed him through his sufferings, for without them Job wouldn't have learned, as intimately, the paramount importance of knowing and trusting God. He wouldn't have developed the relationship with God that he ultimately cultivated. Nothing in life can possibly compare to fellowship with God. This is not to trivialize the horrible deaths God permitted Satan to visit on Job's family, or the suffering any human beings experience. But it is to say, as noted above, that from an eternal perspective God works all things for the good of His people (Romans 8:28).

The Book of Job may seem discouraging because it implies that our omnipotent God permits suffering when He has the power to prevent it. But He also reveals to us that He is in control and will manage our affairs consistent with our best interests—provided we respond in faith. This doesn't mean we will always recognize the benefits, or that they will occur in the short term. But we can derive comfort from the scripturally revealed truth that He is not the apathetic god of the deists. As He shows us in Job, He is an active and sovereign God Who beneficently oversees His universe.

In the Book of Job God doesn't illustrate His incomparable, indescribable majesty and our comparative impotence simply to humiliate us. He does it to convince us that we can trust Him. He shows Job and us that there is abundant evidence that He is trustworthy and that when we place our trust in Him, He will bring us through our difficulties to a better end and will change us as a result, mainly through developing a deeper relationship with Him. By revealing His infinite glory and perfection to us while simultaneously demonstrating His desire to condescend and deal with us on an intimate, personal level, He shows us just how loving He is. In trusting Him and relying on His strength instead of our own, we can become more like Him. Through the fires of suffering He refines us.

In experiencing this suffering, Job directly encounters God, comes to know Him, and becomes a changed man. Ironically, Job's suffering can be seen as a gift of God's grace because it unites him with God.

God doesn't wish suffering and pain on us, but as we've seen, to make us capable of love and of having a loving relationship with Him, He had to give us free will. In making us free, He necessarily gave us the option of choosing evil. Sin and evil lead to pain and suffering in the world. This is not to say that everyone who suffers does so as a result of his own sinful actions. But the presence of sin in the world is what ultimately leads to suffering.

I also believe that if there were a more suitable way for God to have created us in His image—free, moral beings capable of love and loving relations—and without opening up the possibility of evil, He would have done so, because in creating us the way He did, He knew that we would sin. He thus knew that in order to redeem us so that we could enjoy a relationship with Him, His nature would require Him to send His Son to save us, which would involve immeasurable suffering by the Son and therefore also the Father, Who is in perfect harmony with the Son.

CHRIST, THE ULTIMATE MEDIATOR

Before leaving the subject of Job, I want to share one last insight. At one point, Job becomes so exasperated at God's supposed arbitrary treatment of him that he cries out for a mediator who will act as an umpire between him and God. At first this may seem ludicrous because Job is asking God to help him find an advocate against Himself. In a sense, he is asking God to act against His own interests. Job recognizes that God is all-powerful, yet appeals to Him to provide a mediator who will put Him in His place.

But on deeper reflection this isn't so far-fetched, for isn't this a fore-shadowing of what actually occurred when God sent His Son to be an advocate for us? Isn't Jesus Christ the Ultimate Mediator between our sinfulness and God's perfect justice? Isn't that the essence of the gospel—that by believing in Christ, by putting our faith and trust in Him as our Mediator, He will bridge the gap between our sinfulness and God's justice? By living a sinless life and taking on our sins, He makes possible our eternal life in His presence.

So while it may seem, in human terms, that God would be acting against His own interests by providing a mediator, this is not the case at all. God *wants* to provide a mediator to redeem us because He loves us. He is not compromising His justice or His standards by providing Jesus to us as our mediator. To the contrary, by doing so, He has made possible our reconciliation to Him and our ability to have a permanent loving relationship with Him without compromising His holiness.

In the end, this is the real, complete, and most fulfilling answer to the question of evil. The answer is Jesus Christ. God suffered with us when He didn't have to. God is the ultimate answer because He suffered in Christ. He was so intent on creating us that He subjected Himself to the world of suffering necessitated by our infusion with (and abuse of) free will.

THE "CROSS SMASHES TO SMITHEREENS" THIS TERRIBLE CARICATURE OF GOD

Christianity is the only religion in which God suffers along with us. And to suffer and die is the very reason Christ came into the world, as Bishop Fulton Sheen explains, because His death was necessary for our redemption. The God of the universe is actually sitting beside us and feeling our pain—"and He weeps."[10] God went to the cross to suffer for our evil.

In *The Cross of Christ*, the late John Stott, a brilliant Christian evangelist and author, acknowledges that human suffering is one of the main obstacles to our faith: "The fact of suffering undoubtedly constitutes the single greatest challenge to the Christian faith, and has been in every generation. Its distribution and degree appear to be entirely random and therefore unfair. Sensitive spirits ask if it can possibly be reconciled with God's justice and love."[11]

In fact, Stott admits that but for the cross, he too would have insurmountable problems with Christianity: "I could never myself believe in God, if it were not for the cross. The only God I believe in is the One Nietzsche ridiculed as 'God on the cross.'"[12] But the fact that God was willing to suffer Himself makes Him a God who demonstrably loves us and Who can relate to us through His sufferings. As Stott movingly explains,

> For the real sting of suffering is not misfortune itself, nor even the pain of it or the injustice of it, but the apparent God-forsakenness of it. Pain is endurable, but the seeming indifference of God is not. Sometimes we picture him lounging, perhaps dozing, in some celestial deck-chair, while the hungry millions starve to death. We think of him as an armchair spectator, almost gloating over the world's suffering, and enjoying His own insulation from it. Philip Yancey has gone further and uttered the unutterable which we may have thought but to which we have never dared to give voice: "If God is truly in charge, somehow connected to all the world's suffering, why is He so capricious, unfair? Is He the cosmic sadist Who delights in watching us squirm?" Job had said something similar: God "mocks the despair of the innocent" (Job 9:23). It is this terrible caricature of God which the cross smashes to smithereens. We are not to envisage Him on a deck-chair, but on a cross. The God Who allows us to suffer,

once suffered Himself in Christ, and continues to suffer with
us and for us today.[13]

Ravi, as usual, provides the exclamation point:

> God alone is the absolute expression of love that is never
> separated from holiness. God cannot be at the same time holy
> and unloving or loving and unholy. In turning our backs upon
> Him, we lose the source of defining love, live with the pain of
> unholiness, and suffering remains an enigma—leaving our
> blemished characters in search of a moral law and our finite
> minds crying out for an answer.... When we come to Jesus
> Christ at the cross, where love, holiness, and suffering com-
> bine, we find both the answer to why we suffer and the
> strength to live in this mortal frame for Him.... Where love
> is possible, there pain is also possible. Where the resurrection
> is promised, there is also the promise of tears wiped away.
> Heaven is the confirmation of our choice, to love Him and to
> be with Him. That is the hope of everyone who is a follower
> of Jesus Christ, whom to know is life eternal.[14]

I do not pretend to have all the answers to the problems of evil, suffering, and pain in the world, and some of those I've shared in this
chapter will probably not be satisfying to one who is currently suffering.
I don't ever want to presume to place myself in the shoes of someone who
is feeling unbearable pain and pretend I, or anyone else, can offer mag-
ical words or even some glib citation to Scripture that will instantly make
everything better.

Words alone cannot possibly eradicate the anguish, agony, and griev-
ing that human beings endure. But Christianity does offer the one ultimate answer, Jesus Christ, Who will sustain all who place their trust in
Him. Countless people who had given up all hope finally found their
rest in Christ, Who, if we'll place our faith and abide in Him, will truly
give us a peace that surpasses all understanding. We know that we can
trust Him because He voluntarily suffered and died on our behalf. We

know we can relate to Him and Him to us precisely because, for our sakes, He voluntarily endured every kind of indignity that we can possibly experience ourselves. His offer is not for us to embrace an abstract intellectual belief in His existence. It is to develop a real and intimate personal relationship with Him. In that relationship, the Bible assures us, we will find enduring peace and fulfillment. Please believe it. Please act on it. You won't regret it.

CONCLUSION

At the beginning of this book I told you that I began my adult spiritual journey as a nonbeliever. I was constantly seeking God, searching for answers, and trying to understand why I couldn't bring myself to believe in Christianity. Different people planted various seeds in the garden of my life, but my faith didn't finally blossom until that last seed was planted, which was the discovery of the messianic prophecies.

Many other seeds helped lead me to that final moment of belief—I'm sure I was and remain unaware of half of them. But what I do know is that in my case, in my life, Christian apologetics had a profound impact. Studying theology and Bible doctrine was also crucial. It is because of my experiences that I decided to write this book. While I believe it is the work of the Holy Spirit that brings people to God, He sometimes does so through human agents, and so there is nothing futile about Christians evangelizing and defending the faith. In fact, we are commanded to do so.

Based on my own personal experiences with other people, I think that many nonbelievers haven't spent a great deal of time studying the Bible or exploring Christian theology. That is why I was determined to include in this book not just the arguments advanced by classical Christian apologists, but also a discussion of what Christians believe. It's wonderful to convince someone that Christianity's truth claims are supported by substantial evidence, but what good is defending the faith if the person to whom you are defending it ends up knowing very little about it after you've presented your case?

Therefore, apologetics and theology go hand in hand. Indeed, for me, theology and the Bible are the best apologetic of all. As I've said throughout this book, I find Christ's teachings, the letters of the New Testament writers, and the history and teachings in the remainder of the Bible intellectually, emotionally, and spiritually attractive, and probative of the truth of Christianity. I am excited about Scripture—from individual verses, to chapters, to books, to the entire Bible as an integrated whole. I could not have written a book of this sort without sharing my enthusiasm for the Bible and for theology, because I believe many readers are ripe for these ideas and will find them as exhilarating as I do, and I trust that this could make a difference in their lives.

As I believe I've shown in this book, there is an enormous amount of evidence that the Bible is historically reliable and that it was written by real men who were united in their commitment to truth. I believe the evidence shows, well beyond a reasonable doubt, that the Bible is the inspired Word of God, and that it teaches that God entered this world in human form when Jesus Christ was born, that Christ lived a sinless life, that He was crucified, that He died, and that He was resurrected. I believe all these things, and I encourage you to believe them as well, because if they are true, your acceptance or rejection of them—your decision whether to place your saving faith in Jesus Christ—will, the Bible tells us, affect your eternal destiny.

I also agreed to undertake this project because I believe I can relate to skeptics, having been one for many years. I don't look down on skeptics; in fact I believe I understand their perspective. But I also know that nonbelievers don't have to remain that way. The Holy Spirit beckons all to come to Jesus Christ in faith.

I could never be smug about my faith. I readily confess that I still have doubts about some things, and that I can't completely understand certain things God did in the Old Testament. I have read explanations for them that make sense to me and satisfy me, however, including why God took the drastic actions that He did—not for the purpose of exterminating the human race, but to preserve it; not out of vindictiveness, but out of love.

While I don't understand everything entirely, I am also not playing mind games with myself. I have approached these problems with the goal of discovering the truth, and I have tried to confront potential obstacles, not avoid them. On balance these struggles have been a positive influence for me because they have spurred me to study further and more deeply immerse myself in God's Word. Without putting aside my critical faculties, without abandoning my God-given ability to reason, but by embracing it, I have weighed all the evidence in support of Christianity and have concluded that it is absolutely true—and it's not even a close call.

If you are looking for reasons not to believe, I suppose you will find them. And if you are close-minded toward the supernatural or toward a Christian worldview, I concede that you will continue to resist these ideas. But if you approach the evidence with an open mind and open heart, I think you might be surprised how God will begin to convince you that He is Who He has revealed Himself to be—in creation, in nature, in His incarnation, and in His Bible.

Even if you intellectually assent to the truth of Christianity, you will still need to take that further step of faith and place your trust in Jesus Christ. When you do, you will find that He will change your life. He will begin to give you peace and fulfillment—and this is something that cannot be taught in a book, but must be experienced.

In complete honesty, the world makes no sense to me apart from the biblical, Christian worldview. If you have difficulty comprehending any of this, try to unshackle yourself from the cultural bombardment you've experienced in your life. Even if it makes you feel uncomfortable, just give it a shot. Give the Bible a fair hearing. Don't read it grudgingly, but openly. Ask God to unveil its meaning for you. Ask Him into your heart. Ask Him to reveal Himself to you so that you will acquire an assurance that surpasses all understanding. You may have a fast, sudden epiphany, or God may choose to reveal Himself and His truths to you over time. Every person's experience is different.

I have tried not to sound sarcastic as I have discussed the ideas of certain naturalists and Darwinists who truly do believe things that are much more far-fetched and implausible—and I dare say, based on far less persuasive evidence—than the things I believe, as a Christian. But naturalists and Darwinists have controlled the culture and our educational establishment for most of my lifetime. Many of them ridicule Christian beliefs and Christians' intellectual prowess. But many Christians are intellectuals and many intellectuals are Christians—and that might just shock you if you follow the mainstream media's coverage of these issues.

Great peer pressure is brought to bear in many circles against Christianity. Please realize that and try to divorce yourself from it. Open your minds and let the Bible and the evidence speak for themselves. You may be surprised.

You may have heard or read about Pascal's wager. In his famous *Pensées*, seventeenth-century French mathematician and Christian philosopher Blaise Pascal wrote that reasonable people should bet on the existence of Christ and the truth of Christianity because if they are correct they will have attained eternal life, and if they are wrong they will have lost nothing.

Though Pascal has always been my favorite philosopher since I first read him in college, I have long believed that his "wager" formulation is flawed. One cannot become a Christian simply by casually casting his lot as one and saying, "Hey, I'm a Christian, so I'm saved." He first must believe that Christianity's essential truth claims are true and, more important, place his trust—his saving faith—in Christ. He must ask Jesus Christ to save him from his sins and believe that He can and will.

But I do think we can extract an important point from Pascal's suggestion, and I urge you to consider it. I would modify his wager to tell you that you have nothing to lose, and potentially everything to gain, by honestly investigating the evidence and reading, studying, and meditating on the Bible, and prayerfully inviting God into your heart to illuminate His truths for you. There is no downside to you in embarking on such a venture if Christianity is in fact hogwash. But you have everything to gain if by undertaking this mission, you find that Christianity is true and you eventually take the step of faith by placing your trust in Jesus Christ.

Don't be offended by the notion that you must have saving faith in Christ. Don't assume that God is making you jump through unnecessary hoops. He is the One Who suffered for *you*. He did this so that you could live. He doesn't ask you to believe because He is on a divine ego trip, but because He loves you and wants you to latch on to Him in order to be saved from your sins.

You must know that you can't do that for yourself. I know that I can't. You must know that you need a Savior. I know that I do. Jesus Christ is our Savior. He is asking you to appropriate His offer for eternal salvation by trusting Him to save you. You must not be passive about it. You have a choice. He will meet you nine-tenths of the way, he will come all the way to that last fraction of a percent, but in the end, you must accept His offer and allow Him to do the work. Indeed, He has already finished all the work on your behalf. Don't let it go to waste in your life.

So I humbly encourage you to take this bet. It's one you can't lose, and even if you end up remaining a nonbeliever, you will have enriched yourself in the process by studying the most marvelous work ever written by the hand of man—and the mind of God.

God bless you.

ACKNOWLEDGMENTS

First, I give all the thanks and glory to Jesus Christ, but there simply are no words sufficient to communicate it. I know, however, that He knows the depth of my gratitude for *everything*, including pursuing me, not giving up on me, forgiving me, and dying on the cross for me.

I thank everyone at Regnery Publishing, with whom I continue to enjoy a tremendous working relationship and whose professionalism and competence make the entire book writing experience enjoyable instead of drudgery. I especially want to thank Marji Ross for her ongoing support and confidence, and for her wisdom in all aspects of the publishing business. I am particularly grateful to Harry Crocker, who first approached me with the idea for this book. I can't thank him enough for that and for his friendship, mentorship, counsel, and enthusiasm for every project with which I've been involved. Maria Ruhl did a wonderful job copy editing and proofing the manuscript and was a joy to work with on this book.

This is the third consecutive book in which I have worked with the greatest editor ever, Jack Langer, whose unique editing skills are perfectly suited for my weaknesses. He is an artist at tightening my writing and smoothing the flow. In the process, he never makes any suggestions that change the substance, unless I've made a mistake, which sometimes happens. He is incredibly conscientious, industrious, and cooperative—amazingly easy to work with.

Many thanks as always to my buddy Greg Mueller and his team at Creative Response Concepts for quarterbacking the promotion and marketing of this book along with the excellent marketing staff at Regnery.

I want to put in a plug for Logos Bible Software—the most powerful and useful software I have ever used. With this software I have at my fingertips almost twelve thousand books that are fully accessible and searchable. Without this software my research and writing would have taken months longer and would not have been as fruitful. I can't praise this product enough and would encourage anyone serious about the Bible and theological study to get it.

There are so many people who have influenced my spiritual life and development that it would be impossible to list them all. No one has been more important than my wife Lisa, my best friend and mother of our awesome children, who was patient and understanding through my doubting years, always confident I would come to Christ. There is a reason I made sure that she was the first to read my completed manuscript. She diligently read every page and made invaluable and insightful suggestions, helping to clarify potentially confusing passages.

My friend Dr. Steve Johnson helped to guide me through the beginning phases of my journey and helped keep me on the right theological path early on and away from error. Thank you so much, Steve.

Ron Watts, my extraordinary pastor and friend, has been an enormous blessing to me and to every other member of his congregation. His Christian example and leadership have helped La Croix become an amazingly successful, seeker-friendly, biblically solid church with a balanced approach to theology, discipleship, and service. His consistently outstanding sermons have educated, inspired, and uplifted thousands. The entire staff of La Croix is Christ-centered and focused on spreading the gospel to the "unchurched." They impart to the congregation the essential messages of service and discipleship, and help to train all members with the skills necessary for both.

My friend Frank Turek has not only been a wonderful source for my biblical and theological mentorship, but performed for me an essential role in this project. When I was finished with the manuscript I wanted it vetted by someone schooled in both theology and apologetics, so I asked Frank to review my work and save me from any egregious errors. He undertook the task immediately and enthusiastically and did, in fact, make a number of immensely useful suggestions. Frank is always willing to help and never asks for credit, but I will tell you that his suggestions were invaluable and clarifying. Thank you so much, Frank.

I want to thank my friend Ravi Zacharias, whose incomparable intellect, winsomeness, and teaching have meant more to me than I can properly express. Thanks also to Ravi's right-hand "man," my good friend Danielle DuRant, for her support and her important suggestions.

Many thanks to Dr. Richard Land, president of Southern Evangelical Seminary, for his encouragement and for his work for the Kingdom. Thanks also to Eric Gustafson at Southern Evangelical Seminary for his suggestions early on in this process, for finding certain materials for me, and for his support.

I owe a major debt to Dr. Norman Geisler for his friendship, support, and voluminous writings on the subjects of apologetics and theology, which have greatly deepened my understanding of these subjects.

A big thank you to Josh McDowell, whom I've never met, but whose books and teachings have been instrumental in my theological and apologetics studies. Josh is a tireless and meticulous researcher and contagiously enthusiastic ambassador for Jesus Christ. There is no telling how many people Josh has reached, but I can safely say we're all immeasurably grateful.

Thanks to my friend Michelle Malkin for her steadfast support and friendship through the years and for the vitally important work she does for this nation.

I want to express my gratitude to Lee Strobel, whose books on apologetics have enlightened thousands, including me, and whose dogged investigation of the truth claims of Christianity help bridge the important credibility gap that sometimes exists between believers and skeptics.

My friend Sean Hannity has always been supportive of all my books and other professional endeavors. Sean is a wonderful Christian man who practices what he preaches and, despite his success, remains humble and leads his life as if his guiding principle were the golden rule, always treating everyone with respect, compassion, and generosity.

Mark Levin is one of my very best friends whose loyalty exceeds anything any friend would ever deserve. I can always count on his support and counsel, and I'm forever grateful for both.

I want to thank my father and mother for raising my brother and me in a wonderful, happy Christian home, and for taking us to a special church, Centenary United Methodist, where we were first exposed to the love of Christ and the glories of a supportive Christian community. I will always love that church and its congregants, and consider them family. All the foundations were laid in that environment without which I could never have become a believer and follower of Jesus Christ.

I am very grateful to my grandparents, paternal and maternal, for their Christian example. My uncles, Manley and Stephen Limbaugh Sr., are both role models as hard-working Christian and family men who have always been there for me. My aunts Mary and Anne have also been extremely loving and supportive, and both have set the standard for Christian service through their lives. I am immeasurably grateful that our entire extended family is so close. I don't deserve to be this blessed.

Finally, I want to thank my brother Rush again for inspiring me, for opening up doors for me directly and indirectly, and for doing wonderful work for this nation we both love from the bottom of our hearts. While he has been unfairly maligned more than anyone I know, years from now, if America is able to right its course back toward its founding principles and Christian moorings, people will come to recognize the invaluable role he played in that godly mission. He never complains and always marches on, doing the work of ten people and having the impact of millions. God bless you, Rush, for being the best brother a brother could have.

NOTES

CHAPTER 1: From Skeptic to Believer

1.   Franklin's letter offers a captivating portrait of the great man's thinking on religion. He wrote to Stiles, "You desire to know something of my Religion. It is the first time I have been questioned upon it: But I do not take your curiosity amiss, and shall endeavour in a few Words to gratify it. Here is my creed: I believe in one God, Creator of the Universe. That He governs it by his providence. That he ought to be worshipped. That the most acceptable service we can render to him, is doing good to his other children. That the soul of man is immortal, and will be treated with Justice in another Life respecting its conduct in this. These I take to be the fundamental principles of all sound religion, and I regard them as you do, in whatever sect I meet with them. As to Jesus of Nazareth, my opinion of whom you particularly desire, I think the system of

morals and his religion as he left them to us, the best the world ever saw, or is likely to see; but I apprehend it has received various corrupting changes, and I have with most of the present dissenters in England, some doubts as to his divinity: though it is a question I do not dogmatize upon, having never studied it, and think it needless to busy myself with it now, when I expect soon an opportunity of knowing the truth with less trouble. I see no harm however in its being believed, if that Belief has the good consequence as probably it has, of making his doctrines more respected and better observed, especially as I do not perceive that the Supreme takes it amiss, by distinguishing the believers, in his government of the world, with any particular marks of his displeasure. I shall only add respecting myself, that having experienced the goodness of that Being, in conducting me prosperously through a long life, I have no doubt of its continuance in the next, though without the smallest conceit of meriting such goodness." "Letter from Benjamin Franklin to Ezra Stiles," March 9, 1790, available on Beliefnet, http://www.beliefnet.com/resourcelib/docs/44/Letter_from_ Benjamin_Franklin_to_Ezra_Stiles_1.html.

2.   In his notes from the convention, James Madison reported that Franklin addressed the group. "I have lived, Sir, a long time," said Franklin, "and the longer I live, the more convincing proofs I see of this truth—that God governs in the affairs of men. And if a sparrow cannot fall to the ground without his notice, is it probable that an empire can rise without his aid?" A deist simply could not have made this statement. "Benjamin Franklin's Request for Prayers at the Constitutional Convention," July 28, 1787, available on Beliefnet, http://www.beliefnet.com/resourcelib/docs/21/Benjamin_ Franklins_Request_for_Prayers_at_the_Constitutional__1.html.

3.   Christian Business Men's Committee of USA, *First Steps* (Chattanooga, TN: CBMC Publications, 1983), 3.

4.   R. A. Morey, *Satan's Devices* (Las Vegas, NV: Christian Scholars Press, 2003), 126.

5.   Leland Ryken, *Words of Delight: A Literary Introduction to the Bible* (Grand Rapids, MI: Baker Academic, 1992), 36.

6. Franz Delitzsch, *A New Commentary on Genesis*, trans. Sophia Taylor, 2 vols. (Edinburgh: T. and T. Clark, 1894), 2:275.

7. J. F. Walvoord and R. B. Zuck, Dallas Theological Seminary, *The Bible Knowledge Commentary: An Exposition of the Scriptures*, vol. 2 (Wheaton, IL: Victor, 1985), 231.

8. Some critics argue that the word that is translated "virgin" in this passage means a "young woman" rather than "virgin," but, according to the ESV Study Bible, the term actually refers specifically to a "maiden," which means "a young woman who is unmarried and sexually chaste, and thus has virginity as one of her characteristics." More importantly, Matthew, in his gospel, did apply this prophecy to the virgin birth of Christ (Matt. 1:23).

9. G. K. Chesterton, *Orthodoxy* (New York: John Lane Company, 1909), ix.

10. Douglas Groothuis, *Truth Decay: Defending Christianity against the Challenges of Postmodernism*, Kindle ed. (Downers Grove, IL: Intervarsity Press, 2000), locations 604–6.

11. Rev. Hugh McIntosh, *Is Christ Infallible and the Bible True?* (Minneapolis, MN: Klock and Klock Christian Publishers, Inc., 1902), 282.

12. M. J. Erickson, *God in Three Persons: A Contemporary Interpretation of the Trinity* (Grand Rapids, MI: Baker Books, 1995), 193.

13. J. Locke, G. Berkeley, and D. Hume, *The Harvard Classics 37, The English Philosophers of the 17th and 18th Centuries; Hume, "Of Miracles"* (New York, NY: P.F. Collier & Son), 397.

14. C. H. Spurgeon, *Spurgeon's Sermons, The Infallibility of Scripture*, electronic ed., vol. 34 (Albany, OR: Ages Software, 1998).

15. McIntosh, *Is Christ Infallible and the Bible True?*, 429.

16. Ibid.

17. R. H. Mounce, *Romans*, vol. 27 (Nashville, TN: Broadman & Holman Publishers, 1995), 212.

18. G. Campbell Morgan, *The Teaching of Christ* (New York; London; Edinburgh: Fleming H. Revell Company, 1913), 13.

19. Rev. Charles Spurgeon delivered two excellent sermons on the subject of seeking that illuminate this issue. C. H. Spurgeon,

Spurgeon's Sermons, Good News for Seekers, electronic ed., vol. 22 (Albany, OR: Ages Software, 1998).

20. Alister E. McGrath, *Mere Apologetics: How to Help Seekers and Skeptics Find Faith* (Grand Rapids, MI: Baker Books, 2012), 109.

21. Blaise Pascal, *The Harvard Classics 48 Thoughts, Letters, and Minor Works*, ed. C. W. Eliot, trans. W. F. Trotter, M. L. Booth, and O. W. Wight (New York: P. F. Collier & Son, 1908), 138.

22. Blaise Pascal, *The Harvard Classics 48: Blaise Pascal: Thoughts, Letters, and Minor Works*, ed. C. W. Eliot, trans. W. F. Trotter, M. L. Booth, and O. W. Wight (New York: P. F. Collier & Son, 1910), 140.

23. Ibid.

24. Walvoord and Zuck, Dallas Theological Seminary, *The Bible Knowledge Commentary*, vol. 2, 403.

25. Ramond C. Ortlund Jr., *A Passion for God* (Wheaton, IL: Crossway Books, 2002), xix.

26. Ravi Zacharias, *Cries of the Heart* (Nashville, TN: Thomas Nelson, 2002).

27. J. N. Oswalt, *The NIV Application Commentary: Isaiah* (Grand Rapids, MI: Zondervan Publishing House, 2003), 200.

28. R. Johnson, C. Sanders, and M. S. Heiser, *TH101 Introducing Bible Doctrine I: Theology, Divine Revelation, and the Bible* (Bellingham, WA: Lexham Press, M. S., 2013).

29. Alister McGrath, *Intellectuals Don't Need God and Other Modern Myths: Building Bridges to Faith Through Apologetics* (Grand Rapids, MI: Zondervan, 2010).

30. W. Hendriksen and S. J. Kistemaker, *Exposition of the Gospel According to Luke, Vol. 11* (Grand Rapids, MI: Baker Book House), 736.

31. Ravi Zacharias, *Beyond Opinion: Living the Faith That We Defend* (Nashville, TN: Thomas Nelson, 2007), introduction.

32. William Lane Craig, *Reasonable Faith: Christian Truth and Apologetics*, rev. ed. (Wheaton: IL: Crossway Books, 1994), xiv.

33. Douglas Groothuis, *Christian Apologetics: A Comprehensive Case for Biblical Faith*, Kindle ed. (Downers Grove, IL: InterVarsity Press, 2011), location 176 of 10010.

34. Jeffrey M. Spencer, "An Examination and Evaluation of the Brownsville Revival," *Southern Evangelical Seminary: Christian Apologetics Journal* 2, no. 1 (1999): 6.

CHAPTER 2: "Aha" Moments, Part 1

1. Fulton J. Sheen, *Life of Christ* (New York: McGraw-Hill Book Company, Inc., 1958), 9.

2. Ibid., 19.

3. Ibid., 19–20.

4. Ibid., 20.

5. Ibid.

6. My friend, Christian apologist Frank Turek points out that critics dismiss the point that God reveals Himself in the Bible because many people don't have the Bible. To that, Frank responds that while everyone does not have the Bible, they do observe creation and they possess their own conscience. If they respond to those "lights," God will make the Gospel available to them, as He rewards those who seek Him.

7. William Barclay, ed., *The Gospel of John*, vol. 2, John 14:11 (Philadelphia, PA: Westminster John Knox Press, 1975).

8. D. A. Carson, *The Gospel According to John* (Leicester, England; Grand Rapids, MI: Inter-Varsity Press; W.B. Eerdmans, 1991), 128.

9. Carl F. H. Henry, *God, Revelation and Authority*, vol. 2 (Wheaton, IL: Crossway Books, 1999), 17.

10. Ibid.

11. Douglas Groothuis, *Truth Decay: Defending Christianity against the Challenges of Postmodernism*, Kindle ed. (Downer's Grove, IL: InterVarsity Press, 2000), locations 600–3.

12. Ben Witherington, *The Indelible Image: The Theological and Ethical Thought World of the New Testament: The Collective Witness*, vol. 2 (Downers Grove, IL: InterVarsity Press, 2010), 173.

13. W. A. Criswell, *Great Doctrines of the Bible*, vol. 1 (Grand Rapids: Zondervan Publishing House, 1982), 76–77, quoted in T. George

and D. S. Dockery, eds., *Theologians of the Baptist Tradition* (Nashville, TN: Broadman & Holman Publishers, 2001), 241.

14. W. A. Criswell, *Why I Preach That the Bible Is Literally True* (Nashville, TN: Broadman Press, 1969), 66, quote in T. George & D. S. Dockery, eds., *Theologians of the Baptist Tradition* (Nashville, TN: Broadman & Holman Publishers, 2001), 241.

15. R. C. H. Lenski, *The Interpretation of the Epistle to the Hebrews and of the Epistle of James* (Columbus, OH: Lutheran Book Concern, 1938), 141.

16. Ibid., 144.

17. Ibid., 147.

18. F. F. Bruce, *The Book of the Acts* (Grand Rapids, MI: Wm. B. Eerdmans Publishing Co., 1988), 471.

19. Ray C. Stedman, *Adventuring through The Bible, A Comprehensive Guide to the Entire Bible* (Nashville, TN: Discovery House Publishers, 1997), 29–31.

20. A copy of the entire book of Isaiah was found among the Dead Sea Scrolls, some 150 years before Christ was born, which proves it couldn't have been written after the fact.

CHAPTER 3: "Aha" Moments, Part 2

1. Romans 8:28, 31, 32, 35, 37–39.

2. Ravi Zacharias, *Deliver Us From Evil, Restoring the Soul in a Disintegrating Culture* (Nashville, TN: W Publishing Group, A Division of Thomas Nelson, Inc., 1997).

3. Ibid.

4. Normal L. Geisler, *Systematic Theology, Volume Four: Church, Last Things* (Minneapolis, MN: Bethany House Publishers, 2002), 501.

5. Allen P. Ross, *Creation and Blessing: A Guide to the Study and Exposition of Genesis* (Grand Rapids, MI: Baker Books, 1998), 68.

6.   D. K. Stuart, *Exodus*, vol. 2 (Nashville, TN: Broadman & Holman Publishers, 2006), 372.

7.   This is not to say that all Old Testament commands apply to us today. Some, for example, do not, as they were put into place for the people (and theocracy) of ancient Israel.

8.   Charles H. Spurgeon, *The Metropolitan Tabernacle Pulpit Sermons*, vol. 39 (London: Passmore & Alabaster, 1893), 524.

9.   Charles H. Spurgeon, *Spurgeon's Sermons*, electronic ed., vol. 39 (Albany, OR: Ages Software, 1998).

10. *Word in Life Study Bible*, electronic ed. (Nashville, TN: Thomas Nelson 1996).

11. Spurgeon, *Spurgeon's Sermons*, electronic ed., vol. 39.

12. A. C. Myers in *The Eerdmans Bible Dictionary* (Grand Rapids, MI: Eerdmans, 1987), 856.

13. W. S. La Sor, D. A. Hubbard, and F. W. Bush, *Old Testament Survey: The Message, Form, and Background of the Old Testament*, 2nd ed. (Grand Rapids, MI: William B. Eerdmans Publishing Company, 1996) 528.

14. Ibid.

15. Cyril J. Barber, *2 Chronicles: The Faithfulness of God to His Word Illustrated in the Lives of the People of Judah* (Ross-shire, Scotland: Christian Focus Publications, 2004), 97.

16. Thomas F. Thorance, *The Christian Doctrine of God, One Being Three Persons* (Edinburgh, Scotland: T&T Clark, 1996), 238.

17. Barber, *2 Chronicles*, 98.

18. Ron Rhodes *The Challenge of the Cults and New Religions* (Grand Rapids, MI: Zondervan, 2001), 187.

19. Timothy J. Keller, *The Timothy Keller Sermon Archive* (New York City, NY: Redeemer Presbyterian Church, 2013).

20. Fulton J. Sheen, *Life of Christ* (New York: McGraw-Hill Book Company, Inc., 1958), 10.

21. Mark Driscoll, *Mark Driscoll Sermon Archive 2005–2009* (Bellingham, WA: Logos Bible Software, 2009).

22. Philip Yancey, *The Jesus I Never Knew*, Kindle ed. (Grand Rapids, MI: Zondervan, 1995), location 249 of 4799.

23. Got Questions Ministries, *Got Questions? Bible Questions Answered* (Bellingham, WA: Logos Bible Software, 2010).
24. A. W. Tozer and R. Eggert, *The Tozer Topical Reader*, vol. 2 (Camp Hill, PA: WingSpread, 1998), 202.
25. J. M. Boice, *Acts, An Expositional Commentary* (Grand Rapids, MI: Baker Books, 1997), 148.
26. Ibid.

CHAPTER 4: Paradoxes of Christianity, Part 1

1. James Anderson, *Paradox in Christian Theology: An Analysis of Its Presence, Character, and Epistemic Status* (Milton Keynes, UK; Waynesboro, GA: Paternoster, 2007), 1.
2. G. K. Chesterton, *Orthodoxy* (New York: John Lane Company, 1909), 150.
3. S. S. Buzzell, "Proverbs," in J. F. Walvoord and R. B. Zuck, eds., *The Bible Knowledge Commentary: An Exposition of the Scriptures*, vol. 1 (Wheaton, IL: Victor Books, 1985), 907.
4. Millard J. Erickson, *Christian Theology*, 2nd ed. (Grand Rapids, MI: Baker Book House, 1998), 181.
5. Thomas Aquinas, Fathers of the English Dominican Province, *Summa Theologica*, complete English ed. (Bellingham, WA: Logos Bible Software, 2009), STh., III, q. 46 a. 3, resp.
6. D. Fortner, *Basic Bible Doctrine* (Danville, KY: Don Fortner, 2003), 293.
7. Erickson, *Christian Theology*, 2nd ed., 834.
8. Ibid., 835–36.
9. Josh McDowell and Sean McDowell, *77 FAQs about God and the Bible* (Eugene, OR: Harvest House Publishers, 2012).
10. Charles H. Spurgeon, *Christ in the Old Testament: Sermons on the Foreshadowing of Our Lord in Old Testament History, Ceremony, and Prophecy*, electronic ed. (Chattanooga, TN: AMG Publishers, 1997), 370.

11. Robert G. Tuttle, *Sanctity without Starch* (Bristol Books, 1992), 127.

12. I am not certain that Catholics would completely agree with this statement. They might believe that sanctification is also part of the justification process. See David G. Bonagura Jr., "Faith or Works? A Different Approach," The Catholic Thing, November 11, 2012, for a discussion of this and related issues, http://www.thecatholicthing. org/columns/2012/faith-or-works-a-different-approach.html.

13. William Hendriksen and S. J. Kistemaker, *Exposition of Colossians and Philemon*, vol. 6 (Grand Rapids: Baker Book House, 1964), 85.

14. T. R. Schreiner, *1, 2 Peter, Jude*, vol. 37 (Nashville: Broadman & Holman Publishers, 2003), 298.

15. Richard Foster, *Celebration of Discipline* (New York: Harper Collins, 1978), 7.

16. Jerry Bridges, *The Pursuit of Holiness* (Colorado Springs: Navpress, 1978), 8.

17. Ravi Zacharias, *Cries of the Heart* (Nashville, TN: Thomas Nelson, 2002).

18. Douglas Groothuis, *Christian Apologetics: A Comprehensive Case for Biblical Faith*, Kindle ed. (Downers Grove, IL: InterVarsity Press, 2011), location 4447.

19. Blaise Pascal, *The Harvard Classics 48: Blaise Pascal: Thoughts, Letters, and Minor Works*, ed. C. W. Eliot, trans. W. F. Trotter, M. L. Booth, and O. W. Wight (New York: P. F. Collier & Son, 1910).

20. Norman L. Geisler, *Systematic Theology, Volume Three: Sin, Salvation* (Minneapolis, MN: Bethany House Publishers, 2004), 227; Rolland McCune, *Systematic Theology of Biblical Christianity: The Doctrines of Salvation, the Church, and Last Things*, vol. 3 (Allen Park, MI: Detroit Baptist Theological Seminary, 2010), 94.

21. R. H. Stein, *The New American Commentary, Luke*, vol. 24 (Nashville: Broadman & Holman Publishers, 1992), 230.

22. Erickson, *Christian Theology*, 2nd ed., 1023.

23. Daniel Fuller, *The Unity of the Bible: Unfolding God's Plan for Humanity* (Grand Rapids, MI: Zondervan, 1992).

24. Warren W. Wiersbe, *Wiersbe's Expository Outlines on the Old Testament* (Wheaton, IL: Victor Books, 1993), 46.

25. J. F. Walvoord and R. B. Zuck, Dallas Theological Seminary, *The Bible Knowledge Commentary: An Exposition of the Scriptures*, vol. 1 (Wheaton, IL: Victor Books, 1985), 55.

26. Wiersbe, *Wiersbe's Expository*, 111.

27. Ray Comfort, *The Evidence Bible: Irrefutable Evidence for the Thinking Mind* (Gainesville, FL: Bridge-Logos, 2003), 142.

28. Ibid.

29. John R. W. Stott, *The Message of Romans: God's Good News for the World* (Leicester, England; Downers Grove, IL: InterVarsity Press, 1994), 187.

30. These Old Testament ceremonial laws were indeed perfect for their time as applied to the nation of Israel. They were essential for getting the Israelites to separate themselves from sin and from other cultures. But they were not intended to have universal application for all people in all times.

31. The New Testament references for the restatements of the other nine commandments are as follows: 1) Acts 14:15; 2) 1 John 5:21; 3) James 5:12; 4) n/a; 5) Eph. 6:1; 6) 1 John 3:15; 7) 1 Cor. 6:9–10; 8) Eph. 4:28; 9) Col. 3:9–10; 10) Eph. 5:3.

32. Wayne A. Grudem, *Systematic Theology: An Introduction to Biblical Doctrine* (Leicester, England; Grand Rapids, MI: Inter-Varsity Press; Zondervan Pub. House, 2004), 444.

33. J. I. Packer, *Concise Theology: A Guide to Historic Christian Beliefs* (Wheaton, IL: Tyndale House, 1993).

34. Norman L. Geisler, *Systematic Theology*, vol. 2, "God, Creation" (Minneapolis, MN: Bethany House Publishers, 2003), 302.

35. Ibid., 292.

36. L. T. Jeyachandran, "The Trinity as a Paradigm for Spiritual Transformation," in Ravi Zacharias, *Beyond Opinion: Living the Faith That We Defend* (Nashville, TN: Thomas Nelson, 2008).

37. Lewis Sperry Chafer, *Systematic Theology*, vol. 1 (Grand Rapids, MI: Kregel Publications, 1993), 382.

38. Charles H. Spurgeon, *The Metropolitan Tabernacle Pulpit Sermons*, vol. 20 (London: Passmore & Alabaster, 1874), 40.

39. Erickson, *Christian Theology*, 2nd ed., 754.

40. Ibid., 740.

41. Grudem, *Systematic Theology*, 542; J. Hastings, J. A. Selbie, and J. C. Lambert, eds., in *A Dictionary of Christ and the Gospels: Aaron–Zion. Edinburgh*, vol. 1 (New York: T&T Clark; Charles Scribner's Sons, 1906), 808.

42. William Newell, *The Book of Revelation* (Chicago: Moody Press, 1935), 346.

43. M. R. DeHaan, *Portraits of Christ in Genesis* (Grand Rapids, MI: Kregel Publications, 1995), 50.

44. J. F. Walvoord and R. B. Zuck, Dallas Theological Seminary, *The Bible Knowledge Commentary: An Exposition of the Scriptures*, vol. 2 (Wheaton, IL: Victor Books, 1985), 59.

45. R. H. Stein, *The New American Commentary, Luke*, vol. 24 (Nashville, TN: Broadman & Holman Publishers, 1992), 293.

46. William Hendriksen and S. J. Kistemaker, *Exposition of the Gospel According to Matthew*, vol. 9 (Grand Rapids: Baker Book House, 1953–2001), 884.

CHAPTER 5: Paradoxes of Christianity, Part 2

1. Timothy Keller, *The Timothy Keller Sermon Archive, The Grace of God* (New York City: Redeemer Presbyterian Church, 2013).

2. R. E. Gingrich, *The Book of 2 Corinthians* (Memphis, TN: Riverside Printing, 2000), 47.

3. D. K. Lowery, "2 Corinthians," in J. F. Walvoord and R. B. Zuck, eds., *The Bible Knowledge Commentary: An Exposition of the Scriptures*, vol. 2 (Wheaton, IL: Victor Books, 1985), 554.

4. M. J. Harris, "2 Corinthians," in F. E. Gaebelein, ed., *The Expositor's Bible Commentary: Romans through Galatians*, vol. 10 (Grand Rapids, MI: Zondervan Publishing House, 1976), 320.

5. D. M. Martin, *1, 2 Thessalonians*, vol. 33 (Nashville: Broadman & Holman Publishers, 1995), 61.

6. S. J. Kistemaker and W. Hendriksen, *Exposition of the Second Epistle to the Corinthians*, vol. 19 (Grand Rapids: Baker Book House, 1953–2001), 44.

7. P. H. Davids, *The First Epistle of Peter* (Grand Rapids, MI: Wm. B. Eerdmans Publishing Co, 1990), 55.

8. G. W. Bromiley, ed., in *The International Standard Bible Encyclopedia, Revised*, vol. 2 (Grand Rapids, MI: Wm. B. Eerdmans Publishing Co. 1979–1988), 1141.

9. Mark Driscoll, *Mark Driscoll Sermon Archive 2005–2009* (Bellingham, WA: Logos Bible Software, 2005–2009).

10. Maryam Rostampour and Marziyeh Amirizadeh, "Captive in Iran," an interview with the Christian Broadcasting Network, YouTube, published July 4, 2013, http://www.youtube.com/watch?v=mDXH2DQQxks.

11. Ibid.

12. Ibid.

13. Ibid.

14. Ibid.

15. Ibid.

16. Maryam Rostampour and Marziyeh Amirizadeh, *Captive in Iran* (Tyndale Momentum, 2013), 220.

17. Ibid., 268.

18. Rostampour and Amirizadeh, "Captive in Iran," an interview with the Christian Broadcasting Network, YouTube.

19. Rostampour and Amirizadeh, *Captive in Iran*, 288.

20. R. L. Alden, *Job*, vol. 11 (Nashville, TN: Broadman & Holman Publishers, 1993), 102.

21. J. D. Barry, M. R. Grigoni, M. S. Heiser, M. M. Custis, D. Mangum, and M. M. Whitehead, *Faithlife Study Bible* (Bellingham, WA: Logos Bible Software, 2012).

22. M. G. Easton, *Easton's Bible Dictionary* (New York: Harper & Brothers, 1893).

23. R. C. Van Leeuwen, "Book of Proverbs," in C. Brand, C. Draper, A. England, S. Bond, E. R. Clendenen, and T. C. Butler, eds.,

Holman Illustrated Bible Dictionary (Nashville, TN: Holman Bible Publishers, 2003), 1337.

24. John MacArthur Jr., *The MacArthur Study Bible*, electronic ed. (Nashville, TN: Word Pub, 1997), 877.

25. Benjamin B. DeVan and Thomas W. Smythe, "The Character of Jesus Defended," *Christian Apologetics Journal 5*, no. 2 (Southern Evangelical Seminary, Electronic Copyright 2006): 120.

26. William Hendriksen and S. J. Kistemaker, *Exposition of the Gospel According to Luke*, vol. 11 (Grand Rapids: Baker Book House, 1978), 830.

27. DeVan and Smythe, "The Character of Jesus Defended," 120.

28. Norman L. Geisler, *Systematic Theology, Volume One: Bible* (Minneapolis, MN: Bethany House Publishers, 2002), 220.

29. R. Johnson, C. Sanders, and M. S. Heiser, *TH101 Introducing Bible Doctrine I: Theology, Divine Revelation, and the Bible* (Bellingham, WA: Lexham Press, 2013), segment 40.

30. Geisler, *Systematic Theology, Volume One: Bible*, 253.

31. Carl F. H. Henry, "The Authority and Inspiration of the Bible," in F. E. Gaebelein, ed., *The Expositor's Bible Commentary: Introductory Articles*, vol. 1 (Grand Rapids, MI: Zondervan Publishing House, 1979), 8.

32. T. Cabal, C. O. Brand, E. R. Clendenen, P. Copan, J. P. Moreland, and D. Powell, *The Apologetics Study Bible: Real Questions, Straight Answers, Stronger Faith* (Nashville, TN: Holman Bible Publishers, 2007), 1850.

33. E. D. Radmacher, R. B. Allen, and H. W. House, *The Nelson Study Bible: New King James Version* (Nashville: T. Nelson Publishers, 1997).

34. Cabal et al., *The Apologetics Study Bible*, 1054.

35. J. M. Wilkins, *The NIV Application Commentary: Matthew* (Grand Rapids, MI: Zondervan Publishing House, 2004), 495.

36. J. Edlin, *Daniel: A Commentary in the Wesleyan Tradition* (Kansas City, MO: Beacon Hill Press of Kansas City, 2009), 144.

37. *King James Version Study Bible*, electronic ed. (Nashville: Thomas Nelson, 1997).

38. William Lane Craig explains the Molina in much greater detail here. Cabal et al., *The Apologetics Study Bible*, 1850.

39. Timothy J. Keller, *The Timothy Keller Sermon Archive, Sermon: Sin as Slavery, The Faces of Sin, March 17, 1996* (New York City: Redeemer Presbyterian Church, 2013).

40. Norman L. Geisler, *Knowing the Truth about Creation: How It Happened and What It Means for Us* (Ann Arbor, MI: Servant Publications, 1989), 13.

41. Ibid.; Plotinus, *The Enneads*, trans. Stephen MacKenna (London: Faber and Faber Limited, 1966), 1.8.7.

42. Geisler, *Knowing the Truth about Creation*, 13; See Plato, *Timaeus in Collected Dialogues of Plato*, Edith Hamilton and Huntington Cairns, eds. (New York: Pantheon Books, 1964), 27ff.

43. C. Vaughan, "Colossians," in F. E. Gaebelein, ed., *The Expositor's Bible Commentary: Ephesians through Philemon*, vol. 11 (Grand Rapids, MI: Zondervan Publishing House, 1981), 166; and Geisler, *Knowing the Truth about Creation*, 13; Mary Baker Eddy, *Science and Health with Key to the Scripture* (Boston, MA: Published by the Trustees under the Will of Mary Baker G. Eddy, 1934), 480–584.

44. Millard J. Erickson, *Christian Theology*, 2nd ed. (Grand Rapids, MI: Baker Book House, 1998), 402.

45. Charles C. Ryrie, *Ryrie Study Bible: New International Version*, expanded ed. (Chicago: Moody Publishers, 1994), 1927; and John MacArthur Jr., *The MacArthur Study Bible*, electronic ed. (Nashville, TN: Word Pub, 1997), 1974.

46. Daniel L. Akin, *The New American Commentary, 1, 2, 3 John*, vol. 38 (Nashville: Broadman & Holman Publishers, 2001), 213.

47. Timothy Keller, "The City of God," *The Timothy Keller Sermon Archive* (New York City: Redeemer Presbyterian Church, 2013).

48. R. Mohrlang and Gerald L. Borchert, *Cornerstone Biblical Commentary, Vol 14: Romans and Galatians* (Carol Stream, IL: Tyndale House Publishers, 2007), 55.

49. H. H. Rowley, *The Unity of the Bible* (Philadelphia, PA: Westminster Press, 1953), 80.

50. James M. Boice, *The Epistles of John: An Expositional Commentary* (Grand Rapids, MI: Baker Books, 2004), 34.

51. Martyn Lloyd-Jones, *The Assurance of Our Salvation: Exploring the Depth of Jesus' Prayer for His Own: Studies in John 17* (Wheaton, IL: Crossway Books, 2000), 287–88.

52. B. B. Barton, *John* (Wheaton, IL: Tyndale House, 1993), 66.

53. R. C. Sproul, *Does Prayer Change Things?*, vol. 3 (Lake Mary, FL: Reformation Trust Publishing, 2009), 8.

54. Gary C. Newton, *Growing toward Spiritual Maturity* (Wheaton, IL: Crossway Books, 2004), 52.

55. Sproul, *Does Prayer Change Things?*, vol. 3, 10.

56. John F. MacArthur, *The Freedom and Power of Forgiveness*, electronic ed. (Wheaton, IL: Crossway Books, 1998), 8.

57. Michael P. Green, ed., *Illustrations for Biblical Preaching: Over 1500 Sermon Illustrations Arranged by Topic and Indexed Exhaustively*, revised edition of: The expositor's illustration file (Grand Rapids: Baker Book House, 1989).

58. Charles F. Stanley, *The Gift of Forgiveness* (Nashville, TN: Oliver Nelson, 1991), 3.

59. Ibid.

60. Ibid., 177.

61. Clark Pinnock, *Biblical Revelation* (Chicago: Moody, 1971); cited by John F. MacArthur, *Introduction to Biblical Counseling: Basic Guide to the Principles and Practice of Counseling*, electronic ed. (Dallas, TX: Word Pub, 1997), 88.

CHAPTER 6: Jesus Christ, Fully Human and Fully Divine

1. Charles C. Ryrie, *Basic Theology: A Popular Systematic Guide to Understanding Biblical Truth* (Chicago, IL: Moody Press, 1986, 1999), 247.

2. R. D. Culver, *Systematic Theology: Biblical and Historical* (Ross-shire, UK: Mentor, 2005), 118.

3. Ryrie, *Basic Theology*, 247.

4. Ibid., 250.
5. K. J. Vanhoozer, C. G. Bartholomew, D. J. Treier, N. T. Wright, eds., *Dictionary for Theological Interpretation of the Bible* (London; Grand Rapids, MI: Baker Academic, 2005), 366; and G. T. Kurian, *Nelson's New Christian Dictionary* (Nashville, TN: Thomas Nelson Publishers, 2001).
6. C. Brand, C. Draper, A. England, S. Bond, E. R. Clendenen, T. C. Butler, and B. Latta, eds., *Holman Illustrated Bible Dictionary* (Nashville, TN: Holman Bible Publishers, 2003), 656.
7. L. A. Nichols, G. A. Mather, and A. J. Schmidt, *Encyclopedic Dictionary of Cults, Sects, and World Religions* (Grand Rapids, MI: Zondervan, 2006), 400.
8. Fulton J. Sheen, *The Life of Christ* (New York, NY: McGraw-Hill Book Company, Inc., 1958), 22.
9. C. H. Spurgeon, *The Metropolitan Tabernacle Pulpit Sermons*, vol. 22 (London: Passmore & Alabaster, 1876), 493–94.
10. J. D. Barry, M. R. Grigoni, M. S. Heiser, M. Custis, D. Mangum, and M. M. Whitehead, *Faithlife Study Bible* (Bellingham, WA: Logos Bible Software, 2012).
11. Ryrie, *Basic Theology*, 237.
12. Warren W. Wiersbe, *The Bible Exposition Commentary*, vol. 1 (Wheaton, IL: Victor Books, 1996), 570.
13. Ryrie, *Basic Theology*, 238.
14. John F. Walvoord, *Jesus Christ Our Lord* (Galaxy Software, 2008, digitized version of: Chicago, IL: The Moody Bible Institute of Chicago, 1975), 25.
15. Ibid., 22.
16. Ibid.
17. Ibid., 23.
18. John Piper, J. Taylor, and P. K. Helseth, *Beyond the Bounds: Open Theism and the Undermining of Biblical Christianity* (Wheaton, IL: Crossway Books, 2003), 108; S. J. Lawson, *Foundations of Grace* (Lake Mary, FL: Reformation Trust Publishing, 2006), 47.
19. John MacArthur Jr., *The MacArthur Study Bible* (Nashville, TN: Word Publishing, 1997), 803.
20. Ibid., 1941.

21. Ajith Fernando, *The Supremacy of Christ* (Wheaton, IL: Crossway Books, 1995), 218.

22. In the kenosis, Christ gave up this glory, which consisted, in part, in the voluntary non-use of His prerogatives and powers as the Second Person of the Trinity, something He did in order to become the God-man/servant for purposes of redemption. Those sovereign powers and prerogatives have been restored to Him in His ascension/exaltation (Phil. 2:9; although as in eternity past He exercises them according to the functional subordination within the triune God). Rolland McCune, *A Systematic Theology of Biblical Christianity, Volume 2: The Doctrines of Man, Sin, Christ, and the Holy Spirit* (Allen Park, MI: Detroit Baptist Theological Seminary, 2009), 239.

23. John Piper and Justin Taylor, eds., *The Supremacy of Christ in a Postmodern World* (Wheaton, IL: Crossway Books, 2007), 76–77.

24. J. I. Packer, *Concise Theology: A Guide to Historic Christian Beliefs* (Wheaton, IL: Tyndale House, 1993).

25. J. D. Grassmick, "Mark," in J. F. Walvoord and R. B. Zuck, eds., *The Bible Knowledge Commentary: An Exposition of the Scriptures*, vol. 2 (Wheaton, IL: Victor Books, 1985), 189.

26. Sheen, *The Life of Christ*, 319.

27. Ibid., 32–33.

28. Millard J. Erickson, *Christian Theology*, 2nd ed. (Grand Rapids, MI: Baker Book House, 1998), 740.

29. Sheen, *The Life of Christ*, 22.

30. R. F. Youngblood, F. F. Bruce, and R. K. Harrison, *Nelson's New Illustrated Bible Dictionary* (Nashville, TN: Thomas Nelson Publishers, 1995).

31. T. F. Torrance, *The Christian Doctrine of God, One Being Three Persons* (Edinburgh, Scotland: T & T Clark Ltd., 1996), 22.

32. John Piper, *Seeing and Savoring Jesus Christ* (Wheaton, IL: Crossway Books, 2004), 22.

33. C. S. Lewis, *Mere Christianity* (C.S. Lewis Pte. Ltd., 1952), 55.

34. Piper, *Seeing and Savoring Jesus Christ*, 23–24.

35. Fernando, *The Supremacy of Christ*, 45.

36. I am borrowing some of these points from Ajith Fernando, *The Supremacy of Christ*, 45.

37. Fernando, *The Supremacy of Christ*, 45.

38. G. Campbell Morgan, *The Teaching of Christ* (New York; London; Edinburgh: Fleming H. Revell Company, 1913), 3.

39. Ibid., 8.

40. Fernando, *The Supremacy of Christ*, 44.

41. Rev. Hugh McIntosh, *Is Christ Infallible and the Bible True?* (Minneapolis, MN: Klock and Klock Christian Publishers, Inc., 1902), 58.

42. Joachim Jeremias, *The Prayers of Jesus* (Naperville, IL: Allenson, 1967).

43. G. Campbell Morgan, *The Teaching of Christ* (New York; London; Edinburgh: Fleming H. Revell Company, 1913), 11–12.

44. Ibid., 13.

45. Fernando, *The Supremacy of Christ*, 39.

46. Ray Comfort, *The Evidence Bible: Irrefutable Evidence for the Thinking Mind* (Gainesville, FL: Bridge-Logos, 2003), 1357.

47. Stephen Neill, *The Supremacy of Jesus* (London: Hodder and Stoughton, 1984), 68; Fernando, *The Supremacy of Christ*, 40.

48. R. T. France, *Jesus the Radical* (Leicester: InterVarsity Press, 1989), 46.

49. Fernando, *The Supremacy of Christ*, 43.

50. Morgan, *The Teaching of Christ*, 5.

51. William Hendriksen and S. J. Kistemaker, *Exposition of the Gospel According to John*, vol. 1 (Grand Rapids, MI: Baker Book House), 72.

52. D. L. Allen, *The New American Commentary: Hebrews* (Nashville, TN: B & H Publishing Group, 2010), 119.

53. Ibid., 123.

54. J. F. Walvoord and R. B. Zuck, Dallas Theological Seminary, *The Bible Knowledge Commentary: An Exposition of the Scriptures*, vol. 2 (Wheaton, IL: Victor Books, 1985), 781.

55. Allen, *The New American Commentary: Hebrews*, 123.

56. Ibid., 124.

57. John also said, "And we know that the Son of God has come and has given us understanding, so that we may know Him who is true; and we are in Him who is true, in His Son Jesus Christ. He is the true God and eternal life" (1 John 5:20). The Apostle Paul wrote, "To them belong the patriarchs, and from their race, according to the flesh, is the Christ, who is God over all, blessed forever. Amen" (Romans 9:5); "Waiting for our blessed hope, the appearing of the glory of our great God and Savior Jesus Christ" (Titus 2:13); "For in Him the whole fullness of deity dwells bodily" (Col. 2:9). Peter said, "To those who have obtained a faith of equal standing with ours by the righteousness of our God and Savior Jesus Christ" (2 Peter 1:1).

CHAPTER 7: The Amazing Bible, Part 1: Unity

1. Norman L. Geisler, *Systematic Theology, Volume One: Introduction, Bible* (Minneapolis, MN: Bethany House Publishers, 2002), 245 et seq.
2. Ibid., 246.
3. M. Water, *The New Encyclopedia of Christian Martyrs* (Alresford, Hampshire, England: John Hunt Publishers Ltd, 2001), 326.
4. Ibid., 564.
5. Ibid.
6. Ibid., 933.
7. J. MacDonald, *God Wrote a Book* (Wheaton, IL: Crossway Books, 2002), 16.
8. United Bible Society, *Scripture Language Report 2000*, posted at www.Biblesociety.org/wr_358/slr_2000.htm, as accessed on 1/29/02.
9. MacDonald, *God Wrote a Book*, 14.
10. Ibid.
11. The Gideons International website is available here, http://www. gideons.org/?HP=USA&sc_lang=en.
12. MacDonald, *God Wrote a Book*, 15.

13. Lewis Sperry Chafer, *Systematic Theology*, vol. 1 (Grand Rapids, MI: Kregel Publications, 1993), 29.
14. Daniel P. Fuller, "The Importance of the Unity of the Bible," p. 65, cited by T. D. Alexander and B. S. Rosner, eds., in *New Dictionary of Biblical Theology* (Downers Grove, IL: InterVarsity Press, 2009).
15. Mark Eastman and Chuck Missler, *The Creator Beyond Time and Space* (Costa Mesa, CA: The Word for Today, 1996), 101.
16. Walter A. Elwell, in *Evangelical Dictionary of Biblical Theology* (Grand Rapids: Baker Book House, 1996).
17. Colin N. Peckham, *The Authority of the Bible* (Scotland, Great Britain: Christian Focus Publications, 1999), 13–15.
18. H. H. Rowley, *The Unity of the Bible* (Philadelphia, PA: The Westminster Press, 1953).
19. Ibid., 27.
20. Ibid.
21. Ibid.
22. Ibid.
23. Ibid.
24. John Piper, in Daniel P. Fuller, *The Unity of the Bible: Unfolding God's Plan for Humanity* (Grand Rapids, MI: Zondervan, 1992).
25. James Orr, *The Problem of the Old Testament* (New York: Charles Scribner's Sons, 1907), 31–32, quoted by Daniel P. Fuller in *The Unity of the Bible: Unfolding God's Plan for Humanity.*
26. Orr, *The Problem of the Old Testament*, 31–32, quoted by Daniel P. Fuller in *The Unity of the Bible: Unfolding God's Plan for Humanity.*
27. Fuller, *The Unity of the Bible: Unfolding God's Plan for Humanity.*
28. Ibid.
29. Ibid.
30. Ibid.
31. Ibid.
32. Ibid.
33. Martin Lloyd-Jones, *Triumphant Christianity*, vol. 5 (Wheaton, IL: Crossway Books, 2006), 53.
34. Ibid., 52.

35. Ravi Zacharias, "Questions I Would Like to Ask God," Ravi Zacharias International Ministries, January 22, 2014.

36. Fuller, *The Unity of the Bible: Unfolding God's Plan for Humanity*.

37. Larry R. Helyer, *The Witness of Jesus, Paul and John: An Exploration in Biblical Theology* (Downers Grove, IL: InterVarsity Press, 2008), 74.

38. Ibid.

39. Alfred Edersheim, *Bible History: Old Testament*, vol. 1 (Oak Harbor: Logos Bible Software, 1997), xii.

40. Helyer, *The Witness of Jesus, Paul and John*, 74.

41. Warren W. Wiersbe, *Wiersbe's Expository Outlines on the Old Testament* (Wheaton, IL: Victor Books, 1993), 13.

42. Edersheim, *Bible History: Old Testament*, vol. 1, xii.

43. Helyer, *The Witness of Jesus, Paul and John*, 81.

44. Fuller, *The Unity of the Bible: Unfolding God's Plan for Humanity*, 22.

45. W. A. Elwell in *Evangelical Dictionary of Biblical Theology* (Grand Rapids: Baker Book House, 1996).

46. Helyer, *The Witness of Jesus, Paul and John*, 79.

47. Peckham, *The Authority of the Bible*, 27.

48. Ibid., 28.

49. Walter A. Elwell in *Evangelical Dictionary of Biblical Theology* (Grand Rapids: Baker Book House, 1996).

50. Walter C. Kaiser Jr., *Recovering the Unity of the Bible* (Grand Rapids, MI: Zondervan, 2009), 21.

51. C. A. Myers in *The Eerdmans Bible Dictionary* (Grand Rapids, MI: Eerdmans, 1987), 1024.

52. F. F. Bruce, "Typology," in D. R. W. Wood, I. H. Marshall, A. R. Millard, J. I. Packer, and D. J. Wiseman, eds., *New Bible Dictionary* (Leicester, England; Downers Grove, IL: InterVarsity Press, 1996), 1214.

53. John F. Walvoord, *Jesus Christ Our Lord* (Galaxy Software, 2008, digitized version of: Chicago, IL: The Moody Bible Institute of Chicago, 1975), 67. Pharaoh also regarded Joseph as one who had the Spirit of God (Gen. 41:38).

54. Mark Driscoll and G. Breshears, *Doctrine: What Christians Should Believe* (Wheaton, IL: Crossway, 2010).

55. A. G. Fruchtenbaum, *The Messianic Bible Study Collection*, vol. 70 (Tustin, CA: Ariel Ministries, 1983), 30.

56. Maxie D. Dunham and L. J. Ogilvie, *Exodus (Vol. 2) in The Preacher's Commentary* (Nashville, TN: Thomas Nelson Inc., 1987), 288.

57. Walvoord, *Jesus Christ Our Lord*, 73.

58. Walter A. Elwell, *Evangelical Dictionary of Biblical Theology* (Grand Rapids: Baker Book House, 1996).

59. Fruchtenbaum, *The Messianic Bible Study Collection*, vol. 70, 31.

60. Walter C. Kaiser Jr., *Recovering the Unity of the Bible* (Grand Rapids, MI: Zondervan, 2009), 22.

61. Ibid.

62. Helyer, *The Witness of Jesus, Paul and John*, 80.

63. Walter A. Elwell in *Evangelical Dictionary of Biblical Theology*.

64. Ibid.

65. Peckham, *The Authority of the Bible*, 18.

66. Robert A. Morey, *How the Old and New Testaments Relate to Each Other* (Las Vegas, NV: Christian Scholars Press, 2002), 31.

67. Steve Moyise, *The Old Testament in the New: An Introduction* (London: T&T Clark International, 2001), 1.

68. Walter A. Elwell in *Evangelical Dictionary of Biblical Theology*.

69. Roger Nicole, "The Old Testament in the New Testament," in F. E. Gaebelein, ed., *The Expositor's Bible Commentary: Introductory Articles*, vol. 1 (Grand Rapids, MI: Zondervan Publishing House, 1979), 617.

70. Ibid.

71. Roger Nicole, "The Old Testament in the New Testament," in Gaebelein, ed., *The Expositor's Bible Commentary: Introductory Articles*, vol. 1, 624–25.

72. David L. Baker, *Two Testaments, One Bible* (Downers Grove, IL: InterVarsity Press, 1976).

73. Elwell in *Evangelical Dictionary of Biblical Theology*.

74. Daniel P. Fuller, *The Unity of the Bible: Unfolding God's Plan for Humanity* (Grand Rapids, MI: Zondervan, 1992), 33.

75. Carl F. H. Henry, *God, Revelation, and Authority*, vol. 4 (Wheaton, IL: Crossway Books), 460.
76. Walter C. Kaiser Jr., *Recovering the Unity of the Bible* (Grand Rapids, MI: Zondervan, 2009), 20.
77. Ibid., 21.

CHAPTER 8: The Amazing Bible, Part 2: Prophecy

1. J. Barton Payne, *Encyclopedia of Biblical Prophecy* (Grand Rapids, MI: Baker Books, 1973), 3.
2. Alfred Edersheim, *Prophecy and History in Relation to the Messiah* (Wipf and Stock Pub, 2005).
3. Walter A. Elwell and B. J. Beitzel, in *Baker Encyclopedia of the Bible* (Grand Rapids, MI: Baker Book House, 1988), 1782.
4. M. Water, *Bible Prophecy Made Easy* (New Alresford, Hampshire, England: Hunt & Thorpe, 1998), 44.
5. Payne, *Encyclopedia of Biblical Prophecy*, 9.
6. G. W. Bromiley, ed., "Prophet; Prophecy," in *The International Standard Bible Encyclopedia, Revised*, vol. 3 (Grand Rapids, MI: Wm. B. Eerdmans, 1986), 986.
7. Payne, *Encyclopedia of Biblical Prophecy*, 5.
8. Ibid., 13.
9. Ibid., 14.
10. John F. Walvoord, *The Prophecy Knowledge Handbook* (Wheaton, IL: Victor Books, 1990).
11. Payne, *Encyclopedia of Biblical Prophecy*, 15.
12. Arnold G. Fruchtenbaum, *Israelology: The Missing Link in Systematic Theology*, revised ed. (Tustin, CA: Ariel Ministries, 1994), 334.
13. J. A. Martin, "Isaiah," in J. F. Walvoord and R. B. Zuck, eds., *The Bible Knowledge Commentary: An Exposition of the Scriptures*, vol. 1 (Wheaton, IL: Victor Books, 1985), 1055.
14. Herodotus, *Herodotus, with an English translation by A. D. Godley*, A. D. Godley, ed. (Medford, MA: Harvard University

Press, 1920), Hist. 2, 141. See also J. Skinner, *The Book of the Prophet Isaiah, Chapters I.–XXXIX. With Introduction and Notes* (Cambridge: Cambridge University Press, 1987), 269.

15. Gary V. Smith, *Isaiah 1–39*, E. R. Clendenen, ed. (Nashville, TN: B & H Publishing Group, 2007), 31.

16. M. Water, *The Christian Book of Records* (Alresford, Hants, UK: John Hunt Pub, 2002), 31.

17. Walter A. Elwell and B. J. Beitzel, in *Baker Encyclopedia of the Bible*, 32.

18. M. A. Macleod, "Sharezer," in G. W. Bromiley, ed., *The International Standard Bible Encyclopedia, Revised* (Grand Rapids, MI: Wm. B. Eerdmans, 1988), 451.

19. J. A. Martin, "Micah," in J. F. Walvoord and R. B. Zuck, eds., *The Bible Knowledge Commentary: An Exposition of the Scriptures*, vol. 1 (Wheaton, IL: Victor Books, 1985), 1485.

20. Josh McDowell, *Josh McDowell's Handbook on Apologetics*, electronic ed. (Nashville, TN: Thomas Nelson, 1997).

21. John F. Walvoord, *The Prophecy Knowledge Handbook* (Wheaton, IL: Victor Books, 1990).

22. Hugh Ross, "Fulfilled Prophecy: Evidence for the Reliability of the Bible," in Reasons to Believe, August 22, 2003.

23. Chuck Missler, *Prophecy 20/20: Profiling the Future through the Lens of Scripture* (Nashville: Thomas Nelson, 2006).

24. Walvoord, *The Prophecy Knowledge Handbook*.

25. Josh McDowell and Don Stewart, *Answers to Tough Questions* (Nashville, TN: Thomas Nelson Publishers, 1993).

26. Tony Evans, "Prophecy, God's Eternal Drama, 'The Key to Prophecy,'" Tony Evans.org, 8.

27. A. C. Gaebelein, *Fulfilled Prophecy: A Potent Argument for the Inspiration of the Bible* (Bellingham, WA: Logos Bible Software, 2009), 10–11.

28. Walvoord, *The Prophecy Knowledge Handbook*.

29. Got Questions Ministries, *Got Questions? Bible Questions Answered* (Bellingham, WA: Logos Bible Software, 2010).

30. Hugh Ross, "Fulfilled Prophecy: Evidence for the Reliability of the Bible."

31. Walvoord, *The Prophecy Knowledge Handbook*.

32. Ibid.

33. M. G. Easton, in *Easton's Bible dictionary* (New York: Harper & Brothers, 1893).

34. Walvoord, *The Prophecy Knowledge Handbook*, 223–24.

35. Renald E. Showers, *The Most High God: Commentary on the Book of Daniel* (Bellmawr, NJ: Friends of Israel Gospel Ministry, Inc, 1982).

36. Ibid.

37. Ibid.

38. Ibid.

39. Ibid.

40. J. D. Hays, J. S. Duvall, and C. M. Pate, in *Dictionary of Biblical Prophecy and End Times* (Grand Rapids, MI: Zondervan Publishing House, 2007), 19.

41. Walvoord, *The Prophecy Knowledge Handbook*.

42. Ibid.

43. Norman L. Geisler, *Baker Encyclopedia of Christian Apologetics* (Grand Rapids, MI: Baker Books, 1999), 178–79.

44. Stephen R. Miller, *New American Commentary, Daniel*, vol. 18 (Nashville: Broadman & Holman Publishers, 1994), 290.

45. Walvoord, *The Prophecy Knowledge Handbook*.

46. Gleason L. Archer, *New International Encyclopedia of Bible Difficulties* (Grand Rapids, MI: Zondervan Publishing House, 1982), 292.

47. Leon J. Wood, *A Commentary on Daniel* (Grand Rapids, MI: Zondervan, 1975), 280.

48. Archer, *New International Encyclopedia of Bible Difficulties*, 293.

49. New International Version (1984).

50. Citing Harold Hoehner, who thoroughly researched this prophecy and the corresponding dates, Josh McDowell shows that the calculation involves using the Jewish prophetic year of 360 days. Hoehner writes, "Multiplying the sixty-nine weeks by seven years for each week by 360 days gives a total of 173,880 days. The difference between 444 B.C. and A.D. 33 then is 476 solar years. By multiplying 476 by 365.24219879 or by 365 days, 5 hours, 48

minutes, 45.975 seconds [there are 365 1/4 days in a year], one comes to 173,855 days, 6 hours, 52 minutes, 44 seconds, or 173,855 days. This leaves only 25 days to be accounted for between 444 B.C. and A.D. 33. By adding the 25 days to March 5 (of 444 B.C.), one comes to March 30 (of A.D. 33) which was Nisan 10 in A.D. 33. This is the triumphal entry of Jesus into Jerusalem." See Josh McDowell, *Evidence for Christianity* (Nashville, TN: Thomas Nelson Publishers, 2006), 235. Of course many dispute this precise dating and I am not insisting on it, although I think a strong case can be made for it. I just think it is astonishing that the prophecy comes anywhere close to being accurate. See also John F. Walvoord, *The Prophecy Knowledge Handbook* (Wheaton, IL: Victor Books, 1990).

51. I acquired a great deal of the interpretive insights on this passage from Dr. Thomas Howe, from whom I took an online course at Southern Evangelical Seminary, Old Testament Survey 2. I also borrowed a few insights from *The Bible Knowledge Commentary*: J. A. Martin, "Micah," in J. F. Walvoord and R. B. Zuck, eds., *The Bible Knowledge Commentary: An Exposition of the Scriptures* (Wheaton, IL: Victor Books, 1985).

52. S. J. Kistemaker and William Hendriksen, *Exposition of James and the Epistles of John*, vol. 14 (Grand Rapids: Baker Book House, 1986), 300.

53. Robert. J. Morgan, *Evidence and Truth: Foundations for Christian Truth* (Wheaton, IL: Crossway Books, 2003), 53, and Josh McDowell, *Evidence for Christianity* (Nashville, TN: Thomas Nelson Publishers, 2006).

54. Morgan, *Evidence and Truth*, 53, and McDowell, *Evidence for Christianity*.

55. McDowell, *Evidence for Christianity*.

56. Peter Stoner and Robert C. Newman, *Science Speaks* (Chicago: Moody Press, 1976), 102–9, reported by McDowell, *Evidence for Christianity*, 231–32.

57. Stoner and Newman, *Science Speaks*, 109–10, reported by McDowell, *Evidence for Christianity*, 231–32.

58. McDowell, *Evidence for Christianity*, 231.

CHAPTER 9: The Amazing Bible, Part 3: Reliability and Internal Evidence

1. The twelve points are: 1) Truth about reality if knowable. 2) Opposites cannot both be true. 3) It is true that the theistic God exists. 4) Miracles are possible. 5) Miracles performed in connection with a truth claim confirm the truth of God through a messenger of God. 6) The New Testament documents are reliable. 7) As witnessed in the New Testament, Jesus claimed to be God. 8) Jesus' claim to be God was proven by a unique convergence of miracles. 9) Therefore, Jesus was God in human flesh. 10) Whatever Jesus (Who is God) affirmed as true, is true. 11) Jesus affirmed that the Bible is the Word of God. 12) Therefore, it is true that the Bible is the Word of God and whatever is opposed to any biblical truth is false. Norman L. Geisler and Frank Turek, *I Don't Have Enough Faith to Be an Atheist* (Wheaton, IL: Crossway Books, 2004), 28. Dr. Geisler has also written a separate book exclusively dealing with this twelve-point approach. Norman L. Geisler, *Twelve Points That Show Christianity Is True*, Kindle ed. (Matthews, NC: Bastion Books, 2012), location 3720.
2. Norman L. Geisler, *Christian Apologetics* (Grand Rapids: Baker Book House, 1976), 305.
3. Norman L. Geisler, *Twelve Points That Show Christianity Is True*, Kindle ed. (Matthews, NC: Bastion Books, 2012), location 3720.
4. Norman L. Geisler, in Lecture 4 of the Apologetics 501 Course at Southern Evangelical Seminary.
5. Gary R. Habermas, *The Historical Jesus* (Joplin, MO: College Press Publishing Company, 2005), 15.
6. B. J. Rudge, "The Da Vinci Code: Historical Fact or Historical Fiction," *Journal of Biblical Apologetics* (2008): 50.
7. Ibid.
8. Dan Brown, *The Da Vinci Code* (New York: Doubleday, 2003), 235.
9. Rudge, "The Da Vinci Code: Historical Fact or Historical Fiction," 52.

10. Pliny, *Letters*, trans. William Melmoth, rev. by W. M. L. Hutchinson (Cambridge: Harvard University Press, 1935), vol. II, X:96.

11. Lee Strobel, *Finding the Real Jesus*, Kindle ed. (Grand Rapids, MI: Zondervan, 2008), location 215.

12. Ibid., location 220.

13. Ibid., location 215.

14. Ibid.

15. Ibid., location 361.

16. Ronald H. Nash, *The Gospel and the Greeks: Did the New Testament Borrow from Pagan Thought?* (Phillipsburg: NJ: P & R Publishing, 1992), 2–3.

17. Ibid., 68–69.

18. Ibid., 69.

19. Gordon H. Clark, *Thales to Dewey* (Jefferson, MD: The Trinity Foundation, 1985), 195.

20. T. W. Manson, *On Paul and John* (London: SCM, 1963), 136–37.

21. Ibid.

22. Craig L. Blomberg, *Making Sense of the New Testament: Three Crucial Questions* (Grand Rapids, MI: Baker Academic, 2004), 18–19.

23. Ibid., 19.

24. Ibid.

25. Ibid., 21.

26. Norman L. Geisler, *Christian Apologetics* (Grand Rapids: Baker Book House, 1976), 305.

27. Josh McDowell cites C. Sanders, in *Introduction to Research in English Literary History* for these three tests. Josh McDowell, *Evidence for Christianity* (Nashville, TN: Thomas Nelson Publishers, 2006), 58.

28. Josh McDowell cites C. Sanders, in *Introduction to Research in English Literary History* for these three tests. McDowell, *Evidence for Christianity*, 60.

29. Geisler, *Christian Apologetics*, 305.

30. Philip Schaff, *Companion to the Greek Testament and the English Version* (New York: Harper and Brothers, 1883), 86.

31. J. H. Greenlee, *The Text of the New Testament: From Manuscript to Modern Edition* (Peabody, MA: Hendrickson, 2008), 1–2.

32. Blomberg, *Making Sense of the New Testament: Three Crucial Questions*, 145.

33. Geisler and Turek, *I Don't Have Enough Faith to Be an Atheist*, 236.

34. Ibid., 237–38.

35. Geisler, *Christian Apologetics*, 313.

36. Blomberg, *Making Sense of the New Testament: Three Crucial Questions*, 26.

37. Geisler and Turek, *I Don't Have Enough Faith to Be an Atheist*, 240.

38. Ibid., 241.

39. Blomberg, *Making Sense of the New Testament: Three Crucial Questions*, 26.

40. Geisler, *Christian Apologetics*, 313.

41. Geisler and Turek, *I Don't Have Enough Faith to Be an Atheist*, 275.

42. Blomberg, *Making Sense of the New Testament: Three Crucial Questions*, 33–36.

43. Ibid., 27.

44. Ibid., 145.

45. Mark L. Strauss, *Four Portraits, One Jesus: A Survey of Jesus and the Gospels* (Grand Rapids, MI: Zondervan, 2007), 387.

46. Norman L. Geisler, "The New Testament Is Historically Reliable," PowerPoint presentation, 2014.

47. Josh McDowell, *Evidence for Christianity* (Nashville, TN: Thomas Nelson Publishers, 2006), 60.

48. Ed Komoszewski, M. James Sawyer, and Daniel B. Wallace, *Reinventing Jesus, How Contemporary Skeptics Miss the Real Jesus and Mislead Popular Culture*, Kindle ed. (Grand Rapids, MI: Kregel Publications, 2006), location 632.

49. Blomberg, *Making Sense of the New Testament: Three Crucial Questions*, 22.

50. Strauss, *Four Portraits, One Jesus*, 387.

51. John A. T. Robinson, *Can We Trust the New Testament?* (Grand Rapids, MI: William B. Eerdmans Publishing Company, 1977), 36.

52. Norman L. Geisler, "Updating the Manuscript Evidence for the New Testament," September 2013.

53. J. D. Barry and L. Wentz, eds., in *The Lexham Bible Dictionary* (Bellingham, WA: Lexham Press, 2012).

54. Barry and Wentz, eds., in *The Lexham Bible Dictionary*; J. Daniel Hays and J. Scott Duvall, *How the Bible Came to Be (ebook short)* (Grand Rapids, MI: Baker, 2012); Geisler, *Christian Apologetics*, 306.

55. Gary R. Habermas, *The Historical Jesus: Ancient Evidence for the Life of Christ* (Joplin, MO: College Press Publishing Company, 1996), 55.

56. Komoszewski, Sawyer, and Wallace, *Reinventing Jesus*, location 720.

57. Schaff, *Companion to the Greek Testament and the English Version*, 180.

58. Lee Strobel, *The Case for Christ: A Journalist's Personal Investigation of the Evidence for Jesus* (Grand Rapids, MI: Zondervan, 1998), Chapter 3.

59. Geisler, *Christian Apologetics*, 307.

60. Komoszewski, Sawyer, and Wallace, *Reinventing Jesus*, location 456.

61. Norman L. Geisler, "Updating the Manuscript Evidence for the New Testament," September 2013; Komoszewski, Sawyer, and Wallace agree that these variations do not affect foundational beliefs. Komoszewski, Sawyer, and Wallace, *Reinventing Jesus*, location 560.

62. Komoszewski, Sawyer, and Wallace, *Reinventing Jesus*, location 967.

63. Ibid., location 1103.

64. Blomberg, *Making Sense of the New Testament: Three Crucial Questions*, 23.

65. Norman L. Geisler, An Evaluation of McGowen's View on the Inspiration of Scripture, *Bibliotheca Sacra*, 2010, 167.

66. Archibald T. Robertson, *An Introduction to Textual Criticism of the New Testament* (Nashville: Broadman, 1925), 22.

67. Schaff, *Companion to the Greek Testament and the English Version*, 177.

68. Norman L. Geisler, "The New Testament is Historically Reliable," PowerPoint presentation, 2014.

69. Schaff, *Companion to the Greek Testament and the English Version*, 178. Even New Testament scholar Bart Ehrman admitted in the paperback version of *Misquoting Jesus* that he doesn't disagree with Professor Bruce Metzger's position that the essential Christian beliefs are not affected by textual variants in the manuscript tradition of the New Testament. Bart D. Ehrman, *Misquoting Jesus*, Harper One paperback ed. (New York, New York: HarperCollins, 2005), 252.

70. Frederic Kenyon, *The Bible and Archaeology* (New York: Harper, 1940), 288.

71. Komoszewski, Sawyer, and Wallace, *Reinventing Jesus*, location 709.

72. Frederic Kenyon, *Our Bible and the Ancient Manuscripts* (Eyre and Spottiswoode, 1895).

73. Norman L. Geisler, "The New Testament is Historically Reliable," PowerPoint presentation, 2014.

74. Geisler, *Christian Apologetics*, 314.

75. Strauss, *Four Portraits, One Jesus*, 387.

76. Norman L. Geisler, "The New Testament is Historically Reliable," PowerPoint presentation, 2014.

77. Paul N. Benware, *Survey of the New Testament (Revised)* (Chicago, IL: Moody Press, 1990), 285, and Norman L. Geisler, "The New Testament is Historically Reliable," PowerPoint presentation, 2014.

78. Geisler, *Christian Apologetics*, 314.

79. Dan Story, *Defending Your Faith* (Grand Rapids, MI: Kregel Publications, 1997), 44.

80. J. P. Moreland, *Scaling the Secular City: A Defense of Christianity* (Grand Rapids, MI: Baker Academic, 1987), 138.

81. Geisler and Turek, *I Don't Have Enough Faith to Be an Atheist*, 283–84.

82. Moreland, *Scaling the Secular City*, 139.
83. F. F. Bruce, *The New Testament Documents, Are They Reliable?*, Kindle ed. (Grand Rapids, MI; Cambridge, U.K.: William B. Eerdmans Publishing Company, 1943), location 517.
84. Ibid.
85. Story, *Defending Your Faith*, 43.
86. Moreland, *Scaling the Secular City*, 138.
87. Blomberg, *Making Sense of the New Testament: Three Crucial Questions*, 43–44.
88. Ibid., 44.
89. Ibid., 45.
90. Geisler and Turek, *I Don't Have Enough Faith to Be an Atheist*, 297.
91. Strauss, *Four Portraits, One Jesus*, 388.
92. Moreland, *Scaling the Secular City*, 140.
93. William M. Ramsay *The Bearing of Recent Discovery on the Trustworthiness of the New Testament* (London; New York; Toronto: Hodder and Stoughton, 1915), 82–83.
94. Blomberg, *Making Sense of the New Testament: Three Crucial Questions*, 29.
95. Moreland, *Scaling the Secular City*, 140.
96. Blomberg, *Making Sense of the New Testament: Three Crucial Questions*, 29.
97. G. N. Stanton, *Jesus of Nazareth in New Testament Preaching* (Cambridge: Cambridge University Press, 1974), 70–77.
98. C. H. Dodd, *New Testament Studies* (Manchester: Manchester University Press, 1953), 1–11.
99. Moreland, *Scaling the Secular City*, 140.
100. Geisler, *Christian Apologetics*, 316.
101. Dan Story, *Defending Your Faith* (Grand Rapids, MI: Kregel Publications, 1997), 41. Another fine source examining the evidence is Warner Wallace's *Cold Case Christianity*.
102. American Jurisprudence, 2d, Evidence, Section 1203, Ancient Documents, 2014.
103. See Gleason L. Archer's *Encyclopedia of Bible Difficulties* (Grand Rapids, MI: Zondervan, 1982); Norman L. Geisler and Thomas

A. Howe, *When Critics Ask* (Wheaton, IL: Victor Books, 1992); Walter C. Kaiser Jr., Peter H. Davids, F. F. Bruce, and Manfred T. Brauch, *Hard Sayings of the Bible* (Downers Grove, IL: InterVarsity Press, 1996).

104. John Warwick Montgomery, *The Law above the Law* (Minneapolis, MN: Bethany, 1975), 87–88.

105. Josh McDowell, *Evidence for Christianity* (Nashville, TN: Thomas Nelson Publishers, 2006), 75.

106. Clifford A. Wilson, *Bible and Spade*, vol. 1, no. 1, 1972, 8.

107. Ibid., 9.

108. Strauss, *Four Portraits, One Jesus*, 388.

109. Blomberg, *Making Sense of the New Testament: Three Crucial Questions*, 36.

110. Gleason L. Archer, *New International Encyclopedia of Bible Difficulties* (Grand Rapids, MI: Zondervan Publishing House, 1982), 12.

111. Josh McDowell, *Evidence for Christianity* (Nashville, TN: Thomas Nelson Publishers, 2006), 76.

112. A similar list is compiled by Norman Geisler and Tom Howe in *When Critics Ask: A Popular Handbook of Bible Difficulties* (Wheaton, IL: Victor Books, 1992), 19.

113. McDowell, *Evidence for Christianity*, 78.

114. Norman L. Geisler, *Baker Encyclopedia of Christian Apologetics* (Grand Rapids, MI: Baker Books, 1999), 100.

115. Geisler and Turek, *I Don't Have Enough Faith to Be an Atheist*, 362.

116. T. Cabal, C. O. Brand, E. R. Clendenen, P. Copan, J. P. Moreland, and D. Powell, *The Apologetics Study Bible: Real Questions, Straight Answers, Stronger Faith* (Nashville, TN: Holman Bible Publishers, 2007), 345.

117. Ibid., 347.

118. Ibid., 346.

119. H. .H. Rowley, *The Unity of the Bible* (Philadelphia, PA: The Westminster Press, 1953), 11–12.

120. *The ESV Study Bible* (Wheaton, IL: Crossway Bibles, 2008), 2585.

121. Ibid.

122. Ibid.

123. B. K. Waltke, "Textual Criticism of the Old Testament," in F. E. Gaebelein, ed., *The Expositor's Bible Commentary: Introductory Articles*, vol. 1 (Grand Rapids, MI: Zondervan Publishing House, 1979), 212.

124. Josh McDowell, *Evidence for Christianity* (Nashville, TN: Thomas Nelson Publishers, 2006), 106.

125. *The ESV Study Bible* (Wheaton, IL: Crossway Bibles, 2008), 2585.

126. Waltke, "Textual Criticism of the Old Testament," in Gaebelein, ed., *The Expositor's Bible Commentary: Introductory Articles*, 212.

127. Gleason Archer Jr., *A Survey of Old Testament Introduction*, 3rd. ed. (Chicago: Moody Press, 1994), 27.

128. *The ESV Study Bible* (Wheaton, IL: Crossway Bibles, 2008), 2587.

129. Cabal et al., *The Apologetics Study Bible: Real Questions, Straight Answers, Stronger Faith*, 346.

130. McDowell, *Evidence for Christianity*, 115.

131. Archer Jr., *A Survey of Old Testament Introduction*, 29.

132. McDowell, *Evidence for Christianity*, 130.

133. Norman L. Geisler, *Baker Encyclopedia of Christian Apologetics* (Grand Rapids, MI: Baker Books, 1999), 99.

134. Ibid., 100.

135. Ibid.

136. Geisler and Turek, *I Don't Have Enough Faith to Be an Atheist*, 358; Geisler, *Baker Encyclopedia of Christian Apologetics*, 100.

CHAPTER 10: The Amazing Bible, Part 4: Reliability and External Evidence

1. Eusebius of Caesarea. *An Ecclesiastical History to the 20th Year of the Reign of Constantine* (London: Samuel Bagster and Sons, 1847), Book III, Chapter 39.

2. Ibid.

3. J. R. Michaels, "Apostolic Fathers," in G. W. Bromiley, ed., *The International Standard Bible Encyclopedia, Revised*, vol. 1 (Wm. B. Eerdmans, 1979–1988), 210.

4. T. Donner, "Some Thoughts on the History of the New Testament Canon," *Themelios,* No. 3, 1982, vol. 7, 26.

5. Michaels, "Apostolic Fathers," in Bromiley, ed., *The International Standard Bible Encyclopedia, Revised,* vol. 1, 210.

6. Josh McDowell, *Evidence for Christianity* (Nashville, TN: Thomas Nelson Publishers, 2006), 150; Norman L. Geisler, in *Baker Encyclopedia of Christian Apologetics* (Grand Rapids, MI: Baker Books, 1999), 81.

7. Gary R. Habermas, *The Historical Jesus: Ancient Evidence for the Life of Christ* (Joplin, MO: College Press Publishing Company, 1996), 278.

8. Ibid.

9. Ibid.

10. F. Josephus and W. Whiston, *The Works of Josephus: Complete and Unabridged* (Peabody: Hendrickson Publishers, 1987), section 200.

11. Craig L. Blomberg, *Making Sense of the New Testament: Three Crucial Questions* (Grand Rapids, MI: Baker Academic, 2004), 47–48.

12. Mark Pierson, *Global Journal of Classical Theology,* 2009, 7.

13. Craig Evans, "Jesus in Non-Christian Sources," in J. B. Green and S. McKnight, eds., *Dictionary of Jesus and the Gospels* (Downers Grove, IL: InterVarsity Press, 1992).

14. W. C. Robinson, "Exaltation of Christ," in Bromiley, ed., *The International Standard Bible Encyclopedia, Revised,* vol. 2, 216; Harold W. Hoehner, *Ephesians: An Exegetical Commentary* (Grand Rapids, MI: Baker Academic, 2002); Pliny the Younger, *Epistulae* 10.96.

15. Paul Barnett, *Is the New Testament Reliable?* (Downers Grove, IL: InterVarsity Press, 2003), 14.

16. R. P. Martin and P. H. Davids, eds., in *Dictionary of the Later New Testament and Its Developments* (Downers Grove, IL: InterVarsity Press, 1997).

17. C. Keith, "Introduction: Jesus outside and inside the New Testament," in L. W. Hurtado, ed., *Jesus among Friends and Enemies: A Historical and Literary Introduction to Jesus in the Gospels* (Grand Rapids, MI: Baker Academic, 2011), 7.

18. Mark Pierson, *Global Journal of Classical Theology*, 2009, 7.
19. Gregg R. Allison, *Historical Theology: An Introduction to Christian Doctrine* (Grand Rapids, MI: Zondervan, 2011), 413.
20. Blomberg, *Making Sense of the New Testament: Three Crucial Questions*, 50.
21. R. F. Youngblood, F. F. Bruce, and R. K. Harrison, Thomas Nelson Publishers, eds., in *Nelson's New Illustrated Bible Dictionary* (Nashville, TN: Thomas Nelson, Inc, 1995).
22. Edwin Yamauchi, "Archaeology and the New Testament," in F. E. Gaebelein, ed., *The Expositor's Bible Commentary: Introductory Articles*, vol. 1 (Grand Rapids, MI: Zondervan Publishing House, 1979), 648.
23. Youngblood et al., eds., in *Nelson's New Illustrated Bible Dictionary*.
24. Ibid.
25. Walter C. Kaiser Jr., "How Has Archaeology Corroborated the Bible?," in T. Cabal, C. O. Brand, E. R. Clendenen, P. Copan, and J. P. Moreland, eds., *The Apologetics Study Bible: Real Questions, Straight Answers, Stronger Faith* (Nashville, TN: Holman Bible Publishers, 2007), 1148.
26. Kaiser Jr., "How Has Archaeology Corroborated the Bible?" in Cabal et al., eds., *The Apologetics Study Bible*, 1148.
27. Youngblood et al., eds., in *Nelson's New Illustrated Bible Dictionary*.
28. Ibid.
29. Joseph M. Holden and Norman Geisler, *The Popular Handbook of Archaeology and the Bible* (Eugene, OR: Harvest House Publishers, 2013), 201.
30. Ibid., 181.
31. Merrill Unger, *Bibliotheca Sacra*, 1959, 155.
32. Blomberg, *Making Sense of the New Testament: Three Crucial Questions*, 56.
33. Edwin Yamauchi, *The Stones and the Scriptures*, 99, 116, in Norman L. Geisler *Christian Apologetics* (Grand Rapids: Baker Book House, 1976), 325.
34. Ibid., 314.

35. Colin N. Peckham, *The Authority of the Bible* (Scotland; Great Britain: Christian Focus Publications, 1999), 105.

36. Mark L. Strauss, *Four Portraits, One Jesus: A Survey of Jesus and the Gospels* (Grand Rapids, MI: Zondervan, 2007), 386.

37. Ibid.

38. Norman L. Geisler and Frank Turek, *I Don't Have Enough Faith to Be an Atheist* (Wheaton, IL: Crossway Books, 2004), 256.

39. Norman L. Geisler, *Baker Encyclopedia of Christian Apologetics* (Grand Rapids, MI: Baker Books, 1999), 47.

40. F. F. Bruce, *The Book of the Acts* (Grand Rapids, MI: Wm. B. Eerdmans Publishing Co, 1988), 409.

41. Ibid., 326.

42. A. N. Sherwin-White, *Roman Society and Roman Law in the New Testament* (Oxford: Oxford University Press, 1965), as cited in Paul Barnett, *Is the New Testament Reliable?* (Downers Grove, IL: InterVarsity Press, 2003), 156.

43. Yamauchi, "Archaeology and the New Testament," in Gaebelein, ed., *The Expositor's Bible Commentary*, vol. 1, 647; W. M. Ramsay, *The Bearing of Recent Discovery on the Trustworthiness of the New Testament* (Grand Rapids: Baker, 1953 repr. of the 1915 edition).

44. William M. Ramsay, *St. Paul the Traveller and the Roman Citizen* (1895), 8.

45. William M. Ramsay, *The Bearing of Recent Discovery on the Trustworthiness of the New Testament* (London; New York; Toronto: Hodder and Stoughton, 1915), 82.

46. Merrill F. Unger, *Archaeology and the New Testament* (Zondervan, Grand Rapids, 1962), 245.

47. Colin N. Peckham, *The Authority of the Bible* (Scotland; Great Britain: Christian Focus Publications, 1999), 105.

48. Merrill F. Unger, *Archaeology and the New Testament* (Zondervan, Grand Rapids, 1962), 158.

49. Peckham, *The Authority of the Bible*, 108–9.

50. F. F. Bruce, *The New Testament Documents, Are They Reliable?* (Grand Rapids, MI: Wm B. Eerdmans Publishing Company, 1943), 95.

51. Peckham, *The Authority of the Bible*, 102.

52. John McRay, *Archaeology and the New Testament*, Kindle ed. (Grand Rapids, MI: Baker Academic, a division of Baker Publishing Group, 1991), location 197 of 9657.

53. Paul Barnett, *Is the New Testament Reliable?* (Downers Grove, IL: InterVarsity Press, 2003), 160; Cabal et al., eds., *The Apologetics Study Bible*, 1149.

54. Holden and Geisler, *The Popular Handbook of Archaeology and the Bible*, 348.

55. John McRay, *Archaeology and the New Testament*, Kindle ed. (Grand Rapids, MI: Baker Academic, a division of Baker Publishing Group, 1991), location 197 of 9657.

56. Yamauchi, "Archaeology and the New Testament," in Gaebelein, ed., *The Expositor's Bible Commentary*, vol. 1 (Grand Rapids, MI: Zondervan Publishing House, 1979), 656.

57. Ibid., 667.

58. Colin N. Peckham, *The Authority of the Bible* (Scotland; Great Britain: Christian Focus Publications, 1999), 105.

59. Ibid., 103.

60. Ibid., 104.

61. *The ESV Study Bible* (Wheaton, IL: Crossway Bibles, 2008), 2592.

62. Josh McDowell, *Evidence for Christianity* (Nashville, TN: Thomas Nelson Publishers, 2006), 30; Norman L. Geisler and M. Water, *The Bible and Science Made Easy* (Alresford, Hampshire: John Hunt Publishers Ltd, 2001), 28.

63. M. Water, *The Bible and Science Made Easy*, 29.

64. Dan Story, *Defending Your Faith* (Grand Rapids, MI: Kregel Publications, 1997), 36.

65. J. A. Thompson, *The Bible and Archaeology*, 3rd ed., fully revised (Grand Rapids, MI: W.B. Eerdmans Pub. Co, 1982), 18.

66. Ibid., 26–27.

67. McDowell, *Evidence for Christianity*, 150; Norman L. Geisler, in *Baker Encyclopedia of Christian Apologetics* (Grand Rapids, MI: Baker Books, 1999), 50.

68. Eugene H. Merrill, *Journal of Dispensational Theology*, Volume 13, Number 39.

69. Joseph M. Holden and Norman Geisler, *The Popular Handbook of Archaeology and the Bible* (Eugene, OR: Harvest House Publishers, 2013), 205.
70. Ibid., 209–10.
71. William H. Shea, "Numeirah," in *Bible and Spade*, vol. 1, no. 4, 1988, 22; Norman L. Geisler, in *Baker Encyclopedia of Christian Apologetics* (Grand Rapids, MI: Baker Books, 1999), 50; McDowell, *Evidence for Christianity*, 136
72. William H. Shea, "Numeirah," in *Bible and Spade*, vol. 1, no. 4, 1988, 22.
73. Ibid.
74. B. Halpern, "Text and Artifact: Two Monologues?," in N. A. Silberman and D. Small, eds., *The Archaeology of Israel: Constructing the Past, Interpreting the Present*, vol. 237 (Sheffield: Sheffield Academic Press, 1997), 335.
75. Cabal et al., eds., *The Apologetics Study Bible*, 406.
76. Timothy Paul Jones and Randall Price, *Why Trust the Bible?* (Torrance, CA: Rose Publishing, 2008).
77. Ibid.
78. Ibid.
79. Ibid.
80. Ibid.
81. Ibid.
82. Ibid.

CHAPTER 11: Truth, Miracles, and the Resurrection of Christ

1. Amy Orr-Ewing, in Ravi Zacharias, *Beyond Opinion: Living the Faith That We Defend* (Nashville, TN: Thomas Nelson, 2008).
2. Norman L. Geisler and Frank Turek, *I Don't Have Enough Faith to Be an Atheist* (Wheaton, IL: Crossway Books, 2004), 28.
3. John Ankerberg and John Weldon, *Ready with an Answer* (Chattanooga, TN: ATRI Publishing, 2011).

4. Dan Story, *Christianity on the Offense: Responding to the Beliefs and Assumptions of Spiritual Seekers* (Grand Rapids, MI: Kregel Publications), 1998), 30.

5. William Hendriksen and S. J. Kistemaker, *Exposition of Philippians*, vol. 5 (Grand Rapids: Baker Book House, 1953–2001), 198.

6. Francis A. Schaeffer, "The God Who Is There," in *The Complete Works of Francis A. Schaeffer: A Christian Worldview*, vol. 1 (Westchester, IL: Crossway Books, 1982), 6.

7. Carl F. H. Henry, *God, Revelation, and Authority*, vol. 1 (Wheaton, IL: Crossway Books, 1999), 16.

8. Schaeffer, "The God Who Is There," in *The Complete Works of Francis A. Schaeffer*, vol. 1, 5.

9. Douglas Groothuis, *Truth Decay: Defending Christianity against the Challenges of Postmodernism*, Kindle ed. (Downers Grove, IL: InterVarsity Press, 2000), location 26 of 3542.

10. Millard Erickson, *Christian Theology*, 2nd ed. (Grand Rapids, MI: Baker Book House, 1998), 161.

11. Groothuis, *Truth Decay*, Kindle ed., location 269 of 3542.

12. Ibid., location 279 of 3542.

13. E. Fahlbusch, and G. W. Bromiley in *The Encyclopedia of Christianity*, vol. 4 (Grand Rapids, MI; Leiden, Netherlands: Wm. B. Eerdmans; Brill, 2005), 197.

14. Groothuis, *Truth Decay*, Kindle ed., location 288 of 3542.

15. Erickson, *Christian Theology*, 2nd ed., 162.

16. 16 Ibid., 161.

17. E. Fahlbusch and G. W. Bromiley, in *The Encyclopedia of Christianity*, vol. 4, 299.

18. Stanley J. Grenz, David Guretzki, and C. F. Nordling, in *Pocket Dictionary of Theological Terms* (Downers Grove, IL: InterVarsity Press, 1999), 77.

19. Orr-Ewing, in Zacharias, *Beyond Opinion*.

20. Douglas R. Groothuis, "How Should a Christian Understand Postmodernism?," in T. Cabal, C. O. Brand, E. R. Clendenen, P. Copan, J. P. Moreland, and D. Powell, *The Apologetics Study*

Bible: Real Questions, Straight Answers, Stronger Faith (Nashville, TN: Holman Bible Publishers, 2007), 1385.

21. Ronn Johnson, Carl Sanders, and Mike Heiser, *TH101 Introducing Bible Doctrine I: Theology, Divine Revelation, and the Bible* (Bellingham, WA: Lexham Press, 2013), Segment 30.

22. Richard Rorty, *Consequences of Pragmatism: Essays 1972–1980* (Minneapolis: University of Minnesota Press, 1982), xxxv; "Solidarity or Objectivity?," in *Post-Analytic Philosophy*, eds. John Rajchman and Cornel West (New York: Columbia University Press, 1985), 3–4. See Erickson, *Christian Theology*, 2nd ed., 44.

23. Groothuis, *Truth Decay*, Kindle ed., location 318 of 3542.

24. Ibid., location 341 of 3542.

25. Ibid., location 347 of 3542.

26. Ibid., location 357 of 3542.

27. Michael J. Anthony, W. S. Benson, D. Eldridge, and J. Gorman, in *Evangelical Dictionary of Christian Education* (Grand Rapids, MI: Baker Academic, 2001), 589.

28. The Barna Group, "Barna Survey Examines Changes in Worldview Among Christians over the Past 13 Years," March 6, 2009.

29. Groothuis, *Truth Decay*, Kindle ed., location 308 of 3542.

30. Ravi Zacharias, "An Evangelical Understanding of Postmodernism," YouTube, February 11, 2011.

31. A. McIntosh, *Genesis for Today: The Relevance of the Creation/ Evolution Debate to Today's Society*, 3rd ed. (Leominster, UK: Day One, 2006), 135–36.

32. Schaeffer, "The God Who Is There," in *The Complete Works of Francis A. Schaeffer*, vol. 1, 133–34.

33. Alister McGrath, *Mere Apologetics: How to Help Seekers and Skeptics Find Faith* (Grand Rapids, MI: Baker Books, 2012), 133.

34. Francis J. Beckwith and Greg Koukl, *Relativism: Feet Firmly Planted in Mid-Air* (Grand Rapids, MI: Baker Books, 1998), 20.

35. Winfried Corduan, *No Doubt about It: The Case for Christianity* (Nashville, TN: Broadman & Holman Publishers, 1997), 39.

36. Norman Geisler, "Is Truth about Reality Knowable?" PowerPoint Presentation, 2014.

37. Ibid.

38. Thomas L. Friedman, "The Real War," *New York Times*, November 27, 2001.
39. Geisler and Turek, *I Don't Have Enough Faith to Be an Atheist*, 94.
40. Norman L. Geisler, in *Baker Encyclopedia of Christian Apologetics* (Grand Rapids, MI: Baker Books, 1999), 722.
41. P. D. Feinberg, "Cumulative Case Apologetics," in S. N. Gundry and S. B. Cowan, eds., *Five Views on Apologetics* (Grand Rapids, MI: Zondervan, 2000), 149.
42. Geisler and Turek, *I Don't Have Enough Faith to Be an Atheist*, 25.
43. Norman L Geisler, "God Exists," PowerPoint Presentation, 2014.
44. Dan Story, *Defending Your Faith* (Grand Rapids, MI: Kregel Publications, 1997), 27.
45. Normal L. Geisler, *Systematic Theology, Volume One* (Minneapolis, MN: Bethany House Publishers, 2002), 27.
46. J. P. Moreland, *Scaling the Secular City: A Defense of Christianity* (Grand Rapids, MI; Baker Academic, 1987), 34.
47. Geisler, *Systematic Theology, Volume One*, 27.
48. Dan Story, *Defending Your Faith* (Grand Rapids, MI: Kregel Publications, 1997), 27; Geisler, *Systematic Theology, Volume One*, 27.
49. Got Questions Ministries, *Got Questions? Bible Questions Answered* (Bellingham, WA: Logos Bible Software, 2010).
50. Geisler and Turek, *I Don't Have Enough Faith to Be an Atheist*, 95.
51. Ibid., 171.
52. Ibid., 176–77.
53. Dan Story, *Defending Your Faith* (Grand Rapids, MI: Kregel Publications, 1997), 27; Geisler, *Systematic Theology, Volume One*, 27.
54. Norman L. Geisler, "Are Miracles Possible?" PowerPoint Presentation, 2008.
55. William Lane Craig, *Reasonable Faith: Christian Truth and Apologetics*, rev. ed. (Wheaton, IL: Crossway Books, 1994), 126.
56. Ibid., 154.

57. Antony Flew, "Miracles," in Paul Edwards, ed., *The Encyclopedia of Philosophy* (New York: Macmillan, 1967), 5:346.

58. Norman Geisler, *Miracles and the Modern Mind: A Defense of Biblical Miracles* (Grand Rapids, MI: Baker Book House Company, 1992), 14.

59. Norman L. Geisler, "Are Miracles Possible?" PowerPoint Presentation, 2008.

60. Ibid.

61. David Hume, *The Harvard Classics 37: The English Philosophers of the 17th and 18th Centuries*, C. W. Eliot, ed. (New York: P. F. Collier & Son, 1910), 400.

62. Geisler and Turek, *I Don't Have Enough Faith to Be an Atheist*, 206.

63. Ibid.

64. Norman L. Geisler, "Miracles Can Confirm a Message Is from God," PowerPoint Presentation, 2011.

65. Geisler, "Are Miracles Possible?"

66. Geisler, "Miracles Can Confirm a Message is from God."

67. David Hume, *The Harvard Classics 37*, 401.

68. Ibid., 397.

69. Moreland, *Scaling the Secular City*, 159.

70. Steven D. Mathewson, *Risen: 50 Reasons Why the Resurrection Changed Everything* (Grand Rapids, MI: Baker, 2013).

71. Some critics, for example, advance the "swoon theory," arguing that Jesus just appeared to be dead, but that He did not actually die on the Cross. See Josh McDowell, *Evidence for Christianity* (Nashville, TN: Thomas Nelson Publishers, 2006).

72. Norman L. Geisler, in *Baker Encyclopedia of Christian Apologetics* (Grand Rapids, MI: Baker Books, 1999), 127.

73. Norman L. Geisler, "Jesus Was Confirmed to be God by Miracles," PowerPoint Presentation, 2008.

74. Geisler, in *Baker Encyclopedia of Christian Apologetics*, 128.

75. *The Journal of the American Medical Society 255*, no. 11 (March 21, 1986): 1463, cited by Josh McDowell, *Evidence for Christianity* (Nashville, TN: Thomas Nelson Publishers, 2006).

76. Josh McDowell cites Michael Green in Josh's *Evidence for Christianity*, 273.

77. Geisler, in *Baker Encyclopedia of Christian Apologetics*, 128.

78. Norman L. Geisler, *The Battle for the Resurrection* (Eugene, OR: Wipf & Stock Publishers, 1992), 77.

79. David Strauss, *A New Life of Jesus*, vol. 1 (London: Williams and Norgate, 1879), 412, cited in Geisler, *The Battle for the Resurrection*, 78.

80. Gary R. Habermas, *The Historical Jesus: Ancient Evidence for the Life of Christ* (Joplin, MO: College Press Publishing Company, 1996), 158.

81. Ibid.

82. Moreland, *Scaling the Secular City*, 160.

83. Habermas, *The Historical Jesus*, 160.

84. Ibid., 161.

85. Moreland, *Scaling the Secular City*, 161.

86. Habermas, *The Historical Jesus*, 160–65.

87. Ibid., 172.

88. Ibid., 160.

89. Gary R. Habermas, "How is the Transformation of Jesus' Disciples Different from Other Religious Transformations?," in Cabal et al., *The Apologetics Study Bible*, 1565.

90. Ibid.

91. Ibid.

92. Geisler, in *Baker Encyclopedia of Christian Apologetics*, 651–55.

CHAPTER 12: Science Makes the Case—for Christianity

1. J. Coffey, *Smooth Stones: Bringing Down the Giant Questions of Apologetics* (Adelphi, MD: Cruciform Press, 2011).

2. E. Harrison, *Masks of the Universe* (New York: Macmillan, 1985), 252, 263.

3. Arno Penzias, quoted in Denis Brian, *Genius Talk* (New York: Plenum, 1995), 164.

4. Mark Mittelberg and Lee Strobel, *The Questions Christians Hope No One Will Ask: (With Answers)* (Carol Stream, IL: Tyndale, 2010).

5. Richard Dawkins, "Ignorance Is No Crime," *Free Inquiry* magazine, 21, no. 3, 2001.

6. John Lennox, in Ravi Zacharias, *Beyond Opinion: Living the Faith That We Defend* (Nashville, TN: Thomas Nelson, 2008).

7. J. P. Moreland, *Scaling the Secular City: A Defense of Christianity* (Grand Rapids, MI: Baker Academic, 1987), 197.

8. Ibid.

9. Ibid., 199.

10. C. John Collins, *Science and Faith: Friends or Foes?* (Wheaton, IL: Crossway, 2003).

11. John Lennox, in Zacharias, *Beyond Opinion*; Malcolm Browne, "Clues to the Universe's Origin Expected," *New York Times*, March 12, 1978, 1.

12. Survey by Edward J. Larsen and Larry Withan, "Scientists Are still Keeping the Faith," *Nature* 386 (April 1997), 435–36.

13. John Lennox, in Zacharias, *Beyond Opinion*.

14. Moreland, *Scaling the Secular City*, 197.

15. R. C. Lewontin, "Billions and Billions of Demons," *The New York Review*, January 9, 1997, 31.

16. Nancy Pearcey and Charles B. Thaxton, *The Soul of Science: Christian Faith and Natural Philosophy* (Wheaton: IL: Crossway Books, 1994), 38.

17. Ibid., 12.

18. Loren Eiseley, *Darwin's Century* (Garden City, NY: Doubleday, 1958, Doubleday Anchor Books, 1961), 62, quoted by Pearcey and Thaxton, *The Soul of Science*, 17–18.

19. Pearcey and Thaxton, *The Soul of Science*, 18.

20. Rodney Stark, *For the Glory of God: How Monotheism Led to Reformations, Science, Witch-hunts, and the End of Slavery* (Princeton: Princeton University Press, 2003), 149.

21. Michael J. Behe, William A. Dembski, and Stephen C. Meyer, *Science and Evidence for Design in the Universe*, vol. 9 (San Francisco: Ignatius Press, 2000), 11.

22. Pearcey and Thaxton, *The Soul of Science*, 12.

23. Michael Denton, *Evolution: A Theory in Crisis*, 3rd ed. (Chevy Chase, MD: Adler and Adler, 1986), 66–67.

24. Richard Dawkins, *The Blind Watchmaker: Why the Evidence of Evolution Reveals a Universe without Design* (London: Penguin Books, 1987).

25. Michael J. Behe, William A. Dembski, and Stephen C. Meyer, *Science and Evidence for Design in the Universe*, vol. 9 (San Francisco: Ignatius Press, 2000), 11–12.

26. Ibid., 12.

27. Peter Atkins, "The Limitless Power of Science," in John Cornwell, ed., *Nature's Imagination* (Oxford: Oxford University Press, 1995), 125.

28. John Lennox, in Ravi Zacharias, *Beyond Opinion: Living the Faith That We Defend* (Nashville, TN: Thomas Nelson, 2008).

29. Ray Comfort, *Scientific Facts in the Bible: 100 Reasons to Believe the Bible is Supernatural in Origin* (Alachua, FL: Bridge-Logos, 2001), 11–16.

30. John A. Bloom, "How Can Modern Medicine Relate to the Old Testament?" in H. B. E. Staff, *If God Made the Universe, Who Made God? 130 Arguments for Christian Faith* (Nashville: B&H, 2012).

31. Josh McDowell, *Josh McDowell's Handbook on Apologetics*, electronic ed. (Nashville, TN: Thomas Nelson, 1997).

32. Ibid.

33. Norman L. Geisler and Frank Turek, *I Don't Have Enough Faith to Be an Atheist* (Wheaton, IL: Crossway Books, 2004), 74.

34. Kurt P. Wise, *Faith, Form, and Time: What the Bible Teaches and Science Confirms about Creation and the Age of the* Universe (Nashville, TN: Broadman & Holman, 2002), 81–82.

35. J. P. Moreland, *Scaling the Secular City: A Defense of Christianity* (Grand Rapids, MI: Baker Academic, 1987), 33.

36. Geisler and Turek, *I Don't Have Enough Faith to Be an Atheist*, 81.

37. Ibid., 83.

38. Wise, *Faith, Form, and Time*, 81–82.

39. Robert Jastrow, *God and the Astronomers* (New York: Norton, 1978), 14, quoted by Geisler and Turek, *I Don't Have Enough Faith to Be an Atheist*, 84.

40. Note that chance is not a cause, it is a word we use to describe mathematical possibilities. There's no force in existence called "chance." As Frank Turek quips, when scientists use "chance," they might as well say "they don't know."

41. Denton, *Evolution: A Theory in Crisis*, 3rd ed., 328.

42. Michael Behe, *Darwin's Black Box, The Biochemical Challenge to Evolution* (New York: The Free Press, 1996), 39.

43. Charles Darwin, *Origin of Species*, 6th ed. (New York: New York University Press, 1872), 154.

44. Fazale Rana, *The Cell's Design: How Chemistry Reveals the Creator's Artistry* (Grand Rapids, MI: Baker Books, 2008), 18.

45. Jonathan M, "Michael Behe Hasn't Been Refuted on the Flagellum" *Evolution News and Views*, March 15, 2011.

46. Rana, *The Cell's Design*, 19.

47. Ibid.

48. William A. Dembski and H. F. Schaefer III, *Mere Creation: Science, Faith & Intelligent Design* (Downers Grove, IL: InterVarsity Press, 1998), 41.

49. Josh McDowell, *Josh McDowell's Handbook on Apologetics*, electronic ed. (Nashville, TN: Thomas Nelson, 1997).

50. T. Cabal, C. O. Brand, E. R. Clendenen, P. Copan, J. P. Moreland, and D. Powell, *The Apologetics Study Bible: Real Questions, Straight Answers, Stronger Faith* (Nashville, TN: Holman Bible Publishers, 2007), 832.

51. S. Burgess, *Hallmarks of Design: Evidence of Purposeful Design and Beauty in Nature*, rev. ed. (Leominster, UK: Day One Publications, 2002), 16.

52. Ibid.

53. Geisler and Turek, *I Don't Have Enough Faith to Be an Atheist*, 116.

54. Stephen Meyer, *The Return of the God Hypothesis* (Seattle: Discovery Institute Center for the Renewal of Science and Culture, 1998), 23, in John Lennox, in Ravi Zacharias, *Beyond Opinion:*

Living the Faith That We Defend (Nashville, TN: Thomas Nelson, 2008).

55. Rana, *The Cell's Design*, 162.

56. Leonard M. Adleman, "Computing with DNA," *Scientific American*, August 1998, 54–61.

57. Paun, Rozenberg, and Salomaa, *DNA Computing*, 1–6; Adleman, "Computing with DNA," 54–61.

58. Rana, *The Cell's Design*, 163–64.

59. I am not contending that such evidence alone establishes the Christian God. But when you combine this evidence with other evidence from science, philosophy, and history you can conclude it is the Christian God.

60. David Foster, *The Philosophical Scientists* (New York: Barnes & Noble Books, 1993), 83.

61. Joe Coffee, *Smooth Stones: Bringing Down the Giant Questions of Apologetics* (Adelphi, MD: Cruciform Press), 2011).

62. Ibid.

63. Charles Darwin, *On the Origin of Species* (Cambridge, MA: Harvard University Press, 1964), 280.

64. Coffee, *Smooth Stones*.

65. Geisler and Turek, *I Don't Have Enough Faith to Be an Atheist*, 152–53.

66. Jonathan Wells, *Icons of Evolution* (Washington, DC: Regnery Publishing, Inc., 2000), 39.

67. Ibid, 41.

68. Denton, *Evolution: A Theory in Crisis*, 286.

69. Wells, *Icons of Evolution*, 209.

70. Ibid., 211.

71. Ibid., 211–12.

72. Geisler and Turek, *I Don't Have Enough Faith to Be an Atheist*, 153–54.

73. Wells, *Icons of Evolution*, 221.

74. Denyse O'Leary, "Does the Evidence Point to Mankind's Fully Natural Origin?" *Evolution News and Views*, April 14, 2014.

75. Dr. Daniel Janosik, "How to Think About Evolution," Southern Evangelical Seminary, 2014.

76. Got Questions Ministries, *Got Questions? Bible Questions Answered* (Bellingham, WA: Logos Bible Software, 2010).

77. Paul Davies, *The Cosmic Blueprint* (New York: Simon and Schuster, 1988), 203.

78. Fred Hoyle, "The Universe: Past and Present Reflections," *Annual Review of Astronomy and Astrophysics* 20 (1982): 16.

79. Stephen C. Meyer, Evidence for Design in Physics and Biology: From the Origin of the Universe to the Origin of Life. In *Science and Evidence for Design in the Universe*, vol. 9 (San Francisco: Ignatius Press, 2000), 57.

80. Got Questions Ministries, *Got Questions? Bible Questions Answered* (Bellingham, WA: Logos Bible Software, 2010).

81. Ibid.

82. Norman L. Geisler, *Baker Encyclopedia of Christian Apologetics* (Grand Rapids, MI: Baker Books, 1999), 26.

83. Got Questions Ministries, *Got Questions? Bible Questions Answered* (Bellingham, WA: Logos Bible Software, 2010).

84. Ibid.

85. Ibid.

86. Geisler, *Baker Encyclopedia of Christian Apologetics*, 26–27.

87. Douglas Groothuis, *Christian Apologetics: A Comprehensive Case for Biblical Faith*, Kindle ed. (Downers Grove, IL: InterVarsity Press, 2011), location 4113 of 10010.

88. Colin McGinn, *The Mysterious Flame* (New York: Basic Books, 2000), 5; Groothuis, *Christian Apologetics*, Kindle ed., location 4136).

89. Groothuis, *Christian Apologetics*, Kindle ed., location 4136 of 10010.

90. Ross, *Beyond the Cosmos*, 137.

91. Groothuis, *Christian Apologetics*, Kindle ed., location 4194 of 10010.

92. Frank Turek argues that this is a self-defeating position. For if the brain and the mind are identical then there would be no way to rely on any research purporting to support that claim. If every thought is the result of a blind material process, then there is no reason to

trust any thoughts, including the thought that the mind is the brain. Materialism defeats itself.

93. Groothuis, *Christian Apologetics*, Kindle ed., location 4285.

94. Cabal et al., *The Apologetics Study Bible*, 624.

95. Ibid.

96. Howard Robinson, *Matter and Sense* (Cambridge: Cambridge University Press, 1982); Groothuis, *Christian Apologetics*, Kindle ed., location 4202.

97. Groothuis, *Christian Apologetics*, Kindle ed., location 4210.

98. Ibid.

99. Ibid.

100. "Free will could be the result of 'background noise' in the brain, study suggests," The Independent, June 21, 2014, http://www.independent.co.uk/news/science/free-will-could-be-the-result-of-background-noise-in-the-brain-study-suggests-9553678.html.

101. "Charles Darwin to W. Graham, July 3, 1881," in Francis Darwin, ed., *The Life and Letters of Charles Darwin* (1897; reprint, Boston: Elibron, 2005), 1:285; Groothuis, *Christian Apologetics*, Kindle ed., location 4397.

102. Victor Reppert, *C. S. Lewis's Dangerous Idea* (Downers Grove, IL: InterVarsity Press, 2002); and Victor Reppert, "The Argument from Reason," in William Lane Craig and J. P. Moreland, eds., *Blackwell Companion to Natural Theology* (Malden, MA: Wiley-Blackwell, 2009); Groothuis, *Christian Apologetics*, Kindle ed., location 4413.

103. Groothuis, *Christian Apologetics*, Kindle ed., location 4427.

CHAPTER 13: Pain and Suffering

1. R. C. Sproul, *What Can I Do with My Guilt?*, first ed., vol. 9 (Orlando, FL: Reformation Trustm 2013), 25–26; Waybe A. Grudem, *Systematic Theology: An Introduction to Biblical Doctrine* (Leicester, England; Grand Rapids, MI: Inter-Varsity Press; Zondervan Pub. House, 2004), 445.

2. Norman L. Geisler in *Baker Encyclopedia of Christian Apologetics* (Grand Rapids, MI: Baker Books, 1999), 62.
3. Ibid., 220.
4. If you want to be hyper-technical you could say it's not the best world right now, but it's the best possible way to the best possible world given free creatures.
5. Millard J. Erickson, *Christian Theology*, 2nd ed. (Grand Rapids, MI: Baker Book House 1998), 448–49.
6. Ravi Zacharias, *Cries of the Heart* (Nashville: Thomas Nelson, 2002).
7. H. B. E. Staff, *If God Made the Universe, Who Made God? 130 Arguments for Christian Faith* (Nashville: Holman Bible Publishers, 2012).
8. W. S. La Sor, D. A. Hubbard, and F. W. Bush, *Old Testament Survey: The Message, Form, and Background of the Old Testament*, 2nd ed. (Grand Rapids, MI: William B. Eerdmans Publishing Company, 1996), 482.
9. By this I am not suggesting, of course, that Christ deserved to die, only that God's perfect justice had to be satisfied and thus He sent the innocent Christ to suffer for our sins so that our sins would be atoned for and wiped clean. This was an act of pure, unmerited grace.
10. Joe Coffey, *Smooth Stones: Bringing Down the Giant Questions of Apologetics* (Adelphi, MD: Cruciform Press, 2011).
11. John R. W. Stott, *The Cross of Christ* (Downers Grove, IL: InterVarsity Press, 1986), 311.
12. Ibid., 335.
13. Ibid., 329.
14. Zacharias, *Cries of the Heart.*

INDEX